HOMOSEXUALITY IN ISLAM

HOMOSEXUALITY IN ISLAM

Critical Reflection on Gay, Lesbian, and Transgender Muslims

Scott Siraj al-Haqq Kugle

ONEWORLD

A Oneworld Book

Published by Oneworld Publications 2010
Reprinted 2012, 2013

A CIP record for this title is available
from the British Library

ISBN 978–1–85168–702–2 (Hbk)
ISBN 978–1–85168–701–5 (Pbk)

Typeset by Jayvee, Trivandrum, India
Cover design by Design Deluxe
Printed and bound by Lake Book Manufacturing Inc., USA

Oneworld Publications
10 Bloomsbury Street
London WC1B 3SR
England

CONTENTS

Preface

Bismillah al-rahman al-rahim ... In the name of God, the compassionate One, the One who cares.

All praise belongs to God, the singular and subtle One, who created the universe and made humankind reflect its diversity. All thanks be to God, who made from one human being two, and from two made many and declared, *we created you all from a male and female and made you into different communities and different tribes.* Glory be to God who made a multitude in which each is unique and urged them to reflect upon their differences, overcome their egoistic judgment of others, and find the good in each reflected in others – *so that you should come to know one another, acknowledging that the most noble among you is the one most aware of God* (Qur'an [Q.] 49:13). Then to God they are called and all return. So let us each revere that God, the forbearing One, the One who is just.

Muslim communities, like all other religious groups, face the challenge of confronting diversity. Like other groups, Muslims hesitate and stumble – sometimes inflicting violence along the way – before dealing justly with people in their diverse ranks who are different in appearance, language, ethnicity, creed, or bodily ability. Among the diverse ranks of people are some who are different in gender identity or sexual orientation. Such people are always a small minority yet they appear in every culture and religious community. This book is about the challenge before contemporary Muslims to acknowledge, understand, and accept the diversity in their midst, especially with respect to sexual orientation and gender identity. It contributes to the ongoing process of meeting that challenge and urges Muslims actively to reconsider prejudgments they may hold about gay, lesbian, or transgender members of their communities.

Muslims have profound resources for dealing theologically and ethically with diversity, but often ignore them when facing difference and conflict. In their long history, Muslims have intensively dealt with sectarian differences. Through this debate, the classical Islamic sciences developed one of their best characteristics – the tolerance for diversity of interpretation of sacred texts; this is expressed in the words of Abu Hanifa, the renowned jurist, who is reported to have said, "We know this [position] is one opinion, and it is the best we can arrive at, [but if] someone arrives at a different view, then he adopts what he believes [is best] and we adopt what we believe [is best]."[1] This book invokes that long tradition of tolerance within the faith – which is often ignored or lost in contemporary Muslim communities – in searching for a faith-based response to gay, lesbian, and transgender Muslims.

For many Muslims, dealing with homosexuality or transgender issues is a matter of sin and heresy, not difference and diversity. But when pressed, such Muslims often have no clear idea of what homosexuality means, or simply deny that there are any homosexual people in Muslim families and communities. But there are Muslims who face issues squarely with open minds and humble hearts; they may read this book and grapple with the issues it raises. Even if this book does not convince them, it may encourage them to see the issues in a new light, and in that sense it will have succeeded.

Why talk about gay, lesbian, and transgender Muslims now? We must talk about them because they exist and are suffering – and are increasingly refusing to bear suppression in silence. Some turn to their religious tradition with faith-filled criticism, seeing it as not merely part of the problem but as essential to possible solutions. This book is based upon the experiences and hopes of those who are not content to wait for their Muslim sisters and brothers gradually to come to tolerate them. It offers theological reflection on the insights arising from lesbian, transgender, and gay Muslims' efforts to build support groups to help them reconcile their sexual orientation and gender identity with the Islamic faith. Their struggle beckons Muslims to pay attention to this minority community's experiences and insights before dismissing them or opposing them.

In that spirit and hope, I offer this book to the public. In the end, only God knows best. I seek protection with God, the One who opens possibilities (*al-fattah*), the loving One (*al-wadud*), the One with subtle grace (*al-latif*).

Acknowledgements

This book presents my own theological reflections, but it is built upon the experience of many others who have shared their knowledge and wisdom and resources with me. I cannot begin without offering them acknowledgement and gratitude.

This book was written under the auspices of a two-year fellowship from the Institute for the Study of Islam in the Modern World (I.S.I.M.) at the University of Leiden. I am grateful for the Institute's intellectual and financial support for this project, and for those who helped me refine my project, especially Khalid Masud, Asef Bayat, Martin van Bruinessen, and Abdulkader Tayob. I acknowledge with many thanks the scholars and institutions that invited me to address their members and field questions on this issue, such as Linda Herrera at the Institute for the Social Sciences in The Hague, Kamran Ali and Hina Azam at the University of Texas at Austin, and Malek Moazzam Doulat at Occidental College in Los Angeles.

I am especially grateful to my students on the course "Gender and Sexuality in Islamic Societies," offered at Swarthmore College and the University of Cape Town, whose questions helped me frame this study. The book began with an article written while I was teaching at Swarthmore College, an institution that has supported and nourished my growth as an intellectual attentive to ethical and political questions. I am grateful to faculty members at Swarthmore – especially Pieter Judson, Farha Ghannam, Steven Hopkins, Mark Wallace, and Pallabi Chakravorty – who offered me friendship infused with the quest for knowledge.

I have been blessed with the opportunity to learn at the feet of able scholars in many countries, both Muslims who are dedicated to intellectual renewal of their faith and non-Muslims who are deeply knowledgeable about Islam. I cannot name them here, for some may not want to be associated with a controversial project such as this. Yet I am deeply grateful for their generosity and strive to put all I have learned from them to sincere use in this book. I wish to thank two colleagues in particular from the Progressive Muslim movement who pushed me to think harder about this book and its ethical ramifications. Kecia Ali read the manuscript with the careful scrutiny of a specialist in Islamic law and her suggestions have improved it in countless ways.[1] Amina Wadud has shaped feminist approaches to Islam, and has thereby influenced this book, since gay, lesbian, and transgender people benefit from the strength of the feminist movement.[2] As both a Muslim interpreter of the Qur'an and as a political ally in the fight against injustice, Wadud has offered this book energy and support for which I am deeply grateful.

I have also been blessed with parents who shielded me from poverty, pushed me always to strive for the truth no matter how dangerous that path may be, and supported me in studying, researching, and writing, even if destiny has taken me beyond the horizons of their own experience. While traveling over those horizons, I have found many friends, comrades, and loved ones. I offer sincerest thanks to my sisters of the heart – Rukhsana, Rubina, Farah, Bushra, and Saʿdiyya – who have shown me the true meaning of trust, sincerity, and love. Many friends have shared their own discoveries in research into the topic, and I am grateful to Jamal Bakeer, Faris Malik, Daayiee Abdullah, Rusmir Musić, and Nicholas Heer for their their knowledge and experience. I thank Sameer Ashar, Brett Summers, David Anthony, and Kimee Kimura for their unconditional friendship. My thanks and admiration also goes to those whose courage to speak has shaped this book – those few whose interviews are quoted here and the many others who are not quoted, along with all of those who shared their experiences with me, urged me to write, and helped me find the strength to do so.

Finally, I give a quiet word of thanks to my *murshid*, my spiritual guide, who upholds the spiritual path of those who hold the Prophet Muhammad's most important teaching to be, "All people are God's family, and God loves those most who do the most good for God's family," despite our division into nations, tribes, and factions.[3] If any good comes to my human family from researching, writing, and publishing this book, may reward for it accrue to those who urge us toward *ihsan* – to do what is good for others and beautifies their lives. If any harm comes from this, let the sole responsibility be mine, for the opinions in this work are to be attributed solely to me.

Illustrations

Introduction

O people, we created you all from a male and female
And made you into different communities and different tribes
So that you should come to know one another
Acknowledging that the most noble among you
Is the one most aware of God

Qur'an 49:13

The most noble is the one most aware of God. This is not just incitement for all Muslims to increase their awareness of God – it is also a warning to pursue a policy of social tolerance. The implication of this verse is that no Muslim is better than another because of any of the social categories that we use to classify ourselves, such as race, ethnicity, economic class, or gender. Or even sexual orientation. A gay or lesbian Muslim is no less than a heterosexual Muslim, except by the intangible criterion of pious awareness of God (*taqwa*). A transgender Muslim is no less than other Muslims who have not struggled with their own gender identity and faced the stigma of changing gender classification, except by awareness of God.

Most Muslims cherish reciting this verse to oppose the evils of racial superiority, ethnic chauvinism, and class arrogance. Yet some see this verse as a call to justice that rings far beyond its terse words. Progressive Muslims extend its implied meaning beyond its explicit wording, to condemn also male sexism, gender injustice, and social stigmatizing of homosexuals. This verse is often cited in the internet discussions of members of a support group for Muslims who are lesbian, gay, or transgender in the U.S., called Al-Fatiha Foundation. Its members see themselves as a community of people – like the tribes and communities of the Qur'anic verse – who are a natural result of human diversity as it is created by God's divine will. Many of them refuse to accept the allegation that they are sinful or perverse or sick, as many Muslim authorities regularly assert. They accept that they are merely human, as are all other Muslim believers, and that God judges them according to their awareness of God. They strive to surrender to God's will, not to the criticism of others informed more by social prejudice than by awareness of God.

This book was inspired by the courageous work of Al-Fatiha Foundation and by the author's involvement in its activities. Discussions with its members and sympathy with their sense of urgency sparked me to write an essay entitled "Sexuality, Diversity and Ethics" in a volume of essays by scholars in the Progressive Muslim movement.[1] That essay questioned whether Muslims needed to condemn fellow believers who were homosexual in order to be faithful practitioners of their religion. This book expands upon that original essay, reflecting systematically and thoroughly on Islam from the point of view of gay, lesbian, and transgender believers. The argument engages the full range of the Islamic religious tradition and its complex texts – from Qur'an as scripture and *hadith* as oral teachings to *fiqh* as legal rulings and the *shari'a* as a rhetoric of orthodoxy. For this reason, the argument becomes rapidly complicated. Yet it can be presented here in this introduction in simple terms and common language.

This book asserts that some human beings simply are homosexual by disposition rather than by choice. There has always been a very small minority of homosexual women and men in every human community, though societies define them in different ways, languages have different terms to describe them, and belief systems have different reactions to their presence. Some societies accept them and some condemn them, but none has ever prevented them from being present – whether openly or under suppression. What causes them to be present is open to question. As a Muslim, I assert that they – like all natural phenomena – are caused by divine will, though biological processes or early childhood experiences are inportant means by which they come into being. Whether the "cause" is God's creation, biological variation, or early childhood experience, homosexuals have no rational choice in their internal diposition to be attracted to same-sex mates. The Qur'an mentions them obliquely and does not assess them negatively, but it also does not deal with their existence as a minority social group. Instead, the Qur'an addresses the majority who are oriented toward the other sex, that is heterosexuals whose sexual urge can result in procreation and replication of the social order. Where the Qur'an treats same-sex acts, it condemns them only insofar as they are exploitative or violent.

However, the Islamic tradition is based on more than the Qur'an. Later texts, like hadith reports and fiqh decisions, stigmatize homosexuals and criminalize their relationships. The question is whether these negative assesments in oral tradition and jurisprudence are in accord with the Qur'an as scripture, and whether these other non-scriptural sources of authority are authentic and reliable for Muslims. Asking these questions opens the possibility for Muslims to take a reformist approach to their own religious tradition. The reformist or progressive approach must take into account new possibilities for human fulfillment in increasingly non-patriarchal societies like those evolving under democratic constitutions, where Muslims are living as minority communities and fellow citizens. In these new environments, it is possible for homosexual relationships to be based on ethical reciprocity, trust, justice, and love, just as heterosexual relationships ought to be based on these values in the ethical vision of the Qur'an. What matters is not the sex of the partner with whom one forms a partnership, as long as that partnership is contractual on par with legal custom. Rather, what matters is the ethical nature of the relationship one has within the constraints of one's internal disposition, which includes sexual orientation and gender identity.

This is the argument of this book in the simplest terms. The argument runs up against resistance from two sources. The first source of resistance is the Islamic tradition's being built on a variety of texts and teachings, some of which support this argument and some of which oppose it. A major task of this book is to assess how primary and essential sources of Islam support this argument while specifying how secondary and inessential teachings that oppose it can be reconciled. The second source of resistance is the patriarchal culture of most Muslims, with its misogynist and homophobic elements. This patriarchal culture is independent of Muslim religious tradition but often finds support in some of its teachings.

The challenge faced by this book is a challenge shared by all reformist and progressive projects within a religious tradition. The challenge is to separate what is imposed by culture from what is essential to faith, on the one hand, and to sift what is essential to faith from what is enshrined in religious tradition, on the other hand. This book is a small contribution to this larger project. It offers systematic theological reflection upon the experience of transgender, lesbian, and gay Muslims, and argues that insights gleaned from their experience are integral to the wider movement of progressive reform among Muslims. Their experiences are being articulated today in ways that were impossible only a decade ago.

There is currently an international network of advocacy and support groups for lesbian, gay, bisexual, and transgender Muslims. Though each is embedded in a distinct national environment, these allied groups share many concerns and exchange ideas. The groups include the Inner Circle in South Africa (formerly called Al-Fitra Foundation); Al-Fatiha Foundation in the U.S.; the Salam Queer Community in Canada; Imaan and the Safra Project, both in the U.K.; the Yoesuf Foundation and Habibi Ana Foundation, both in the Netherlands. They focus on building confidence, raising consciousness, and encouraging *ijtihad* – independent or original analysis based on intellectual effort and ethical discretion – in the interpretation of religion and law.[2] These Islamic groups are found mainly in secular democratic nations with Muslim minority communities where lesbian, gay, and transgender Muslims can voice controversial opinions, appeal for rights, and articulate alternative views of Islam without overwhelming fear of persecution. Chapter 1 will present a case study that demonstrates the urgency and potency of the activist work of these support groups in a courtroom drama in which I was an active participant.

In preparing this book, I have interviewed leaders and participants in these support groups to understand their lifestories, how they came to value Islam despite struggling with Muslim families and communities that rejected them, and how they see Islamic spirituality fueling their activist work. These support groups are possible because of increasing social tolerance of homosexual and transgender people in secular democratic societies, and their members argue for more tolerance within the Islamic tradition upheld by minority communities within these societies. A concern for tolerance is shared by other Muslim scholars in the progressive Islamic movement, and their writings are required reading among members of these support groups. The Islamic legal scholar Khaled Abou El Fadl has stated most clearly the baseline issue of whether Islam can and should be tolerant. "The Qur'anic discourse, for instance, can readily support an ethic of diversity and tolerance. The Qur'an not only expects, but even accepts the reality of difference and diversity within human society ... the Qur'an asserts that diversity is part of divine intent and purpose in creation ... The classical commentators of the Qur'an did not fully explore the implications of this sanctioning of diversity or the role of peaceful conflict resolution in perpetuating the type of social interaction that would result in people *knowing each other* (Q. 49:13) ... In fact, the existence of diversity as a primary purpose of creation, as suggested by the verse above, remained underdeveloped in Islamic theology."[3] Abou El Fadl's writings on Islamic law are a major force in trying to redress this underdeveloped aspect of Islamic theology, and his ethical clarity and intellectual vivacity have moved me and so many others.

However, Abou El Fadl's vision of Islam as expecting and accepting diversity exists more in potential than in actuality. Other progressive Islamic scholars have pointed out the limitations of tolerance. Feminist Muslim scholars have continuously pointed out how tolerance of diversity is significantly lacking in Islamic communities with regard to gender, one of the most fundamental markers of difference in all human communities. The fact that women's dignity and equality are treated as an issue of "minority rights" – when women are numerically equal (or greater than) men and are indispensably central to the well-being of all human communities – is indicative of the depth of the problem and the reluctance of men and the institutions they establish and run to justly deal with it. If Muslims' tolerance of diversity is stretched to the limit regarding women's rights, then imagine how it is stretched to the breaking point in dealing with lesbian, transgender, and gay rights.

But, in reality, justice is not served until comfortable concepts like "tolerance" are stretched to the point where they almost break. People are profoundly different even if they belong to the same culture, religion, community, or even family. Difference based on sexual orientation and gender identity takes us to the extremes of individual identity. It pushes religious mores and family authority to their practical horizons. Yet looking squarely at the issues of sexual orientation and gender identity helps us affirm universal values. It helps us define what it means to be human, to be considered an authentic creation of God, to be imbued with dignity and worth despite chronic social stigma and religious condemnation. Progressive Muslim scholars urge us to recover the tolerance inherent in the Islamic message and to assert a values-based religious ethic. The issue of how religious tradition deals with conflicts over sexual orientation and gender identity is an important test case to find and expand the limits of the Muslim community's response to the challenge of diversity.

This book concentrates upon the Qur'an as the ever-full spring of Islamic belief, practice, and spiritual development. While maintaining a focus on the Qur'an in Chapter 2, the book's scope expands to include hadith in Chapter 3, fiqh debates in Chapter 4, the flexibility of *shari'a* to accomodate same-sex marriage in Chapter 5, and fatwa politics that shape opinions toward transgender experience in Chapter 6. In practice, Muslims base their religiosity upon these sources – oral reports, legal debates, and the rhetoric of contemporary authorities – as much as on the Qur'an itself. In this book, I quote the Qur'an in *italics* in order to set off the meaning of God's speech from other kinds of discourse. Immediately after each quotation from the Qur'an is given the chapter and verse, to facilitate readers looking up the scriptural passages. I have not relied upon any single English translation of the Qur'an, but have rather compared many translations and reconciled them with my own understanding of the Arabic text, as I have sufficient knowledge of the language to do so. The English translations of Qur'an given in this book are my own, though I acknowledge with great respect the translators who have meditated on the Qur'an before me.[4] For those readers who question the faith of anyone so audacious as to write about homosexuals as part of God's will in creation, I have explained in other essays how I am a Muslim and what sources in the Islamic tradition nourish my faith.[5]

Many Muslims cling to presumptions when it comes to issues of sexuality and gender, and feel that they already know "what Islam says" without reflecting on whether they have based their opinion on patriarchal culture or knowledge of religion. The theologian Abu Mansur al-Maturidi (died 943) reminds us that in accepting tradition and acting upon it we need to rely on reason: "The human being is specially endowed with the moral responsibility to manage the affairs of the created world, to meet people's needs through labor, to seek the most beneficial circumstances for their powers of reason and choose what is best for them and while protecting them from what is contrary to this – there is no way to achieve this except by using discernment through reasoned research into the nature of things."[6] When we direct discerning reason toward our own religious tradition, we find that many values that we Muslims commonly attribute to Islam do not come from the Qur'an or the Prophet Muhammad's example but rather from patriarchal culture.

Patriarchy is the ideology instituting the dominance of elder heterosexual males over all others, specifically women of all ages, younger men, and minority males who do not accept patriarchal roles that reinforce masculine power. Patriarchy existed before the advent of the Qur'an and the Prophet Muhammad's example, both of which challenged patriachy in some ways. After the Prophet's death, Muslims inscribed patriarchal values deep into Islamic culture, allowing the Islamic *shari'a* to compromise the Qur'an's ethical voice. Because of this, Muslims in the past did not seriously consider the issue of women's social equality, did not offer dignified roles for lesbian and gay people, and did not countenance transgender people in Muslim communities. Rapid changes in society under the impact of modernity, along with advances in scientific knowledge in fields of psychology, sociology, and genetic biology, make reassessing the classical *shari'a* a vital necessity. In addition, the voices of marginalized groups – like women, lesbian, gay, and transgender Muslims – insist on justice after such a long-imposed silence. Previously marginalized groups offer important ethical insights toward non-patriarchal interpretation of Islamic scripture, insights not available to those who have not suffered similar experiences of existential exclusion.

The goal of this book is to show that lesbian, gay, and transgender Muslims offer constructive critique of classical Islamic thought. Islamic theology has previously untapped resources to comprehend them and give them a dignified role in contemporary Islamic communities. As al-Maturidi reminds us, our sincere practice of Islam depends upon constant application of discernment through reasoned research into the nature of things. Such research may change our view of religion depending on new developments in politics, social organization, and scientific understanding. All these things impact our view of sexuality and gender, and demand that we apply reason to scripture and scrutiny to custom.

Reasoned research into the nature of things requires attentive observation of lived reality. The theological reflections offered in this book are informed by interviews with Muslim activists who work with support groups for transgender, lesbian, and gay believers in five different nations on three continents: South Africa, the U.S., Canada, the U.K., and the Netherlands. These activists are very diverse in terms of sexuality, gender, and ethnicity.[7] Despite this wide diversity, all those interviewed share many things in common besides being not heterosexual. They are Muslims as defined by personal identity or spiritual faith, many of them striving to practice the rituals of Islam in their daily lives to the extent and depth possible in their particular situation. All those interviewed are participants in support groups for lesbian, gay, and transgender Muslims, groups that see religious belief and practice as important factors in the well-being and integrity of their members.

All these interviews were undertaken in "Western" countries, meaning countries that are secular democracies in which Muslims form a minority and in which religious custom (Christian or that of any other religion) does not form an explicit legal basis for national law. In these Western countries, Muslims live as citizens even if they are a religious minority (and often belong to ethnic minorities as well), yet the democratic nature of the state allows them religious freedom to worship according to their conscience. It also allows gay, lesbian, and transgender Muslims to establish support groups with differing amounts of legal protection from their own religious community and family pressure. The fact that those interviewed live in Western secular democracies does not lessen their authenticity as Muslims. Rather, living in the West allows them to speak openly and organize legally around their identity as sexual and gender minorities, and to creatively interpret their religious tradition, Islam, in ways barred to many who live in Muslim-majority nations in the Middle East, Africa, and Asia.

Although this book does not present interviews with these activists, I have based theological reflection about Islamic ethics, norms, and texts upon their insights. In the future, I hope to present their lifestories in their own words in a separate book. These interviews show how transgender, lesbian, and gay Muslims embrace their religious tradition, through personal spiritual experience, through struggle with family and community, and through wrestling with the meaning of scripture. However, in this book I take their insights as lived reality and ask what resources the Islamic tradition has to offer them to help resolve the conflicts they experience between Islam (as a religion imposed by family, community, and history) and their existential condition as members of a sexual and gender minority. Their narratives were taken as pointers to explore the Islamic tradition and search for resources to build a sex-positive and sexuality-accepting interpretation of Islam which would not reject gay, lesbian, and transgender believers solely because of their gender identity or sexual orientation. The theological approach laid out here is one of progressive Islamic faith, which seeks to protect the vulnerable from suffering and injustice perpetuated by patriarchal religious authorities, not by discarding religion but rather by liberating religion from the domination of these well-entrenched authorities. Thus liberated, the religion can itself become liberating for those who are vulnerable and oppressed, as it was in the beginning.

This requires us to ask whether Islam can be other than what straight Muslims say it must be. This question, so simple on the surface, is actually very complex. To venture an answer requires that we delve into detail about the Qur'an, hadith reports of the Prophet Muhammad's teachings, and fiqh or norms developed by Muslim jurists in medieval times. Those who adhere to Islam as a religious commitment have to deal with these texts, whether they are theologians, specialist scholars, or common believers. Yet simply quoting Islamic texts with regard to transgender, lesbian, and gay believers without critiquing and reinterpreting the texts only perpetuates the injustice done to them in the name of religion.[8] For this reason, I have endeavored to make the foundation of this study the voices of contemporary Muslims who speak in their own ways and represent their own struggles as gay men, lesbian women, or transgender people whose identification as either male or female does not come easily.

This book has limitations that I openly admit. Whereas many Muslims will see its argument as "radical," some progressive readers may see its argument as "conservative." The book is conservative in that it assumes Islamic belief in the existence of the one God, the sacredness of the Qur'an as the speech of God, and the sincerity of the Prophet Muhammad's mission to spread its message. It is conservative in its aim to nourish the faith of those who hold these beliefs and to help gay, lesbian, and transgender Muslims to find ways to retain their faith despite great obstacles. It is conservative in valuing the principles of the Islamic tradition even as it argues against some of that tradition's normative texts and dominant authorities. Some gay, lesbian, and transgender readers despair at the prospect of a call for acceptance from within the religious tradition, and see religion as part of the problem rather than a resource in its resolution; to such readers this book may seem too conservative or even naive.

There is another aspect of this book's argument that may seem "conservative" to some readers, especially those active in progressive politics and secular human rights. This book restricts its discussion to people who are homosexual (lesbian or gay) and transgender. It presents a theory of sexual orientation and gender identity that accepts and assumes these categories. It focuses mainly upon homosexuals – gay men whose identity is largely and indelibly shaped by their sexual attraction to other males, and lesbian women whose identity is similarly shaped by sexual attraction to females. It focuses also on transgender people – those born as or perceived to be men but who identify as women (male-to-female transgender) and those born as or perceived to be women but who identify as men (female-to-male transgender). Transgender people are quite distinct from homosexuals but their experience of divergence from patriarchal norms resonates with that of homosexuals. All these categories assume that "gender" is a real category that structures the experience of people, even as they diverge from patriarchal norms built upon gender. Homosexuals diverge from it in that they are sexually oriented toward people of the same gender, and transgender people diverge from it in that they identify as the opposite gender to that which they are perceived or ascribed to be. They all question the norm because of their inherent disposition rather than because of any conscious decision, learned behavior, or curable disease.

To argue as this book does that homosexual and transgender people behave the way they do because of their inherent disposition may strike readers as "conservative." Lately, intellectual trends in gender and sexuality studies have labeled this argument as "essentialist." They contrast it with an approach labeled "constructivist" that sees all social categories – including homosexual and transgender (or even male and female) – as inherently unstable and socially conditioned categories. Although such constructivist approaches give us insight into the linguistic flexibility of categories and the great variety of social systems that posit them, these approaches are relatively flimsy as the basis for a call to protect the rights of living persons or to urge religious reform. On the contrary, "essentialist" approaches are more useful to mount a political campaign to actually change social relations rather than just comment upon them.

This book therefore posits that there are real categories of people who can be called gay, lesbian, and transgender. They form identifiable groups because of their inherent disposition which – whatever its original cause – manifests in clearly discernable behaviors. The terms used to describe them may differ from culture to culture or change from era to era (as might the social stigma attached to them), but the fundamental categories are persistent and the psychological processes that push people to manifest behavior that places them in these categories is persistent. So this study takes up these three categories of people as the basis of its analysis.

Of course, there are other categories of people who do not conform to patriarchal norms.[9] The largest category that I do not discuss in this book is "bisexual." Why choose to deal with gay men, lesbian women, and transgender people while excluding discussion of bisexuals? The answer has to do with scholarship, with politics, and with religion. This book seeks to make an Islamic and especially Qur'an-based argument for accepting sexuality and gender minorities. In the Qur'an, I find oblique but potent scriptural reference to gay men, lesbian women, and transgender persons; the speech of God does not condemn them but rather observes them as part of a diverse creation, as detailed in Chapter 2. Therefore, theological reflection based on the Qur'an can find firm foundation for these three categories of people.

In the Qur'an, I do not find any such positive acknowledgement of bisexual people, defined as those men or women who feel sexual attraction to both male and female partners and do not find fulfillment with only one or the other. If this book included discussion of bisexuals without a scriptural reference upon which to base a reformist analysis, the theological basis of its argument would be diluted. Other reasons that it does not discuss bisexuals are political and scholarly. Bisexuality is controversial in contemporary gay and lesbian communities, for many see bisexuals as challenging their identities in destructive ways, especially in environments where lesbian and gay people are not secure. Though many groups are established to support gay, lesbian, transgender, and also bisexual people, there is often a sense of resentment against bisexuals because they fulfill same-sex desires while still conforming – at least partially or publicly – to heterosexual norms. When discussion turns to Muslim communities, the political delicacy of this question becomes even more pronounced.

In many Muslim communities, from the classical period to modern nations, a kind of "behavioral bisexuality" is widespread. In societies that are segregated by gender, like many Muslim communities, access to opposite-sex partners is restricted and marriage is expensive, so same-sex acts may be common. Such behavioral bisexuality – in which a male may find sexual release with another male while still desiring fulfillment with a female – is driven not by identity and inner disposition but rather by thwarted sexual urges that find release through means that the actor finds pleasurable but less than ideal. In a patriarchal environment where homosexual identity is severely censured, the same men who behave in bisexual ways might also condemn their same-sex partners, make homophobic statements, or participate in violence against those seen as homosexual. Such behavioral bisexuals do not perceive themselves to be homosexual even though they participate in acts of "situational homosexuality." In such environments among men, a basic categorical difference is drawn between a partner who takes a penetrating role in intercourse (who perceives himself to be simply an "active" male who is not blameworthy) and a partner who takes a penetrated role (who is perceived as "passive" and therefore not really male – as effeminate or diseased or sinful). Such a behavioral bisexual desires sexual intercourse with women and may marry and procreate even if he indulges in same-sex intercourse before marriage or while married. When this kind of behavioral bisexuality is common (either because intercourse with females is restricted or because active males expect pleasure from whomever allows her- or himself to be penetrated), it obscures "dispositional homosexuality" wherein a man sexually desires another male or a woman desires another female due to inward disposition. Because analyzing "dispositional homosexuality" within an Islamic framework is the aim of this book, discussion of bisexuality – especially behavioral bisexuality of the type described above – is beyond its scope and also against its grain.

Many books have focused on behavioral bisexuality in Muslim communities and on its effect of creating social categories based upon differential sexual roles for "active" versus "passive" participants in homosexual intercourse and relationships. Such books are written from the perspective of sociology, literature, travelogue, and journalism.[10] But if one takes Islamic theology – and especially the Qur'an – as one's starting point for making a positive assessment of homosexuality, then this kind of bisexuality is a distraction. It is such behavioral bisexuality that drove classical Muslim jurists to condemn sodomy (*liwat*) with harsh penalties and charge that early heterosexual marriage was a "cure" or preventative measure against it. Some gay Muslim activists who are trained in Islamic theology have even suggested that the Qur'an condemned the Tribe of Lot for acts that fall into this category of behavioral bisexuality, for they were basically married and heterosexual men who engaged in sexual intercourse with men for reasons other than their internal disposition – specifically, they used rape and sexual abuse to assert dominance and humiliate the Prophet Lot.[11] This debate will be discussed in detail in Chapter 2. Suffice it to say that, from a basis in the Qur'an, one can differentiate between homosexuality based upon internal disposition and behavioral bisexuality that is most often situational, driven by heterosexual deprivation, penetrative lust, or social aggression.

Of course, not all are bisexual only in behavior. There are also people who are "dispositional bisexual" due to their sexual orientation. They are attracted to both males and females either at the same time (concurrent bisexuality) or in series (sequential bisexuality) in a disposition that is of long duration and deep impact, such that they develop an identity rooted in this attraction and the behavior it shapes. In contemporary Western societies, this type of disposition and subculture is the main reference to "bisexuality." Meanwhile sociological research and human rights activists refer to other kinds of behavioral or situational bisexuality as "male-to-male" sex, indicating that such sexual activity is not driven by identity or disposition but rather by other forces. Although the idea that some bisexuals may have an innate disposition that shapes their sexual orientation is closer to the concerns of this study, it is beyond the study's scope. This study addresses directly the question of whether God intends some men and women to be of homosexual disposition, and if so what the consequence of that insight would be for homosexual Muslims and their co-religionists. It also addresses the related but distinct question of whether God creates some people in the "wrong body" such that their gender identity does not match their ascribed gender, a condition that drives them to transgender behavior to change their ascribed gender to harmonize with their internal identity. But this book does not venture the next step to ask whether God intends some men and women to be dispositionally bisexual. To address that question would call into question the definitiveness of sexual orientation and also the discreteness of gender difference which are assumed by gay men, lesbian women, and transgender people.

These categories – male gender, female gender, and sexual orientation toward one's own gender – provide the existential terrain upon which gay, lesbian, and transgender people negotiate their identities and life choices. Such people challenge the way patriarchal societies enforce heterosexual behavior to regulate the boundaries between these categories, but they do not challenge the existence of the categories of gender difference (meaning that female and male are real categories that differentiate people on the basis of gender) and sexual orientation differential (meaning that homosexual and heterosexual are real categories that differentiate people on the basis of their object of sexual attraction). In contrast, dispositional bisexuality challenges the idea that these categories are psychologically firm and socially forceful. Therefore, to focus on bisexuality in this study would be to dilute its focus and undermine the political and theological force of its argument.

Every book has limits. I endeavor here only to establish groundwork for discussion of the issues, not to give final verdicts. If we Muslims cannot establish a baseline understanding of lesbian and gay members of our community, then how can we move on to more ambiguous and varied phenomena like bisexuality in all its variations? This study intends to start a dialogue rather than to have the last word or negate other approaches to the issue. This dialogue is only beginning, and it is hoped that others will consider its blind spots or neglected topics to be invitations for their own contribution. Its major goal is to give heterosexual Muslims a new understanding of homosexual and transgender Muslims, and open a new way for homosexual and transgender Muslims to gain new confidence in themselves within their religious community, its beliefs, and its rituals. That is a large enough task for one book. Non-Muslims can also learn from its arguments about Islam as a religion and its potential for flexible adaptation and progressive change. Bisexuals, though neglected here, can also learn from this book's source-critical approach and liberation theology method; perhaps bisexual activists and scholars representing their experiences will take up these tools in their own search for justice within an Islamic framework, and no doubt when they do they will disagree with some of basic premises of this study. I will be the first to welcome their efforts and read with eagerness their conclusions.

Further limitations are imposed by the need to choose terminology. Those readers familiar with lesbian, gay, bisexual, and transgender politics will notice that I have refrained from using the term "queer." Queer is a term that has been in the not-so-distant past directed against homosexuals in English-speaking environments to insult or punish. In the past two decades, activists and scholars have reappropriated the term "queer" with positive connotations, to describe in one label all varied identities that question patriarchal heterosexuality. In their writings, "queer" means the whole community of lesbian, gay, bisexual, and transgender people along with others who question patriarchal norms. Although some people do identify with the label "queer," many readers find it disorienting, overly intellectual, or polemical. To make this study accessible to the greatest number of people, I persist in using the terms "gay," "transgender," and "lesbian." These terms denote three different kinds of people who have much in common even as they are clearly differentiated from each other, and these terms are more recognizable to general readers. The term "queer" refers to all these varied kinds of people as one single group – those defined as "different" due to sexual orientation and gender identity – in an overtly politicized way to which not all members of those groups subscribe. I have used the term "queer" in previous articles and fully explained its use and nuances there.[12] It is hoped that those who do identify as queer will derive benefit from this book and can adopt its arguments to their own distinctive position even if the book avoids this term.

Some sociological writings use the term "non-heterosexual" as a clinical label to refer to lesbian, gay, bisexual, transgender, and queer persons (often reduced to the acronym L.G.B.T.Q.). While "non-heterosexual" has the merit of being a single-word term, it has the demerit of being defined as a negation – it includes all behaviors that are not heterosexual and all identities that do question the normality of heterosexuality. Therefore, it does not refer to any positive content in the personalities of people who adopt such identities or perform such behaviors; there are consequently no actual people who self-identify as "non-heterosexual." To do so would suggest that they strive to be everything that heterosexuals are not, which is not an accurate description of transgender, lesbian, or gay people; their difference from others in their families and religious community has only do to with sexual orientation and gender identity, not with all other values or qualities. They share much with others, even if they are seen as radically "different." This book tries to facilitate their struggle to assert their common humanity, religious affiliation, and spiritual aspiration while also affirming their difference. To use the term "non-heterosexual" to describe this book's protagonists would undermine their essential message. The term may be apt in clinical sociology, but is not adequate in the context of theology as in this book.

In short, the book reflects theologically on the struggles of lesbian, gay, and transgender Muslims by examining critically and constructively the Qur'an, hadith, and Islamic legal rulings. It hopes to provide a bridge between Islam as a tradition and Muslims as living people. The interviews I have undertaken have the unshakable authenticity of recording individuals speaking in their own voices of their own existential struggles in their own living contexts. They are traces of personal *jihad* or struggle with one's commitments. Those interviews are not fully recorded in this book, though it does quote some activists and has based its theological reflection on their insights. But theological reflection does not have the inviolable value of a first-person account of someone's own experience and is limited by being still in process as one person's attempt to discover the truth through research and reflection. It is an offering of intellectual *ijtihad* or struggle to ascertain what is right, based on one's understanding of the Qur'an, the Prophet's example, jurists' deliberations, and the Islamic community's discourse.

Chapter 1

Islam on Trial: A Case Study

When the earth quakes her violent shakings
And the earth bears forth her weighty burdens
The human being declares, "What is with her?"
That day, she speaks of what's happened with her
All that her Lord has inspired to her
That day people come forward, each differently
To witness their deeds
So whoever does an atom's weight of good
Sees its consequence
And whoever does an atom's weight of harm
Sees its consequence

Qur'an 99:1–8

There comes a day in every life when the unwanted truth bursts forth, with dire consequences that send us into upheaval. We usually try to avoid that day, sometimes with indifferent negligence, sometimes with strategic silence, sometimes with lying avoidance. Nevertheless, the truth comes. The Qur'an insists that the day of truth comes, so it is better that we face the consequences now and live up to our responsibilities to God and to our neighbors than to wait until death overtakes us.

In this brief chapter, Surat al-Zilzal or "The Earthquake," the Qur'an describes the cataclysm of cosmic accountability that will overshadow each of us, surely after death but also certainly, in small forerumblings, in our lives. Events have a way of piling up so that what we strive to avoid comes to slap us in the face and we are shaken violently, suddenly made aware "to see our deeds." This chapter was one of the earliest revealed to the Prophet

Muhammad, and it conveys a core teaching of Islam: the inevitable accounting of facing God directly – without intermediary, without helper, without excuse.

This chapter is the first of the Qur'an that I remember having read, long before I could read its powerful rhyme in Arabic or understand its potent play of gendered pronouns that give the earth its personified role in the cosmic cataclysm. Reading this single chapter, just eight tense verses, laid the seeds that would later grow into the love of learning Arabic, branch into becoming a professor of Islamic studies, and eventually, many years later, flower into the spiritual aspiration to become a Muslim.

However, I really didn't understand the verse, despite its importance to me, until the day I was called to testify in court in the summer of 2002. Fortunately, I was not standing accused, but was rather called upon as an expert witness. The case was at an immigration court in Arlington, Virginia. The Immigration and Naturalization Service of the U.S. (I.N.S.) was seeking to deport a Moroccan man, twenty years old, whom we will call "Mehdi" in order to keep his identity anonymous. He had overstayed his year-long visa to enroll in college, and was arrested on his community college campus, only weeks after having begun his first semester, only days after the events of September 11, 2001 (9/11). After spending many months in an I.N.S. holding facility, Mehdi applied for political asylum to stay in the U.S., as a homosexual, "because he had been persecuted and abused with the acquiescence of the Moroccan government on account of his sexual orientation."[1] He charged that he fled Morocco after having suffered past persecution and can establish in court "a well-founded fear of future persecution based on his membership in his social group as a homosexual" such that he could appeal against I.N.S. deportation back to Morocco under the United Nations Convention Against Torture and Other Cruel, Inhuman or Degrading Treatment or Punishment, known as the "Convention against Torture." The case was complicated, and the U.S. does not have a positive track record on allowing asylum on the basis of homosexuality. Questions arose not only about the veracity of his story but over the status of homosexuality in Islamic law and culture as it is practiced in Morocco. I was called upon in the case to speak about Islam as a religion and Islamic culture in Morocco, for I had lived and studied there for several years, was writing a book on Islamic law and ethics in Morocco, and taught an undergraduate course on gender and sexuality in Islamic cultures. In addition, I served on the *shari'a* advisory board for an advocacy group that works to support gay, lesbian, bisexual, and transgender Muslims in the U.S., Al-Fatiha Foundation. It was an honor to be called to witness in court, but the experience was a bit of an earthquake for me and shook me from my complacency.

I was accustomed to wearing jeans in a university classroom, but now I was wearing a suit. I was used to having an hour to explain a point about Qur'anic interpretation or Islamic legal reasoning in all its ambiguity and detail, but now I had to answer in sound bites. I took it for granted that students could listen to provocations in my lecture and come back tomorrow to ask for clarification or counter-argument with "the real truth" constantly questioned and refined, but now I had only one chance to speak before a decision was made. Before, I hoped my words would convey information mixed with a little wisdom, but now my words were operations of power, upon which a life depended. I had written about jurisprudence (both Islamic and Western) safely from a scholarly armchair, but now I was implicated from the witness chair in the very exertion of power that I had sought to understand from an observer's safe distance.[2] It was as if the world had been overturned in an upheaval that revealed some truths that were weighty to bear.

The case in court and my role in it inspired me to write this book. The case brought up many questions that the courtroom proceedings could not address adequately. This book seeks to address them in great detail and in the widest context, for the way we Muslims treat homosexuality and transgender experiences in our communities reveals much about our religious tradition, our practical interpretation of Islam, which may or may not live up to its essential principles and high ideals. In fact, it reveals how we Muslims have allowed many distortions of Islam to conform to cultural prejudices that are deeply ingrained but not inevitable.

The Trial

However discomforting it was for me to be in court, it was far, far worse for the young man whose hearing it was. After all, he was on trial, not me. Mehdi's own day of upheaval had occurred long before, not in court but in the apparent safety of his family home in a modern city of industry and trade in northern Morocco. He had grown up in a prosperous family, as the only son with four sisters. His father was a merchant marine captain who was a respected community member – both religiously pious and politically conservative – with friends well placed in government and the civic elite. Mehdi grew up hiding his homosexual orientation, owing to fear that revealing it would be dangerous and result in family strife, social ostracism, and bodily harm. In his testimony, Mehdi said, "I never disclosed my sexual orientation to my friends because I knew they would despise me. My friends openly spoke of their desire to kill anyone who was gay, and my personal experiences told me that these were not simply idle threats."[3] However, at age thirteen, his mother found him in a compromising position with a friend, a boy his own age. "As punishment, my mother slapped me twice across the face and held me forcibly while she heated a fork over the stove, which she then pressed against my hand, causing excruciating pain and leaving a scar that I still have. My mother told me that I had committed a very shameful sin, and she threatened to tell my teacher so that everyone at school would know of my sin and, more frighteningly to me, she said that if I met my friend again that she would tell my father." At fifteen, he had a sexual relationship with another adolescent male, a friend of a friend who was visiting his city for the summer. At the end of the summer, the friend left and Mehdi managed to repress his sexual feelings while continuing his schooling.

All this while he heard stories of young gay or lesbian people in his town and how they were treated. When he was thirteen, a teenage girl in his neighborhood was murdered while her parents were gone for the weekend. On going to the scene of the crime, "I noticed that the iron bars had been removed from one of the windows and the phone cable had been cut. I overheard some neighbors talking and saying that the victim was a lesbian woman ... I also overheard that the police knew it wasn't a robbery because nothing had been taken." Because no one was ever arrested for the murder, he concluded that the victim had been murdered for being a lesbian: an "honor killing" that her own family might have engineered. Three years later, another incident drove the danger of his situation home more clearly. The elder brother of one of his neighborhood friends, like many Moroccans, went to college in Germany and he used to return every summer for vacation. One summer, this friend's brother did not return from Germany. The other college students who came back "told everyone they saw that [he] hadn't returned because they had discovered that he was gay. I heard them say that they were afraid to do anything to him in Germany and that they wished he would return because 'it would be easy to get him in Morocco.'" Everyone knew that the police would look the other way and that in situations of violence directed at gay or lesbian Moroccans "The police would not protect me from violence at the hands of my family or others."

Despite this adverse social climate, or perhaps because of it, Mehdi threw himself into schoolwork. He excelled in math and physics to the point that his family rewarded him with his own bank account and passport in preparation for adulthood. At age seventeen, his parents gifted him a tourist visa to the United States, to spend a summer in New York and broaden his horizons. At this point, he felt confident enough to tell his mother that he was gay: the reasons for this confession were not clear, but could have come from discussion about future marriage plans, from discussion of his past "indiscretions," or simply from a sense of integrity in desiring adult honesty with one's mother.

"My mother's reaction was dramatic. She turned bright red, hit me in the face, and screamed at me for bringing disgrace to the family. When she prepared to leave the house, I knew that she was going to tell my father, and that terrified me." He took his clothes, wallet, passport, and all the money from his checking account and fled, staying for ten days at the home of a school friend while making plans to fly to New York.

But it was not so easy to escape confrontation. His father tracked him down and intercepted him in an airport in Europe. The father could not convince him to return to Morocco, so they agreed that they would travel together to New York and complete his trip as planned, then return together to Morocco later. "I was terrified because I could tell that he was angry and intended to punish me, but I did not know what to do. Therefore I let him take my money, my passport, and my return ticket." But on the second night in New York, he decided to flee a second time. He removed his papers and money from his father's wallet and hid out in a mosque in Queens. He spent the night at the mosque and then traveled further from New York. He has not seen his father since.

After some months in the U.S., he tried to contact his family indirectly, through the school friend with whom he had stayed upon setting out from home in Morocco. That friend answered the phone, yelled "Faggot!" and hung up. "I realized then that I could never go home to Morocco. My family had 'outed' me to the world. If my family were still considering whether to accept me again, they would not have told anyone else of my sexual orientation. The fact that my friend knows that I am gay means that my family has made the decision that I have brought shame on the family that cannot be ignored. I am certain that my family will do whatever it can to rid itself of this shame." In his deposition to the court, he concluded, "If I am deported to Morocco, my family will find me and punish me, and the authorities in Morocco will not protect me. Apart from the punishment I would suffer at the hands of my family, I know that if I am deported to Morocco I would also be persecuted by the government."

The role of government and police in the persecution of gay men and lesbian women in Morocco and other Muslim-majority states is controversial. The situation is made more complex by the ambiguous role of religion in law and state. An analysis of the written laws is not enough to understand the actual situation, however, because the police sometimes enforce an unwritten code of morality that is deeply influenced by conservative interpretations of Islam. Further, the police would not interfere with extended families, neighborhood associations, or conservative religious parties who assert moral order at a local level without reference to national law and without the restraint of legal requirements.

Mehdi's lawyer asserted, "The Moroccan government's history of persecuting homosexuals and its refusal to prevent or prosecute such persecution by non-governmental actors demonstrates that my client's fear [of persecution based on sexual orientation] is well founded." The lawyer contended that Mehdi could never take refuge with the police, for gay people are regularly exposed to "humiliation and harassment, at least" and would most likely be handed over to the family patriarch, "to be tortured or killed" at the family's discretion, and called this "state-sanctioned homophobia." Because homosexual sex acts are a crime that is "actively prosecuted in Morocco," homosexuals cannot seek protection from the police, because to do so may lead to arrest and prosecution on charges of homosexuality. "Apart from the danger of imprisonment, most police officers in Morocco are unwilling to protect homosexuals and may even participate in the anti-homosexual violence by committing physical and sexual assault against those suspected of being gay. Once arrested, homosexuals are often subject to physical and sexual assault by the police officers that arrest them, the prison guards who detain them, and even other detainees."

The lawyer's case spelled out the situation in absolute terms, in quick strokes of black and white. This was quite necessary, as under U.S. immigration law, it is very difficult to apply for asylum on the grounds of sexual orientation. The lawyer would have to prove beyond a reasonable doubt that Mehdi, if deported back to Morocco, would face torture or persecution leading to bodily harm either directly by government agents or indirectly with the connivance of government agents. U.S. law in general does not recognize homosexual orientation as grounds for legal protection against discrimination, so applications of asylum must be judged on the grounds of exposure to torture or cruel and inhuman punishment in the home country. Mehdi had not been publicly exposed as gay in Morocco and had not been arrested or suffered systematic discrimination outside his family. Therefore, his lawyer argued that Morocco's social climate, governmental system, and religious tradition are such that Mehdi would suffer bodily harm if deported.

The case raises important questions about how Islam as a religious tradition treats homosexuality. Or, more exactly, how Muslims as religious agents treat homosexual women and men in a systematically negative way that could be categorized as an infringement of their inalienable human rights. The seemingly simply question, "What does Islam say about homosexuals?" is not easy to answer. Islam, after all, has no voice. Only Muslims have voices. Only they speak in the name of Islam, and Muslims speak from distinct social and political contexts that shape how they practice and represent their religious tradition. Islam is a complex tradition with many variations, internal contradictions, and creative ambiguities. This is true even if those who discuss homosexuality do not normally admit any ambiguity or variation, whether condemning homosexuals or protecting them. I was called to testify in the court hearing to clarify the nature of Islam, its stance on homosexuality, and variations in Islamic practice among Moroccan Muslims.

In my university classes, public speeches, and published writings, I usually assert that Islam does not inherently and essentially condemn homosexuals, especially if homosexuals as people are distinguished from particular sexual acts commonly associated with them. I take this stance because I believe it to be true, and also because this stance can further the cause of internal reform in the Islamic tradition based upon its own intellectual resources and moral principles. However, in the courtroom I found myself answering questions in ways that led to the opposite conclusion: that Islam is deeply patriarchal and enshrines profoundly anti-homosexual sentiments and enforces legal rulings that severely curtail the welfare and human dignity of homosexuals in Muslim communities. My intellectual and moral position against saying that Islam's condemnation of homosexuals is essential to the religion is a response to universal concerns; in response to particular concerns, my testimony in Mehdi's case was that Islam as practiced in Morocco can easily lead to curtailed freedom, systematic discrimination, and bodily harm sanctioned by religion and perpetrated by the state. In court, it did not matter what Islam essentially is or could become in the future – what mattered was how Islam was practiced here and now by one Moroccan youth's family and community. In the interest of justice, one life deserved protection even if it meant seriously simplifying my presentation of Islam. The Qur'an warns us that no life is dispensable: *Whoever kills an innocent life, it is as if he had killed all of humanity. And whoever gives life to one, it is as if he had revived all of humanity* (Q. 5:32).

Reflecting upon this experience, I decided to write this book. It addresses many issues raised by Mehdi's court hearing. These issues came up in court in a highly rhetorical way, to establish whether the U.S. government should offer Mehdi asylum, rather than to determine the true character of Islam in all its complexity. This book aims to determine the true character of Islam, as seen through the experiences of lesbian, gay, and transgender Muslims, people like Mehdi and other activists who advocated for his legal protection. Their experiences urge us to reexamine the Qur'an and other foundational texts that Muslims consider sacred or authoritative in their theological and legal tradition, to determine if Islam is inherently and unavoidably against homosexual or transgender people.

There is an unprecedented new context for this detailed attention to Islam and homosexuality. Since 9/11, the public has grown increasingly aware of the violent agenda of Muslim extremists, an agenda that consistently includes upholding a death sentence for homosexuals in Muslim communities, whether or not this is stipulated in the national legal code where these communities reside. These events have accelerated discussions between Muslim groups about whether Islam condones such violence, what the real Islamic beliefs and ethics are, and how Islam accords with "secular" notions of universal human rights. At the same time, transgender, gay, and lesbian Muslim activists have begun to speak out more clearly and to establish organizations to encourage new thinking on the issue and support the welfare of vulnerable members of Muslim communities.

There is currently an international network of advocacy and support groups for lesbian, gay, bisexual, and transgender Muslims, as documented in the Introduction. Mehdi got in touch with one of these groups, which advocated his case. While in I.N.S. detention, he had spoken with a representative of Catholic Social Services, which was trying to ensure that the rights of illegal immigrants in detention since 9/11 were being protected, especially those from Arab and Muslim backgrounds. Mehdi told the representative that he had overstayed his visa because of his homosexual orientation and fear of punishment upon return to Morocco; the representative in turn informed a civic organization that advocates for legal protection of gay and lesbian youth, who in turn contacted Al-Fatiha Foundation. That organization helped secure legal representation for Mehdi and helped his lawyer access press articles, expert witnesses, and personal testimonies, including my own, to mount his asylum case. This book is based on the voices, ideals, and insights of lesbian, gay, and transgender Muslim activists who build and run these advocacy groups, as they negotiate their own personal struggles with religion, identity, family, and community and advance their reform-oriented insights into their own religious tradition, to which many still adhere despite overwhelming obstacles. Their experiences put human faces on the abstract issues of sexuality and authority in the Islamic tradition.

Islam on Trial

Since 9/11, Islam as a religion has been on trial in the West, and Muslims have differed sharply among themselves about whether to testify in the courts of journalism and public policy, and over whose testimony is credible. One could argue that Islam has been on trial since 1978, after the Iranian Revolution and subsequent oil crisis derailed Western assumptions about economic progress, slowly pushing secular advances out of the spotlight and casting attention on to religion. These events first pushed the West into uneasy alliances with Sunni fundamentalists and extremists, from the Wahhabi monarchies of the Gulf states to the Mujahideen and Taliban forces in Afghanistan. The first Gulf War revealed how flimsy that alliance was, as Muslim extremists turned against the U.S. and its allies, globalizing their revolt against local monarchies and authoritarian regimes that tried to rule by a balance of religious rhetoric and secular stability. These political developments overshadowed the crucial issues of women's rights, religious pluralism, and sexual diversity. Militant Muslim extremists raised the stakes with these issues by selectively enforcing elements from the Islamic tradition, driven more by political ideology than by faithful and intellectually honest adherence to tradition; this book terms such a strategy "neo-traditionalist." Militant Muslims from the neo-traditionalist movement vociferously demand a return to patriarchy as authentic religion while condemning with violence as scapegoats any vulnerable people who challenged their authority. The people challenging their authority include women's rights advocates, religious dissenters (in minority or non-Muslim communities, secularist citizens, leftist parties, or free-thinking intellectuals), and homosexuals.

Discussion of Islam and sexual orientation is never neutral and disinterested, even in the best of peaceful times. Our times are far from peaceful and discussion of religion is at the heart of current "culture wars" and justification of violence against innocent people, whether in the guise of terrorism or the uniform of warfare. This makes a book such as this one very tricky to write, perhaps even dangerous. But it makes writing the book now, in this context of Islam on trial, more urgent than it has ever been.

The strategy that this book will use to steer through the minefields of politicized religion and religious politics is to insist on local context and humanizing stories when discussing Islam. In that light, let us return to the hearing of Mehdi and his lawyer's strategy to highlight how Islam persecutes homosexuals, owing to its intrinsic nature and the manner by which it is practiced in Morocco. Mehdi's lawyer cited testimony of the program officer for the North Africa and Middle East region at the International Gay and Lesbian Human Rights Commission (I.G.L.H.R.C.). A practicing lawyer and U.S. citizen of Moroccan ancestry, he conducted fact-finding and research trips to Morocco, Tunisia, and Lebanon during which he interviewed gay and lesbian citizens, along with civic leaders, activists in human rights organizations, and officials at embassies.

His testimony in the hearing reports that "Most orders of Islam, including those practiced in Morocco, view homosexuality as an abomination, a violation of the natural order intended for mankind by Allah. Certain passages of Islam's most sacred text, the Qur'an, are cited as authoritative with respect to Islamic proscriptions against homosexual conduct. In the hadith, a set of writings purporting to set down statements made by the Prophet Muhammad himself and held by many Muslims to be persuasive authority if not binding guidelines that all Muslims must follow, the Prophet is said to have instructed his followers that homosexuality is a crime punishable by death."[4] To substantiate this claim, Mehdi's lawyer appended excerpts from guidebooks on Islam written by neo-traditionalists, those who claim to represent "traditional" Islam in new conditions of ideological debate. One such neo-traditionalist, Ahmad Sakr, writes that, "As far as homosexuality is concerned, Islam prohibits it completely and condemns it. Any male person who practices it is to receive the penalty in this world as well as in the hereafter. Any society that condones homosexuality is to be penalized all together: those who practice it, those who condone it, and those who defend it. In as much as Islam prohibits the practice of homosexuality among male persons, it also prohibits the sexual relationship of females among themselves. It is an abnormal behavior and it leads to psychological, moral, medical, social and religious abnormalities to the individuals and to society."[5] Ahmad Sakr quotes from the Qur'an to illustrate his condemnation of male homosexuality but not his condemnation of lesbians, and we will investigate why in Chapter 2. This unusual textual maneuver alerts us at the outset that representing what Islamic tradition says is not as simple as neo-traditionalists would like us to think.

In supplementing the arguments above, Abd al-Rahman Doi cites the Qur'an and also hadith. "Sodomy or homosexuality is an unnatural act of sex to satisfy one's passion ... The Prophet is reported to have said, 'If a man commits an act of sex with a man, they both are adulterers and if a woman commits such acts with a woman, then both of them are adulteresses [for whom the punishment is death].' Homosexuality is on the increase in the civilized Western world and homosexual clubs and unions are founded in the various countries of Europe and America that had only a few years ago considered homosexuality to be a major crime. If this is the sign of civilization, freedom and liberation, the less said the better."[6] The neo-traditionalist scholar cites hadith that claim to communicate verbatim teachings of the Prophet Muhammad, but does not discuss the troublesome issue of how to assess the authenticity of these reports or reconcile their multiplicity and mutual contradictions, a topic we will investigate in Chapter 3. Without such critical and progressive engagement with scriptural and legal texts, both Muslims and non-Muslims will treat as authoritative the narrow and shallow view of neo-traditionalists like the two cited above. They were presented during the hearing as authoritatively defining Islam's condemnation of homosexuality.

However, the full context of Islamic legal rulings is far more complicated. They are based upon the Qur'an and hadith, but were deduced from these texts through a process of rational analogy shaped by cultural assumptions and political expedience over a three-century-long process. Both Sunni and Shi'i orthodoxies represent the cumulative collection of legal decisions, the *shari'a*, as the immutable expression of God's will, based on the Qur'an and the Prophet Muhammad's directives.[7] Behind this representation, however, lies the fact that that the *shari'a* encompasses diversity between different interpretations as well as disagreement on the details of rulings and debate about the principles of deducing rulings themselves. Far from the monolithic façade that neo-traditionalists present, Islamic law of the classical period provides varied rulings about homosexual acts which embody deep and unresolved differences of opinion, as we will explore in Chapter 4. In addition, Islamic law is rarely applied directly in modern nation states with a Muslim majority. Most nation states with a Muslim majority enforce legal systems based on parliamentary legislation, autocratic command, or bureaucratic protocol; their rules and laws may be influenced by Islamic custom or ethics, but cannot realistically be said to enforce the *shari'a* in its classical form. Their rules and norms must be designed to govern all citizens in secular life, whereas the *shari'a* is designed to guide Muslims (in sacred ritual as well as secular interaction) and does not apply at all to non-Muslim citizens of nations even if the majority of citizens are Muslim by belief or heritage. In addition, the *shari'a* cannot be applied at all as enforceable law in Muslim minority communities, such as those living in pluralistic secular democracies in Europe, North America, and South Africa.

Many Muslims disavow opening up debate about unresolved differences of opinion from earlier times and shy away from controversial debates. Perhaps they feel it would damage people's piety to discuss difficult topics, as if the acknowledgment of ambiguities might shake people's faith. Or perhaps they do not feel qualified to return to the sources of theological debates, and deny the qualifications of others who do. This reticence toward open, frank discussions of diversity is even more acute when the issues involve sex and sexuality. Many contemporary Muslims feel shame in talking about sex. However, none of these attitudes is really Islamic, and when we look back at the theologians and jurists of Islam's classical age we may be amazed how bold and open they were. No topic was too insignificant or too intimate to discuss, and enlightened discussion illuminated by returning to the Qur'an could be trusted to increase the faith of those involved, even if they could not agree on a particular topic's resolution.[8]

There is no better spokesperson for this attitude and its practical application than Ibn Hazm (died 1064). He was a theologian and jurist, who wrote a commentary on the Qur'an and composed studies of legal issues that argued for continuing scrutiny of hadith and juridical logic in their application. He was an ethicist and social critic, who tried to integrate insights from philosophy and logic into theological debate. Informed by his active participation in politics and his abiding interest in literature, Ibn Hazm was one of the only Muslim theologians to put forward a deep psychological understanding of human nature which reveals how and why we fall in love. I summon him as a guide in the endeavor of this book.

Ibn Hazm was an interpreter of the Qur'an who was quite sensitive to issues of gender and sexuality and was relentless in exploring the contradictions in his community's conclusions about the sacred text. For instance, he held that women could be Prophets and upheld his opinion in detailed readings of the Qur'an itself, even though most in his patriarchal society believed that women were inherently inferior to men (in physique, in reason, and in piety) and therefore God would never entrust to women the authority of bearing divine messages to humanity.[9] Ibn Hazm was primarily educated and raised by women who were highly skilled in intellectual and artistic pursuits, so his experience allowed him to critically appraise and boldly disagree with the biases of his patriarchal culture, even though they were deeply inscribed in his religious tradition.

On such delicate issues, he outspokenly assessed his community's differences of opinion, both theological and legal, and critiqued any drive to close down debate. For instance, Ibn Hazm believed that homosexual acts were a crime, but totally disagreed with other Muslim jurists about the reason why this was so and the rationale for the penalties such acts incurred. He asserts that the punishment for homosexual acts as a crime is not is not based upon the Qur'an. This book will address his legal opinion in detail in Chapter 4. His is an important and subtle argument that urges us, now almost one thousand years after his lifetime, to reassess popular notions in Muslim communities about the acceptability of gay, lesbian, and transgender believers in their midst and at their margins.

Above and beyond his specific legal rulings or scriptural interpretations, Ibn Hazm acknowledged that love is love, whether it is hetero- or homosexual in orientation. He was an avid fan of love poetry and acknowledged that much of the best poetry written by Muslims was homoerotic, addressed by male poets to a beloved who is also male. In his famous study of Andalusian love poetry, *The Neck Ring of the Dove*, he mingles homoerotic love poetry with hetero-oriented love poetry, making no distinction between them and recognizing them all as beautiful expressions of love. In his study of Ibn Hazm's life and influence, the ethicist Abu Laylah notes that "Ibn Hazm knew the weakness of human nature and the strength of temptations. Concerning the sins and faults which emerge from physical temptations, and which inhibit faith and doctrine, we find that Ibn Hazm is tolerant and forgiving. He is sympathetic with men who love women, even with men who love boys [sic]."[10] Abu Laylah says "men who love boys" because of the Platonic framework in which same-sex attraction was understood in medieval Islamic culture, in which men usually (but not exclusively) fell in love with younger men or men who had not yet reached socially defined maturity.[11] As Ibn Hazm demonstrates, many Muslim authors, ethicists, and intellectuals saw hetero- and homoerotic love as being equally love. Both approaches were valuable as love, and both were potentially a spiritual training ground for loving God. This is an issue they considered independently from whether specific sex acts were legal or illegal.

Ibn Hazm may not agree with the arguments of this book, but were he alive today I have confidence that he would see the wisdom in posing the arguments. He eagerly probed the consensus of his Islamic community, testing their arguments against the touchstone of research and fearlessly raising objections to the conclusions of common piety and chauvinistic self-righteousness. In his era when holding slaves was common and legal he defended their inherent human rights; in his society which was a kingdom based on aristocratic privilege he argued that the state should provide all people free education.[12] He also argued that Islam must be practiced in accord with scientific observation and disciplined reason, calling upon the resources of logic and philosophy. In his world-embracing optimism, he saw all knowledge – whether it came from sacred or secular disciplines of learning – as leading to a greater knowledge of God and a greater appreciation of divine wisdom in the perpetual creation and re-creation of the world in which we live.

Ibn Hazm's influence was largely lost after the passing of Arab Andalusia. Many elements of the brilliant Spanish Islamic culture were embraced by Morocco and other North African Muslim societies that shared with it common roots and complex interactions. But Ibn Hazm's influence is largely suppressed, because he was critical of the Maliki school of law that dominated North Africa; no community currently follows his teachings based upon the Zahiri school of law. Rather, Ibn Hazm's insights were left as a written legacy for later generations, as potential pointers for later reformists who might find in them inspiration and guidance in totally altered situations. The case of Mehdi reveals just how altered contemporary situations have become from the classical Islamic times of Ibn Hazm. As Moroccans, Mehdi's community and family continue to live out the Islamic culture inherited from Arab Spain, yet the relations of power between the Euro-American West and the Arab Islamic world have radically changed. In that light, we return to the court case at hand.

Local Realities and Global Interactions

For an example of the complexity of the contemporary situation, we may note that Mehdi grew up in a constitutional monarchy that preserves some elements of traditional Islamic governance tempered by modern European practice introduced through French and Spanish colonial domination. The Moroccan king rules as a descendant of the Prophet, but shares symbolic power with a parliament. In the court hearing, this was expressed as: "The legal system of Morocco is based on Islamic law, with some areas (i.e., business law) supplemented by French and Spanish civil law. The personal laws which govern marriage, inheritance, filiations and sexual relations are all based on Islamic law." The Moroccan law forbidding homosexual acts may embody Islamic social ethics but does not enforce in detail the rulings of the *shari'a.* As interpreted by the Maliki legal school that dominates the North African region, sexual penetrative acts between men should be punished according to the rules for fornication outside of marriage: lashing for an unmarried perpetrator and death for one already married. In contrast, Moroccan law stipulates that homosexual activity is illegal pursuant to section 489 of the Moroccan Penal Code, which specifies a penalty of six months' to three years' imprisonment and a fine of 120–1,000 dirhams (approximately U.S.$1,040–8,700).

Homosexual activity, however defined – as a major sin in religious law or a crime in secular law – is a crime actively prosecuted in Morocco, as shown by evidence from newspapers, court trials, and personal testimonies. If held in police custody, homosexual Moroccans often face abuse, as attested by a staff member of A.L.C.S. (Association de Lutte Contre le S.I.D.A., a Moroccan association to combat the spread of A.I.D.S.) who has collected testimony of gay men and male sex-workers, who were sometimes raped in police custody and forced to have anal or oral sex against their will with the arresting officers. Those who end up in jail often face a worse regime of abuse: rape by prison guards or even being "rented out" by the guards for coerced sex with prison officials or other inmates.[13] Police often charge alleged homosexuals with moral offenses that are less burdened by proof of actual sex acts, such as obscene behavior, public lewdness, contempt of monotheistic faiths, or "abuse and exploitation of Islam" (a crime usually applied to fundamentalists, extremists, and terrorists). Even without active police prosecution, the laws exist as a threat hanging over anyone who is alleged to be or perceived to be a homosexual, rendering them vulnerable to harassment, exploitation, or blackmail by community members or government representatives.

Moroccan government representatives disavow these assertions of a hostile or dangerous climate for homosexual men and women. Many Moroccan intellectuals would support the government spokespersons. I was fortunate to participate in a masterclass on feminism with Fatima Mernissi, the renowned sociologist from Morocco's premier university and advocate for women's rights in Islamic communities. When I brought up the subject of homosexuality to ask her advice on the project of writing this book, she answered firmly that there was no persecution of homosexuals in Morocco. She even denied that there had ever been systematic persecution or suppression of homosexuals in Islamic history more broadly conceived. In Islamic culture, she asserted, sex is a private matter and not a matter for public discussion. The problem, she stated, is that in recent years globalization of culture, satellite television, and internet access have caused sex to invade the public space, eroding the previous ethic of tolerance under silence.[14] Of course, many Moroccan homosexuals lead their lives without coming to violent harm in prisons, without being persecuted by family or neighborhood, without being condemned by religion. But they do so under the cover of silence, always in fear of being exposed to the discourses of power: family honor, religious respectability, and state authority.[15]

However, the religious climate among Moroccans, in their home country and adopted diasporic homes, is drifting toward fundamentalist ideological versions of Islam and a militant rejection of modernism as capitulation to Euro-American dominance. Morocco's authoritarian monarchy has been a buffer against this trend, which has been felt much more strongly in Egypt, the Levant, and the Arabian Peninsula (and which has caused an outright civil war in neighboring Algeria). Upon the ascension to power of King Mohammad VI in July 1999, there were hopes for liberalization, widening of democratic participation, and progressive reform of family law. However, there was also fear that in order to strengthen his fragile position he might pass restrictions on social and moral issues in order to take the wind out of fundamentalist sails and bolster the Islamic legitimacy of his rule. One easy way to do this is by restricting women's ambition to achieve greater legal protection and cracking down on homosexual activities. The new King of Morocco seems to be resisting this option. In 2004, he supported a major reform of family law (called the "Moudawana"), which had been heavily informed by Islamic legal norms, reforms that give women greater equality with men in matters of marriage, divorce, and child custody. Yet, though these reforms are significant for women who marry, they leave homosexual men and women just as vulnerable to persecution by the state and victimization by families as they were before. In contrast to the Moroccan King, though, the Egyptian regime under President Hosni Mubarak has lately pandered to Islamic fundamentalists through high-profile arrests of gay men to buttress the authority of his autocratic regime.[16]

Fatima Mernissi pointed out that rhetoric that stigmatizes homosexuality as a pathological disease and outright attacks on homosexual persons are both "warning signs" of fundamentalist movements gaining strength (whether in Christian, Jewish, or Islamic contexts). There are disturbing signs that Morocco is affected by the region-wide rise of Islamic fundamentalism that finds an easy target in homosexuals. In 1999, the popular Arabic magazine *al-Majallah* focused an issue on the topic of homosexuality in Islamic countries. An interview was solicited from an Islamic scholar from al-Azhar, the preeminent Islamic university in Egypt, which is widely respected in the wider Sunni world; his call for the execution of all homosexuals was published in *al-Majallah*, which is widely available in Morocco. Its contents were reprinted the next week in the Moroccan daily *al-Ittihad al-Ishiraki*, the newspaper sponsored by the Union Socialiste des Forces Populaires (U.S.F.P.), the governing political party at that time and the main outlet for opinions on policy.[17] The Moroccan newspaper reports, like those elsewhere in the Arabic-language press, have been sensationalist and lurid to the point of framing homosexuality as Satan worship that threatens Islam.

Beyond Rhetoric to Personal Realities

The testimonies of a court hearing – whether in Cairo or in Virginia – do not reflect everyday reality. Trials mark unusual circumstances that come to the attention of the state. Mehdi was unusual in fleeing from his family and having the means to run far, not just across international borders but to the U.S. Most Moroccan youth have to find quieter means of coping with the limitations placed upon them by family, community, and state in the name of religion and moral order. However, the unusual nature of court hearings can reveal quotidian realities of social life. The way Mehdi's mother used family honor to shame her son into obedience is routine in Islamic families, as is her seamless interweaving of religious imagery into the coercive fabric of family control. From the interviews with gay, lesbian, and transgender Muslim activists that inform this book, it is clear that disentangling family expectations from religious beliefs is very difficult – for many it may be impossible – but it is the key to reconciling one's homosexual orientation with one's Muslim identity. We also observed how Mehdi's mother branded him with fire, a kind of family punishment that resonates with the Islamic past when companions of the Prophet, a few years after his death, punished an allegedly homosexual man with death by fire, as we will investigate in Chapter 4.

Mehdi's story also reveals to us how homosexuals in Muslim communities are silenced by shame and never given an opportunity to rationally discuss their sexuality, openly interpret their own religion, or express their own sense of morality based on their experiences of faith. For this reason, this book was written only after long interviews with lesbian, gay, and transgender Muslim activists who, by fortunate opportunity, intense ethical struggle, and great personal risk, have carved out a space in their outer lives and inner consciences to reconcile their homosexuality with their Islamic faith. Their insights emerge from the dark background of silence forced upon their many others sisters and brothers who, for lack of opportunity, education, or audacity, never arrive at a place of critical reflection about the interaction of their sexuality and their faith. We have observed how Mehdi escaped from his father and took refuge in a mosque, a strange irony that resonates with many others interviewed for this study. Though some gay, lesbian, and transgender Muslims may abandon their faith, many others refuse to relinquish their identity as Muslims. They retain their religious belief in the revelation of the Qur'an and their personal practice of Islamic rituals, even as they are persecuted or ostracized in their religious communities. The activists upon whose insights this book is based are those who have not relinquished the struggle, though they may be at very different places in the long journey of reconciling Islamic faith with homosexual or transgender experience.

They are the voices of men and women who have founded and run support groups for lesbian, gay, and transgender Muslims, groups like al-Fatiha in the U.S. which helped successfully secure asylum for Mehdi. His court hearing ended with the I.N.S. lawyer, who was commissioned to persuade the judge to deport Mehdi, arguing for the judge to uphold his asylum request, having been thoroughly convinced of the honesty of his story and the gravity of the danger that would face him if he returned. The judge concluded the court hearing by congratulating Mehdi on his courage, welcoming him as a legal resident of the U.S., and hoping that he would abide by the law in order to qualify for American citizenship in a few years.

Mehdi walked from the courthouse shaking his head in disbelief. "These past years are as if I had been living in black-and-white," he said, "but now, slowly, I'm beginning to see color again." He is currently living in the brightest colors possible – he passed his general education qualifying exams, has qualified for scholarships to begin college, and plans to study accounting and finance. "At this moment, although life is a little bit hard between school and work, I cannot complain. This great country gave me what my own country – Morocco – could not give. People who were complete strangers came to rescue me from a terrifying jail and opened their house to me, while the others helped raise money to cover my expenses while my case was pending." Some earthquakes destroy while others remove obstacles, shaking down mountains that previously seemed unmovable. Some upheavals, while terrifying, cause hidden truths to be revealed with a clarity that only comes through trial. In the end, *Whoever does an atom's weight of good sees its consequence, and whoever does an atom's weight of harm sees its consequence* (Q. 99:7–8).

Chapter 2

Liberating Qur'an: Islamic Scripture

> Remember when you were few
> and oppressed to the ground
> And feared that people would carry you off by force
> But God gave you shelter, aiding and strengthening you
> And provided for your welfare
> that you might give thanks
>
> Qur'an 8:26

Islam began as protest against a system of oppression. The Qur'an announced that belief in one God would lead the fledgling Muslim community through a process of liberation. Like the Israelite Tribes under the leadership of Moses, whose story the Qur'an narrates, the Muslims too would leave a state of oppression. They would traverse the desert of struggle, cross the river of promise, and create a new community in which they could live in a state of blessed well-being. Muslims left suffering as an oppressed minority in Mecca and moved to Medina where they founded a commonwealth based on monotheistic belief which would break down old hierarchies and divisions.

This is the core narrative that shapes Muslim self-understanding, even if Muslims have not always lived up to its ideals of struggle, transformation, and liberating solidarity. It is an ideal that has moved many Muslims in South Africa as they faced the seemingly intractable apartheid system (enforced as it was with sophisticated weapons, international recognition, nationalist legitimacy, mineral wealth, and even nuclear weapons). They found strength in scriptural exhortations to struggle against injustice and oppression, whether in the

Qur'an's telling of the Exodus narrative or in the Muslims' own flight to Medina. In South Africa, Muslims as well as Jews and Christians developed very powerful intellectual and spiritual currents of liberation theology as they searched for the power, inspiration, and solidarity to resist apartheid. They remembered the Qur'anic words of consolation quoted at the head of this chapter: *Remember when you were few and oppressed to the ground.* Those who seek liberation from this oppression through belief in God are told to uphold justice: *don't betray God and the Prophet, and don't betray your responsibilities to others entrusted to you* (Q. 8:66–67).

In South Africa, lesbian, gay, and transgender Muslims also take courage and hope from these words. Despite their small numbers, they have created a support group, called the Inner Circle, which organizes discussion groups, spiritual retreats, conferences, and media interventions. The support group's members have grown up as strangers within their own families, feeling utterly alone and under constant fear of being found out and punished. Most are convinced that they are the "the only one." Therefore, taking ownership of one's identity and admitting one's inner identity to the point of joining a group is a major step, and fostering this process is a key function of a support group. Muhsin Hendrix, one of the founders of this support group, stated, "I believe that just because I am gay does not mean I can't practice Islam or be a Muslim and I've used the Qur'an to back up this belief."[1] He enjoyed a solid madrasa education and has experience teaching in one, but he also faced persecution when he began to come out as gay. Instead of suffering alone, he resolved to reach out and find others in his same position and with them to build a community. He says, "I realized that I'm not alone – these people are going through the very same things that I'm going through. But I've managed, because of my in-depth relationship with God, to reconcile the two. I was completely comfortable saying to the world that I'm gay and I'm Muslim. I wanted to help other people to get there."[2] The support group he directs was born from an earlier group that Muhsin and others formed in 1998, Al-Fitra Foundation. They took the term *al-fitra* from the Qur'an as the name for the group: "The message then was to let people know that [homosexuality] is not a pathology, that it is [one's] nature – you were either born that way or even if you were conditioned to be that way through society, it was when you were too young to have a decision in that. So it is part of your *fitra* – your nature." This chapter will explore below the resonance of this term, *fitra* or "nature," in the Qur'an and its importance for understanding sexual orientation from an Islamic point of view.

Muhsin explained that his approach to Islam may be characterized as liberation theology, based upon the insight that God's will works with and through those who suffer oppression. He states that the central principle of the Qur'an is solidarity with the oppressed, such that openness to God's presence and message is conditioned by how committed one is to justice for those who are deemed weak and who suffer in their vulnerability. Many lesbian, gay, and transgender Muslims share with Muhsin his admiration for liberation theology, even if they have not experienced it first hand in an existential struggle as in South Africa.

The liberation theology approach of transgender, gay, and lesbian Muslims provides a profound interpretation of the Qur'an. Its central principle – striving for justice in solidarity with the oppressed – lets gay, transgender, and lesbian Muslims join a wider coalition of reformers. It lets them join all women, youth, racial minorities, and others who are marginalized or disempowered by the political–religious system that rules them. From the position of being an oppressed minority, they hear the Qur'an's voice from a particularly sensitive position, when it insistently asks Muslims, *Why don't you struggle in the way of God and on behalf of those who are oppressed? On behalf of those men, women and youth who say "O Lord! Help us to escape from this town whose people oppress us, give us a guardian appointed by you, and grant us aid from one close to you"* (Q. 4:75).

Oppression and Resistance in the Qur'an

The Qur'an encourages solidarity with the oppressed and this is an essential component of its message. It is inseparable from the divine charge to act with justice and responsibility. The Qur'an calls those who are oppressed *al-mustad'afun fi al-ard* or those who are made weak and held down. The Arabic phrase is very subtle. The oppressed are "deemed weak" by others who grab power for themselves, but they are not actually weak. They suffer in their vulnerability but actually have great strength and resilience. God is on their side. They hear God's message clearly because of their condition of vulnerability, suffering, and oppression. Their endurance, pain, and patience render them open to hearing God's voice and accepting God's message when Prophets come. In standing up against their oppression they enact God's will in the world, to the surprise of those who are accustomed to wielding power and thinking themselves gods.[3]

The story of the Prophets is the narrative of those who hear the speech of God because their ears are opened by suffering oppression and struggling against it with endurance and patience. The message of the Prophets, such as Lot, Salih, Moses, and Muhammad, is not just to believe in one God and reject the worship of false idols. It is also to sacrifice one's own well-being to protect the poor, the vulnerable, the strangers, and those who suffer, without which worship is incomplete, indeed hypocritical. This chapter will revisit the stories of Lot and Salih in detail later, but here we should note how each Prophet stood with the oppressed and was denounced by the powerful of their society, those who "considered themselves greater" because they arrogated for themselves wealth, prestige, and ideological truth.

Salih was the Prophet sent to the prosperous people of Thamud, as the Qur'an tells. The chief of those who acted proudly and thought themselves better than others said to those of his people whom they oppressed and considered weak, "Do you think that Salih is a messenger sent by his Lord?" They answered, "We believe in the message that he brings" (Q. 7:75). Lot was the Prophet sent to the wealthy Cities of the Plain (which included Sodom and Gomorrah, though they are not named as such in the Qur'an). When he tries to protect the weak, poor, and homeless with a Prophetic ethic of generous hospitality, his people oppress him and prove him weak by violating his dignity and abusing his guests. Similarly, Moses stands up against some of his own people who try to rebel against him and throw his status as Prophet under their feet by worshiping the golden calf. Moses said, *Terrible is what you have done behind my back after I left! You have turned your back on the order of your Lord ... Surely the people try to render me weak and they have almost killed me – so let my enemies not rejoice over my defeat or count me among those who are unjust* (Q. 7:150). In narrative after narrative, the Qur'an clearly links idolatry to injustice, and shows that people oppose their Prophets by oppressing them along with their followers and rendering them weak. God blesses those whom the strong and arrogant deem weak, those who suffer injustice and are ground into the dirt as a result of the social system and its power relationships that the powerful build into idols, fashioning divinity out of their own drive to power. *Surely Pharaoh exalted himself over the land ... but we desired to bless those who were oppressed into the ground and deemed weak, to make them the leaders in righteousness and make them inherit [our presence]* (Q. 28:4–5).

Yet when those who are weak and oppressed rise up and come to power; they can end up quickly oppressing others. The Israelite Tribes were oppressed in Egypt under Pharaoh's idolatrous ego, as the Qur'an narrates.[4] Yet when the Israelite Tribes tasted freedom from oppression, they turned against their Prophet, trying to oppress Moses and render him weak. Like the Israelite Tribes, the Muslim community also has a history mixed with success and failure. Their initial fervor in standing up for the weak and dispossessed was galvanized by the Prophet Muhammad, himself an orphan, and his earliest followers were slaves, women, ethnic minorities, and other marginalized outsiders. In their fervor, the earliest Muslims established an innovative new commonwealth, based on a brother-and-sisterhood of belief, shared wealth, and mutual protection. Their experiment conflicted with Arab tribal forces in Mecca and later Jewish sectarian forces in Medina, the two forces that defined the status quo of military might, trade profits, and religious legitimacy in Arabia.

The initial success of the Muslims' experiment, however, rendered it liable to compromise and retrogression. Muslims increasingly turned to fighting external enemies in order to bolster their mutual solidarity, while allowing old tribal pride and patriarchal values to creep back into their community. As warfare generated power and profits, Muslims returned to the old inequalities and hierarchies. They began keeping slaves even though the Qur'an urged them to free slaves. They began acting as patriarchs even though the Qur'an declares the moral equality of men and women. They began living in luxury even though the Qur'an warns against the hoarding of wealth. Within a few generations, the Muslims' experimental commonwealth of liberation became an empire that rivaled Rome. The Qur'anic message of liberation was interpreted as an Islamic charter for domination.

The Qur'an is still with us and its message is not lost. Its message of liberation still reverberates in its words and imagery, sometimes explicitly and other times implicitly. Whether that message is heard and embodied by Muslims is only a matter of how it is interpreted by them. Liberation theology argues that the existential condition of those who interpret shapes their interpretation. The poor, the vulnerable, and the suffering are in an existential position to actively hear the scriptural message and its call toward justice. They have a privileged position as interpreters of scripture precisely because they are in a disempowered position, because they are oppressed within their society.

Islamic Liberation Theology

Liberation theology is a distinct way of "talking about God." Liberation theology works from within religious traditions to stand against the drive to power of patriarchal and priestly elites who speak for those traditions. Liberation theology tries to restore the courage of those who are oppressed, confident that those who suffer truly understand God's message and, in standing against such injustice, embody God's will in this world. Whether they are professional theologians or community activists, Muslims with an orientation toward liberation theology seek to restore the voice of the dispossessed and let them speak the truth of their own experiences, for their experience of injustice should guide the community's understanding of its religious commitments and moral duties. Gay, lesbian, and transgender Muslim activists have taken up this challenge. Muhsin Hendrix is directly aware of these wider connections. He was inspired by the South African theologian and political activist Farid Esack, who led a movement called the Call of Islam which actively embraced the anti-apartheid struggle.

Farid Esack's book entitled *Qur'an, Liberation and Pluralism* articulates the religious principles of liberation theology in Islam with clarity and depth. It is required reading among lesbian and gay Muslim activists.[5] Esack's work synthesized progressive Islamic thinking with passionate political activism. Esack argued not only that Islam's essential goal is the liberation of believers from all forms of oppression, but also that the ongoing and ever-renewed drive toward justice will liberate the Qur'an from prior interpretation that used scripture to justify various forms of oppression. In his view, the Qur'an is both liberating and in need of liberation. To fulfill its promise of liberation, Muslims must first free the Qur'an from partial, limited, and corrupted interpretations that enshrine injustice.

In the context of South African apartheid, the immediate goal of Esack and others who participated in this struggle was liberation from the oppression of racial hierarchies and the systems of inequality and poverty that they enforced. From complementary angles, many Muslim women took up this challenge by identifying patriarchal social systems as causes of oppression: women like Fatema Mernissi, Amina Wadud, Asma Barlas, and Kecia Ali, among many others. Such feminist Islamic scholars point out how patriarchy limits women's equality and spirituality but also compromises men's well-being and leads to the social ills of authoritarianism. They are joined by a growing number of male scholars like Khalid Abou El Fadl and Omid Safi who support feminist critiques and see them as crucial to freeing men from social roles that are rooted in injustice and aggression. As a group, these activist-scholars, both female and male, articulate an Islamic liberation theology that seeks both to free Muslim women from inequalities and also to free the Qur'an from male-dominated interpretations that limit its spiritual potency.[6] Gay and lesbian Muslim theologians, whether in formal or informal ways, also join this broad movement that is only made stronger by having so many fronts. This wider movement that has absorbed the ethical spark and intellectual tools of liberation theology has come to be known as the movement of Progressive Muslims, a rubric that seems to have been first applied in South Africa and subsequently spread to Muslim communities living in North America and Europe.[7] It has articulated the need for Muslims to interpret the Qur'an anew to recover its initial egalitarian and liberating message. It has also provided the intellectual tools to carry out such interpretation. In doing so, Progressive Muslim activists and scholars aim to revive the Islamic tradition from within.

Gay, lesbian, and transgender Muslim activists see themselves and the advocacy organizations that they are building as part of this wider movement.[8]

Their perspective on the Qur'an is rooted in their particular existential experience as a minority defined by sexual orientation and gender identity, but it has a much wider relevance that resonates with the perspectives of other minority groups. As Muslims, however, their voices are rooted in the Qur'an and accountable to its ideals and pronouncements. What questions do they ask of the Qur'an and what answers does it provide them? How does their approach to the Qur'an challenge previous interpretations? How does it stimulate interpretation as a perpetual challenge for Muslims as a community in every age?

Principles and Tools of Qur'an Interpretation

Transgender, lesbian, and gay Muslims participate in this Progressive Muslims movement, and their well-being depends upon its outcome. The aim of this wider movement is to revive the Islamic tradition from within. It aims to "prune" the tradition of old branches that may have once been vital but are now dead and serve only to justify injustice in the name of religion. In pruning the living tree of Islam, they hope to revive the flow of its life-giving sap, clearing the way for new growth in hopes of future fruit.

There is certainly some dead wood to pruned back. Muslims have produced a very rich but dense literature of interpretation (*tafsir*) of the Qur'an. The density of this literature is an expression of reverence for the Qur'an but also a sign of how difficult it is to apply the Qur'an directly to issues of social organization and legal rules. For example, the fourth caliph Imam 'Ali faced Khariji rebels who insisted that he simply "apply" the Qur'an's judgment without interpretation. In that situation of armed conflict, Imam 'Ali gathered the people and brought out a copy of the Qur'an and as he touched the book he exclaimed, "O Qur'an, speak to the people!" The people gathered around 'Ali, saying, "O 'Ali, do you mock us? It is only paper and ink and it is we [human beings] who speak on its behalf." To this, 'Ali stated, "The Qur'an is written in straight lines between two covers. It does not speak by itself. It needs proper interpreters, and the interpreters are human beings."[9]

Imam 'Ali was right to demonstrate that it is always human beings who speak for the Qur'an – they interpret its words according to their own commitments and political positions. This means that interpretation is always ambiguous and contested. This ambiguity allows gay, lesbian, and transgender Muslim activists to articulate an interpretation of the Qur'an that is "sexuality-sensitive," attentive to homosexual experiences, and accommodating to their presence among Muslims. They contend that the Prophet Lot condemned same-sex rape and denounced the use of sex as coercion against the vulnerable, and that the men of Sodom and Gomorrah committed lustful violence against Lot's guests not out of sexual appetite but in order to deny Lot's Prophetic mission by denying him the authority and dignity of giving hospitality to guests and strangers. This chapter will later provide details about such alternative scriptural interpretation and will argue that it is a more literal and more contextual reading of the sacred text than one informed by patriarchal and homophobic prejudice.[10]

Lesbian, gay, and transgender Muslims approach the Qur'an with a dual strategy of resistance and renewal. They resist previous interpretations, but advocate on behalf of new interpretation that is arguably better – more accurate, more insightful, or more ethical – than previous interpretations. In terms of resistance, they focus on resisting previous interpretations of the story of the Prophet Lot, a story that many claim condemns homosexuality. They also query other verses that speak about transgressions particular to women, which a few interpreters claim condemn lesbian acts. In terms of renewal, transgender, lesbian, and gay Muslims focus on verses that affirm their presence in God's message, in moments when the Qur'an values diversity in creation and pluralism within human communities, both on a universal plane and in specific discussions of the Prophet Muhammad's community in Medina. Between renewal and resistance, they celebrate the fact that changing historical conditions open new opportunities to generate insights into the meaning of the Qur'an, meaning that was always there but was obscured by the limitations of previous conditions. Prior interpretations are limited by the conceptual and political commitments of human beings who were just as frail and fallible as we are when they engaged in interpretation.

Before this chapter turns to the interpretation of specific verses of the Qur'an, it is essential to discuss the principles and tools of interpretation. It is critical that we be clear about this before diving into the Qur'an's words, because many Islamic authorities would forbid "common Muslims" from engaging in interpretation at all, especially if they are from the margins of communal life (like women, youth, the poor, or people from sexual and gender minorities). If one adds up these so-called marginal people, one finds that they constitute the vast majority of Muslims; so the majority of Muslims are not given the tools to interpret the Qur'an and are denied the very right to interact directly and personally with the Qur'an. Of course, one needs a certain level of knowledge to engage in interpretation. But those with such knowledge should engage in consultation with others whose experience may speak to and through the Qur'an, even if their level of formal knowledge of Arabic and Islamic sciences is not sufficient to allow them complete mastery over the interpretive arts.[11] Societies that restrict the pursuit of religious knowledge and suppress the spiritual quest for meaning betray an essential element of the Qu'ranic message. As Muslims, our interpretation will be richer if there are more varied voices asking questions of the Qur'an.

A sexuality-sensitive interpretation of the Qur'an is an understanding of its words and message that takes into account the reality of sexuality and sexual orientation among the people who read and follow it. A sexuality-sensitive interpretation would be explicitly non-patriarchal. It would not presume patriarchal values of male supremacy; it would not assume that all readers of Qur'an are (or should be) heterosexual in orientation. It would avoid imposing ideas of human nature that are obsolete (such as medieval Muslim assumptions based on philosophy, medicine, or psychology, largely adopted from Hellenic norms in the Middle East that have long been proved crude and unscientific). In this sense, sexuality-sensitive interpretation of the Qur'an would complement and support gender-sensitive interpretation of the scripture (to which feminist Islamic scholars, both women and men, are dedicated) as well as race-sensitive and class-sensitive interpretations.

Such progressive approaches to interpretation are based upon seven principles: (1) the inherent dignity of all human beings as bearing the breath of God;[12] (2) the sacredness of life such that all persons may pursue the highest spiritual aspirations of well-being in this world and salvation in the next; (3) the ethic of pluralism, for God creates diversity as an ethical challenge to meet the other, care for the other, and understand the other as a way of coming to fully know oneself; (4) order with justice, for God's message is eternal yet complex, announcing principles and promoting their flexible application in ever-changing social circumstances;[13] (5) God's speech is meaningful, such that interpretation is the right and obligation of all Muslims to discover what God intends behind, within, and through scripture's words (within the constraint of the linguistic limits and grammatical construction of the words);[14] (6) faith complements reason, such that the Qur'an must be understood in the light of observed experience, scientific exploration, and reasoned argument about human nature; (7) love is the goal, for, though the Qur'an urges us to build societies based on moral order requiring rules and laws, the deeper goal behind this order is the promotion of loving sincerity between each person and God, between individuals of the faith community, between members of every family, and between sexual partners.[15]

These seven principles must guide the interpretation of the Qur'an. But interpretation must be carried out with specific tools. Many of these tools were specified by early Muslim scholars who engaged in interpretation (*tafsir*), and others have been added to the interpreter's toolbox by modern Muslim thinkers.[16] These tools include: (1) striving for linguistic accuracy such that all interpretations of the Qur'an that conform to the grammatical conventions of

Arabic are possible and authentic meanings;[17] (2) maintaining the Qur'an's primacy – in its own use of language, its own retelling of narratives, and its own principles – rather than falling back on cultural prejudice, pre-Islamic patterns, or related scriptural traditions; (3) affirming the Qur'an's integrity, such that its interpretation should not be limited to a word-for-word translation, a phrase-by-phrase explanation, or a verse-by-verse assertion but should refer back to other uses of terms or ideas in the whole Qur'an;[18] (4) clarifying the Qur'an's context, for, though scripture is eternally relevant, the context in which the Qu'ran was revealed shapes the language and form in which its message is expressed;[19] (5) focusing on principles, for ethical principles are the core of the Qur'an's guidance, and interpretation brings them forth from the language of the Qur'anic message; (6) restraint in imposing rules until one has fully explored whether a rule is in accord with underlying principles conveyed in the Qur'an; (7) embracing moral optimism, for our understanding of the Qur'an is not determined solely by the technical tools of interpretation (like grammar, linguistics, Arabic poetry, history of the early Islamic community, and comparison with other scriptures) but is also shaped by our attitude toward life. How one interprets the Qur'an depends upon how one conceives human nature, what role one understands sexual activity to play in human relationships, what worth one assigns to gender differences, and how one thinks political authority should work in the community.[20]

These seven tools reveal how complicated the task of interpreting scripture really is. When believers use such linguistic, rational, and ethical tools to interpret scripture under the guidance of the seven principles laid out above, they can proceed with interpretation. However, the process is always one of debate and dispute. It is an ongoing process that is never complete or free of contestation. Though believers understandably crave certainty, the ambiguities inherent in interpretation actually play a positive role – they keep us both intrepid and humble in the constant search for a most holistic and just interpretation.

In the Islamic tradition, interpretation of the Qur'an is an aspect of *ijtihad* – the struggle to understand. It is the struggle to commit all one's resources – spiritual, intellectual, literary, and political – to understanding a matter of faith. It shares a common linguistic root with the Arabic word *jihad*, meaning a struggle in the more overtly physical sense, with moral suasion, legal compulsion, or physical coercion. The two types of struggle are integrally related. The custodians of power most often oppose those who engage in *ijtihad* (who struggle for an understanding of religion through which they can dedicate themselves to God with full sincerity and clear conscience). The latter often face violence or its threat, both actual violence and symbolic violence.

For lesbian, gay, and transgender Muslims, the struggle must be non-violent even when they are faced with violence or its threat. This is because their struggle is primarily with their own families and immediate communities. Persuasion rather than coercion is the only strategy that will work, even if their families and communities suppress them or treat them with violence. The Qur'an also encourages believers to struggle with words rather than fists, saying *Summon them to the way of your Lord with wisdom and good counsel, and argue with them by means that are more wholesome* (Q. 16:125). But before they can speak to community or family, transgender, lesbian, and gay Muslims must struggle with themselves, with the fear they internalized as they were raised. If this fear becomes rooted deep in the psyche, it can lead to self-loathing and result in self-destructive behavior. Denying the ones who oppress you the ability to dominate your inner life is often a more decisive form of resistance to oppression than a counter-punch.

Just such a non-violent strategy is the gay, transgender, and lesbian Muslim effort to assert their own interpretation of Qur'an as a fuller and better interpretation. It denies their oppressors the means to marginalize and silence them; it invites them to rise above the violence of exclusion and to recognize that both sides share core values. In this way, lesbian, gay, and transgender Muslims can turn to the Qu'ran for a symbolic affirmation of their humanity and worth. Through its verses, they call upon God to provide them inner strength and resolve to face a struggle that is intensely inward but also outward, which integrates the psychological and the political. With this background about the principles of interpretation, its tools, and its high stakes, we can turn to the specific verses that gay, lesbian, and transgender Muslims consider.

Diversity and Sexuality

In the Qur'an's view, diversity is a positive reality in the created nature of things. Diversity and multiplicity in the cosmos, in humanity, and among social groups are an integral part of God's creative will. They are an indispensable challenge to our moral systems. Islamic feminists have explored the Qur'anic description of gender, such as in the verse: *O people, stay aware of your Lord who created you all from a single self and created from it its mate and spread from those two many men and women* (Q. 4:1). The creation of women was not a mistake, a lessening of the moral standard, or a faulty copying of the perfect male (as suggested by later patriarchal interpretations in Islam encoded in the *shari'a*).[21] Diversity in gender is intimately related to diversity in human communities among tribes, sects, nations, and civilizations: *O people, We created you all from a male and female and made you into different communities and different tribes, so that you should come to know one another, acknowledging that the most noble among you is the one most aware of God* (Q. 49:13). There is a moral purpose behind the single God's creation of different and seemingly contradictory human types: it challenges us to restrain our egoistic aggrandizement, practice ethical compassion toward others, protect the vulnerable in their socially defined difference, and through this to stay conscious of God's presence. *If God had willed, God would have made you one single community, but rather God brings whomever God wills within divine compassion – yet the unjust oppressors have no guardian and no helper* (Q. 42:8).

Our human diversity is often cause for exclusion and violence, but it is actually God's way of challenging us to rise up to the demands of justice beyond the limitation of our individual egoism and communal chauvinism. Deep diversity confronts us with a bewildering pattern of differentiation. Difference often leads us to exclude others in hopes of building a firm community or with ambition to create a hierarchy of power to assert some moral order. However, the Qur'an warns us against going to extremes to exclude others, reminding us that not a single life is dispensable: *Whoever kills an innocent life, it is as if he had killed all of humanity. And whoever gives life to one, it is as if he had revived all of humanity* (Q. 5:32). All people, despite the apparent and real differences, are part of a greater whole. Safeguarding the dignity of each is essential to achieving one's own dignity and upholding the rights of each is integral to securing justice for oneself.

The diversity of human communities is not just in appearance, but also in the subtler hues of language and shades of belief. The Qur'an says, *One of God's signs is the creation of the heavens and the earth and the diversity of your tongues and your colors, in which there are signs for those who know* (Q. 30:22). The Qur'anic term for "color" (*lawn*), in the richness of Arabic metaphors, can refer not just to visible hues but to other sensations like the "taste" of different dishes of food or aromas.[22] Our diversity as human beings goes much deeper than color of the skin or surface appearance, and extends into the inner core of our personalities where language, concepts, beliefs, and experiences lie. With such a radically positive assessment of human diversity on the epistemological and ethical levels, one can justifiably wonder whether the Qur'an addresses diversity in sexuality as well.

What do we mean by sexuality? Deep in the core of the human personality lies our sense of sexuality, which is far more subtle and pervasive than mere sexual acts. By sexuality, we mean a kind of self-awareness that is not just an urge like lust, but rather a passion that grants us emotional fulfillment, sparks in us expansive joy, and urges us toward existential coming-to-completeness through encountering another person in a way that unites body, soul, and spirit. Sexual acts bring us as close as possible to "tasting" another person, not just in bodily sensations, but also in comprehending the other person's sense of self. Just like tasting food, one comes to sense another's presence by merging her or him with one's own body, dissolving the barrier between self and other through harmonious movement, intense intimacy, and ecstatic rapture. This is why sexual acts are so powerful. This is why sexuality is such an intimate part of each individual's personality and an integral component in each person's appreciation of beauty or apprehension of emotional intensity.

Sexuality is made up of many components, making its manifestation in any individual unique. These components include strength of sex drive, frequency of sexual contact, a continuum of style from aggressively passionate to delicately tender, and variation in intensity of response. An integral component of sexuality is sexual orientation, that is, whether one is attracted to a partner of the same gender or the opposite gender (or perhaps to both and possibly to neither). Is this concept found in scripture or in Islam? Classical Islamic theologians and jurists discussed "sexuality" (though in a way deeply prejudiced by male dominance), but they did not reflect systematically on what we call "sexual orientation." Before we turn to their opinions, upon which the classical Islamic tradition is based, we need to develop a sufficiently subtle model based on the Qur'an for understanding personality and how sexual orientation is related to it.

Nature and Personality

Sexual orientation is one of the "color" differences that make people distinct from each other. Yet those who oppose homosexuality call it "unnatural" or against human nature. In contrast, lesbians and gays attest that their sexual orientation expresses their innate personality and sense of self that are so deep as to be beyond rational capacity to alter; transgender people assert the same of their gender identity. Clinical research by professional psychiatric associations support this attestation, and most have removed homosexuality from the category of "personality disorder" and disavowed techniques previously claimed to be able to "correct" sexual orientation. The argument is over what constitutes human nature. From an Islamic perspective, we can ask: How does God create human beings? What role do sexuality and sexual orientation play in the personality? Do human beings choose their sexual orientation? Is it alterable by choice or habit? Are we morally accountable for sexual orientation if it is part of the sub-rational elements of personality? The questions raised are profound and the answers are not obvious.

Modern psychiatry increasingly holds that sexual orientation is an inherent part of an individual's personality. Elements effecting sexual orientation may be genetic, influenced by hormonal balances in the womb, and shaped by early childhood experiences, the cumulative effects of which unfold during adolescence and early adulthood.[23] Most psychiatrists in the West (and increasingly among professionals in Muslim communities) assert that one's attitude toward one's sexual orientation is largely cultural, but that the orientation itself is not cultural. The behavior deriving from one's sexual orientation is subject to rational control and clinical modification, but the underlying sexual orientation is not. In pre-modern times, philosophers also observed that sexual orientation was largely determined outside the choice of the individual; lacking knowledge of genes, hormones, and psychiatric research, they usually speculated that determination was by astrological influences.[24] The personal accounts of lesbian and gay Muslims testify to the early and deep feeling of being different, followed by long and difficult struggles to understand that this difference was due to homosexual orientation and to find ways of explaining this to family and friends while striving for emotional satisfaction within the limits of one's sexual possibilities. Today, Muslim communities are undecided as to whether to accept modern psychiatric research. Professional psychiatrists in countries with modern medical systems have renounced the idea that homosexuality is a pathology that must be "cured" by changing one's sexual orientation. They hold that one's internal disposition cannot be changed even if outward behavior can be. Most clinical therapists have renounced the idea of changing a patient's sexual desire or behavior, and instead help the homosexual client deal with unresolved childhood traumas caused by rejection by family, society, and religion.

As professionals in Muslim communities slowly adopt clinical approaches based on research and modern medicine, they advocate a non-judgmental approach. At the same time, neo-traditionalist Muslims caricature homosexuality as a crime, a disease, or an addiction, and they have a wide audience. Many Muslims are willing to accept modern medical knowledge and techniques in an ad hoc manner to solve particular problems, but shy away from developing a coherent theory of the human personality based either upon medical practices and scientific discoveries or upon their own religious scripture. However, the Qur'an offers many insights into a theory of personality, and we can integrate into them new complexities revealed by contemporary psychiatry so that our notions of morality may be firmly grounded in the reality of human personality.

Personality is made up of many levels, and in the Qur'an one finds reference to at least four basic levels: outer appearance, inward disposition, genetic pattern, and inner conscience.[25] The outer form in which we appear is *sura*; the

Qur'an says, *O human being, what has deceived you from your generous Lord who created – well-shaped God made you and balanced set you and into whatever form [*sura*] God desired God composed you* (Q. 82:6–8). Many other verses describe the stages in which God creates each person's form or *sura*, in the mother's womb as a physical growth and later after breathing into it the spirit, as a new being with consciousness, and continuing to develop and grow through birth, infancy, childhood, and adolescence. *Sura* unfolds into fullness as we reach adulthood, act autonomously as a moral agent, and are held accountable for our actions. However, our personality consists of far more than our outward appearance and rational actions.

From experiences in infancy and childhood, each person develops an inward disposition, a set of traits, potentials, or characteristics that are more or less innate, which the Qur'an calls *shakila*. This disposition determines how we react to experiences and profoundly shapes our potential to have faith. *We reveal of the Qur'an that which is healing and compassion for the believers yet which gives the oppressors nothing but loss. When we bless people they turn away and act proudly, but when harm brushes them, they despair. So say, "All act according to their own disposition [*shakila*], yet your Lord knows best who is on the most guided path"* (Q. 17:82–83). Disposition is made up of factors beyond our conscious decision and often beyond our awareness: childhood experiences, infant memories, emotional and intellectual capabilities. In short, it is our psyche through which the ego manifests.

Genetic inheritance is a third level of our personality. Through contemporary science, we are discovering that genetic patterns in our biological material not only determine our outward form but also greatly affect psychic disposition. The Qur'an refers to this material substrate of organic life by pronouncing, *We created the human being from a quintessence of clay* (Q. 23:12). In Arabic, this is called *tabi'a* (one's "physical stamp" that determines one's temperamental nature), a term adopted not from the Qur'an but from Greek science as it was translated into Arabic and became Islamic science. From this genetic stamp embedded deep in our organic tissue the Qur'an depicts the development from zygote to fetus to infant, referring to this intimate relationship between genetic material, biological organism, and moral agency: *Then we made the human being a spermazoid firmly embedded, then we created from the spermazoid a clot of mucus and created from the mucus a lump of flesh, then created from the flesh bones, then clothed the bones with muscle, then we transformed it into another creation – so blessed be God, the best of creators!* (Q. 23:13–14). The concept of genetic inheritance certainly complicates discussions of morality. As a Muslim, I uphold that the choices we make based upon genetic potential and constrained by environmental limitations generate our moral worth; I certainly do not argue that genetics determines everything about us in a way that excuses moral failings, any more than I would agree with pre-deterministic theology which imagines that God wills the corrupt and unjust oppressors into hell by fiat (a position toward which much of classical Sunni theology veers dangerously close). However, moral worth must not be pre-judged, and each person must be given a reasonable chance to assess her or his potential for growth and ground for sincerity, based upon a realistic, reasonable, and compassionate assessment of one's own position and personality. *God does not make persons responsible for what is beyond their capacity* (Q. 2:286), for everyone has the capacity to apprehend God, as the Qur'an optimistically affirms.[26]

This Qur'anic verse indicates the fourth layer of personality, which is one's inner conscience nestled subtly within one's outer appearance and accessible only through one's inward disposition. This is the part of our personality in which our true humanity lies. It is our original nature or *fitra*, the deep core of our being that touches on the spirit and stays aware of the presence of God. Our outer form may grow and decay and our inward disposition may become refined or lapse into rawness, but our inner conscience remains fresh if our awareness is not distracted from it. *Set your face to the moral challenge [*din*] in a pure way, according to the original nature [fitra] upon which God based humanity, for there is no changing the creation of God* (Q. 30:30). We were created to be aware of God's presence (through all of God's qualities, majestic and awe-inspiring qualities as well as beautiful and love-invoking qualities), and nobody is excluded from this original nature that is never lost. This *fitra* provides us with our conscience; it is the seat of intention and sincerity by which actions will be judged for their moral worth, as the Prophet is reported to have taught: "Surely actions are by intentions and each will get that for which they intend."[27]

Sexual acts, too, should be judged by the intention with which they are performed, an intention formed within the heart of sincerity and fully colored by the filter of inward disposition before being expressed through the physicality of apparent action. Sexual orientation is latent within each individual, emerging in complex interactions between the genetic *tabi'a* and early childhood *shakila*. Current research is pushing slowly but steadily toward the conclusion that sexual orientation is largely inherent. Psychiatrists are investigating early childhood experience, chemists are discovering hormonal influence during fetal development before birth, and biologists are uncovering genetic inheritance that is fully present at conception. The cause of sexual orientation and gender identity probably lies in a combination of such factors. Whatever the exact balance of causes, sexual orientation is in place before rational thought or adolescent maturity. Judging sexual acts without a theory of sexuality will lead to injustice and will betray the most fundamental Islamic teaching that actions are assessed by the intention behind them.

Confronting the Tribe of Lot

Classical Islamic theologians and jurists interpreted the Qur'an without a fully developed theory of sexual orientation based on experimental science. Although the Prophet's life provided a model of sexuality-positive morality, classical jurists and theologians discussed sexuality in mainly negative terms, as the power of lust. For example, the great theologian Fakhr al-Din Razi (died 1209) claims that the power of lust leads to unrestrained and immoral acts, including sex.[28] The key term in their discussion is *shahwa*, meaning lust or sensual desire. However, the Qur'an uses this term in nuanced ways – sometimes positively and sometimes negatively – to mean desire as appetite and the pleasurable delight of consuming. The Qur'an uses *shahwa* as a verb in conjunction with eating and drinking as well as sexual intercourse, which are all pleasures promised to souls in heaven.[29] On a more worldly level, the Qur'an warns of *shahwa* as desire for all domestic delights that give the soul satisfaction and the body ease, which if unbridled can become lustful: *Made beautiful to people is the love of desires, for women and children and treasures hoarded of gold and silver and well-bred horses and livestock and crops – that is a transient worldly life given them by their Lord, but with God is the best return* (Q. 3:14). Clearly, *shahwa* as lust is harmful, for it distracts one from God's presence, incites greed, and leads to immoral deeds. "Desires" appear in the plural, to show the variety of directions lust can move: toward food, sex, pride in family (the mention of children), wealth (mention of gold and silver), status and power (mention of horses).

These objects of desire and their pleasurable consumption are not bad in themselves, so they are not prohibited outright. Rather, the psychic state of the desire, *shahwa*, as craving makes such consumption lustful and potentially destructive. They are bad when bodily pleasures are saturated with egoistic pride. For this reason, the Qur'an juxtaposes the term *shahwa* with another term, *bagha*, meaning ardent desire or covetousness.[30] *Bagha* is less about bodily pleasure or concupiscence and more about getting egoistic satisfaction, about getting one's way.[31] If pursuing pleasure for egoistic purposes transgresses moral bounds, it becomes *fahisha*, a term the Qur'an uses to mean "immorality" that is strongly condemned. Yet the Qur'an asserts that seeking and desiring are not bad in themselves; it depends upon their intent and sincerity. If one seeks and desires while acknowledging the bounty of God (*fadl*) and giving thanks for getting one's way (*shukr*) without damaging others or transgressing their rights, then braving the dangerous waves of desire may not be reprehensible: *It is God who made subservient the sea, that you may eat from it fresh flesh and extract from it ornaments to wear, so you see the ships cleaving through it, that you might seek your desires from God's bounty and that you may give thanks* (Q. 16:14). God demands from believers mindfulness, sincerity, and thanks for every benefit whether it is corporal delight or egoistic desire.[32] Sex is included with food, wealth, and power as among our desires, which might be good or bad depending more on the intent, intensity, and ethical comportment of the desiring than on the specific object or experience desired. The Qur'an warns everyone about sexual lust, regardless of sexual orientation or marital status. Even heterosexual sex with one's legal spouse can be lustful, as implied by the above-quoted verse (Q. 3:14), if it leads to greed, selfishness, harm, or abuse.

The Qur'an speaks in subtle ways about sexual desire among other kinds of desires, but does it contain indications about sexual orientation? Its language specifically addresses heterosexual people. This is no surprise, since they constitute the vast majority in any society, including the Prophet Muhammad's immediate environment in Arabia. In one sense, heterosexual relationships are very important for society at large, since procreation, child-rearing, and family lineage are consequences of heterosexual relationships. This is especially true for a small society under threat, as was the early Muslim community. For this reason, the Qur'an directly addressed heterosexual adultery along with legitimacy and inheritance. In contrast, the Qur'an does not clearly and unambiguously address homosexuals in the Muslim community, as there is no term in the Qur'an corresponding to "homosexual" or "homosexuality." This is true despite the fact that many classical Muslim jurists identify the Qur'anic narrative of Lot's struggle with his Tribe (*qawm lut*) as addressing homosexual sex or, more specifically, male-to-male anal penetration. The Prophet Lot's Tribe means the people of Sodom and Gomorrah, as described in the Torah. All Muslim interpreters condemn how the men of Lot's Tribe rejected Lot's authority over them by trying to deprive him of the right to extend hospitality and protection to strangers, to the extent of demanding to use the male strangers in coercive same-sex acts. However, some classical interpreters who were jurists read into the scriptural text the conclusion that Lot was sent primarily to forbid anal sex between men, which was the principle act of Lot's Tribe which constituted their infidelity. These jurist interpreters created a legal term, *liwat*, as a shorthand for "the act of the people of Lot," meaning anal intercourse, and it corresponds to the English term "sodomy." By creating a new term – *liwat* – jurist interpreters of the classical period cemented the close association of Lot's Tribe with male anal intercourse. A corresponding term, *luti*, was created to mean a sodomite or one who commits such an act.[33] However, neither term is found in the Qur'an itself, leading sexuality-sensitive interpreters to question how jurists have read into the scriptural text terms and concepts that are not literally there.

Gay, transgender, and lesbian Muslims resist this singular focus on same-sex acts and charge that focusing only on this actually distorts one's reading of the story. The story is really about infidelity and how the Tribe of Lot schemed for ways to reject his Prophethood and his public standing in their community. Same-sex acts were only one of a range of actions that constituted their infidelity – from murder and robbery (as mentioned in Q. 29:29) to other repugnant acts in their assemblies (which commentators claim included public nudity, gambling, and idolatrous worship). In putting forward this interpretation, gay and lesbian Muslims are not "rejecting" the whole classical tradition of *tafsir*, as some opponents have accused. Rather, they renew the tradition by fueling debate, through which the tradition was originally built.

There are certainly multiple currents and contradictions within the *tafsir* literature. Gay and lesbian Muslims, for instance, build upon the interpretation of Ibn Hazm, the famous jurist and scholar of Andalusia. He asserted that the Tribe of Lot was destroyed for their attitude of infidelity (*kufr*) and their violent rejection of the Prophet sent to them, and that this rejection was expressed in their whole range of criminal deeds, only some of which were sexual in nature.

> God's act [of retribution] against Lot's Tribe is not due to the reasons they [other interpreters] suppose [that is, their practice of anal penetration between men]. Rather, God says of them, *The tribe of Lot considered the warning a lie. We sent upon them a storm of stones [destroying all] except Lot's family, for them we saved at dawn as a favor from us. In this way we reward those who give thanks. He [Lot] warned them of our violent retribution but they obstinately denied the warning. They strived to alienate his guest from him but we blinded their eyes, [declaring] "Now taste my punishment and my warning!"* (Q. 54:33–37). God also says, *When our messengers came to Lot he was distressed on their account and felt he could not protect them, but they said, "Do not fear and do not grieve – we are rescuing you and your family, all except your wife, for she is one of those left behind"* (Q. 29:33) … God has declared a clear text [*nass*] declaring that the Tribe of Lot had disbelieved [in his Prophethood] and therefore sent upon them a storm of stones. The [divine] stoning which punished them was not for one type of immorality [*fahisha*] in specific, but was rather for their infidelity and rejection [*kufr*]. Those who claim that stoning is the punishment for this immorality [anal sex between men] are not following the command of God unless the one guilty of it is a rejecter of God's Prophet [*kafir*]. Their claim that the Qur'an justifies the

> punishment of stoning [for this sex act] is null and void, since their action contradicts the explicit meaning [*hukm*] of its words.[34]

Ibn Hazm delves into the narrative to find the ethical principle that Lot's Tribe violated and for which they were all punished. That principle was rejecting their Prophet and the ethical guidance he brought. They rejected him in a variety of ways, and their sexual assault of his guests was only one expression of their inner intention to deny Lot the dignity of being a Prophet and drive him from their cities. Ibn Hazm interprets the Qur'an as a jurist, but he is a jurist who relies on the Qur'an's explicit language rather than relying on cultural presumptions or reports about what the Prophet's companions might have done.

Ibn Hazm was no gay activist, but he may have been the first "sexuality-sensitive" interpreter of the Qur'an. He sets a precedent that lesbian and gay Muslim interpreters can follow and refine. His interpretation was informed with a subtle theory of human nature, far more so than most classical *tafsir* writers. In particular, he followed the first three principles of interpretation that we clarified earlier in this chapter (primacy of the Qur'an, attention to context, and articulation of principles), because he was not only a jurist but also an ethicist and literary author who brought to bear on the Qur'an a poet's sensitivity to language. In addition, he fearlessly challenged the orthodoxy of his day, especially if he perceived it to assert unjust laws based on irrational or fanciful interpretation of the Qur'an. Though he accepted that anal sex between men was a crime (*jurm*) and was forbidden by Islamic law, he cautioned that it not be exaggerated in importance by homophobic hysteria. As an authoritative jurist who served as the chief judge of Cordoba, he noted correctly that the Qur'an does not forbid it in language that implies the legal force of specific punishment; he therefore concluded that analogy to adultery or heterosexual fornication (*zina'*) are not justified and that sodomy should be prevented by discretionary punishment. These are juridical distinctions that will be discussed in detail in Chapter 4. For now, let it suffice to note Ibn Hazm's tone of voice when he says, "It is necessary to stop this practice by means that do not destroy life, human dignity or livelihood … We seek refuge with God from raging against any act with either more or less anger than God has in defending divinely guided morality [*din*], and from legislating based upon our personal opinion and thereby forging corrupt systems of law."[35] His legal critique was fueled by his understanding that there are Muslims who are homosexual whose faith is no less than that of other Muslims and whose lives are just as dear. With a perspective informed by "platonic love," he could clearly distinguish between sex and love, between acts and dispositions.

In interpreting the story of the Tribe of Lot, Ibn Hazm goes back to the earliest moments in the Qur'an that speak of this tribe. He finds that these early verses all stress the infidelity of his tribe and how they rejected Lot's prophethood, rather than obsessing about the sexual details of their assault upon him. These earliest moments are the most universal in tone and ethical in content. Ibn Hazm also notes that it is impossible that Lot's Tribe was destroyed solely or primarily because of male-to-male sex, because Lot's wife was also destroyed along with all the women and children of their tribe. To make his point, Ibn Hazm cites the Qur'an: *God strikes an example of those who reject belief in the wife of Noah and the wife of Lot. They were both under [the household authority] of two of our righteous servants but they betrayed them both. But their betrayal did not avail them against God, and it was declared "Both of you enter the fire with those condemned!"* (Q. 66:10). Lot's wife was guilty of infidelity and betrayal for denying her husband's role as Prophet, just as the men in her community were guilty, and so she was destroyed with them.[36] The role of male-to-male sex acts is marginal to the essence of the story and its moral lesson.

The contemporary interpretation of gay and lesbian Muslims independently confirms the medieval approach of Ibn Hazm. They come to similar conclusions because they share similar assumptions, principles, and strategies. Like Ibn Hazm, they contradict other interpreters who focus very narrowly on anal penetration between men and ignore the wider context of sex in the story of Lot. For example, when the early exegete al-Tabari (died 923) interprets a verses in which Lot admonishes some men from his tribe for "perpetrating the immorality [*al-fahisha*]" (Q. 7:80–81), he writes, "The immorality that they perpetrate, for which they are punished by God, is penetrating males sexually [*ityan al-dhukur*]. The meaning is this: it is as if Lot were saying, 'You are, all of you, you nation of people coming to men in their rears, rather than coming to those whom God has approved for you and made permissible to you of women.'"[37] Al-Tabari clearly uses a strategy of definition and substitution: he defines the nature of "the immorality" as anal sex and then substitutes this definition back into the Qur'an, even daring to rewrite the dialogue with this definition integral to Lot's speech ("it is as if Lot were saying ... "). Because al-Tabari is primarily a jurist, he does not pursue a broader reading of the Qur'an's story of Lot to discover its deeper themes or compare the Qur'an's use of the term "immorality" (*fahisha*) here to other uses where it describes actions that are clearly not anal penetration or same-sex acts or even sexual acts as all. The scholar Amreen Jamel has addressed this ambiguity in detail, in an article that aims to discover whether the Qur'an uses the term *fahisha* to mean only or even primarily same-sex acts, and concludes that its does not.[38] Clearly, al-Tabari did not intend to give a full and searching interpretation of the

Qu'ranic terms and themes, but rather wanted to link jurists' rulings about male-on-male sex to the Qur'an, to claim that the Qur'an itself justifies these legal rulings.

There is no opportunity here to give details of al-Tabari's interpretive logic, which I have written about elsewhere.[39] Because his interpretation of Lot's narrative focused on juridical rulings, it will be dealt with in Chapter 4, which assesses homosexuality in Islamic jurisprudence or *fiqh*. Suffice it to say here that most of the classical interpreters, following al-Tabari's example, discussed sex acts with almost exclusive attention to anal sex between man and man (sometimes extended to anal sex between man and woman). This tradition of interpretation is so prevalent that many translators of the Qur'an (who may or may not admit that all translation is actually interpretation) use terms like "homosexuality" or "unnatural sex" or "crime against the laws of nature" in interpreting these verses.[40] Of course, we must be careful not to rely on translations of the Qur'an to substitute for full interpretation of the Qur'an, which in order to be full must not only define the meaning of words and phrases, as al-Tabari strives to do, but also explain the book's deeper themes and wider contexts, which al-Tabari neglects to do. What is clear from this brief discussion is that al-Tabari and other classical interpreters never discussed sexual orientation as an integral aspect of personality, which greatly limits their interpretation.

If they had, they would not have read the narrative of Lot and his tribe as addressing homosexual acts in general, but rather as addressing male rape of men in particular. The acts would appear analogous to soldiers using rape as a weapon (as happened in the Yugoslav wars against both men and women) or to interrogators using sexual acts as tools of domination (as happened in Abu Ghraib, Guantanamo Bay, and other prisons). Applying a psychological theory of sexual orientation, it appears that the men of Lot's Tribe were actually heterosexual men attempting to aggressively assert their power against other vulnerable men. These latter "men" were the angels who appeared in their city as strangers and wayfarers, to whom Lot offered hospitality and protection in assertion of his Prophetic authority. The mob's attempt to rape the men was motivated by their wish to reject the Prophetic authority of Lot and assert their own egoistic status and power, rather than by sexual desire and bodily pleasure.

This line of interpretation makes more sense of the many verses that comprise the story of Lot than does the classical interpretation that Lot's prophethood was about forbidding sex between men of homosexual orientation. The verses should be read in context, as inter-referential, in order to interpret the meaning of any particular word or phrase. *[Recall] Lot when he said to his people, "Do you commit the immorality that nobody in the wide world has done before? You do the men in lust [*shahwa*] besides the women – indeed you are a* *people who transgress!" His people answered him with nothing but, "Drive them out of your town, for they are people who make themselves to be purer!" So we delivered him and his followers, except for his wife – she was one of the goners* (Q. 7:80–83).[41] If the immorality were sex acts by men with men, then why was Lot's wife also destroyed by God's punishment? Clearly, she was involved in "the immorality," the network of idolatry and exploitation that characterized the city's population, including women and children who were not involved in the sex acts. This question was asked by the theologian Ibn Hazm, almost a thousand years ago, when he accused other classical Muslim interpreters of the Qur'an of ignoring the details of the Lot story and misconstruing its essential message: "They forget that the perpetrators of this act from among the Tribe of Lot were infidels [*kafir*], as stated explicitly in the Qur'an, who denied their prophet's warning [*kadhaba bi'l-nadhar*], for their women and children were punished along with them who were not among those who perpetrated this [sexual] act."[42]

The men who attacked Lot's guests with the intent to rape them had wives and children, as they *do the men in lust besides the women* [*min dun al-nisa'*], as the Qur'an (27:55) emphasizes through its grammar. It makes definite both "the men" whom they are sexually assaulting and "the women" with whom they already have sexual relationships. That the Qur'an makes these nouns definite (with *al-* or "the") alerts the attentive reader to the specificity of Lot's condemnation. He is not talking about men in general who have sex with other men in general rather than with women in general. He is denouncing the men who sexually assault these specific men (those who are vulnerable as strangers and taken under his protective hospitality) while leaving aside the sexual relationships they already have with the women who are their wives. This fact warns us that their crime was not homosexuality in a general way or even sex acts per se; rather it was their intention that made their actions immoral. Their sexual assault was driven by their infidelity and their rejection of their Prophet.

In another verse, Lot challenges his attackers: *Do you do males from the wide world and leave what mates God has created for you? Indeed you are people exceeding in aggression!* (Q. 26:165–166). Here Lot specifies that these men already have mates (*azwaj*), wives whom God has created for them, and yet they aggressively exceed the bounds of propriety by demanding Lot's guests in disregard for the rights their spouses have over them. The issue here is the men's disregarding their spouses to attack strangers. But a critic could argue that the gender of their victims is actually the problem, whereas the men's leaving their spouses is just a necessary condition. Another verse addresses the question of gender directly, as Lot confronts his assailants: *His tribe came to him rushing at him and before this they had been practicing bad deeds. Lot said, "O my people, these are my daughters – they are purer for you so be mindful of God and do not humiliate me over my guests!"* (Q. 11:78). Some readers might rush to judge that Lot is saying women are purer for the men who are rushing at him, meaning that women are more suitable for sex and are legal as spouses for men. However, to read these verses as an assertion that heterosexual desire is normative takes it totally out of context.

Would anyone believe that a Prophet would offer his daughters to assailants intent on rape, as if their raping women would make the act "pure"? Rather, Lot makes a sarcastic comparison to show his assailants how wrong it is to rape guests over whom he has extended protective hospitality. Both he and his tribe know that it is far from pure to take his daughters, whose dignity he protects; Lot argues that assaulting his guests is even worse in his sight than fornicating with his daughters. Far from giving them license to rape his women, he is expressing, with sarcasm born of despair, that vulnerable strangers are as valuable to him as his own children. On the surface, he may appear to talk about the correct gender for men's sexual orientation, but in reality he is preaching that both men and women deserve protection from rape and humiliation. Such protection, extended to both women and men, is a consequence of the ethic of care that fuels his Prophetic mission. This ethical message comes through clearly in another verse's narration of these events: *Lot said, "Surely these are my guests, so do not dishonor me – stay mindful of God and do not humiliate me." They said, "Have we not forbidden you [granting others protection] from the wide world?" Lot said, "These are my daughters, if you are intent on doing it"* (Q. 15:68–71). The comparison by gender is only to emphasize to his audience that strangers of either gender deserve the same protection one gives to daughters. Offering the assailants his daughters is a sarcastic critique of their behavior with his male guests. Lot's own actions urge us not to obsess about whether the intended crime is a same-sex act or a heterosexual act but rather to delve deeper and perceive that violence and coercion in sex is the essential issue.

In conclusion, one can argue that the story of Lot is not about homosexuality at all. Rather, Lot criticizes using sex as a weapon. Lot condemns sex acts that are coercive, like rape. This is a critique of male sexuality driven by aggression and the urge to subjugate others by force, not of male homosexuality in particular. It is incidental to the story that his guests, who are the targets, are male. One can imagine the same story with guests who are female and it would exert the same force and convey the same moral message, if the Islamic imagination allowed angels to appear as women. Jurists who have interpreted the story to be about homosexual acts have missed the point.[43]

Beyond Lot's Tribe

This alternative interpretation holds that some men of Lot's tribe were guilty of assault and rape, rather than consensual same-sex acts or homosexual orientation. It is based on reading the whole narrative of Lot, in all its details, rather than isolating the same-sex nature of the mob's attack as the reason for God's wrath against them. This alternative interpretation not only makes clearer sense of the whole narrative of Lot, but also gives deeper understanding of wider context in the Qur'an of Lot's narrative. The narrative about Lot is not told in one go. The Qur'an refers to incidents of his story in various places, which is why interpreters have to cite various chapters in order to piece the story together. Some of these incidents refer to the infamous sexual assault while others refer to the Tribe of Lot's other crimes, their idolatry, their rejection of Lot's prophetic mission, or the journey of the angels in male form to the tribe's prosperous cities. The Qur'anic narrative strategy fragments the story, making it easier for patriarchal interpreters like al-Tabari to focus solely on the same-sex act and ignore the wider context. Why does the Qur'an tell the story in this way?

The Qur'an has its own unique structure, which sets it off as distinct and unique from other scriptures like the Torah or the Gospels. The way it fragments the narratives of past prophets, like Lot, is part of its beauty and power. It always tells of incidents in Lot's story in the context of the stories of other prophets with similar missions. Mention of Lot and his tribe always comes within a series of other prophets: Noah, Salih, Hud, Shu'ayb, and Moses, for example. The tribes and nations to whom each of these Prophets were sent found innovative ways to drive the Prophets from their midst and undermine their authority. On the surface of the narratives, each tribe found different ways of attacking their Prophet, but the underlying intention is the same, namely, to call a lie the Prophet's warning that there is life after death, moral accountability, and a day of judgment.

The intention to reject and belittle their Prophet is what the Tribe of Lot has in common with the other destroyed peoples who rejected their Prophet and the message brought to them to believe in one God and act justly. The earliest revelation that mentions Lot simply tells that *the people of Lot treated the warning as a lie . . . they accosted his guests but we blinded them* (Q. 54:33–37), with no mention of sex acts. This early revelation, the first moment that the Qur'an mentions Lot, gives us a key to understand properly the importance of the story and its underlying meaning. Lot's Tribe was punished for infidelity and rejecting their Prophet; raping his protected guests was one way they rejected his authority. Lot should not be taken separately from the other Prophets, for the Qur'an mentions his experience of rejection in parallel with that of other Prophets.

This becomes clear when we compare the stories of different Prophets, as the structure of the Qur'an compels us to do. Comparing their stories helps to explicate the common principles underlying their experiences, in the same way that comparison of observations in scientific experimentation allows us to find principles of structure and motion in the physical universe. The Qur'an most often mentions Lot in close association with the Prophet Salih.[44] Just as Lot was sent as a Prophet to the people of Sodom and Gomorrah, Salih was sent to the people of Thamud, who built powerful cities that dominated wealthy trade routes. Like those in Sodom and Gomorrah, the powerful elite of Thamud grew arrogant, hoarded their wealth, and refused to share equitably resources to protect the poor and vulnerable. Salih revealed his people's ethical corruption by introducing a "sacred she-camel" on God's order, charging his people to allow this animal to roam their land and drink freely of their water, to be protected and cherished though she was vulnerable and had no owner.[45] The sacred she-camel of Salih is a living metaphor for the poor and vulnerable people living under the rule of Thamud: if the elite would accept Salih's charge and care for the sacred camel they might reflect upon their own treatment of poor people and more justly share their resources. But the elite of Thamud rejected Salih's prophethood, ridiculing the God who sent him and the message that he brought. Instead of attacking him directly, they attacked his sacred she-camel, tied her up, and slaughtered her (Q. 7:77). Why did they kill the camel of Salih? To reject the authority of the Prophet who protected her and call a lie the belief in the one God who sent him. As a consequence, God destroyed the cities of Thamud with what appears from the Qur'anic description to have been a volcanic eruption involving a quaking earth and choking clouds of dust and gas.

Would anyone take seriously an interpretation of the Qur'an that claimed the people of Thamud were a unique society that hated camels? If one applied to the story of Salih the interpretive strategy that classical scholars (like al-Tabari) apply to the story of Lot, this is what one must assert. Yet no interpreter claims that they perverted nature with a lust for camel blood that corrupted their inner dispositions, just because they slaughtered the sacred she-camel of Salih. None claims that Salih was sent to Thamud specifically to forbid the slaughtering of camels. No interpreter reads Salih's story as relevant to the crime of camel theft or animal murder; none charges that such an act is a major sin and an offense punishable by death. Nobody suggests that a Muslim who appropriates or kills a camel not rightfully belonging to her or him should be punished by asphyxiation in a legal ruling that approximates how God razed the people of Thamud in a volcanic eruption.

Anyone suggesting such an interpretation of Salih's narrative would be gently reminded that they had missed the basic point of the story. Yet the same logic of interpretation is applied to Lot's narrative and accepted by most Muslims, who claim that Lot's Tribe was unique in committing homosexual acts, that Lot was sent with a Prophetic mission specifically to forbid these acts, that the entire tribe (men, women, and children) were destroyed because they perpetrated homosexual acts or accepted homosexuality in their midst, and that Muslims must punish with death anyone found guilty of such acts or attitudes. Despite the fact that they apply such logic only to Lot and not to other Prophets and that none of these conclusions is a "literal" reading of the Qur'an, most Muslims strenuously resist any critique or suggestion that this is not an adequate understanding of these verses. Gay and lesbian Muslims are not the only ones to point out these blatant contradictions in how the Qur'an is interpreted by classical scholars. Ibn Hazm, himself a classical scholar, pointed out this faulty logic a thousand years ago, but was largely ignored.[46]

The Qur'an tells the story of Lot together with narratives of other Prophets, like Salih and many others, often inter-splicing different episodes. The Qur'an emphasizes that the same principles are revealed by each of these stories about early Prophets and the elites of every tribe who reject them.[47] The Qur'an retells these stories in specific contexts, often to encourage the Prophet Muhammad and his followers to have patience, endure rejection, and suffer through persecution without retaliating unjustly. The Prophet Muhammad and his followers should embody the ethical principles of these narratives and enact a Prophetic ethic of care that protects the poor, the vulnerable, and the marginalized against unjust exploitation and unfair distribution of resources. This is the ethical principle that the Muslim community can deduce from the narrative of Lot once it has been liberated from the narrow interpretation of jurists and a patriarchal obsession with anal sex.

Long before lesbian and gay interpreters of the Qur'an put forward these ideas as keys to reinterpreting the significance of Lot's Tribe, Ibn Hazm had the same insights. He was critical of how his fellow classical interpreters justified the death penalty for homosexuals. They claimed that the death penalty of stoning for anyone caught in same-sex penetrative acts is based upon the Qur'an's explicit language in a literal reading of the Lot story, but Ibn Hazm boldly disagreed. The interpretation of other classical jurists ignores the explicit wording of the Qur'an and misconstrues God's intent in revealing it in this form. Ibn Hazm argues that "God says *The tribe of Lot considered the warning a lie. We send upon them a storm of stones* … (Q. 54:33), but it is not permissible in our *shari'a* to punish a liar with stoning to death [*rajm*], even one who lies about a Prophetic warning. Some Muslim jurists rely on this verse to rule death-by-stoning for those who commit 'the act of Lot's Tribe' [male-on-male anal intercourse] … but they forget that the perpetrators of this act were infidels. … They also forget that God says *He [Lot] warned them of our violent retribution but they obstinately denied the warning. They strived to alienate his guests from him but we blinded their eyes, [declaring] 'Now taste my punishment and my warning!'* (Q. 54:36–37). If these jurists truly follow their own fallacious principle, then they must gouge out the eyes of anyone who tries to wrest away a guest from another, because God blinded the eyes of those in Lot's Tribe when they [tried to] wrest away his guest, in addition to God stoning them when they did it to males [*lamma atu al-dhukur*] in order to call the Prophet a liar [*kafiru*]. Whoever isolates one of these events, which are interrelated to the others, makes rulings in God's pure religion that are not based on proof or evidence from God's speech."[48] Later in chapter 4, we will deal in detail with legal rulings in the *shari'a*; it is sufficient here to note that the legal punishment of stoning is not based on an exact and thorough reading of the Qur'anic verses that describe what happened to Lot's Tribe. God stoned them, but for what reason? As Ibn Hazm points out, God's stoning them is divine punishment and does not constitute a command for Muslims to stone others – to do that is to arrogate God's authority for oneself and twist God's speech as it narrates events of the past.

So why does God narrate these events in the Qur'an? God relates Lot's story in its distinct Qur'anic form, interrelated to the stories of other prior Prophets and their rejection, in order to make a deep point. They are mentioned in order to reinforce Muhammad's own mission of Prophethood. The story of Lot is intimately connected to the Qur'an denouncing how the Prophet Muhammad's own tribe and surrounding Arabs found ways to persecute him and reject his message. The narrative's purpose is not to legislate about same-sex acts but to dramatize an ethical principle – that the powerful in society twist religion to justify their wealth and status, corrupting whatever moral insights it might otherwise provide, and they therefore oppose the Prophetic messages that come to remind humanity to stay conscious of God, do good, and enact justice. It is the disempowered who hear the Prophetic message clearly, and the message is only followed fully when the disempowered are protected and cherished as an integral part of the human family.

An interpretation of Lot's Tribe that takes events out of context and severs Lot's prophetic mission from that of other Prophets is not a good interpretation. It justifies injustice in the name of righteousness. Lesbian, gay, and transgender Muslim activists put forward an alternative interpretation to restore the story of Lot's Tribe to its wider context, provide a deeper ethical understanding of God's intent in revealing it, and criticize the way the Islamic community has legislated on narrow and partial interpretations of it. They point out that anti-homosexual bias was common in the patriarchal religious cultures that preceded Islam, especially among Jews and Christians who so deeply influenced early Muslims' interpretation of their own religion. Whether consciously or subconsciously, classical interpreters relied upon these earlier understandings, rather than on the exact words of the Qur'an, to say that Lot came primarily to forbid same-sex penetration.

However, even if Lot's mission is understood to denounce homosexual acts or homosexuality as a psychological orientation, against all suggested above, that does not mean that Muslims are obliged to follow the specific commands of Lot in the realm of law. This brings up another strategy essential to classical Islamic interpretation – the question of "abrogation" (*naskh*). Interpreters and jurists upheld the importance of abrogation, which is the idea that revelation of God's message happens in the unfolding of chronological and historical time. Earlier revelation is either confirmed by later revelation or erased (*mansukh*) and revised by later revelation (*nasikh*), depending on the situation of the community to which God reveals divine speech. This theory was first elaborated to explain how the Qur'an could give the same general message as earlier scriptural revelations while differing from them in ritual and legal details. Later, Muslim jurists applied the theory of abrogation to explain how earlier verses of the Qur'an were revised or replaced by later verses of the Qur'an, while all verses remained integral parts of the Qur'anic message and its written text. The theory and its practical implications are so important that many classical scholars, such as Ibn Hazm, wrote an entire book on the subject.[49] Those classical interpreters who rule that the story of Lot's Tribe justifies the death penalty by stoning for same-sex penetration fail to apply this interpretive principle, just as they fail to uphold the primacy of the Qur'anic wording, in its exact uniqueness, against earlier Christian and Jewish understandings of the same story derived primarily from the Torah.

Even if jurist interpreters were right that Lot condemns same-sex acts between men, this would not necessarily apply to Muslims because the Qur'an's revelation abrogates the legal force of earlier revelations and the legal systems put in place by earlier Prophets who brought them. In other words, Muslims are not obliged to follow Christian mores (even though Muslims regard Jesus as a Prophet who brought a revealed message that is a divinely inspired guide for a religious community) and Muslims are not required to follow Judaic law (even though Muslim revere Moses as a Prophet and respect the Torah). Muslims will only follow as law those aspects of earlier dispensations that are confirmed by the Qur'an and were put into practice by the Prophet Muhammad. The complex theological idea of abrogation defined Islam as a new religion, independent from the religious communities founded upon the earlier Prophets' teachings, like the Christians and Jews.

The urge to condemn homosexuality among Muslims was reinforced by the Jewish and Christian traditions that surrounded them. Early Muslim interpreters relied upon Jewish and Christian sources to understand the story of Lot, sources that were already saturated with a culture of homophobia and misogyny. By relying on earlier interpretations of other Middle Eastern religious communities, early Muslims created a continuity of cultural prejudice that affected their interpretation and diluted the theory of abrogation. Their interpretation of the Lot story as condemning male-to-male sex acts relied more upon cultural presumptions than on a close and attentive reading of the Qur'an's words.

From this perspective, Muslims must look to the behavior and decisions of the Prophet Muhammad as a guide to norms and laws, rather than to stories of pre-Islamic Prophets like Lot, even if the latter are narrated by the Qur'an as examples from history. The body of traditional reports (*hadith*) which the Muslim community preserved offers us no incident in which the Prophet Muhammad punished anyone in his community for same-sex acts, either between two men or between two women. This is an issue we will investigate more fully in Chapter 3. Long before gay and lesbian Muslim activists made these observations, Ibn Hazm applied the theory of *naskh* to critique Muslim interpretations of the story of Lot. He asked, "Do we [Muslims] have a duty to obey those *shara'i'* [the legal and ritual systems set up by Prophets before Muhammad] and what they forbid, or is it not allowed for us to follow anything in them, on principle, except what is in them conformed by our own legal system which we are ordered to obey by an explicit text in Muhammad's name only? ... I will mention now the areas in which some Muslim have made mistakes in the religion, by ruling according to other *shari'a* systems and making them into proofs and evidence [for Muslims to obey] when in reality they are not. The truth is that it is not permissible to rule according to anything in them [legal systems of prophets prior to Muhammad] in Islam."[50] Ibn Hazm includes the regulations of the Prophet Lot in the record of previous *shari'a* systems that are rendered null and void by the coming of Islam based upon the revelation to Muhammad. The only points of such prior Prophetic revelations to have continuing relevance as ritual guide or legal rule are points explicitly confirmed by Muhammad's revelation.

In conclusion, one can argue that the story of Lot is not about homosexuality at all. That is a plausible and accurate reading of the Qur'an, especially if one takes into account the wider context of the Lot story. However, even if Muslims insist that the Prophet Lot was condemning homosexual acts – or specifically same-sex penetration – it is questionable whether Muslims are obliged to follow a point of law based upon a Prophetic mission prior to the final Prophet,

Muhammad. The theory of abrogation, which is central to Muslims' conceptions of their religion as distinct and unique, calls such a legalistic interpretation of Lot's story into question. Muslim jurists who interpret the Qur'an have long realized that basing legal rulings to forbid homosexual acts on the Lot story is problematic. They have scanned the Qur'an for other verses that are more explicitly legal and linked more clearly to Muhammad's dispensation. Yet even those verses, as we will see, do not appear to refer unambiguously to homosexual activities.

If Two Commit the Immorality

Of course, homosexuality does not just involve men whom we call gay, but also women whom we call lesbian. Lesbians face a dual challenge, first as women in Muslim communities that are largely patriarchal, and second as women who are sexually attracted to other women. For many lesbian Muslims, the first challenge is the most difficult, since before one can even discuss sexual orientation, one must address whether women are treated as full human beings, legally autonomous agents, morally equal to men, and subjects with sexual drives that deserve satisfaction beyond their role in procreation. Muslim jurists and interpreters in the classical period produced some female-affirmative decisions. They acknowledged that women enjoy sex and are entitled to satisfaction from their partners, affirming the existence and potency of female orgasm and ejaculation. They emphasized the equal participation of male and female liquids in conception, imagining the egg and sperm to be equal and autonomous agents who come together to draw up a contract of mutual obligation, in radical contrast to earlier Hellenic, Jewish, and Christian theories of sex and fertility in which only the man and his sperm were active agents.[51] Most jurists not only asserted the legality of non-reproductive sexual intercourse but also affirmed its positive role in cultivating pleasure and generating tenderness between partners. They even lauded foreplay, caressing, and sexual activity for pleasure (not restricted to procreative intent) as following the *sunna* of the Prophet Muhammad.

Practice often did not live up to this discourse presenting a positive view of women's sexuality and sexual pleasure. Local communities and individual families stressed the "uncleanness" of women's sexual organs owing to menstruation, and often spun this into a theory of women's inherent moral brokenness. Though Muslims generally accept that women desire sexual satisfaction, patriarchal men often exaggerated such desire into an uncontrollable force that overwhelms women and corrupts their rational faculties, justifying male control over their movements and social interactions. Too often, discussion of female sexuality was reduced to urging women to satisfy the male prerogative of penetration and preventing any social, spiritual, or intellectual activity of women that might threaten this prerogative. In general, Muslim jurists did not attentively address sexual acts between two women, because they defined sexual intercourse as penile penetration. They never asked the obvious question of whether penetration, whether with a male penis or anything else, is the epitome and extent of female sexual satisfaction.

The story of Lot does not address sexual acts between women. There are no other verses in the Qur'an that clearly and unambiguously address same-sex acts between women, which is known in Arabic sources as *sihaq* or "rubbing" (a direct translation of the Greek term for "tribadism"). The term *sihaq* is not used by the Qur'an (just as the term *liwat* is not). Nevertheless, some interpreters have searched for a reference to same-sex acts between women in the following verse: *As for those of your women who commit the immorality [*al-fahisha*], have four from among yourselves bear witness against them. If they do witness, then confine them [the women] to their rooms until death causes them to perish or until God makes for them a way [of release]. And for any two from among you [men] who commit it, then punish the two of them, then if they repent and reform then leave the two alone, for indeed God is forgiving and merciful* (Q. 4:15–16). This is certainly a confusing series of verses. It speaks to men of the Muslim community about an "immorality" that might be committed by a group of their women or a pair from among themselves. What could this "immorality" refer to? A tenth-century Mu'tazili interpreter, al-Isfahani, seems to have been the first to argue that this verse concerns "immorality" identified as same-sex acts between women. This suggestion was repeated by later interpreters like al-Zamakhshari and al-Baydawi in medieval times, and in modern times Rashid Rida has revived this previously marginal opinion.[52]

They concluded that the "immorality" referred to in these verses is lesbian sexual intercourse. They drew this conclusion because of the insistence on four eye-witnesses to "the immorality," which is the same requirement for punishing heterosexual intercourse without a contract, even though the punishment required here is not similar at all to that for fornication (lashing) or adultery (stoning). Why should interpreters assume the immorality discussed in the verse to be sexual, especially when the grammatical plural "your women" clearly refers to a group of three or more? Arabic has a specific construction for a group of three or more women (represented by the pronoun *hunna*) in contrast to a pair or people (represented by the pronoun *huma)*. What kind of sexual intercourse is this, which is performed by a group of three or more women? The "immorality" it refers to is ambiguous, as the term *fahisha* could refer to a wide range of immoral deeds that are not sexual at all.[53]

The assertion that this verse condemns lesbianism and specifies punishment for homosexual acts is quite flimsy. The language and the context of this verse mitigate against its having anything to do with sexual intimacy between two women. The "immorality" denounced is not specified and the Qur'an applies the term *fahisha* to many types of immoral acts, including adultery, idolatry, and financial dishonesty. Although the first sentence clearly discusses women in the plural, the second sentence that discusses two people committing the immorality is not clearly directed against women, and says *two from among you* [plural group of men], implying "two from among your men" (or "a pair including a woman and a man from among your men"). Whatever the immorality discussed is, it must be something that can be performed by a group of women together to the exclusion of men, and also by pair of men or a twosome consisting of a man and a woman. It is hard to imagine a particular sexual act that could fit this configuration of actors. This prompts the careful interpreter to question whether the immorality discussed here is a sexual act at all.

It is hard to conceive of a group of women and then two men committing the same immoral act if it were referring to homosexual intimacy. Because of this, some scholars have referred to other verses, intent on proving that the Qur'an prohibits lesbianism and sex acts between women. The Qur'an, however, does not give them much to work with. Some Shi'i scholars assert that "the People of Rass," a pre-Islamic Semitic community mentioned obliquely twice in the Qur'an, were a people destroyed because of widespread lesbianism. However, there is not a word in the Qur'an to substantiate such a position.[54] Their efforts illustrate how far interpreters with prejudice will go to find ideas in the Qur'an that are not there in its language and context.

Finally and most convincingly, the context of the two verses cited above, which are the focus for those who think the Qur'an condemns lesbian sex acts, is not about sex or sexuality at all. The verses before and after them are rather about honesty in dividing inheritance to support orphans and the vulnerable. In that context, the immorality condemned in these two verses is more likely financial dishonesty and inheritance swindling, rather than homosexual coupling between women or men. Conventional interpretations often create sexual diversions to bypass ethical teachings on distributing wealth to prevent hoarding, misallocation of funds, and exploitation of the vulnerable.[55] The verses allegedly forbidding lesbian sex actually address financial honesty and fraud, something male jurists and interpreters either misrecognize or obscure. Patriarchal interpretations of scripture often suppress issues of economic injustice and social justice in favor of more narrowly defining ethics in terms of sexual morality.[56]

Positive Identification of Gay, Lesbian, and Transgender Persons in the Qur'an

Gay, lesbian, and transgender interpreters do not just resist the interpretations of past Muslim scholars who claim that the Qu'ran condemns homosexuality, as documented above. They also renew interpretation by citing those moments when the Qur'an mentions gay and lesbian believers in a positive or morally neutral way. Far from explicitly forbidding homosexuality, the Qur'an contains inferences to the existence of homosexual people in the Muslim community; explicating these hints requires interpretation, but so does ignoring them.

During the Inner Circle annual retreat in March 2005, there was an intense dialogue about these issues. Muhsin and his colleague, Daayiee Abdullah from the U.S. (whom we will meet in Chapter 5), both asserted that the Qur'an mentions homosexual people without any moral condemnation or legal sanction. The first mention is in a verse referring to minority groups defined by sexual orientation and gender identity as part of the creative will of God. *To God belongs dominion of the heavens and earth. God creates whatever God wills and gives to whomever God wills females and gives to whomever God wills the males, or pairs them as male and female. And God makes whomever God wills not reproducing, for God is One who knows all, One capable of all things* (Q. 42:49–50). Here the Qur'an seems to mention all possible intersections of gender and sexuality as intentional creations of God. First mentioned are ordinary males and females, as distinct genders who mate with the opposite sex, leading to reproduction. Then mentioned are those who are "paired as male and female," implying the possibility of male and female being joined in one person, alluding to gender-ambiguous people (such as hermaphrodites or transgender people, as discussed in detail in Chapter 6). Then mentioned are those who are "not reproducing" (*'aqim*), alluding to lesbian women or gay men, whose sexual orientation does not lead them to reproductive intercourse.[57] The Qur'an here indicates possibilities without specifying terms to describe the diverse personality types to which its discourse alludes. The Qur'an emphasizes that a righteous man does not necessarily mean a patriarchal heterosexual man, for it explicitly mentions John the Baptist as a man *honorable and not having intercourse* (Q. 3:39). He is a man who does not have sex with women (*husur*) owing to wary abstention and ascetic purity rather than to sexual orientation. But refusing the patriarchal role of heterosexual sex and reproduction does not disqualify him in any way from being considered a righteous man and a Prophet.[58]

The second and third mentions of homosexual people come in verses that discuss modesty and gender separation. These verses will be discussed here for what they reveal about gender difference, attraction, and sexual orientation, rather than reading these verses as mandating dress codes or gender segregation. Whether these norms apply to modern conditions of life is a question central to an Islamic project of gender justice, but this discussion will leave that for others to address in order to stay focused on gender and sexuality minorities. Thus we find a second mention of homosexual people when the Qur'an urges Muslim women to be modest, urging women not to reveal their beauty except to males who are related to them, to children, or men without *irba*, which means "those who have no wiles with women." The Qur'an gives a long and detailed list of kinds of men with whom women can behave more freely. *Let them [Muslim women] not display their beauties except to their husbands, or their fathers, or the fathers of their husbands, or their sons, or the sons of their husbands, or their brothers, or the sons of their brothers, or the sons of their sisters, or their womenfolk, their slaves, or their followers among the men who have no wiles with women or children who do not recognize the sexual nakedness of women* (Q. 24:31). The "followers among the men who have no wiles with women," preceded by "womenfolk" and followed by "children who do not recognize the sexual nakedness of women," suggests that these men (like heterosexual women or pre-adolescent children) have no sexual desire for women and are therefore exempt from the general rule of separation. This can be interpreted as referring to gay men who have no desire or wiles to seduce women. It might also refer to men who are celibate, are eunuchs, are impotent, or who are aged enough to have no sex drive, if that is possible. Classical interpreters thought this verse applied to elderly men or impotent men, whom they assumed were exempt by fiat of age or anatomy. However, with the emergence of the modern social category of "gay men," we should renew the interpretation by extending its meaning to include them.[59] If we do, we conclude that the Qur'an mentions gay men in an indirect but potent way with no condemnation, recognizing the unique characteristic that sets them apart from other adult men – their not sexually desiring women and therefore not being a threatening presence in the intimate company of women.

The third mention comes when Muslim men are urged to be modest and to require household servants and visitors to knock and request permission before entering private chambers during times of potential nakedness or sexual intimacy. The Qur'an addresses men on issues of gender separation and the preservation of domestic privacy for women: *Yet if your children have reached sexual maturity, then require them to ask permission before entering, like those mentioned before, for in this way God clarifies for you God's signs, and God is a knowing One, One most wise. Of the women, those not reproducing who do not wish for intercourse, it is no harm for them to lay aside their clothing as long as they do not overtly display their beauty* [in the company of men] (Q. 24:60). The key term is "those not reproducing" from among the women (*al-qawa'id min al-nisa'*). It describes fertility, meaning withdrawn from reproductive activity, like a field left fallow and not sown with seed or a date palm not pollinated. The Qur'an clarifies that such women do not wish for sexual intercourse, which is the same word in Arabic as for marriage (*nikah*). *Of the women, those not reproducing who do not wish for intercourse* can remove their modest garments as long as they do not brazenly display their beauty. This description could apply to lesbian women. It might also apply to women who are celibate, or old enough that they can no longer become pregnant, or old enough to have no sex drive, if that is possible. Classical interpreters described such women as elderly, beyond the capacity to become pregnant; they allow only the elderly as exemption to the rules guarding against social mixing of opposite-gendered people which might lead to sexual attraction and seduction. However, we know from sexological research that post-menopausal women are still sexually active and often desire intercourse.[60] Therefore, the verse invites a deeper interpretation. It may be that the reason some women are not reproducing is because they do not desire sexual intercourse with men owing to their sexual orientation rather than merely their supposed lack of fertility or libido. Neither the context nor the literal meaning of the words precludes a renewed interpretation in which those who are exempted from heterosexual attraction are not just mentioned but are specially acknowledged as exceptions to the rule and allowed a social place within the family system.

In his presentation to members of the Inner Circle in Cape Town, Daayiee Abdullah concluded, "Those are the two verses [the last two mentioned above] that I use to substantially assert that it [the Qur'an] says, reading it in this context, that we [gay and lesbian Muslims] are there and that we are the creation of Allah." Daayiee, Muhsin, and others in the support group assert that these verses show that the Qur'an does acknowledge the existence of lesbian and gay people within the Muslim community and accepts that their different psychological state in terms of sexual orientation exempts them from the normal gender separation that defines modesty for the heterosexual majority. This study supports that assertion and adds to it the possibility that a third verse also mentions transgender persons in a neutral way. Beyond this, these thinkers reject the conventional interpretations given to the story of Lot's Tribe and the verse about *those of your women who perpetrate the immorality*, arguing that these verses are not about sex acts as an expression of love or care, or even about sex acts as an expression of a distinct sexual orientation. In this way, they dispute those interpreters who claim that the Prophet Lot condemned anal intercourse between men. They protest how modern ideologues have extend this to a condemnation of homosexuality in its psychological and social dimensions, far beyond any discussion of sexual acts.

Such a sexuality-sensitive interpretation accords with both reason and the literal meaning of the scriptural text. Therefore according to classical principles of Qur'anic interpretation or *tafsir*, it deserves recognition as one of several possible meanings that are all valid. From this interpretive perspective, the Qur'anic verses conventionally held to condemn homosexual acts do not actually address homosexuality, and other verses conventionally held to address the non-sexual elderly actually refer to the presence of homosexual members of the Islamic community in a non-condemning way. Without a concept of homosexuality informed by a psychological theory of sexual orientation, one who recites and contemplates the Qur'an misses these inferences. They have gone unnoticed by classical Muslim interpreters and are deliberately ignored by modern interpreters who are neo-traditionalists and assert unsophisticated notions of "human nature."

Such a theory of homosexuality is available to us today in ways that were not articulated in the past. In both the West and in Islamic societies, technical expertise in medical and psychological research supports a more complex definition of human nature outside the purview of traditional authorities (such tribal leaders, patriarchal households, or religious scholars). However, traditional authorities often resist secular definitions of homosexuality, seeing these definitions as a threat to morality, and often seek to marginalize or denounce scientists and clinical professionals. Although the term "homosexuality" first came into use to describe an emerging modern concept that was not available to classical Muslim interpreters, it would be wrong to assume that homosexuals did not exist before there was a clinical name for them. Homosexual women and men have always existed as a minority within every cultural group, even if an abstract term like "homosexuality" was not there to label them. There may have been different social constructions as roles for homosexual people (priest, artist, seer, joker, heretic, criminal, to name just a few examples), and those social constructions change over time and vary between communities, yet the essential psychological element – difference based on sexual orientation and expression – was present in every place beneath the variety of names and concepts. It is essential to bear in mind that what modern researchers mean by "homosexuality" is not at all what classical Muslim scholars meant by "sodomy" (*liwat*). *Liwat* denoted anal penetration as an act, and said nothing about the intention, sexual orientation, or inner disposition of the person performing the act.

Interpretative Debate: Argument by Wholesome Means

The Qur'an commands believers to call others to God through persuasion and to argue with others *by means that are more wholesome* (Q. 16:125). Interpretation of the Qur'an is a process of debate, discussion, and argumentation. It always has been that way among Muslims, about every imaginable issue. There is no reason that issues of sexuality and sexual orientation should be any different. However, many contemporary Muslims shy away from debate. Especially since 1975, with the oil boom fueling the international spread of Wahhabi-informed Islamic fundamentalism, many Muslims have assumed that admitting ambiguity in interpreting the Qur'an is tantamount to heresy. This is a sad collapse of the classical tradition of disciplined argumentation which made Islam such a strong and flexible religion. Gay, transgender, and lesbian Muslims who engage in theological debate hope to contribute to a restoration of this optimistic spirit of dialogue and debate. As they speak out, they find that many Muslims will dismiss them as unqualified for debate (either because they are not madrasa trained or because they are assumed to be "sinners"), or try to silence them by avoiding discussion of the issues they raise.

However, as lesbian, transgender, and gay Muslims persist in speaking out they increasingly find debate partners in Muslims who oppose their interpretations but accept the basic terms of debate. There are contemporary critics of gay and lesbian Muslim activists who accept that the issues must be debated, that the foundation for debate is the meaning of Qur'anic verses, and that homosexuals exist as human beings with a different psychological character from heterosexuals; these opponents claim simply that the Qur'an validates only heterosexuality. There are two approaches to this argument, one stressing ontology and the other stressing morality. The argument stressing ontology (the nature of being) claims that the Qur'an reveals that God created all human beings as heterosexuals such that if one claims to be homosexual one has perverted one's inherent, God-given nature. The argument stressing morality claims that the Qur'an reveals that God wills a norm that is heterosexuality, regardless of one's inherent sense of sexual orientation, such that anyone who acts in homosexual ways is disobeying God's will and command. The first sees homosexuality as a perversion of nature as created by God; the second sees homosexuality as deviation from morality as willed by God. In short the first sees homosexuals as sick; the second sees them as sinful.[61]

Lesbian, transgender, and gay Muslim interpreters, even as they disagree with these opponents, are grateful to them. By engaging in a reasoned argument over the meaning of the Qur'an's words, these opponents tacitly accept the humanity, dignity, and religious commitment of their debate partners.

They do not let disagreement obscure their ethical consideration of the other. This confirms one of the best characteristics of classical Islamic sciences, the tolerance for diversity of interpretation of sacred texts – as expressed in the words of Abu Hanifa, the renowned jurist who is reported to have said, "We know this [position] is one opinion, and it is the best we can arrive at; [if] someone arrives at a different view, then he adopts what he believes [is best] and we adopt what we believe [is best]."[61] Muslim communities in general do not live up to this ideal, though it is deeply enshrined in their classical tradition, and have yet to engage in restrained and informed debate on these issues. However, it is still an ideal that we must work towards.

What is clear from examples like the interpretation of al-Tabari and others in the classical tradition is that anti-homosexual bias can cause interpreters to read into scripture condemnations that are not necessarily there in the exact language and wider context of the Qur'an. At the Inner Circle retreat, a lesbian Muslim responded to discussion of these points by saying, "I have heard somebody saying that as the people of Sodom and Gomorrah who made homosexual acts were killed, so the future punishment for homosexual acts is that on the day of judgment they will rot in their own semen and they won't stop rotting. This is the kind of fear that is manifested in our society ... So this is why most people, I think, fear their Creator rather than try to meet the Creator." New interpretations of the Qur'an can certainly help to clear away the fear and terror that our cultures read into the sacred text, as Daaiyee Abdullah's answer to this response reveals: "I think you are very correct about the aspect of fear ... The only way you get rid of fear is once you read the Qur'an through your brain and your heart, then your answer will come because you are with Allah. When you are connected in that process, then you are really on a solid foundation. Then when people say things ... you empower yourself to recognize that the things people are telling you are not true. So then you are not fearful of the words that they say. In many cases, you end up educating them [those who condemn you]!" In his view, reading the Qur'an is the key to liberating oneself from the prejudice of others, for it puts one in direct communication with God. It reveals that anti-homosexual prejudice is a cultural phenomenon among Muslims and not a scriptural mandate.

This conclusion has radical consequences for the evaluation of the *shari'a* – Islamic custom and law based on a legal reading of scriptural sources. The legal strictures against homosexual acts which are an integral part of the *shari'a* are not based upon clear and compelling language in the Qur'an. Rather, they are based immediately on decisions of the Prophet's followers and later upon *hadith* that circulated in the Prophet's name. That is no surprise to Islamic jurists who know how the law was built, but is a great surprise to most Muslims who are taught that the *shari'a* is a direct expression of divine will. Although assessing the validity of *hadith* is a complex problem and a very difficult topic for Muslim activists, we will try to wrestle with it in Chapter 3. New interpretations of the Qur'an question the rhetoric of infallibility and immutability of *fiqh* or Islamic jurisprudence, a startling idea to many Muslims, and an idea we will examine closely in Chapter 4.

Conclusion

Clearly the problem faced by lesbian, gay, and transgender Muslim activists is more complex than just interpretation of the Qur'an. Yet the Qur'an is the key to unraveling the complexities of Islam as a religious tradition and the Qur'an itself provides the key to arguing with a hostile Muslim community. To conclude this chapter on the Qur'an, we can restate its basic insights. The Qur'an speaks to the issue of homosexuality only obliquely – not directly – and therefore the issue of how one interprets the scripture (with which principles, through which tools, by what assumptions) is of utmost importance. There is no term in the Qur'an that specifically describes homosexual people or acts. Many classical scholars interpret some terms to forbid homosexual sex acts, but there is ambiguity in their method of interpretation and room within the Islamic tradition for alterative interpretations (both in the classical past and in the contemporary present). Although many classical interpreters read the story of the Prophet Lot as forbidding same-sex acts, there is ambiguity in the Qur'an over whether Lot's Tribe was punished because of sexual acts or because of their infidelity, an inner attitude of which their same-sex acts were an overt expression. To clarify this ambiguity, gay, lesbian, and transgender Muslim activists put forward an alternative interpretation. This alternative interpretation – in which Lot condemned his tribe for rape and aggression that happened to be male upon male – makes sense of not only the words of the Qur'an but also its deeper themes and context. In their understanding of the Qur'an, the essential issue is aggressive use of sex as a weapon to reject the teachings of the Prophets and express infidelity toward God, not same-sex acts in general or homosexual orientation in particular. Transgender, lesbian, and gay Muslims find other verses in the Qur'an which speak of their presence in Muslim communities in a non-condemning way and hint at their place in God's creation of a natural world full of diversity.

Chapter 3

Critiquing Hadith: Islamic Oral Tradition

> A man was with the Prophet (peace be upon him) when another man passed by and the former said, "O Messenger of God! I love this man." The Messenger of God asked, "Have you let him know that?" He said, "No." The Messenger of God then said, "Tell him." So he went up to the man and said, "I love you for the sake of God" and the other replied, "May God love you who loves me for the sake of God."
>
> Hadith reported by Anas bin Malik[1]

Hadith are full of surprises. Hadith are reports (often called "traditions") of incidents in which the Prophet Muhammad said or did something that was observed by his followers and passed on orally until later written down. Just when one thinks one knows what the Prophet thought or how he acted in regard to any topic, one finds in the hadith something surprising. For instance, there are many reports that purport that the Prophet condemned homosexual acts and that those who do them earn God's curse, require social repression, or deserve criminal punishment. Yet in a talk I once gave in Canada, a member of the audience who was a gay Muslim from the Philippines reminded me of the report quoted above. He asked whether its reference, to a man who loved another man and was encouraged by the Prophet to speak out about his love, might also be relevant to a discussion of homosexuality. Could the Prophet Muhammad have encouraged a man to speak to another man of his love, yet also commanded a death sentence for a man who has sexual intercourse with another man?

The hadith themselves do not answer such questions; they simply convey a small bit of information along with a chain of narrators upon whom its authenticity rests. The hadith itself conveys nothing of the wider context of the incident it reports, and does not give us the identity of the men involved. Such ambiguity is typical of hadith and poses a major challenge to those who find in hadith a source of Islamic authority second only to the Qur'an. Human interpreters must ask whether the Prophet was speaking of brotherly love, or of platonic love, or of erotic love that could take on sexual expression. It is human interpreters who must resolve questions posed by hadith in their variations and contradictions.

When one enters the world of hadith, one learns to expect contradictions. So much material was attributed to the Prophet Muhammad during the first few centuries of Islam that contradictions are the norm. Hadith scholars and jurists developed techniques to resolve the contradictions, yet ideologues and neo-traditionalists often deny that any contradictions exist at all, as if admitting contradictions and ambiguities would shake their faith. Yet Muslims have, since the beginning, held diverse assessments of hadith and their role in the tradition. Opinions have varied widely. Some followers of the Prophet denounced anyone who narrates reports about him that might compete with the Qur'an as sources of guidance, whereas other followers seem to have become specialists in narrating reports about him. Some of the Prophet's immediate followers destroyed the material on which hadith were written in an attempt to suppress them. Yet within a few generations hadith were compiled into books that became integral to the tradition. Even among those who accepted hadith as integral to Islam, there were major differences on the status granted to them. Jurists insisted that they must be interpreted according to rational scrutiny, sifted with legal principles, and balanced with comparative insight. In contrast, some hadith specialists (like modern Wahhabis) rejected juridical reason and claimed that hadith spoke for themselves and required only literal reading and strict enforcement.

Such divergent views on hadith are part and parcel of the Islamic tradition. Contemporary arguments over their authenticity and interpretation simply revive arguments among the earliest generations of Muslims that were never fully resolved. Medieval scholars confronted these difficulties head on and developed techniques to sift through hadith and judge their credibility; the attempt to discard inauthentic, weak, or forged hadith became part and parcel of Islamic orthodoxy, whose upholders wrote volumes listing supposed hadith that are accepted by many Muslims yet are proved inauthentic. Yet in the contemporary period, bringing up hadith for critical analysis is highly contentious, and those raising the issue risk being condemned as heretical. This reveals a major weakness in contemporary Islamic culture, especially since believers are commanded in the Qur'an to scrutinize any reports about the truth – *lest you harm a community in ignorance and then be sorry for what you have done* (Q. 49:6). Unfortunately, many Muslim scholars have abandoned the faith-based intellectual project to analyze hadith and have largely handed the issue over to neo-traditionalist ideologues who hold written hadith collections to be unquestionably true, rejecting any critical and rational analysis while suppressing the troubling history of these collections.

Common believers are thus left in the dark. Imams and Islamic authorities shut down anyone who probes hadith by stating that she or he does not have the specialized training that one needs to analyze these reports. Yet those who have this training have abandoned their duty to scrutinize the whole body of hadith, and focus instead on selectively quoting hadith to shore up their own vision of orthodoxy.[2]

Can gay, lesbian, and transgender activists be blamed for feeling frustrated when dealing with hadith? Their families and communities quote these reports to oppose them, and refuse to admit that the hadith they cite may be of questionable authenticity. When lesbian, transgender, and gay Muslims try to sort through the reports to make judgments for themselves, they are accused of undermining orthodoxy. Yet many of these activists have enough traditional Islamic education to know that orthodoxy is more complex than families and mosque leaders care to admit. Orthodoxy has a history, and in its history the hadith occupy a place that has been constantly contested.

Asking how one can rely on hadith is not a rhetorical question, but is rather a question every Muslim must ask her- or himself in order to establish faith on a reliable basis. Some contemporary Muslims feel that it is best to focus only on the Qur'an and derive one's Islamic practice from it alone. The Qur'an is a hadith – a report – about God's speech to Muhammad, the authenticity of which is guaranteed by continuous multiple chains of trustworthy narrators (*hadith mutawatir*) from the Prophet's own time to the present. Most other hadith do not have this status and therefore give rise to speculative opinion (*zann*) rather than absolute certainty (*qat'*). These distinctions are central to the Islamic tradition but are most often ignored in contemporary debates. Nowadays people cite hadith without discussing the reliability of the hadith's chain of narration or judging the authenticity of the report's content to assess what level of certainty can be attributed to the knowledge the report conveys. Many activists whom I interviewed note that hadith are used carelessly and that Muslims often enforce their own cultural presumptions or sectarian bias with vague claims that "There must be a reference to some hadith which mentions … " Just mentioning that there must be a hadith that reinforces what you want to say is enough to close down argument and rational debate. Hadith are often an instrument of coercion rather persuasion; they are used in ways that incite reactions based on fear rather than to invite faith-based thinking that is clear.

When lesbian, gay, and transgender Muslims ask hard questions about hadith and how Islamic authorities use them, they speak from a position fully within the Islamic tradition. The struggle of lesbian, transgender, and gay Muslim activists is highly relevant to all Muslims who desire to renew their faith tradition through intellectual clarity. This chapter will document the kinds of hadith that condemn homosexual acts, persons, or attitudes. It will assess the authenticity of such reports and suggest how such reports can be interpreted in alternative ways. It will conclude that the ambiguity in hadith allows for a diversity of opinion among faithful Muslims. Regarding the hadith, there is room for mainstream Muslims to reconsider whether gay, lesbian, and transgender Muslims can be included in their religious community.

This chapter will focus specifically on hadith about homosexuality. Other reports on gender identity, which are often used by Muslim communities to condemn homosexuality in ways that confuse the issue, will also be examined here as an example of ambiguities in hadith transmission (the deeper issues of gender identity, including the hadith that are used to discuss it, will be examined in Chapter 6).

After assessing hadith on these subjects, this chapter concludes that the Prophet Muhammad never condemned an actual person for homosexual relationships or meted out punishment for homosexual intercourse. Reports in which the Prophet is pictured announcing a death penalty for homosexual intercourse are not reliable, as they appear not to have originated with the Prophet himself but rather with a second-generation follower of the Prophet (a follower prone to exaggeration, fabrication, and ideological extremism). Reports in which the Prophet is pictured as describing the damnation of homosexuals in the afterlife are not reliable, as so many of them are demonstrably forgeries that the whole class of reports stands discredited; they are likely attributable to moralists centuries after the Prophet died. In contrast, reliable reports show that the Prophet condemned and banished some individuals exhibiting transgender behavior (which Muslim neo-traditionalists often deploy to condemn homosexuals). However, many reports about this incident have been distorted to make the Prophet's judgment about ethical infractions involving heterosexual attraction appear to condemn transgender behavior itself, which is not true to the original event pictured in the reports.

Before we turn to a detailed examination of these reports about homosexuality, we must present a brief history of hadith collection and the techniques of assessing their textual authenticity. This information is crucial to discussing any individual report and it cannot be assumed that most Muslims know it well.

Hadith Reports: Their Origin and Authenticity

For many Muslims, hadith are integral to the Islamic tradition. However, in the earliest period Muslims practiced their faith without hadith. Writing down hadith was a highly controversial act among the first generations of Muslims. It took several centuries for Muslim scholars to allow written reports to have authority. Considering this gradual evolution with constant dissension, it is surely not heresy to question how hadith were recorded in order to assess, in a balance of faith and reason, whether specific reports carry any authority relating to a specific issue.

At first, the Prophet Muhammad forbade the writing down of reports of what he said or did in everyday life. The Prophet distinguished what he said in revealed language (included in the evolving Qur'an) from what he pronounced of his own opinions, instructions, or decisions. Yet his followers regarded his decisions and opinions as God's guidance for them; in this light, the Prophet forbade them to write down anything that he said or did which was not explicitly the Qur'an.[3]

Though the Prophet Muhammad conditionally allowed some of his followers to write down words of his that were not part of the Qur'an, after his death, the vice-regents were wary of allowing oral tradition to be written down as law. 'Umar was skeptical of some of the Prophet's companions relaying reports that they claimed came from the Prophet.[4] Members of the Prophet's family, like 'A'isha his youngest wife, accused others in the community of spreading false information in the name of Muhammad, and specifically singled out Abu Hurayra (to whom are attributed 5,375 reports, more than double the number attributed to any other companion) as a liar.[5] Another companion, 'Abdallah ibn Mas'ud, washed the ink off pages of a book of hadith, reciting from the Qur'an, *We narrate to you the best of narrations, by our revealing to you this Qur'an* (Q. 12:3).[6]

These examples show how the public narration of hadith was suspect and writing them down was controversial. However, as the Islamic community became an empire it required a system of law. The first systematic writing down of hadith was in legal texts.[7] These cited reports of the Prophet's followers and companions as well as of the Prophet himself without distinguishing between them.[8] Slowly, the texts began to distinguish whether the reports used in legal decisions were attributed to the Prophet and if so by what chain of narrators.[9]

This spawned a new genre called *musnad* texts, which include only reports with an *isnad* (or chain of narration) leading specifically to the Prophet, such as the *Musnad* of Ibn Hanbal (died 855).

Musnad texts distinguished reports that claimed to represent the Prophet's behavior from reports attributed to a follower or companion only, but that did not guarantee that these reports were genuine.[10] Many hadith were in circulation with an *isnad* that was inauthentic. In response, hadith scholars invented tests for probing the veracity of the chain of transmission and its narrators to try to sift true from false. Scholars collected reports that passed these tests into new collections known as *sahih* texts, which include only reports from the Prophet that are considered authentic through discrimination of the quality of their *isnad.*

The scholar Muhammad ibn Isma'il al-Bukhari (died 870) was the first to write such a critical work of hadith, followed by Muslim ibn al-Hajjaj of Nishapur (died 875).[11] Their two *sahih* collections are the basic sources for Sunni discussions of hadith. However, their elaboration of techniques to cull inauthentic hadith from true hadith reveals that inauthentic reports were circulating among Muslims.[12] Reports had proliferated before any systematic scrutiny; the damage had already been done before these scholars dedicated their life to damage control. Later hadith scholars scrutinized the reports collected by al-Bukhari and Muslim and found false or weak hadith that had been allowed into these esteemed collections.[13] In practice, once a hadith was in common usage it remained in circulation whether or not its chain of transmitters stood the test of authenticity.

Once written texts gained the aura of respectability, hadith specialists created their own discipline of knowledge. Under pressure to compile ever more inclusive works of hadith, later authors relaxed the criteria and began recording hadith with solitary chains of transmission or weak chains, of a quality that had been rejected by al-Bukhari and Muslim.[14] In the classical period, these works were standard references for Sunni jurists and theologians.[15] Even though the reports were canonized, they were never considered unassailable or inerrant. Hadith scholars refined their tests of chains of transmission and the reliability of transmitters and fearlessly attacked reports if they were suspected to be weak or false.[16] Our guide Ibn Hazm, a critical Sunni, relentlessly questioned his fellow jurists' use of hadith that he suspected of being unreliable. He applied with restless energy the tools and techniques that hadith scholars had developed to try to authenticate hadith.

This chapter takes inspiration from Ibn Hazm. Below I detail the kind of tests, some classical and some modern, which will be applied to reports about homosexuality in the remainder of this chapter to assess their authenticity.

Discussion of these tests and the resulting classification of reports is somewhat technical, but will be briefly introduced here. Every hadith consists of two parts: the information relayed (*matn*) about the Prophet's words or deeds, and the chain of narration (*isnad*) by which that information was passed down. Thus tests can be divided into two kinds: *isnad* criticism and *matn* criticism.

Classical hadith scholars focused on criticism of the *isnad* in order to certify the authenticity of the information relayed. The first technique in *isnad* criticism is to check whether the chain of narration leads back to the Prophet (*musnad*) or whether it ends with a companion or follower who had assumed that the information came from the Prophet himself (*marfu'*).The second technique is to check whether each link between narrators is plausible; the two narrators of each link must have lived in the same time and place, so that the later narrator could have believably heard the report from the former; if just one link in the chain of narration is not plausible, then the report is considered to have a "cut chain" (*maqtu'*) and cannot give authentic information. The third technique is to check the morality of all the narrators to judge whether they are believers in Islam, not biased by heresy or sectarian partisanship, and not liars. The fourth technique is to check the veracity of each narrator: that he or she is mature with an adequate memory and is not known to have made errors in transmitting information. If these texts of the *isnad* are all positive, then the report is considered a hadith by scholars of the classical period.

The most valuable kind of hadith report is known as *mutawatir*, or "continuously narrated." It has multiple and continuous *isnad*s, or chains of transmission. One hadith scholar defines it thus: "The *mutawatir* is a report that has so many narrators that it is conventionally impossible for them all to have agreed upon its fabrication. This multitude must be fulfilled on all the levels or generations of reporters."[17] *Mutawatir* reports confirm the basic beliefs and ritual practices upon which all Muslims concur.

However, there are very few reports that qualify as *mutawatir* hadith. Our guide Ibn Hazm paid great attention to this issue and maintained that "about 78 hadith reports reach the rare quality of reliability called *mutawatir*."[18] Others scholars think there are even fewer.[19] Scholars differ on exactly how many multiple chains of transmission it takes for a report to be judged *mutawair*; Ibn Hazm, for example, relates hadith that have five, seven, or eight independent chains of narration yet still finds them weak reports (*da'if*) and does not see them as reliable (*sahih*).[20] Although individual assessments differ, it is clear that very few hadith reach the level of *mutawatir*.[21] The vast majority of reports are less than supremely reliable, and hadith scholars in cooperation with jurists devised a complex system of evaluating them. All reports that are not *mutawatir* (with successive and multiple chains of narration) are called *khabar al-wahid* (a solitary report). This means that they have a chain of transmission that, at some point, relies on the word of one narrator unconfirmed by any other.[22] No hadith report about homosexuality or transgender behavior is *mutawatir* in its wording.

Facing these solitary reports, hadith scholars were faced with a quandary. Very strict jurists upheld the theory that only *mutawatir* hadith convey information with certainty whereas all other reports, such as solitary hadith, may help contribute to building an opinion (*zann*) but cannot provide decisive proof. Yet, jurists from earliest generations used these reports, even those which are solitary, in making their decisions long before hadith scholars developed the techniques to authenticate and classify them. So they categorized some hadith with only a single chain of narration as *maqbul* or "accepted," representing a report that scholars have accepted and implemented, even if it has only a single chain of narration. Scholars use the term *sahih* or "authentic" to represent a report consecutively transmitted from one reliable, pious, and accurate reporter to the next all the way back to the Prophet. These were deemed not ultimately confirmed but good enough to use. At a lesser level of reliability are those reports termed *hasan* or "good" which have a continual transmission although its narrators's reliability may not have been confirmed. Scholars rate a report *mawaththaq* or "dependable" (or alternatively *qawi* or "strong") which has a continuous chain of narrators back to the Prophet, though the narrators may be people of dubious morality or questionable reliability.

A report that does not live up to any of these criteria is labeled *da'if* or "defective." Its chain of transmission may contain a gap or a narrator who is immoral or of unknown character or known to lie or fabricate reports. Such weak or defective reports are further placed in sub-categories to specify in what way they are suspect. *Mardud* is "rejected" because of discrepancy in the narration of the reporter or distortion in the text of the tradition. *Mushtabah* is "suspect" because its circumstances of transmission admit doubt and its report is suspect. *Mawdu'* or "fabricated" is a report with a chain of transmission that is not reliable and is falsified; it is not permissible to relate the report except to declare it fabricated. Fabrication is ascertained by the narrator's admission, by evidence of weak wording, or by investigating its transmission.

Classical scholars focused their attention on the *isnad* in order to assess a report's authenticity, but one can also assess the information conveyed by the report, its *matn*. Most classical hadith scholars distrusted rational analysis in assessing hadith and therefore focused on the formal criteria of the chain of transmission. However, modern scholars, with increasing openness to the use of reason to confirm and bolster faith, are turning to *matn* criticism to supplement *isnad* criticism. Classical hadith scholars practiced *matn* criticism, even if it was overshadowed by *isnad* criticism, for they asked whether a report's *matn* contain information that goes against common experience, scientific observation, medical knowledge, or historical and geographical facts. If so, they concluded, it should be rejected as inauthentic even if its *isnad* is plausible.[23]

A second kind of *matn* criticism is linguistic analysis. Classical scholars asked whether the speech that the report attributed to the Prophet contained terms or expressions that the Prophet did not or could not have used. If they did, they were rejected as fabrications even if they had a plausible *isnad*. We find hadith in which the Prophet purportedly condemned various political leaders, sectarian movements, or theological schools that only existed after the Prophet had died.[24] The same kind of linguistic analysis of the *matn* was used to dismiss hadith that condemn later theological groups or predict later political events.[25]

In a similar way, hadith are suspect which picture the Prophet using in a technical way legal terms that were only developed by jurists many generations after the Prophet died. This chapter will question hadith that use the term *liwat* to mean anal intercourse or *luti* to mean one who engages in this act, for such terms developed in specialist juridical circles that did not exist at the time of the Prophet. The Prophet's companions used the more cumbersome and ambiguous phrase "act of the Tribe of Lot" to describe such events, rather than technical terms of Islamic law. Therefore, reports in which the Prophet speaks as if he were a classical-era jurist are of doubtful authenticity and can be dated to a later period through linguistic analysis. Muslims of later generations accepted them as teachings of the Prophet even though they are not; provided with a plausible *isnad*, these reports were incorporated into collections of hadith, as will be documented in the discussion of individual reports below.

In addition to rational and linguistic analysis, we can engage in sociological analysis by examining the historical specificity of the *matn*. Does it relay information in the context of an actual event in the life of the Prophet, rather than a juridical decision that is devoid of context? This was not a technique used in classical times, but modern scholars maintain its usefulness. We know much about the life of the Prophet and his companions through other genres of Islamic literature. In roughly the same era that hadith were being compiled, other authors were recording historical events of the Prophet's life: the history of military adventures (*maghazi*), the biography of the Prophet (*sira*), and the record of poetry and song (*aghani*).[26] Comparing hadith with other accounts of the Prophet's life can thus help us to reconstruct the context of the information conveyed by reports, a context that the hadith format tends to strip away.

Some hadith contain within their *matn* robust information about the context of the event they purport to convey – information like which other people are present with the narrator who hears and remembers the report, how these people interact with the Prophet, what events precipitated the words or deeds of the Prophet, or which topics were up for debate when the Prophet acted in a certain way. Such hadith we can all "embedded reports" because they contain detailed data on the names, characters, events, and issues that surround what the Prophet said or did. Such hadith with rich sociological data embedded in them provide clues as to their reliability, for one can confirm from other historical records whether such people interacted around such events; one can make such a confirmation independent of the *isnad.* Reports with rich details embedded in them are less likely to have been invented or mis-remembered, for they are context specific, exacting to recall, and quite inconvenient to pass on to a later generation. Probability is very high that they relay an actual event, rather than answer a legal or moral question that arose in the Muslim community in later generations.

However, most hadith do not have such historical and social information embedded in the *matn.* Such is the case when a hadith records an opinion or judgment or command of the Prophet in isolation from any actual case involving known persons around him. In that case, the *matn* suggests three possibilities. The first possibility is that the Prophet actually spoke the words as a rule or judgment in a general way meant to apply to his whole community and not to a specific person or incident; in this case, it is logical that he would speak it in a context of many listeners and therefore we would expect the *isnad* of such reports to represent multiple chains of transmission from different hearers in the earliest generations, and if this is not the case then the discrepancy between the form of the *matn* and its supporting *isnad* invites our critical scrutiny. The second possibility is that the Prophet's words were originally spoken in a specific context but, over time and transmission, the narrators stripped it of context that was considered irrelevant, inconvenient, or too hard to remember, and such stripping is a normal characteristic of oral narratives. The stripping changes a descriptive report about what happened into a prescriptive report stating what should happen. We observed above that hadith were remembered, recorded, and collected under pressure from jurisprudence. In the process of transmission, such information would be streamlined or rendered into a form more useful for making legal decisions as details of the event were reduced or eliminated to free the Prophet's words from their immediate social context and transform them and into the form of a general rule to be applied far from its original context. It remains to be seen whether such stripping of contexts changes the actual or possible interpretation of the words that the Prophet is reported to have said.

The third possibility, when a report's *matn* lacks any embedded information that provides its social context, is that the Prophet did not pronounce the words. The Prophet lived in a very tightly knit community and his life was rich with connections to friends, family, and tribe. His interactions were deeply embedded in this context, and many hadith portray him addressing individuals known by name or interacting in events that were widely observed. He made rules and pronounced judgments in the thick of a local community and social context. We have hadith that convey how his decisions were made in a context where the issues were specific and the names of those involved in the affair that triggered a judgment are known. If the *matn* of a hadith is devoid of such detail, chances are high that it is an answer to a legal question from a later period, was attributed to the Prophet informally, and then at a later date was given a formal *isnad*. Local authorities like judges, preachers, or parents might claim that it was based on the Prophet's practice or intent. When hadith criticism was structured, such reports could be given a retrospective *isnad* back to the Prophet and easily incorporated into written collections of hadith texts which included reports with solitary chains of narration. *Isnad* criticism, no matter how conscientiously applied, could not prevent such infiltration of reports with fabricated chains of narration to legitimize them. There is a high probability that a report with a *matn* stripped of contextual information and with a solitary *isnad* is of this type, which reflects the folk wisdom or common opinion of members of the Muslim community in later generations rather than the words of the Prophet himself. When we turn to examine reports on homosexuality, we will find that most of them fall into this category and are therefore of suspect authenticity.

This study tries to take a realist position that is nonetheless nurturing of faith. Muslims must admit that classical categories were codified and critical techniques were defined long after hadith were in wide circulation, first orally and then in written form. We must not imagine that these tests preexisted the reports being tested or that these categories prevented weak hadith from circulating widely. Hadith scholars were fighting an uphill battle: jurists were already citing in legal decisions reports that hadith scholars classified as "weak" and popular preachers were quoting reports that schools classified as "forged." I will document a vivid example of one such case below, in a popular hadith about homosexuality which was long ago declared forged but still circulates. Although we must admire the painstaking effort of hadith scholars and the elaboration of their system, its net effect was not to test each hadith before circulation and therefore limit the number and use of them. Rather its effect was generally to justify the hadith as a corpus that was already in use, even as the scholars claimed to be able to sift out the few fabricated reports from the general body of authentic reports. One can see this in the very optimistic terms for their categories: reports labeled as "good" or "sound" or "authentic" are reports with only solitary chains of transmission which are far below the ultimate standard of reliability (*mutawatir*).

These optimistic labels make very tenuous reports seem more reliable than they are. In addition, jurists and scholars developed other theoretical constructs to get around the unreliability of hadith. Despite the fact that so few hadith achieve the level of reliability called *mutawatir*, scholars advanced the concept that an abundance of reports with only solitary chains of narration or weak chains could, by repetition, amount to the status of "reliable in general meaning" or *mutawatir al-ma'na*, even if, taken individually, they were not reliable in their exact wording. This concept gave jurists and theologians a justification to use reports of solitary narration without entering into exacting criticism of their *isnad*s and discussing their authenticity. However, a skeptical believer may perceive that this concept amounts to believing a rumor simply on account of its widespread repetition while abdicating responsibility for investigating in detail its circumstances of origin.

Every believer must come to her or his own conclusions about hadith, the authenticity of information they convey, and the rightness of how Muslim jurists and preachers utilize them. No single study can provide a universal answer to such sensitive questions that affect one's faith. This chapter will apply critical techniques to individual reports or clusters of similar reports, using methods both traditional and modern to allow readers to assess the skepticism with which many gay, lesbian, and transgender Muslims view these traditions. In these endeavors, this chapter follows the example of Muslim feminist scholars, such as Fatima Mernissi and Amina Wadud, who have in similar ways questioned the authenticity of many misogynist reports.[27] In this way, it becomes clearer that transgender, lesbian, and gay Muslim activists are not isolated. They engage these questions from within the wider fronts of feminist and progressive Muslim movements, whether or not those movements welcome them as equal participants.

A Tradition of Forgery

A Muslim can accept the body of hadith in general, reject them in totality, or take a middle position that accepts them in general while trying to sift them for inauthentic reports. Yet all Muslims must confront the fact that the body of hadith contains forged traditions. Some reports purporting to convey the Prophet's words or actions are falsely attributed to him yet still circulate among Muslims who consider them true. Neo-traditionalists try to minimize this fact by claiming that hadith sciences in classical times weeded out falsifications as hadith were written down and gathered into usable collections. Reformists acknowledge the fact by highlighting how the hadith sciences were created in order to stem the influx of false reports but were not in place early enough to prevent such reports from entering even esteemed collections. More radical critics raise this fact as evidence that the whole body of hadith is suspect and requires either radical revision or dismissal. Putting these generalized reactions to one side for the moment, let us consider hadith that speak of issues involving sexual orientation and gender identity. Within this narrow cross-section of hadith, we find some forged reports.

Let us consider one of the most widely cited reports in Islamic literature on homosexuality. The Prophet was reported to have said, "When the male mounts another male the angels are alarmed and raise a cry to their lord. The wrath of the mighty One comes down upon those [men], the curse covers over them, and the tempters surround them. The earth asks its Lord for permission to swallow them up and the divine throne grows heavy upon those who bear it up, while the angels declare God's greatness and hellfire rears up high." The conservative medieval scholar Ibn Qayyim al-Jawziyya (died 1350) cites this report in his book on love but warns that its chain of transmission is quite weak.[28] A later medieval hadith scholar who was equally conservative but had no particular obsession with homosexuality declared this report to be an outright fabrication (*mawdu'*).[29] The scholar who publicized this judgment was Muhammad ibn Tahir Patani (died 1578), who was known as the "King of Hadith Scholars" in his age and revived in his native South Asia the discipline of hadith criticism. He disparages this supposed hadith through traditional methods of *isnad* analysis in his book entitled *Focusing Attention on Reports that Are Fabrication* (*Tadhkirat al-Mawdu'at*).[30] He rejected it it along with hundreds of others on a myriad of topics. He disparaged the report even though it boasts an *isnad* leading back to Ibn 'Abbas, an esteemed companion (died 686/87) who was the cousin of the Prophet and to whom are attributed 1,660 reports.

Medieval scholars like Patani discovered forged reports but had no success removing them from circulation. Almost five centuries after Patani proved that this particular report was forged, it is still in circulation among Muslim communities. Hadith scholars could pronounce judgment on reports or transmitters but had no means to actualize their judgment. Jurists, preachers, poets, and parents repeated the report without questioning its authenticity. Even in South Asia, where Patani exerted such influence and his books are printed and read, this particular report continues to be cited. In 1879, the reformist Urdu poet Hali echoed its words in his epic moral poem "The Ebb and Flow of Islam" as he chastised Muslims for adopting what he calls the the effeminate and pederastic ways of the Persians and thereby corrupting their moral fiber, which led to colonial rule.[31] In 1960, a religious scholar of the Deoband academy, Mufti

Zafeeruddin, published an Urdu tract against homosexuality in which he cites this supposed hadith. Despite his training as an Islamic scholar and official of one of the Sunni world's most acclaimed madrasas, he cites this report as a true teaching of the Prophet Muhammad without considering its authenticity (even as he notes that Ibn Qayyim, his source for the report, warned that its transmission was weak). In 1971, a second Urdu edition was published with no consideration of the authenticity of this report. His tract was recently translated into English, in 1999, the translation including his use of this fraudulent hadith, with no attempt made to assess its authenticity.[32] This example illustrates how far contemporary Muslims have moved from their intellectual roots in the classical Islamic tradition while representing Islam in an increasingly ideological neo-traditionalist form.[33]

The example above is an extreme case, but not an isolated one. Patani also discredits the famous saying, "The sodomites [*lutiyun*] will be raised on judgment day in the form of monkeys and pigs." The hadith scholar considered its *isnad* from 'Abdallah ibn 'Umar (an esteemed *sahabi* or companion and son of the second caliph, to whom are attributed 2,630 reports) and deemed it false.[34] Despite its attribution to a companion revered for his intimacy with the Prophet and knowledge of the Qur'an, the scholar judged the report to be forged. The link between the report's content and its purported source was illegitimate, and the scholar suggested that it should be cited only to mention its inauthenticity and encourage its removal from circulation. Yet we find it still in circulation. Mufti Zafeeruddin cites it without discussing its origin or status, in order to condemn the homosexual man, whom he calls *Luti*, by writing that "the souls of these evil doers would be with the souls of the Tribe of Lot [in hell] which is a very narrow and restricted place and is greater in punishment than the oven of the fornicators."[35] This wild claim by Mufti Zafeeruddin goes against the spirit of most classical texts that discuss grave sins or "enormities" (*kaba'ir*), in which heterosexual fornication (*zina'*) is usually cited as a more atrocious sin than sodomy (*liwat*).[36]

How to account for these reports and their wisespread use, even after hadith scholars criticize their narration and declare them false? They circulate because they reflect the Muslim community's prejudice, even if they do not convey an authentic teaching of the Prophet. For this reason, they are cited without scrutiny by scholars as well as other members of the community. This insight also allows us to understand how and why they were forged in the first place. We can hear in them the voice of preachers in the generations after the Prophet died.

Preachers and moralists felt themselves responsible for warning Muslims away from what they perceived to be sins, through exaggeration of hellfire and pig-flesh. If such moralistic preaching were not accepted (either by being ignored or challenged), it had to be reinforced and given legitimacy by the claim that it represented the Prophet's words. Those who placed their own words in the Prophet's mouth might do so with the best of intentions, and we should not imagine "hadith forgers" to be infiltrators, hypocrites, or heretics. Most likely they were moral leaders of their community who simply assumed that their own opinion (whether formed from prejudice, moral debate, or learning) echoed that of the Prophet. Most likely, the "forgery" happened over many generations, as sayings of popular preachers, jurists, or community leaders were repeated, recycled, and then remembered as something integral to the Prophet's teachings. What the Prophet "could have said" easily morphed into something the Prophet "must have said" (especially when the report confirmed popular prejudice of the time) and was later transformed into something "the Prophet did in fact say." In this sense, many reports convey to us the opinions of members of the Muslim community (usually one side of a point of hot debate) but not necessarily the opinion of the Prophet himself.

It is clear that Muslim moralists were obsessively concerned with males who practiced anal intercourse. This was a topic of dispute, especially in the later 'Abbasid Empire, when it became fashionable to own slave boys and to prefer sexual intercourse with them to intercourse with wives or female slaves. Many 'Abbasid era writers penned witty debates about whether romance or sex with a male slave (*ghulam*) was more pleasurable than with a female slave (*jariya*) – such as the famous literary debate penned by al-Jahiz (died 868).[37] As the custom became so widespread among aristocracy, the mother of one ruler was worried that her son would become so enanmoured of his slave boys that the would never beget an heir, so she ordered all the slave girls of the palace to dress in the style of fashionable young men.[38] Muslim moralists and jurists responded to these radical transformations of culture by preaching against the seductions of same-sex eroticism in a pederastic mode.

Their opinions were often presented as the literal words of the Prophet, and so we find purported hadith that use the term *ghulam* and denounce anal sex. Yet did the Prophet actually say them? Let us take, for instance, the following report: "God curses whoever kisses a male slave [*ghulam*] with lust. If he caresses him [the slave] with lust God never accepts his prayers. If he embraces him [the slave] he will be lashed with flames on the Day of Judgment. If he fornicates with him [the slave] then God will throw him into the fire." It is commonly retold as a hadith of the Prophet, but the hadith scholar Muhammad ibn Tahir Patani judges that it is a fabrication.[39] He discredits reports in which the Prophet supposedly denounces those male slaves who accept anal penetration – "There is no young man [*amrad*] more shameless than one who allow [himself to be taken from] his behind" – which he judges inauthentic. He rejects a report that warns all men (old or young, slave or freeborn) against anal intercourse – "Whoever take it [sexual penetration] in his behind seven times, God changes his desire for pleasure from his front to his behind" – which he judges to be fabricated.[40]

The scholar who discredited all these reports, Muhammad ibn Tahir Patani, had no motive to encourage homoerotic acts. Although he probably agreed with those who circulated these reports that same-sex intercourse is sinful, he objected to any words being projected on to the Prophet that he demonstrably did not say. Patani notes with engaging honesty that "There are many kinds of people who have fabricated hadith, but those who are gravely damaging are those who belong to communities of righteous asceticism [*zuhd*] who falsely attribute reports to the Prophet in order to have people refrain and then people accept their sayings out of trust in them [due to their righteousness]."[41] He quotes with approval the judgment of Ibn al-Jawzi, "Among those who have forged hadith and lied are those who are overcome with ascetic zeal and neglect proper memorization ... I have not seen anyone lie [about hadith] more than those who a known for their piety and ascetic zeal!"[42] Ironically, the moralists and preachers who strive to do what they see as good for the community have in fact spread falsely attributed reports.

All these reports, judged as forged but continuing to circulate, share certain features when we examine their *matn*. They convey condemnation of homosexuals in moral terms rather than legal terms; they speak of divine punishment on the day of judgment rather than legal punishment. There is a group of reports that do this (one of five categories of reports which address homosexuality in some way, which will be detailed in the next section). The fact that at least five reports in this category are forged should give us cause to scrutinize them when considering others with such exaggerated moralistic imagery or that use the technical term *luti*. Such reports, in any case, are not used by jurists in building the *shari'a* and its legal rulings, addressing as they do the more rhetorical realm of punishments in the afterlife, which is beyond the purview of legal rulings proper. We will consider the hadith that directly affect legal rulings on homosexuality below (which are not forged reports that should be dismissed, but rather reports with solitary chains of transmission, the application of which should be assessed). There is no consensus among Muslim scholars about the extent of forged reports. Contemporary Muslim scholars argue about how many forged reports are still in circulation and also about how early forged reports began to infiltrate the corpus of hadith. The existence of some forged reports that circulated as authentic hadith does not prove that all reports are late creations. However, it does provoke us to explore the historical context in which later Muslim society, generations after the death of the Prophet, did set into circulation condemnations of homosexuality that did not originate with the Prophet himself.

The German Orientalist Joseph Schacht was the first scholar to allege that the hadith as a corpus were written down late (in the second century after the Prophet's death) and therefore represent the legal opinions and moral commentary of later Muslim society. He asserted that *isnad*s were "created" under pressure from the emerging discipline of hadith scholarship, to justify reports and opinions that were already in circulation among jurists, moralists, and political partisans. In Schacht's view, hadith were generated by civil wars, theological debates, and legal arguments which engrossed the first several generations of Muslims after the Prophet death, rather than by the memory of the Prophet's companions passed down through oral tradition. Schacht may have overstated his case, and later Western scholars have modified his theory over the last century and a half. But Schacht's insight does account for some troubling aspects of hadith for which Islamic orthodoxy does not account. These are evident in the case of the two inauthentic reports cited above. First, Schacht's theory accounts for how opinions that are not authentic could continue to circulate under the guise of being hadith. They are not the result of intentional fabrication or occasional misunderstanding but are rather the exception that reveals the norm. The few reports that hadith scholars can with confidence declare to have forged *isnad*s reveal that all or many *isnad*s were in fact created retroactively to anchor opinions and teachings in the Prophet's followers, companions, and eventually the Prophet himself. Those reports whose forged *isnad* is evident after close scrutiny by hadith scholars are simply those that were less convincingly forged. While Schacht may have overstated the case (and making a judgment about what proportion of reports may be forged versus genuinely transmitted involves more faith than science), his theory does account for the persistent presence of forged reports among those initially considered authentic. His theory also accounts for another disconcerting feature of hadith, the unreasonably disproportionate number of attributions to a small number of companions, like Ibn 'Abbas or 'Abdallah ibn 'Umar (as in the above two forged reports). According to Schacht and the Western scholars who followed him, this high density of chains of transmission leading back to only six companions is evidence of manufactured *isnad*s projected retrospectively back to the Prophet through key figures.

Those who were considered popular narrators were often selected in this process, until thousands of reports were attributed to them, even if they were not the closest or most intimate companions. The prime example of this is Abu Hurayra, to whom the highest number of reports are attributed and who has become a very controversial figure in modern assessments of hadith authenticity among both Muslim and non-Muslim analysts.[43] Despite the fact that over five thousand reports are attributed to him (over twice the amount attributed to the next most popular), he was not the closest observer of the Prophet or his most durable friend. Abu Hurayra was a Yemini Arab who converted to Islam when about thirty years old and "served the Prophet" doing odd jobs around his household (according to some reports he cleaned in the women's quarters). He evidently stayed in the Prophet's company in Medina for a limited time.[44] In contrast, many of the closest companions to the Prophet who knew him for decades (such as the first three vice-regents Abu Bakr, 'Umar, and 'Uthman) are almost non-existent in *isnad* chains of narration.

Schacht and his supporters suggest that endless debate over the personality of companions and followers who are named in *isnad*s is useless in proving a report's authenticity. In their view, many hadith (if not all of them) are the product of Muslim opinions and debates one to two centuries after the Prophet died, rather than reports originating during the Prophet's lifetime. They argue that these reports convey information about political, legal, and moral debates of Muslims but tell us very little from the Prophet himself. The existence of some reports which are clearly forged that address homosexual behavior, such as the two cited above, shows that Muslims were hotly debating the issue in a later historical period and that their opinions may have been mis-remembered as the Prophet's own teachings. Schacht's "source-critical" method invites us to consider how an era long after the Prophet's death may have shaped hadith and the opinions they present on matters pertaining to sexual orientation and gender identity.

This chapter argues that the era of the Umayyad Empire and 'Abbasid Empire set the conditions for debates on homosexuality as reflected in the hadith. Many social factors shaped this debate, including use of slaves for companionship as well as work, the rise of a courtesan culture, the assimilation of Hellenic ideals into Arab and Islamic culture, and the increasing seclusion of wives and daughters. Feminist Muslim scholars have also pointed to this era as the time in which Islamic patriarchy was established and then its norms were projected back into the Prophet's own era and teachings. It was in this same era that the Islamic legal and theological tradition was formulated.[45]

A Tradition of Variation

As we have seen, some forged reports occur that speak about homosexuality. They occur in a particular category of reports, those with exaggeratedly vivid descriptions of afterlife punishments for sodomy or which use the technical term *luti* for "sodomite." Muslims may come to different conclusions about how to react to the existence of some forged reports in these categories: some may assert that they are rare forgeries that can be detected and removed from circulation, and some may suspect that other reports that use this language and imagery may well be forged also even if their *isnad* is intact. Still others may suggest that if some forgeries survive in this category Muslims should throw out the whole category of reports.

Even if one did throw out this whole category of reports, it would not affect Islamic law, for that is built upon a different category of reports altogether. As mentioned above, the reports that address sexual orientation and gender identity may be grouped into five different categories on the basis of the content of their reports: (1) reports that speak of divine punishment after death; (2) reports that in which God curses homosexuals; (3) reports that speak of criminal punishment by execution; (4) reports that condemn transgender behaviors; (5) reports that speak of cases involving historically known individuals who engaged in homosexual or transgender behavior. Islamic law is primarily built upon reports in the third and fourth categories, even if it is those in the first and second categories that preachers and families most often use against homosexuals in their community. It is to the reports in the third and fifth categories that we now turn our attention, these being closely related.

The discussion of forged reports above suggests that hadith on the whole may inform us about the opinion of later generations of Muslims but give no guidance about the words or actions of the Prophet. This conclusion certainly makes sense when we confront forged traditions, but it is far from clear that all traditions are forged. Are there any reports that reveal the Prophet addressing a historically verifiable case, that is, interacting with historically known individuals, in which the hadith might be bolstered by other textual sources?

When we examine the Prophet's life, as revealed in the *sira* literature (the Prophet's biography), the *maghazi* literature (events of warfare in the early Islamic community), and the *adab* literature (literary and artistic activity in pre-Islamic times and the early Islamic community), we find many detailed cases where Muhammad deals with sexuality and gender issues. Most of these, however, are about heterosexual cases: these include fornication (*zina'*) between a man and woman, sexual activity between slaves and their owners, discussions about birth control, and arguments between husbands and wives over sexual positions. We find no case in which the Prophet deals with an actual case involving known individuals of homosexual intercourse between two men or two women.

We do find a few cases of the Prophet dealing with effeminate men (*mukhannath*) in the early Islamic community at Medina. The reports dealing with effeminate men are a good example of variation, for they exist in multiple variations in their wording. Variation in wording is very common among hadith, and often these variations suggest that changes occurred over time in the understanding and usage of a particular report. Narrators remembered the wording in particular contexts and for different purposes, which are sometimes revealed by the subtle changes the words of a report undergo.

Hadith do not reveal the Prophet Muhammad dealing with any specific case of known individuals punished, disciplined, or cursed for homosexual behavior. However, there are reports that show him dealing with known individuals who were *mukhannath*. An effeminate man is one who is anatomically male and raised as male but who in adult life dresses and acts in the social role of a woman. The *mukhannath* exhibits transgender behavior rather than homosexual behavior, but Islamic traditionalists often conflate these, assuming that homosexual men behave like women and are therefore addressed by how the Prophet treated effeminate or transgender men. This is not an assumption that is supported by sociological research or actual reported experience of gay and lesbian Muslims. However, we will consider these reports because they are often used to argue against homosexual Muslims.

These reports are found in the *sahih* hadith collection of al-Bukhari. Al-Bukhari's stringent standards eliminated many less reliable reports, and we do not find in his collection many reports about punishments for homosexuality that we find in other collections whose standards were not as strict. For example, in al-Bukhari's collection there are no reports that treat same-sex acts as fornication (*zina'*, or a *hadd* crime). However, al-Bukhari did include several reports about men who appear similar to women and women who appear similar to men; significantly, he includes these reports in the section on clothing rather than in a distinct section on sex acts.[46] Al-Bukhari includes in these linked sections three hadith that exhibit variations upon one incident.

The report with the longest and most detailed text (*matn*) records Umm Salama, a wife of the Prophet, describing an incident between the Prophet and an effeminate man. Other sources give the personal name, Hit, to the *mukhannath*, who was with Umm Salama in her room on the eve of a Muslim army raid against the town of Ta'if. According to the hadith, "The effeminate man said to 'Abdullah, the brother of Umm Salama, 'O 'Abdullah, if God grants that you take Ta'if tomorrow, go after Ghaylan's daughter, for she comes forwards with four and goes away with eight!' Upon hearing this, the Prophet said, 'Don't let those people enter in your [females'] presence.'"[47] The incident is not self-explanatory, and hadith transmitters have offered commentary to explain the specific details of the incident. Hit, like other *mukhannath* in Medina, had a distinct social role. Though anatomically male, he displayed the gendered

Companions:

1 'A'isha bint Abu Bakr al-Siddiq, a wife of the Prophet (died 57AH in Mecca; to her are attributed 2210 reports)

2 Umm Salama, a wife of the Prophet named Hind bint Umiya ibn al-Mughira (died 63AH; to her are attributed 387 reports)

3 Ibn 'Abbas, 'Abdallah (died 68, 71, 72, or 74AH at around the age of 73 in Ta'ifa, to him are attributed 1660 reports)

Second generation followers:

4 'Urwa ibn al-Zubayr ibn al-'Awam al-Madani (died 93, 94 or 95AH)

5 Zaynab bint Umm Salama, daughter of the Prophet

6 'Ikrima

Later narrators:

7 Ibn Shihab al-Zuhri

8 Yunus

9 Ibn Wahb

10 Ahmad ibn Salih

12 Ma'mar

13 Muhammad ibn Thawr

14 Muhammad ibn 'Ubayd

15 'Abd al-Razzaq

16 Muhammad ibn Dawud ibn Sufyan

17 'Abdu ibn Humayd

18 Hisham

19 Zuhayr

20 Malik ibn Isma'il

21 Hisham's father

22 Ibn Numayr

23 Waki'

24 Abu Bakr ibn Abi Shayba

25 Abu Mu'awiya

26 Abu Kurayb

27 Jarir

28 Ishaq ibn Ibrahim ibn Rahawayh

29 Yahya

30 Mu'adh ibn Fudala

31 Qatada

32 Shu'ba

33 Ghandar

34 Muhammad ibn Nashshar

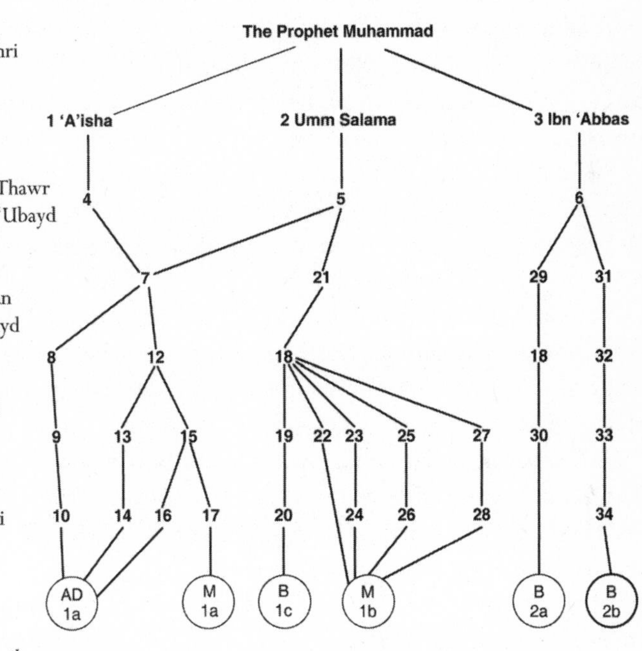

report 1a — The Prophet said, "Oho! I think this one knows what goes on here! Do not admit him [a specific effeminate man] into your [females'] presence!"

report 1b — The Prophet said, "Don't let those people [effeminate men] enter in your [males'] presence"

report 1c — The Prophet said, "Don't let those people [effeminate men] enter in your [females'] presence"

report 2a — The Prophet cursed those effeminate among the men and those emasculine among women and said, "Get them out of your houses"

report 2b — The Prophet cursed those men who resemble women and those women who resemble men

Hadith recorders:

AD Abu Dawud;

M Muslim;

B al-Bukhari

Figure 1 *Isnad* of reports on transgender behavior.

character of a female and was therefore allowed privileged access to the inner homes of women, including the Prophet's own wives. *Mukhannath* were assumed not to have sexual feelings toward women, unlike most gendered males, which exempted them from the normal rules forbidding non-related men from entering in private among the women.

This crucial point is made explicit in a variation of this hadith, as recorded by Muslim ibn al-Hajjaj on the authority of 'A'isha, another wife of the Prophet. She was remembered to have said, "There was a *mukhannath* who used to be admitted to the presence of the Prophet's wives. He was considered one of those lacking interest in women. One day, the Prophet entered when this *mukhannath* was with one of his wives; he [the *mukhannath*] was describing a woman and said, 'When she comes forward, it is with four, and when she goes away, it is with eight.' The Prophet said, 'Oho! I think this one knows what goes on here! Do not admit him into your [females'] presence!' So he was kept out."[48] In this version of the same incident, the narrator recalls the crucial detail that the *mukhannath*, as an effeminate man, was considered one of those lacking interest in women (*min ghayr uli irba*, quoting the words of Qur'an 24:31, a crucial phrase discussed in Chapter 2). However, the *mukhannath*'s comment about another woman shocked the Prophet and caused him to reassess this assumption. The *mukhannath*, Hit, was describing the sensual body of the woman from Ta'if, named "the Daughter of Ghaylan." The rolls of fat across her belly were so beautifully voluptuous that they appeared as "four" lines when she walked toward you, but "eight" lines from behind as, wrapping around her flanks, they tapered out towards her spine. The *mukhannath* described her body to Umm Salam's brother, advising him to go after her in the upcoming raid and capture her beauty for his own enjoyment – and it must be remembered that in the early Islamic community war captivates were treated as slaves, and sexual intercourse with one's slaves was legal and expected.

The *mukhannath* named Hit gave evidence of understanding heterosexual lust in great detail, and the Prophet reacted to his words with shock. There are two possible interpretations of the Prophet's banishing Hit and others like him from Muslim homes. Perhaps he reacted to Hit's inciting one of his Muslim companions to follow his heterosexual lust in a war raid, for Hit used his exemption from gender segregation to reveal the beauty of a woman's body to prying eyes and possibly predatory intentions. Or perhaps the Prophet reacted to Hit's evident knowledge of heterosexual desire, despite his exceptional gender identity as a transgender man who was assumed to be outside of the economy of heterosexual desire, and saw him as not exceptional enough; this possibility is suggested by the one variation that remembers the Prophet as saying, "Oho! I think this one knows what goes on here!" meaning that Hit knows about sexual desire and seduction between women and men, despite his being an effeminate man who is outside the heterosexual gender binary. The hadith do not give us further clues about the Prophet's intention in banishing Hit from his household. The scholar of Arabic literature Everret Rowson, who has best studied the phenomenon of *mukhannath* in the first century of the Islamic community, sums up the situation succinctly: "Al-Muhallab explains that the Prophet 'only barred the mukhannath from the women's quarters when he heard him describe the woman in this way (i.e. her belly-wrinkles) which excites the hearts of men; he forbade him (to enter) in order that he not describe (prospective) mates to people and thus nullify the point of secluding women.' It is not entirely clear, then, to what extent mukhannath people were punished for their breaking of gender rules in itself, and to what extent such measures were taken rather because of the perceived damage to social institutions from their activities as matchmakers and their corresponding access to women."[49]

Other reports describe this incident in different variations. These variations are much condensed and elide most of the personal details of the event. By removing the personal specificity, these various "rememberings" of the event strip away its historical context and create the impression of a general pronouncement; this renders the Prophet's reaction to unique events into the form of a juridical decision. Take for example this report, also recorded in al-Bukhari: Ibn 'Abbas was reported to have said, "The Prophet cursed effeminate men [*al-mutakhannathin min al-rijal*] and masculine women [*al-mutarajjulat min al-nisa'*] and he said, 'Turn them out of your houses.' One of the narrators, Sha'ba, reports the the Prophet turned out a certain *mukhannath*, and that 'Umar followed his example in turning out another."[50] This report preserves the words of the Prophet, "turn them out of your houses," while erasing the context of the actual event and its unique specificity about Hit, the effeminate man named. Without the detailed context, the Prophet appears to make a general command to banish all *mukhannath*, rather than just a specified one. This makes it appear that the Prophet banished them all on account of their unusual gender identity rather than for a specific ethical transgression. This variation of the report not only erases historical context but also adds juridical rationale to the Prophet's pronouncement, which the fuller report did not specify. This report says that the Prophet cursed not only effeminate men but also masculine-acting women (*mutarajjulat*) and generates a juridical decision. It implies that the fault of effeminate men or masculine women is their gender identity rather than any particular transgression of sexual behavior or trespass of ethical norms. In contrast, the reports that preserve the historical context of the event reveal that the Prophet originally banished one of them who had helped heterosexual men act upon their lust for women.

A third variation of this report in al-Bukhari goes even further in remembering the Prophet's words as a juridical pronouncement. This report maintains that Ibn 'Abbas said, "The Prophet cursed those men who appear like women [*al-mutashabbihun bi'l-nisa'*] and those women who appear like men [*al-mutashabbihat bi'l-rijal*]."[51] The original event involved only an effeminate man, but the second report remembers the Prophet as cursing both effeminate men and masculine women; the third report further reduces and rationalizes the Prophet's statement, claiming that he cursed men who appear like women and women who appear like men, using a single technical term, *mutashshabih*, to denote those of one gender who appear like the other gender. Clearly, these variations follow a certain trajectory. They reduce personal detail, eliminate historical context, and create the appearance of general juridical pronouncements when the reports were originally a unique personal response to a discrete ethical challenge.

The reports that derive from this event reveal that hadith do not simply preserve the Prophet Muhammad's words and deeds. Rather, reports are shaped into variations by the memory of those who transmit them. Memory is a slippery thing. The report is determined just as much by the urgent needs of the transmitter and receiver as it is by the actual event it purports to describe. Hadith, as remembered and transmitted over generations before being written down, may preserve a kernel of truth about events in the Prophet's life, but may also be distorted by those who transmit them. The Prophet's words are recorded in multiple variations, often with important omissions or alterations that can have a great impact on how the report is applied in legal decisions. For lesbian, gay, and transgender Muslims, such subtle alterations could mean quite literally the difference between life and death.

To illustrate these stakes, let us return to the original event that generated these variously remembered reports. The *mukhannath* Hit, once welcomed in the Prophet's household as a valuable addition to his wives' social life, was banished from Medina. The hadith that refer to him eliminate the specificity of his ethical transgression and make it appear as if the Prophet condemned all *mukhannath* solely because of their unusual gender identity. Not only this, but these reports' erasure of the specific historical circumstances covers up the fact that Hit continued to live on the margins of the Muslim community. Further variations of these reports recall the details that Hit, the *mukhannath* who was banished, lived in the desert and came into Medina once a week to beg for food. A further variation adds that some members of the Islamic community complained to the Prophet that Hit would die of starvation in his banishment, in response to which the Prophet allowed Hit to come into Medina twice a week to beg for food.[52] Yet another variation recalls that the *mukhannath* whose hands and feet were dyed with henna in the style of women was brought before the Prophet, who banished him from Medina to a place called al-Naqi‘ several miles outside the oasis city. When some of the Prophet's companions asked if it were better to kill the *mukhannath*, the Prophet is reported to have said, "I have been forbidden to kill those who pray."[53]

This last report depicts the Prophet sticking to his principle that fellow Muslims can only be executed for three things – fornication, murder, and apostasy – even if his companions allowed their prejudice against transgender behavior to override their attention to this principle. Classical Islamic commentators on hadith collections provide definitions of *mukhannath* which show how Muslims in the early Islamic era did not assume *mukhannath* to have any sexual activity or even sexual orientation.[54] They found blameworthy only a *mukhannath* who affects effeminate behavior for ulterior motives rather than one who acts thus by inherent nature. They acknowledged that for some rare individuals this behavior was a natural expression of their gender identity, in a phenomenon that we would in today's clinical terminology call "transgender" identity (to be examined more thoroughly in Chapter 6). The hadith documented above about the Prophet's banishing one or several *mukhannath* are most often cited by contemporary Muslims to forbid or discourage homosexuality. This obscures both the distinctive inherent nature of transgender identity as well as confuses the reason for banishing the *mukhannath* who had lived in the Prophet's household, depicting it as a generalized curse on any person who does not fit binary gender norms.

Beyond what this series of hadith can tell us about the Prophet's attitude toward transgender behavior, the reports when examined as a series can also inform us about the process of memory and transmission. They illustrate how reports exist in wide variation even when they reflect an historical incident involving known personalities around the Prophet. Analyzing the *matn* of the reports and comparing them against each other suggests that the process of remembering produces variations and that the variations owe to the pressures upon later generations to remember reports about the Prophet in ways that are applicable to legal decisions and moral judgments that may be far removed from the Prophet's original words and intent. Details are forgotten. Situational contexts are erased. Historical contingencies are transformed into universal generalizations. Even if hadith contain some traces of the historical events of the Prophet's life and teachings, the process of their preservation ensures that they are subtly recast, through generations of selective memory, into forms that may betray as much as convey the Prophet's intent.

A Tradition of Ambiguity

The analysis offered above demonstrates that hadith are susceptible to distorting variation even if each report is supported by a full and reliable *isnad*. In this next section, we will apply *isnad* criticism in addition to *matn* criticism to a set of hadith. We will focus here upon the reports that command punishment for homosexual acts. Although not easily dismissed as forgeries and falsifications, the reports that command legal punishment for homosexual acts are still subject to scrutiny. They are the immediate basis of Islamic law yet they contain many ambiguities that Muslims have a duty to assess with all the tools of traditional Islamic scholarship and modern secular scholarship. We will examine in detail those reports which picture the Prophet Muhammad ordering the death of "those who perpetrate the act of Lot's Tribe."

There are several different reports that give such a command, in different wording and with different conditions. However, they are all reports with solitary chains of narration (*hadith ahad*). None of them qualifies as a *mutawatir* report with multiple chains of transmission in each and every generation of transmission. In the face of this fact, how should they be assessed and how applied? Traditional criticism focusing on *isnad* has given them conditional approval. Hadith scholars have included them in collections that are now seen as canonical, and left it to jurists to decide how to use them. Jurists have used these solitary reports rather uncritically, since they conveniently confirm what was already juridical practice.

The analysis offered above based on *matn* criticism suggests several conclusions. First, those reports with the richest contextual detail about the personalities involved in an incident and its historical situation are most likely to preserve the oldest versions of hadith; they were recounted before there was a clear distinction between hadith (which relate the words or deeds of the Prophet) and *khabar* (which relate the acts and opinions of his followers). Second, anthropological studies of oral literature demonstrate how with time and transmission contextual details are easily lost as they become irrelevant or unintelligible to later generations of hearers. Pressure to remember hadith for the purpose of making legal decisions reinforced this natural process of streamlining reports. Simplification of reports helped to make them general pronouncements of the Prophet rather than his context-specific reactions to real events.

When we apply these insights to the reports in which Muslims are commanded to punish men for homosexual intercourse, we find that there is no hadith about the Prophet actually punishing a known person in an actual historical event. Rather, the only context-rich report of punishment is a *khabar*, a report about the companions of the Prophet. This *khabar* recounts an event that happened shortly after the Prophet's death, when Abu Bakr had become the first vice-regent. During military operations, a commander named Khalid ibn al-Walid wrote back to Abu Bakr in Medina, announcing "that he had found a man in some outlying region who does the deed of the Tribe of Lot." Abu Bakr gathered the leading companions of the Prophet. They debated the issue, because it appears that none of them knew of a precedent for such a phenomenon. The Prophet had left no example to follow, and none of them quoted any hadith transmitting the Prophet's teaching or advice. In the end, 'Ali asserted that in the Qur'an God destroys the Tribe of Lot by raining down on them burning stones, and so suggested that Muslims should punish the man by burning him. The council consented to 'Ali's suggestion, and Abu Bakr ordered the man burned. Some versions of this report even preserve the name of the man punished, as al-Fuja'a, but the report gives no more information about his identity, the fate of his sex partner, or the context in which this event happened.[55]

This is the most historically detailed event for which we have a report. According to our sociological method, we assume that this report is an early one, since it preserves the names and historical contexts of the actors. It is a report about the companions' actions after the Prophet's death and its *isnad* is incomplete: it is assumed to go back to them (*marfu'*) without mentioning the name of each transmitter. These apparent faults of the report are actually characteristic of early reports, when there was no framework to distinguish the Prophet's hadith from the companions' *khabar* and no pressure to supply a complete *isnad*. The report does not present the companions in an ideal way, so we can assume that it reflects the reality of the earliest community. In this report, the companions are confused, call for a council, argue among themselves and arrive at a decision by debate.

The factuality of this event is further confirmed by the existence of other *khabar* that confirm its context. These reports show that companions and followers continued to debate the decision to burn a man alive, which was very contentious. These continuing debates also show that burning was a punishment applied, very confusingly, to both same-sex intercourse and apostasy (*irtidad*) – rebellion against authority by renouncing one's allegiance to Islam.[56] This first event sparked debates among other companions, followers, and later generations of Muslims about the proper punishment, its logic with regard to scriptural interpretation, and its legal analogy with fornication (*zina'*). In later generations, the historical context of this event was lost. It lost the context of an actual event and entered the abstract discussion of legal discourse.

Later generations with a mind for legal logic argued that the punishment for sexual intercourse between two men is analogous to adulterous sexual intercourse between a man and woman. Thus they disparaged the early consensus on burning and argued for punishment by stoning, analogous to the punishment for heterosexual intercourse without a contract (of marriage or ownership). The punishment for heterosexual fornication was death by stoning if the accused was married and lashing if the accused was not married. The earliest sources of hadith are actually legal manuals, like *al-Muwatta'* of the jurist Malik ibn Anas (died 795), composed about a century and a half after the Prophet died. They record the fact that followers (the second generation after the Prophet) in Medina argued for punishment by execution but not by burning, and later specified execution by stoning in order to conform to the analogy with fornication.

One generation after Malik, scholars who were not jurists began to write down collections of reports that freely mixed those stemming from the Prophet with those of his companions and the companions' followers. Legal decisions and local consensus were already being made before hadith were being systematically tested and recorded. In this generation were written the *musannaf* texts of Abu Bakr 'Abd al-Razzaq ibn Hammam ibn Nafi' from Yemen (died 827) and Abu Bakr 'Abdullah ibn Muhammad ibn Abi Shayba from Kufa (died 849). According to the research of the German scholar Arno Schmitt, "In them both we find twenty-sex reports ... only one report has the proper character of being attributed to the Prophet himself: 'You should kill the doer and the one done-to, meaning those who do the act of the tribe of Lot.' And the report continues, 'And whoever commits it with an domestic animal, kill him and kill the animal.'"[57] What we begin to see, as hadith are more systematically collected, is the process of juridical abstraction. This report combines two different phenomena: a man having sexual intercourse with another man and a man having intercourse with an animal. The purported statement of the Prophet establishes a juridical rationale – that both phenomena are analogically related by the act of male penetration in an orifice that should not be available for sexual enjoyment, either because of lack of legal contract between the partners or because of anatomical unsuitability.

In the next generation, Ahmad ibn Hanbal (died 855–56) led the drive to collect reports that were attributed only to the Prophet himself.[58] Ibn Hanbal's *musnad* collection clearly differentiates these reports from sayings of the companions and followers, who had argued among themselves about appropriate punishments and among whom a consensus had built for execution in cases of same-sex male intercourse.[59] Ibn Hanbal records the same report as the earlier *musannaf* texts: "You should kill the doer and the one done-to in those who do the act of the Tribe of Lot, and kill the domestic animal and whoever commits it with the animal, and also one who does it with a close relative you should kill him." He records this on the authority of Ibn 'Abbas via his servant 'Ikrima.[60] He also records a variation, on the authority of the same companion and follower – "The Prophet said 'Whoever you find doing the act of the Tribe of Lot you should kill – the doer and the one done-to'" – without addressing the apparent variation in wording and meaning.[61]

Later hadith collectors, like Ibn Maja (died 887), Abu Dawud (died 889), and al-Tirmidhi (died 892/93), cite the same reports or variations of them on the authority of the same key narrators, Ibn 'Abbas and his slave, 'Ikrima. However, repeated citation of these reports does not establish their reliability. Even if each subsequent hadith collector records them in multiple variations, we find that these reports have only a single chain of narration (they are *ahad* not *mutawatir*). They rely upon a single transmission between Ibn 'Abbas and his servant 'Ikirma. For this reason, the more scrupulous hadith scholars like al-Bukhari and Muslim did not include such reports that call for the killing of "the doer and one done-to" in their *sahih* collections, for they endeavored to limit the reports in circulation to those with reliable narration in each generation back to the Prophet. To make matters more confusing, Abu Dawud also records an *ahad* hadith that relies upon the same key narrators, Ibn 'Abbas and 'Ikrima, and gives a contradictory ruling, saying that those commiting the act of the Tribe of Lot should be stoned specifically, not just killed somehow. The hadith collectors did not see it as their job to resolve these contradictions – that was the work of jurists. Rather they tried to show how these reports, in all their variation and contradiction, each came reliably from the Prophet's mouth.

But did these words come from the Prophet? Most Muslims assume that if scholars recorded the report in their texts during the second and third centuries after the Prophet's death it must accurately reflect the Prophet's own words. However, when we examine with scrutiny the *isnad* behind each of these reports, we find it to go back to the same crucial link. This structure becomes apparent when the reports are taken out of the books (in which they are simply listed as Prophetic reports) and placed in an analytic diagram in which their attribution and derivation becomes evident to critical examination.

Traditional *isnad* criticism focused on two criteria: checking the continuity of the narration's chain (*sanad*) and assessing each narrator's memory and morals (*jarh wa ta'dil*). Although these techniques remain important, they are augmented by modern techniques of analysis that view whole clusters of reports in relation to each other. Such source-critical methods offer new ways

Companions:

1 Ibn 'Abbas, 'Abdallah (died 68, 71, 72, or 74AH at around the age of 73 in Ta'ifa, to him are attributed 1660 reports)
2 Abu Hurayra (died 57, 58, 59 or 78AH near Medina, to him are attributed 5374 reports)

Second generation followers:

3 'Ikrima
4 Sa'id ibn Jubayr
5 Mujahid
6 Abu Salih, father of Suhayl

Later narrators:

7 Suhayl ibn Abi Salih
8 'Asim ibn 'Umar
9 'Abdallah ibn Nafi'
10 Yunus ibn 'Abd al-A'la
11 Ibn Khuthaym
12 Ibn Jurayj
13 'Abd al-Razzaq
14 Ishaq ibn Ibrahim ibn Rahawayh
15 Ayyub
16 Isma'il
17 'Abdallah's father
18 'Abdallah
19 Dawud ibn al-Hasin
20 Ibn Abi Habiba
21 Abu'l-Qasim ibn Abi al-Zannad
22 'Amr ibn Abi 'Amr
23 'Abd al-'Aziz ibn Muhammad (known as Ibn Muhammad al-Darawardi)
24 Abu Salama al-Khuza'i
25 Abu Bakr ibn Khalid
26 Muhammad ibn Sabbah
27 Muhammad ibn 'Amir al-Sawwaq
28 'Abdallah ibn Muhammad ibn Abi Nufayli

Hadith recorders:

IH Ibn Hazm;
IM Ibn Maja;
AD Abu Dawud
T al-Tirmidhi
H Ibn Hanbal

report 1a — The Prophet said, "Whoever you find doing the act of the people of Lot, kill the one doing and the one done-to"

report 1b — The Prophet said, "Kill the one on top and the one on bottom"

report 2 — "Ali ordered a man to be burned alive for sodomy"

report 3a — The Prophet said about those people who do the deed of the people of Lot, "Stone the one on top and the one on bottom, stone them both together"

report 3b — If you find an unmarried man doing sodomy (lutiya), it is said, "He is stoned"

Figure 2 *Isnad* of reports that command killing or stoning.

to assess reports. One such technique, called "common-link criticism," tries to locate when and where the report became publicly known before it was granted a formal *isnad.* This technique takes very seriously the possibility that the words conveyed by hadith originated with the companions, followers, or later generations of Muslim jurists and were later "remembered" as the words of the Prophet himself. The *isnad* attached to the report could represent a post-facto justification for the words that were already in circulation and valued as authoritative religious guidance. By examining the *isnads* of a cluster of indentical or related hadiths, common-link criticism tries to find the one or several persons that each report's *isnad* has in common, and draws the conclusion that this single popularizer of the report was the one who "remembered" it as the Prrophet's own saying.[62]

In Figure 2, I chart the *isnads* of reports that the Prophet ordered, "Kill the one doing and the one done-to" and the related wording "Kill the one on top and the one on bottom." We discover a striking fact: regardless of whether the report is found in Ibn Hanbal's collection, or that of Ibn Maja, al-Tirmidhi, or Ibn Hazm, the *isnad* of each report with this wording converges upon one figure: 'Ikrima. Each report rests upon the claim of 'Ikrima (died 723) that he heard the report from his master, Ibn 'Abbas, the cousin of the Prophet and an important early jurist in Mecca.[63] However, there are no alternative *isnad* routes to confirm 'Ikirma's claim. The reports' authenticity stands or collapses on the reliability of 'Ikrima, their "common link."

Facing a configuration of this type, where all reports with a particular wording converge on one single narrator – the common link – there are three possible conclusions. First, one can conclude that the report is authentic and that only one companion heard it from the Prophet, who told it to only one other in this way until the "common link" source found the means or motivation to broadcast it widely, after which many branching chains of transmission reached later generations who recorded the report. This is the dogmatic Muslim position. Second, one can conclude that the report is inauthentic, since the convergence of each and every *isnad* to a single common link reveals that later Muslims projected its *isnad* to him because of his reputation for being a respected hadith narrator. This is the position of source-critical scholars among Western scholars of Islam and some reformist Muslims, who do not trust *isnads* to represent actual oral transmission of information from the Prophet. Third, one can conclude that the report is possibly authentic but doubtfully so, since it was not widely known before it was spread by a later individual – the common link pointed out by each *isnad* of the report's versions; the report is highly vulnerable to being mis-remembered, distorted, or fabricated by the common link because there are no parallel chains of transmission to confirm the report in its earliest links. The report's authenticity totally depends on this one personality, whose potential weakness, bias, or ulterior motive must be thoroughly scrutinized. This is the position of Muslims who believe that traditional tools of hadith scholarship can continue to be used, along with modern techniques of analysis, to sift reliable from unreliable reports.

This particular cluster of reports calling for the killing of "the doer and the one done-to" in homosexual couplings offers an illuminating test case for the third conclusion. Because the *isnad* of each such report leads back to a common link, it invites a renewed application of traditional hadith scholarship techniques to assess whether the common link could be susceptible to error, in which case the report should be laid aside as unreliable. Let us explore this possibility by returning to the biographical, historical, and political information that Islamic sources provide us about the common link, namely 'Ikrima. He is an important personality among the generations of followers who came after the Prophet's immediate companions. He was a Berber war captive who became a slave owned by the Prophet's cousin, Ibn 'Abbas. In captivity, 'Ikrima became a Muslim and, once manumitted as an adult, acted as an important and controversial figure in the early Islamic empire.

Standard hadith collections include many reports narrated by 'Ikrima, as he was respected as the closest disciple of Ibn 'Abbas, who was renowned for his knowledge of the Qur'an and his intimate familiarity with the Prophet's conduct. However, even though hadith collectors included many reports attributed to 'Ikirma, they expressed reservations about his reports. Some note that Ikrima's reports were mainly from the companions rather than the Prophet himself. Some hadith collections mention that his reports are *marfu'*, assumed to come from the Prophet but without an explicit *isnad* leading back to him beyond the generation of companions.[64] Nevertheless, they included his reports in their *musnad* and *sunan* collections, though al-Bukhari and Muslim were more scrupulous and rejected any report whose attribution to the Prophet was only assumed or suggested rather than explicitly documented.

The reports on our chart, however, are not *marfu'*. They each have explicit chains of narration that claim to lead back to the Prophet, though each chain is single and unconfirmed by alternative routes. The essential link between the hadith scholars who heard and recorded them for posterity and the purported origin with the Prophet is 'Ikrima and his claim to have heard each of them from his master, Ibn 'Abbas. Here, traditional *isnad* criticism provides us with an arsenal of criteria by which to judge 'Ikrima's character and suitability as a narrator. Traditional hadith criticism questions a narrator's qualities of maturity, memory, truthfulness, probity, piety, and moral discernment. It also questions whether a narrator had ulterior motives for narrating hadith which might distort his "remembering," such as political ambitions, heretical loyalties, or extremist zealotry. When we apply these critical criteria to 'Ikrima, we discover a complex personality steeped in ambiguity, which gives us sufficient reason to doubt his accuracy as a narrator of hadith, especially those having to do with sexual morality.

The key quality of a reliable hadith transmitter is an acute memory and scrupulous restraint to stick to the facts, literally as one heard them. Yet 'Ikrima was accused by others in his community of exaggeration. The early biographer Ibn Sa'd mixed admiration for his knowledge with critical comments about the reliability of reports he narrated.[65] The most damaging comment about him is that of a contemporary, Tawus (who knew him well, since he was a student of Ibn 'Abbas), who commented about 'Ikrima, "If only this slave of Ibn 'Abbas would fear God and restrain these hadith of his as one ties up camels [to keep them from wandering afar]."[66] This satirical comment suggests that 'Ikrima, after being freed and achieving status, let his reports exceed the bounds of truthful representation of what he might have learned from Ibn 'Abbas.

Despite 'Ikrima's close association with Ibn 'Abbas, who was highly respected for his intimate knowledge of the Prophet, many hadith specialists suspect 'Ikrima of not being a reliable narrator. The early biographer al-Jazari (died 833) recorded mixed opinions of him: "Several people rejected him, like 'Ulba' ibn Ahmad and Abu 'Amr ibn al-'Ala', while others narrated his reports, like Ayyub and Khalid al-Hadha'. Al-Bukhari relied upon his reports and Muslim quoted him [in reports that were] attached to others. Others called him a liar, like Mujahid and Ibn Sirin."[67] Both Mujahid and Ibn Sirin were respected hadith transmitters in the generation of early followers, and Ibn Sirin in particular became a religious leader in Basra, so he must have known 'Ikrima well through his owner, Ibn 'Abbas. Though 'Ikrima was respected in reports he told about interpreting the Qur'an, he was accused of lying in reporting about questions of ritual and legal norms, according to Fitr ibn Khalifa. Fitr said, "I once said to 'Ata' that 'Ikrima declares that Ibn 'Abbas said, 'The ruling about wiping the slippers [in ritual ablutions] pre-dated the revelation of Qur'an.' 'Ata' replied, "Ikrima lied! For I heard Ibn 'Abbas say, "It is no problem to wipe the slippers even if one has walked through excrement."'"[68] Tawus judged him by saying, "Poor guy ... if he had just kept to what he heard, he would have heard real knowledge." Muhammad ibn Sirin said, "I would be happy if he were one of the saved, but he is a liar [*kadhdhab*]!" The evaluator of hadith narrators Ibn 'Adi (died 975–76) adds evidence that his contemporaries felt 'Ikrima overstepped the bounds of his knowledge by giving reports of the Prophet to decide legal matters of which they suspected he had no real knowledge: "The people of Medina called upon him to give them knowledge when they differed in opinion over certain cases – 'Ikrima gave them reports and they were shocked by what he said."[69] A later jurist of Medina, Sa'id ibn al-Musayyab, used to tell his own servant, "Beware that you never lie about what I say as 'Ikrima has lied about the sayings of Ibn 'Abbas!"[70] Perhaps the most damning opinion of his contemporaries is this anecdote provided by Ibn 'Adi: "Al-Salt ibn Dinar reported, 'I said to Muhammad ibn Sirin, "Ikrima is annoying us and saying things to us that we repudiate." Ibn Sirin replied, "Then ask God to bring him death and rid us of him!"'"[71] Even upon his death, some of his contemporaries snubbed 'Ikrima.[72]

His status as a slave gives us insight into 'Ikrima's ideological beliefs, for he supported the heretical Khariji revolt, which was the most damaging aspect of his personality in the sight of hadith scholars. He was a Berber, of the non-Arab tribes that originally inhabited North Africa. Ibn 'Abbas participated in the conquest of Ifriqiya (the region of Libya and Tunisia) in 647 and acquired 'Ikrima as a slave boy in war booty. Though raised as a Muslim, 'Ikirma was reportedly a partisan of Khariji beliefs. He would have been attracted to this subversive movement that preached the radical equality of all Muslims, non-Arabs as well as Arabs, in an era when pedigree determined one's social prestige and political authority. Berber and African slaves who embraced Islam and were manumitted found themselves free but not equal, and joined people from disaffected Bedouin tribes and radically pious theologians in this movement which ignited sectarian violence.

'Ikrima's own father was most likely killed in the conquest of Berber territories, and he seems to have focused his devotion on his owner, Ibn 'Abbas. As the slave of Ibn 'Abbas, 'Ikrima witnessed first-hand the ideological and theologial struggles that tore apart the early Muslim community and led to the Khariji revolts. Ibn 'Abbas entered political life when 'Ali rose to power as the fourth vice-regent and appointed him as governer of the Iraqi city of Basra. When 'Ali's authority was challenged by Mu'awiya and his Umayyad clan and the two armies met at the battle of Siffin, Ibn 'Abbas was among those dignitaries who signed the treaty, supporting arbitration to resolve the dispute. Ali's acceptance of arbitration caused a faction of his supporters to defect, to "go out" from his camp and political consensus – these were the band that initiated revolt of the Kharijis (meaning "those who go out"). Their political betrayal was justified on ideological and theological terms: 'Ali had negotiated with an opponent they saw as oppressive and morally corrupt, thereby forfeiting his own right to rule as the pure and righteous leader of the Muslim community. To replace 'Ali, they selected from their ranks a new leader, the most righteous among them regardless of race, genealogy, appearance, or status.

'Ali perceived rightly that "those who go out" from his own camp were more dangerous than his overt enemy. They challenged his rule through pious ideology, whereas the Umayyads challenged it only through tribal pride and force of arms. 'Ali directed his army to attack the Khariji camps, and his forces massacred many of them at Nahrawan. At this point, Ibn 'Abbas seems to have doubted his initial support of 'Ali. He resigned from the governorship of Basra and stigmatized 'Ali's killing of his Khariji opponents.[73] The Khariji partisans, in turn, declared 'Ali and his supporters not to be true Muslims and eventually assassinated 'Ali.

Though clearly not a Khariji himself, Ibn 'Abbas harbored some sympathy for their cause and lost confidence in 'Ali because of to his treatment of them. His intimate involvement in the civil war would have exposed his slave 'Ikrima to Khariji ideology, which had a special appeal for him as a non-Arab slave who was also a devoted Muslim. Despite 'Ikrima's intelligence and faith, his owner did not release him from slavery. Thus the Khariji ideology spoke to him, as to the many other slaves and outsiders were called to its radical sense of Islamic justice. Once released from slavery, 'Ikrima is rumored to have acted as a missionary to spread Khariji ideology in Ifriqiya among Berbers who had adopted Islam. Khariji groups became very strong in Ifriqiya, the region of North Africa from which he had originated and whose native language he knew.

Many hadith scholars noted 'Ikirma's Khariji leanings, and this heretical allegiance was enough to make them doubt the veracity of the reports he transmitted in the name of the Prophet. Al-Jazari says of 'Ikrima, "People spoke of him [disparagingly] because of his opinions not because of his narration, because he is accused of holding the doctrines and opinions of the Kharijis."[74] Ahmad [ibn Hanbal] says, "Neither Malik [ibn Anas] nor [Muhammad] ibn Sirin name him as a reliable source in hadith, with the exception that Malik allowed one single hadith from him. I asked him [Malik], 'What is his status?' He answered, 'He believed in the opinions of the Khariji sects, according to doctrines of the Sufriyya. He didn't leave any region without people leaving the consensus [to become Kharijis] in Khurasan, Syria, Yemen, Egypt and North Africa. It is said that the people of North Africa adopted the doctrine of the Sufriyya from 'Ikrima when he presented it to them.'"[75] This anecdote is particularly damning, since Malik ibn Anas, the early jurist of Medina, was an admired source of reports about the Prophet and his companions. To clarify this anecdote, the biographer Ibn 'Adi says on the authority of one of Malik's colleagues, "'Abbas said, 'I once asked Ibn Ma'in, "Did Malik despise 'Ikirma?" He said, "Yes." So I asked, "But didn't he [Malik] narrate a hadith from a man who had learned it from him ['Ikrima]?" He admitted, "Yes ... but just a little something."'"[76] Contemporaries noted 'Ikrima's tendency to exaggerate the extent of his knowledge, perhaps creating reports in the name of his master, Ibn 'Abbas, to confirm his own judgment about legal matters. This was combined with his known ideological bias toward the heretical movement of the Kharijis. Yet it appears that, despite these grave reservations about his reliability and fairness, his reports were still grudgingly accepted by skeptics – at least those having to do with the Qur'an and not having to do with legal judgments.

From the more specific vantage point of examining this cluster of reports about same-sex intercourse, 'Ikrima was passing on reports that had everything to do with legal judgments. On this specific topic, 'Ikrima's ideological commitments to the Khariji movement colored his opinion and affected how he "remembered" hadith. The Khariji groups had very dogmatic and extremist opinions on matters of personal morality, which they enforced with violence. They were the first Muslims to charge that fellow believers who commit sin (as they defined it) were no longer Muslims and were liable to be killed. They combined militant sectarianism with a rigid puritanical and ascetic condemnation of sexual improprieties, traces of which we can observe in these reports transmitted in 'Ikrima's name. Shedding a fellow Muslim's blood for minor sins or improprieties was a part of Khariji dogma.[77]

'Ikrima was influenced by the ideology of a moderate group of Kharijis who devoted their energy to debating morality and sexual impropriety more than to fighting.[78] Their ascetic rigor was even more pronounced as they tried to prove their pietistic superiority to the more overtly militant extremists. They built settled communities and preached separation from other "lapsed" or "nominal" Muslims through rigid moralism and asceticism.[79] Their doctrine spread from Basra to North Africa – perhaps with the aid of 'Ikrima himself – where Berber converts to Islam embraced this Khariji ideology. One Khariji leader, Abu'l-Qasim Samghi ibn Wasul, had reportedly studied under 'Ikrima, then went on to participate in the armed uprising in Tangier.[80]

As they built communities, the Sufriyya groups had to confront moral ambiguities that the militant rebels avoided. They confronted the vexing question of whether one who sinned is an infidel to be killed. In guerilla camps, they could banish or kill a member who sinned. However, settled life forced them into unwilling compromise and legalistic debate. Sexual improprieties were a matter of heated debate among them, and they faced cases of heterosexual fornication in their communities. They argued that an adulterer was not simply a sinner who had abandoned the faith and therefore should be killed as an apostate. Rather, she or he should be classified as an adulterer or *zani* and was not quite as condemned as an infidel or *mushrik*.[81] The adulterer as *zani* held an intermediate position between righteous believer and infidel who was liable to be killed. An adulterer in this intermediate position was somewhat protected by legal rulings on heterosexual fornication, for the Qur'an stipulates lashings as punishment if multiple eye-witnesses can attest to the sexual activity.

Fornication and other ethical ambiguities forced these moderate Kharijis to make more nuanced their understanding of righteousness. The adulterer was a *zani* and not automatically an infidel. As a borderline believer, the adulterer had access to legal protection (witnesses or their lack), expiation through corporal punishment (lashing), and possibly reintergration into the community of believers through repentance. But in facing same-sex activity these Kharijis would not acknowledge any moral ambivalence, as if to compensate for their compromise in cases of heterosexual fornication. Their tentative step toward moderation with regard to heterosexual fornication pushed them to harden their stance on other sexual acts that they saw as sinful. The reports that ʿIkrima publicized reflect this hardened stance. They called for the execution of one found guilty of same-sex intercourse (with the assumption that both "doer" and "done-to" are male), avoiding mention of stoning as the means of execution or other explicit analogy to heterosexual fornication.

In these reports transmitted by ʿIkrima, there is no acknowledgement that a Muslim involved in same-sex intercourse is actually a Muslim – the meaning of the report is that he should be killed as an infidel or apostate rather than treated like an adulterous Muslim. The content of these reports reflects the moralistic boundary definition that is charcteristic of Khariji ideology. The content of these reports demonastrates an eagerness to kill fellow Muslims as unbelievers if they fail to live up to stringent moral standards. These reports show no impact of juridical debates in nascent Sunni and Shiʿa circles about whether same-sex intercourse should be treated analogously to heterosexual fornication, confirming that the reports ʿIkrima remembered and spread reinforced his ideological allegiance to Khariji sectarian thinking. The content of these reports supports the notion that ʿIkrima was a covert Khariji, a fact hinted at in what little biographical knowledge we have about him.

This analysis should give thoughtful Muslims reason to pause before accepting as authentic reports that are traced back to ʿIkrima, the slave of Ibn ʿAbbas. This is especially so when the content of the report involves the killing of fellow Muslims or deals with issues involving ascetic moralism, as these issues were directly influenced by his involvement with Khariji sectarian ideology, which both Sunni and Shiʿi analysts define as the first and gravest Islamic heresy. When we apply traditional tools of hadith science bolstered by modern source-critical techniques in a spirit of non-dogmatic scrutiny, we find multiple and mutually reinforcing reasons to suspect ʿIkrima of not living up the highest standard of impartially reliable transmition of information about the Prophet in regard to this topic of sexual ethics. Whether one generalizes this conclusion, such that ʻIkrima is an unreliable transmitter of reports on any topic, is a matter beyond the scope of this study. That would depend upon one's individual conscience and insight, and one's willingness to discard many reports that are transmitted on his authority.

A Tradition of Debate

We have noted above that there was an actual historical event, after the Prophet had died, of a man being punished with burning for same-sex intercourse. But the specific historical circumstances of this event were gradually blurred and lost. What circulated more widely were general statements that Muslims should kill or stone a man found guilty of such an act. The original event of burning a man was controversial, for there was no precendent for this in the Prophet's example and it seemed to arrogate to a human judge the right to imitate God's action. It sparked a debate, and we can find traces of this in hadith. As the Muslim community matured and dealt with real conflicts, it developed a system of legal argumentation. In theory, hadith are the raw material upon which legal decisions are based (along with the Qur'an, analogous reasoning, and jurists' consensus), yet there is reason to suspect that hadith were often the product of jurists' debates over tentative legal decisions.

Many sayings circulated as legal arguments of later generations before being "remembered" as reports about the Prophet's own rulings. We can observe this dynamic at work if we analyze another cluster of reports that command Muslims to punish with death any man found having same-sex intercourse. This cluster of reports expresses the death sentence in different wording, commanding that both partners should be stoned (*rajm*). It may not seem to make much difference to the severity of the sentence, whether the method be stoning, burning, or killing by other means, most likely with a sword. But from the perspective of establishing whether reports are authentic and reliable the difference in wording is crucial.

When we gather the various recordings of reports that order execution by stoning, we find that they are quite distinct from those which portray the Prophet commanding Muslims to "kill" (*qatl*) or which illustrate how his companions gave the order to "burn" the victim. Variations of the report that commands Muslims to execute by stoning are, like those analyzed above, all *hadith ahad* – reports with single chains of transmission back to the Prophet unconfirmed by multiple parallel chains of transmission. However, unlike those analyzed above, their chains of transmission all lead back to a common link. When we arrange the *isnad*s of these resports in a chart, we find that all the single chains are attributed to Abu Hurayra, a companion of the Prophet who became famous (even infamous) as a transmitter of hadith. More reports are attributed to Abu Hurayra than to any other narrator. Let us delay assessing his controversial personality as a reliable transmitter of reports and focus first upon the content of this cluster of reports.

Many companions of the Prophet assumed that any man found having sexual intercourse with another man should be killed, but they differed over the means of execution. ʿAli's initial decision to burn a man had a few later imitators, but sparked contentious debate. His relative, Ibn ʿAbbas, openly criticized him for burning and ruled that killing by other means was more appropriate and less theologically audacious. These *khabar*, or reports about what companions of the Prophet said and did, give no indication that any direct order from the Prophet existed to enjoin either burning or killing by other means. They were rather decisions taken independently by elders in the community after the Prophet's death and without apparent guidance from the Prophet himself. In the next generation, as Khariji revolts raged, civil war broke out between Muslims over who had the right to rule the expanding empire; partisans of ʿAli fought against supporters of the Umayyad clan, leading to an enduring sectarian conflict between Sunnis and Shiʿa. As Muslim killed fellow Muslim, there was increasing sensitivity to reports that portrayed the Prophet as ordering the killing of other Muslims, for hadith began to circulate for propagandistic purposes.

Just as Khariji partisans of a more moderate orientation began to nuance their position on heterosexual fornication, jurists in Sunni circles were eager to rein in open violence and create legal norms defining crime and regulating execution. Jurists and theologians began to argue that faith is not an either/or option: Muslims should not kill others who disagree with them, over religious or political questions, with impunity. Rather, they argued, faith could grow or wane in the heart, but a Muslim who sins or errs should not be dogmatically banished or summarily killed. They advocated the idea that laws, based on the will of God as expressed in revelation and the Prophet's example, should govern human affairs and restrain sectarian violence. Their arguments gave rise to the notion that there were only a limited number of specifically grave crimes. These were called *hadd* because they transgressed the "boundary" laid down by God's explicit revelation, which called for grave corporal or capital punishment of a Muslim. Otherwise, a Muslim's blood was sacrosanct by her or his verbal profession of faith or basic demonstration of participation in rituals.

The *hadd* crimes were defined by jurists' debate as theft, armed robbery, apostasy, fornication, and false accusation of fornication. The jurists limited the *hadd* crimes to these five, which were specifically stated in the Qur'an along with specific punishment. Killing was the punishment for apostasy and armed robbery, and lashing or stoning was stipulated for fornication. We noted above how controversy broke out early over the punishment for heterosexual fornication. As jurists argued to standardize their punishment for heterosexual fornication and the conditions which limit that punishment, they began to argue that same-sex intercourse was analogous to fornication. With this background, we can understand the cluster of reports that portray the Prophet commanding that men found having same-sex intercourse should be stoned, a punishment analogous to that for fornication.

This position emerged gradually through debate, and we find evidence of it in the *al-Muwatta* of Malik ibn Anas. This is one of the earliest collections of hadith, though its purpose is to give legal rulings according to the customary practice of the people of Medina. It sometimes gives Malik's own opinion, sometimes provides reports of earlier jurists' decisions, often related *khabar* telling of companions' acts, and occasionally provides a hadith attributed directly to the Prophet. The book originates from a time when these various sources of authority were not clearly differentiated, and reflects the organic reality of jurists' debate rather than the tidy reports provided by later hadith specialists. The compiler of *al-Muwatta*, a follower of the jurist Malik, recorded the following entry about sexual intercourse:

> Malik related to me that Yahya ibn Sa'id heard Sa'id ibn al-Musayyab say, "When 'Umar ibn al-Khattab [the second vice-regent] came from Mina, he made his camel kneel at al-Abtah, then gathered a pile of small stones and cast his cloak over them and dropped to the ground. He raised his hands to the sky and said, 'O God, I have become old and my strength has weakened! My flock is scattered! Take me to you, with nothing left undone [in my life] and without any neglect.' Then he went to Medina and addressed the people, saying, 'O People, examples [*sunan*] have been laid down for you and obligations [*fara'id*] have been placed upon you! You have been left with a clear way, unless you lead people astray to the right or left.' He struck one of his hands on the other and said, 'Take care lest you destroy the verse of stoning so that one might say, "We do not find two *hadd* punishments [revealed] in the book of God." The Messenger of God stoned [people for fornication] so we have stoned. By God whose hand holds my soul, had it not been that people might say that 'Umar ibn al-Khattab has added to the Book of God, I would have written, "The full-grown man and the full-grown woman, stone them absolutely." We have certainly recited that [as part of the Qur'an].'" Malik said, "Yahya ibn Sa'id reported that Sa'id ibn al-Musayyab said, '[That very month of] Dhu'l-Hijja had not passed before 'Umar was murdered, may God

> have mercy on him.'" Yahya said that he had heard Malik say, "As for his saying, 'The full-grown man and the full-grown woman' he meant that men or women who have been married should be stoned [if they commit adultery]." Malik related to me that he asked Ibn Shihab about a man who has committed the act of the Tribe of Lot, and Ibn Shihab said, "He is to be stoned, whether or not he is married."[82]

In a single entry in *al-Muwatta*, we encounter a cluster of reports. Indirect reports about the Prophet's conduct mix seamlessly with the decisions of his companions and later authorities of Medina, like Ibn Shihab al-Zuhri and Yahya ibn Sa'id. This one example shows how the legal disputations of later generations mixed jurists' own opinions and clarifications with the pronouncements of followers and companions and occasionally a report of the Prophet. How easy it was for these later sayings to be compounded and "remembered" as simply the Prophet's own position, especially when after Malik's death there was increasing pressure to admit only sayings of the Prophet as foundation for a legal decision.

In this particular example, we find 'Umar, at the end of his life, afraid that the Muslim community will neglect the punishment of stoning for fornication. He insists that he himself stoned adulterers (fornicators who were already married) on the Prophet's example. Further, he claimed that the order to stone fornicators was revealed as part of the Qur'an. This was highly controversial, since the Qur'an as we have it today stipulates only lashing as punishment for fornication. 'Umar insists that he recited the Qur'an's *As for the woman guilty of fornication and the man guilty of fornication, flog each of them with a hundred lashes* (Q. 24:2) with inclusion of the words, "The full-grown man and the full-grown woman, stone them absolutely," words that do not appear in the currently accepted Qur'an.[83] 'Umar complained that these words were left out of the Qur'an and that Muslims were veering toward neglecting the "two *hadd* punishments," by which he meant lashing for fornicators who are not full-grown and stoning to death for those who are full-grown. Malik interrupts the narrative to explain that by "not full-grown" 'Umar meant someone who has not yet been married and has not had the opportunity for legal sexual intercourse; punishment for such a man or woman should be lighter than the stoning execution for those who are "full-grown," whom Malik defines as those who have already married (meaning adulterors).

The collection *al-Muwatta* preserves a debate between various authorities; some like 'Umar were long dead and others like Ibn Shihab or Malik himself were currently dealing with legal issues for their community, a century and a half after the Prophet's death. Malik reveals his juridical thinking when he appends to this discussion of heterosexual fornication a separate report on a different topic. He adds that Ibn Shihab, the renowned jurist of Medina, was asked about a man who commits the act of the Tribe of Lot, clearly intending to mean same-sex anal intercourse. He notes that Ibn Shihab answered, "He is to be stoned, whether or not he is married [*'alayhi al-rajm ahsana aw lam yuhsin*]." Here Ibn Shihab represents the practice of the people of Medina, which he and Malik assume is in continuity with the *sunna* of the Prophet. Neither jurist gives a hadith to back them up and do not feel the need for one.

Their position represents an intermediate development in the changing pattern of punishment for same-sex male intercourse. Burning has been discontinued as against the ethos of the Prophet's teaching. "Killing" (*qatl*) resembles too much the punishment for rebellion or apostasy and has been appropriated by Khariji extremists. So the current practice, reflected in Malik's reports, was stoning to death. However, Malik's elder, Ibn Shihab, is careful to distinguish stoning as punishment for same-sex male intercourse from stoning as punishment for heterosexual fornication or adultery. In the heterosexual case, there is a more lenient punishment of lashing if the guilty party is young and yet unmarried. In the homosexual case, there is no such leniency and "He is to be stoned whether or not he is married."

This demonstrates how, in the early Islamic community, legal rulings were made ad hoc in accord with local community norms. In reaction to this, hadith scholars began to compile reports that were attributed to the Prophet himself. This was part of an effort to enforce standardization across the wide expanse of Islamic territory. The most authoritative of hadith collections, the *Sahih* of Muslim and al-Bukhari, do not contain any reports that depict the Prophet ordering punishment by stoning (or any other kind of execution). However, later generations of hadith collectors widened the net to gather more reports. Ibn Maja, for instance, records a report narrated on the authority of Abu Hurayra: "The Prophet said about those people who do the deed of the people of Lot, 'Stone the one on top and the one on bottom, stone them both together.'"[84] Here we find the same judgment that Malik and Ibn Shihab expressed (in slightly different wording), written approximately one hundred years later as a verbatim order from the Prophet himself. A judgment that was juridical opinion in 795 when Malik died has been "remembered" as a saying by the Prophet a century later when Ibn Maja (died 887) wrote it down as a hadith. Community debate sparked by lack of a clear directive from the Prophet was processed into a form attributed to him.

This hadith reflects jurists' debates in the eighth century, rather than the Prophet's order in the seventh. The *isnad*, therefore, is suspect of being a backward projection to give Malik's juridical decision a more formidable authority – that of the Prophet's example. The purported first hearer and transmitter of this report is Abu Hurayra. He became such a famous source of hadith that many analysts, Muslim and non-Muslim, suspect that his name was a favorite choice for attribution of inauthentic hadith. Fatima Mernissi has subjected Abu Hurayra's credibility to scathing critique, on account of several manifestly misogynist reports that are attributed to the Prophet in his name. She goes so far as to venture a psychoanalytic sketch of his personality based on comments about him in Islamic sources, arguing that his misogyny probably came from his being regarded as an effeminate man (or a man with no sexual desire for women). Other critical Muslim scholars have questioned his credibility as a narrator, citing 'A'isha's condemnation of him as a liar.[85]

We do not have to cover the previously contested territory of Abu Hurayra's reliability in the case of the report under consideration here. When we chart the *isnads*, we find that the two written versions of his report have a common link in a narrator named Yunus ibn 'Abd al-A'la, via whom both Ibn Maja and Ibn Hazm recorded this report. He is depicted as narrator number 10 in figure 2 (see page 102). From Yunus the report became widely known, whereas before him the *isnad* shows only a single person hearing it from a single person. Yunus heard the report, according to the *isnad*, from 'Abdallah ibn Nafi', a personality much maligned by traditional hadith scholars, like Ibn 'Adi. Ibn 'Adi endeavored to analyze the reliability of each person involved in relating hadith, gathering the various verdicts of previous hadith experts before giving his own judgment. About 'Abdallah ibn Nafi', this scholar reports, "Of 'Abdallah ibn Nafi', Ibn Ma'in said, 'Weak,' but at another time he said, 'No, he's not that [weak],' and another time he said, 'His hadith are written down.' 'Ali al-Madini said, '... The hadith reports transmitted by 'Abdallah [ibn Nafi'] are rejected ...'. Al-Bukhari said, 'As for 'Abdallah ibn Nafi', there is disagreement over authenticity of his hadith.' ... In another place, al-Bukhari said, 'His hadith are rejected [*munkir al-hadith*].'"[86] At the end of his varied list of critique, Ibn 'Adi concludes judiciously that "He is among those whose hadith reports have been written down, even though others have differed in their opinion of him."

The hadith scholar, Ibn 'Adi, is caught in a bind. As a narrator of reports, 'Abdallah ibn Nafi' is not reliable, for renowned scholars have rejected his reports, including the much-admired al-Bukhari. Yet, the reports that 'Abdallah ibn Nafi' transmitted have been written down and included in collections that have become canonical and are used by jurists to make decisions that affect Muslims, sometimes making the difference between life and death. Once written down in collections, hadith are hard to dismiss or suppress, even if scholars have criticized his reliability and express grave reservations about his genuineness.

If there remains any doubt about dismissing the hadith under question, we can analyze the next link in its claimed *isnad*. The questionable 'Abdallah ibn Nafi' supposedly heard this report from 'Asim ibn 'Umar; this fourth-generation descendant of the second vice-regent, 'Umar ibn al-Khattab, may have been a good man, but scholars have branded him a disaster in narration. We turn again to Ibn 'Adi, who writes, "Of 'Asim ibn 'Umar, Ibn Ma'in said, 'He is weak – he is worth nothing' [*da'if, laysa bi-shay'*]. Al-Sa'di said, 'His hadith reports are weak.' Al-Bukhari said, 'His hadith are rejected [*munkir al-hadith*].'"[87] Yet because his reports have been included by hadith collectors less scrupulous than al-Bukhari, Ibn 'Adi is forced to conclude that despite his weakness this narrator's reports are "are written down." And therefore we must continue to confront hadith like the one at hand despite evidence that its *isnad* is fabricated and the judgment which is its content originated in jurists' debates after the Prophet had died.

As evident in the analysis presented above, hadith scholars found themselves in a predicament. Reports that had weak or highly suspect *isnad*s were nonetheless needed for legal debates and were already in circulation among jurists long before hadith scholars were asked to certify them. Despite their critiques of individual narrators in the *isnad*, hadith specialists continued to transmit such reports in their written collections as if they were authentic. In the process of moving from the active and ongoing arena of juridical debate to the more inert field of hadith collections, such reports that originated as jurists' decisions were "remembered" as statements of the Prophet.

When hadith scholars confronted the weakness of the chain of narration of such reports, they searched for variations of the same report with alternative chains in order to prop them up. We have an example of this dynamic in the case of the report discussed above. Abu Dawud included in his *sunan* collection a version of this report, purportedly in the words of Ibn 'Abbas, rather than those of Abu Hurayra, to whom the attribution was so weak. According to Abu Dawud, "Ibn Khuthaym said, 'I heard Sa'id ibn Jubayr and Mujahid both saying that Ibn 'Abbas spoke about an unmarried [male] found engaged in anal intercourse [*al-lutiya*] pronouncing, "He is stoned."'"[88] There are several points that are strange about this report, even if its *isnad* is judged to be sound. First, the content of the report contains a juridical term that was not in use during the time of the Prophet or the early generations of his followers. That term is *lutiya*, literally "Lot-ity," an abstract noun derived from the Prophet Lot's name to describe sodomy. "The act of the Tribe of Lot" is used in all early reports, by companions and followers of the Prophet, to describe anal intercourse between two men. *Lutiya* is a theological–legal term the use of which is comparable to "sodomy" in Euro-American Christianity. The fact that the term *lutiya* as "sodomy" or *luti* as "sodomite" occurs in the content of a report reveals that the content does not date from the time of the Prophet or his early followers. Rather it dates from a later period during which jurists' debates generated a technical vocabulary of legal shorthand.

In this report, there are several "layers" to the content text, as later narrators added observations or judgments to the report. The term *lutiya* occurs in an "outer layer" of three layers, as we can hear: "Ibn Khuthaym said, 'I heard Sa'id ibn Jubayr and Mujahid both saying that Ibn 'Abbas spoke about an unmarried [male] found engaged in anal intercourse (*al-lutiya*) pronouncing, "He is stoned."'" It is unclear whether the description of the act in question as *lutiya* is attributed to Ibn Khuthaym or to the earlier narrators whom he heard, namely Sa'id ibn Jubayr and Mujahid. However, the use of the technical term *lutiya* is clearly separate from the core layer of the report, which conveys the purported judgment of Ibn 'Abbas that an unmarried (younger) man who engages in same-sex anal intercourse should be stoned.

A defender of this report might argue that its core (the judgment "He is stoned") may be authentic even if it is wrapped in a textual envelope that uses legal terms dating from a later period. But this argument is untenable, because the core words (that Ibn 'Abbas pronounced, "He is stoned") contradict other reports that portray Ibn 'Abbas arguing that such a person should not be burned but rather killed by other means, most likely with a sword. Of course, stoning is one form of killing, but we have seen above how stoning was specifically used as an punishment for sexual offenses, in later juridical circles, to argue against killing by other means. The circulation of reports that specify stoning was part of the jurists' debate over whether same-sex male intercourse is analogous to heterosexual adultery. This debate flared up after the era of Ibn 'Abbas; reports that advocated stoning took a position against the reports attributed to 'Ikrima which represent his owner, Ibn 'Abbas, supporting the decision to kill one who committed such an offense by means other than stoning. In hadith criticism, if the *matn* of a report contradicts what is known from other reports, then the report is to be discarded even if it may have an apparently sound *isnad*.[89]

It appears that later narrators attributed to Ibn 'Abbas a report whose content clearly contradicts the position that Ibn 'Abbas was known to take on the issue of executing Muslim men for same-sex intercourse. This contradiction is explained by the pressure hadith collectors felt to bolster reports that were already in circulation and upon which juridical decisions depended, reports with doubtful attribution to the Prophet himself. Legal debate gave rise to hadith, rather than the reverse. This reality contradicts the idealistic notion that hadith are simply the raw material for legal decisions.

Tradition of Misapplication

There is one final category of hadith which pertains directly to homosexuality. We noted above five categories of such reports, of which only two deal with legal punishment, and two others have to do with condemning transgender behavior and divine punishment on the day of judgment. The final category consists of reports that picture God cursing anyone who acts like the Tribe of Lot. In contemporary condemnations as well as pre-modern moralistic literature, the Prophet Muhammad's curse is understood to apply to homosexuals. This application is not based upon any evidence within the content of the reports. It depends, rather, on the patriarchal interpretation of the Qur'an which equates "the act of the Tribe of Lot" with homosexual behavior, as we documented in Chapter 2.

The *Musnad* of Ibn Hanbal appears to be the earliest collection to include a report that pictures the Prophet cursing those who act like the Tribe of Lot. He includes at least three versions of this report, each with variations in its wording. Each variation of this report consists of a list of people whom the Prophet Muhammad says are cursed by God. One variation reads, "'Ikrima has said that Ibn 'Abbas reported that the Prophet said, 'God cursed whoever sacrifices an animal to [a deity] other than God, and God cursed anyone who alters the boundaries of the earth, and God cursed anyone who conceals the path for the blind, and God cursed anyone who insults his parents, and God cursed anyone who lords over those who are not his slaves, and God curses anyone who does the deed of the Tribe of Lot – and God curses anyone who does the deed of the Tribe of Lot, and God curses anyone who does the deed of the Tribe of Lot!"[90] According to the report, the Prophet repeated the last phrase three times, a common expression in hadith for emphasis.

What do these items have in common that they should appear together in a list? All actions in the list are immoral transgressions that either infringe upon the rights of God (like making a sacrifice to a false god) or injure others (like misleading the blind). The focus of our analysis is on the last item of the list: the deed of the Tribe of Lot. We have observed that many hadith transmitters assume that this deed is same-sex intercourse, specifically anal penetration between men. Certainly by the time hadith were used in making legal decisions and later as the *shari'a* was formalized (about which we will speak at length in Chapter 4), "the deed" of the Tribe of Lot was defined by a technical term, *lutiya* or *liwat*, which left no ambiguity that anal sex was the meaning. Jurists fashioned the term "lesser *liwat*" to discuss a man's anal penetration of a woman.[91] If we disregard, for the moment, the sexual interpretation given to this phrase by later interpreters and view it only in the context of this report, there is

Companions:
1 Ibn 'Abbas, 'Abdallah (died 68, 71, 72, or 74AH at around the age of 73 in Ta'ifa, to him are attributed 1660 reports)

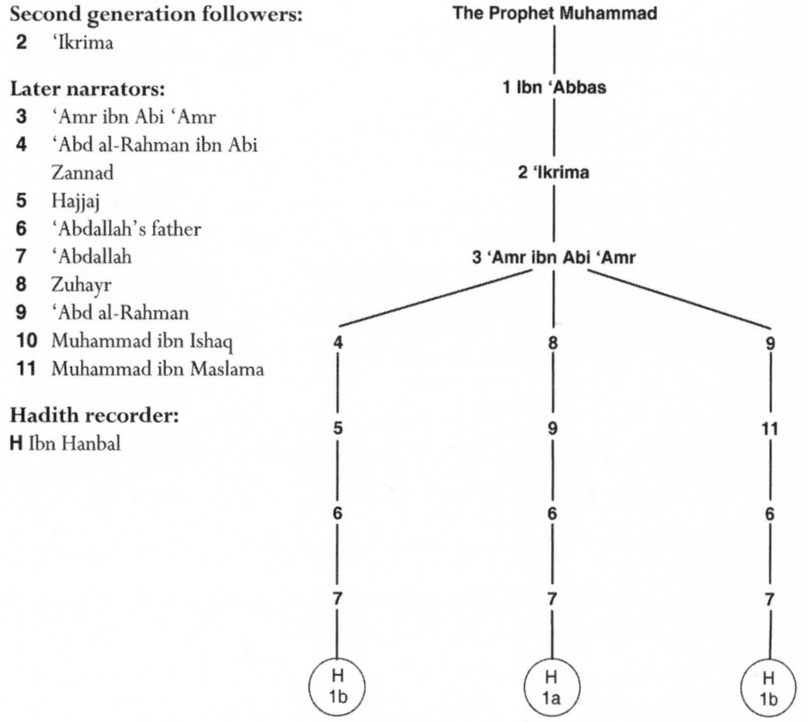

report 1a — The Prophet said, ". . . God curses anyone who does the deed of the Tribe of Lot—and God curses anyone who does the deed of the Tribe of Lot, and God curses anyone who does the deed of the Tribe of Lot!"

report 1b — The Prophet said, ". . . God curses anyone who does the deed of the Tribe of Lot," saying it three times

Figure 3 *Isnad* of reports that God curses those who do the deed of the Tribe of Lot.

nothing intrinsic in the report to encourage us to see the deed of Lot's Tribe as involving sex. As we fully investigate its context, this appears to be a misapplication of the report to support a legal ruling.

We observed in Chapter 2 that sex acts were only one facet of the tribe's rebellion against Lot and his Prophetic message. How one understands the meaning of "the deed" depends upon how one interprets the Qur'an's narration of the story of Lot and the conflict with his tribe. Lot criticized their worship of other gods, their murderous domination of trade routes, and their rejection of his own Prophetic mission, in addition to the attempt on the part of some powerful men of the tribe to rape his male guests. Infidelity and rebellion were the cause of their attempted rape, a sex act designed to humiliate Lot, deny his authority, and drive him from town. The wider context of the hadith's list supports this alternative interpretation of the Qur'anic narrative. It begins with "God cursed whoever sacrifices an animal to [a deity] other than God" in reference to worship of false gods (*shiṛk*) and disbelief in the one true God (*kufr*). The other elements refer to further dimensions of immoral behavior which stemmed from the infidelity of those like the Tribe of Lot: altering "the boundaries of the earth" refers to political rebellion or violent appropriation of others' property, lording it "over those who are not his slaves" refers to coercive domination of the vulnerable, insulting "his parents" refers to contempt for authority, and concealing "the path for the blind" refers to lack of compassion and heartless victimization of those in need of care. Coming at the end of this list, the reference to "the deed of the Tribe of Lot" places their sexual acts (attempted same-sex rape) in the broader context of infidelity, polytheism, rebellion, violent crime, and contempt for humane behavior.

One principle of hadith criticism is that authentic reports from the Prophet convey words and meanings that are complementary to the Qur'an. If a report contradicts the Qur'an, Muslims should discard it as inauthentic or refuse to apply it as authoritative.[92] The Qur'an does speak of God cursing different kinds of people. The most foundational and oft-repeated mention of God's curse is against those who disbelieve in God's unity or associate others with God. *Surely God has cursed the unbelievers and prepared for them a burning fire* is the basic statement of God's curse, through which past nations and tribes who rejected God's message and persecuted God's messengers were destroyed – *cursed wherever they are met, seized and killed with a horrible killing, for such is the example of God with those who have come before and you find no change in God's example* (Q. 33:61–64). In the Qur'an, God curses outright infidels and also lapsed believers, such as some members of Jewish or Christian communities who receive the message of God's unity but backslide into associating other powers with God, thereby abandoning the covenant that was extended to them: *Certainly God made a covenant with the children of Israel … but on account of their breaking the covenant we cursed them and made their hearts hard, for they altered the words from their proper place and neglected some of the message* (Q. 5:12–13).[93] The Qur'an always pairs infidelity with immoral actions that arise from hardened hearts. In this sense, God also curses hypocrites (*munafiqun*) who claim to worship the one God but aim to subvert God's presence with immoral deeds.

The Qur'an hints that this subversion of faith in one God can take the form of crimes that involve sex acts or sexual desire. The first verse cited above speaks about the hypocrites among the Muslims in Medina who accosted or harassed women on the street, including the Prophet's wives. They used sex as a threat and intimidation, as a way of subverting the Prophet Muhammad's authority over them, in a way quite analogous to how the Tribe of Lot used male-on-male rape or the threat of it to reject his prophetic authority over them. In another instance, hypocrites in Medina fomented rebellion against the Prophet Muhammad by accusing his young wife 'A'isha of an adulterous affair.[94] However, the Qur'an revealed his wife's innocence and cursed those who spread false accusation of sexual misdemeanors: *those who accuse believing women who are negligent but faithful [to their marriage] are cursed in this world and the next* (Q. 24:23).

In these examples, based upon real events of sexual tension in Medina, the Qur'an curses those who exploit sexual desire to accuse others or destroy their reputations. Those who exploit sex to gain power and dominate others are mentioned as those cursed by God, especially those who use sex as a threat or insult to reject the authority of their Prophet over them. With this broader perspective of how the Qur'an depicts God's curse, we can return to the hadith in question. Should we understand its mention of those who "do the deed of the Tribe of Lot" to mean homosexuals or anyone (regardless of sexual orientation) who engages in anal intercourse? Such a misapplication of the report ignores both the wider context of the list of immoral deeds the report gives and also the wider context of the Qur'anic statements about God's curse.

Hadith collectors, however, routinely apply this report to legal rulings about homosexuality. Al-Tirmidhi, the author of a major Sunni hadith collection, cites this report, mentioning only the phrase "Cursed is anyone who does the deed of the Tribe of Lot" without the other elements of the list. He cites it in the same entry as the separate hadith, "Whoever you find doing the deed of the Tribe of Lot, kill the doer and the one done-to." Al-Tirmidhi uses one hadith to comment upon the other without feeling the need to interpret their deeper context. Misapplying this report through legal logic is made easier by the fact that this report exists in diverse variations. One variation claims that "'Ikrima has said that Ibn 'Abbas reported that the Prophet said, 'God cursed anyone who alters the boundaries of the earth, and God cursed whoever sacrifices an animal to [a deity] other than God, and God cursed anyone who insults his parents, and God cursed anyone who lords over those who are not his slaves, and God cursed anyone who conceals the path for the blind, and God curses anyone who has sexual intercourse with a domestic animal, and God curses anyone who does the deed of the Tribe of Lot,' saying it three times."[95] In this variation, we find most of the same phrases, but in a different order, and the narrators have, somewhere along the chain of transmission, stopped repeating the last phrase verbatim three times, substituting this with the explanation that it was originally repeated three times. Most importantly, in this variation a new item has been inserted into the list: just before mention of God cursing those who do the deed of the Tribe of Lot it is mentioned that God cursed those who use animals for sexual intercourse. The actual term used, *bahima*, usually applies to a cow or sheep but indicates any four-legged domestic animal. In this variation, inclusion of the element of bestiality intends to deflect the interpretation of "the deed of the Tribe of Lot" from infidelity, rebellion, and rape toward a more narrow and juridically determined meaning of anal intercourse in general.

Jurists regard the issue of bestiality as closely related to same-sex intercourse, especially those who argued that "killing" (*qatl*) is the penalty for such acts. We have seen above how 'Ikrima is remembered as having championed this position, against others who argued for the more explicit stoning, using the analogy (partial or total) with heterosexual adultery. That the report exists in several variations provides evidence of change in the process of transmission. So it may not be accurately transmitted. In addition, the fact that the variation includes additions and interpolations of a juridical character emphasizes how the report may have been "remembered" for legal justification of positions that developed long after the Prophet's death.

Another report attributed to 'Ikrima makes explicit the juridical equation between same-sex intercourse and bestiality: "You should kill the doer and the one done-to, meaning those who do the act of the tribe of Lot. And whoever does it with an domestic animal, kill him and kill the animal."[96] Such reports were integral to juridical debates; the injunction to kill the person and the animal also circulates as an independent report, unconnected to the discussion of same-sex intercourse. One topic of discussion was why one was charged to kill the animal, since it surely cannot be blamed if a person sexually abuses it. For instance, Abu Dawud and al-Tirmidhi record the hadith in which 'Ikrima reports that the Prophet said, "If anyone has sexual intercourse with an animal, kill him and kill it along with him," and adds to the report a discussion by the narrators: "I ['Ikrima] asked him [Ibn 'Abbas], 'What offence can be attributed to the animal?' He replied, 'I have never heard anything about that from the Prophet, but my opinion is that the Prophet disapproved of its flesh being eaten or any benefit taken from it when such a thing had been done to it.'"[97] The fact that this report was generated by juridical discussion more than verbatim report of the Prophet's teachings is indicated by the presence, in both collections that preserve this report, of a totally contradictory report attributed to the same companion: "Ibn 'Abbas said 'There is no *hadd* punishment [of execution] upon one who has sexual intercourse with a domestic animal,' and al-Hakam has said, 'My opinion is that such a person should be lashed to an extent that does not reach the *hadd* punishment,' while al-Hasan [al-Basri] has said, 'His status is that of a fornicator [*zani*].'"[98] These variations lead to direct contradictions, as Ibn 'Abbas is reported upholding opposite opinions. This situation makes an astute reader suspect that all such reports derive from juridical debates among later generations of Muslims; the reports acquired an *isnad* retrospectively back to the Prophet in order to bolster their authority. The fact that jurists in later generations held differing opinions on bestiality (from no *hadd* punishment, to lashing in a form less than *hadd*, to full *hadd* penalty equivalent to that for adultery) would be impossible if there were authentic reports on the topic from the Prophet himself.

We can derive several lessons from this example of a report about God's curse. First, many reports exist in multiple variations of wording, and this variation is not innocent. It reveals the interpolation of new terms or phrases into reports that reflect jurists' arguments long after the Prophet died. When such variation in wording is found, analysts should pay close attention to whether the content of the report goes against the wording or meaning of the Qur'an and focus critical attention upon the *isnad* of reports that appear in variation. This report, about God's curse, exists in many forms and iterations, but the *isnad* of each recording of it is a single chain of narrators purporting to lead back to the Prophet, making it a *hadith ahad* of unconfirmable authenticity. In addition, the single chain of each report leads back to a common link in 'Ikrima, whose trustworthiness and motivations were discussed extensively above. This report about God's curse is highly suspect of distortion or fabricaton owing to evidence in both its chain of tranmission and its content. In addition, the variation in wording give evidence of how its meaning was changed in the process of transmission, giving evidence of later juridical interpolation that made it more liable to be misapplied to condemn same-sex intercourse in a dramatic narrowing of its possible meaning.

Although this report is often cited in reference to homosexuality, there is little in the report itself, in its most concise variation, to favor the interpretation that God curses people for same-sex intimacy. This point depends upon one's understanding of the Qur'an and for what it condemns the Tribe of Lot. The same is true for another set of hadith, which picture the Prophet saying, "What I fear most for my community is the deed of the Tribe of Lot." This is also a *hadith ahad*, the authenticity of which rests with only one companion, Jabir ibn 'Abdallah, who reportedly transmitted it to only one other, Ibn 'Aqil (whose full name was 'Abdallah ibn Muhammad ibn 'Aqil ibn Abi Talib); then from Ibn 'Aqil several others heard it and they later preserved it. Its condemnation of the "deed of the Tribe of Lot" was also appended to a report that apparently addresses heterosexual topics. In it, Jabir reports that "the Prophet said, 'Any person who marries without permission from his family' or it is said by some whoever has sex without permission from his family 'is a whore-fucker [*'ahir*].' And I heard the Prophet saying, 'What I fear most for my community is the deed of the Tribe of Lot.'"[99] We will not pursue a detailed critique of this hadith, because it so feebly endorsed by even those who record it – such as al-Tirmidhi, who expressed doubts about its authenticity. Its chain of transmission is not only single in two generations, but the key transmitter, one of the common links, is a weak reporter, as noted by the hadith critic Ibn 'Adi. He writes of Ibn 'Aqil that "Ibn Ma'in says, 'He is weak in hadith transmission [*da'if al-hadith*].' Once he [Ibn Ma'in] was asked about the hadith transmission of four people: Suhayl and al-'Ala' and Ibn 'Aqil and 'Asim ibn 'Ubaydallah and he replied, 'Ibn 'Aqil and 'Asim are the weakest of these four, while the reports of Suhayl and al-'Ala' are close to correct – but none of their reports constitutes decisive proof.' … Sa'di said, 'One should refrain in doubt about him [ibn 'Aqil], as most of what is reported from him is unsupported.' Ibn al-Falas said, 'I have heard Yahya and 'Abd al-Rahman together narrating reports on the authority of Ibn 'Aqil and other people taking issue with it.'"[100]

Many other reports do not concern homosexual behavior directly but are often cited in argumentation about the topic. There are reports discouraging a man from seeing other men's genitalia and a woman from seeing other women's genitalia, but such reports are categorized under "bathhouse ettiquite" and were not understood to apply to sexual intimacy in committed relationships. Other reports command that two men should not be covered under one sheet or "skin to skin," or that two women should not be under one cover. These reports dealt with the practice of using a sheet to screen oneself from the sight of others while bathing, rather than about sexual contact in the bedroom. Hadith collectors categorized variations of this report under the heading *adab* or social ettiquite – they were understood to apply to strangers, such as travelers, who had to share an intimate space without having a committed relationship.[101] They may apply to "situational homosexuality" in which people who are not homosexual, or do not understand themselves to be in a homosexual relationship, are thrown together by force of circumstance into sharing an intimate space they would ordinarily not choose to share, and warn against sexual activity happening within such circumstances.

Conclusion

By the late medieval period, Islamic scholars had largely given up the struggle to weed out false, weak, or unverifiable reports from the corpus of hadith. Most accept the textual collections of reports as satisfactory, complete, and reliable, even if they register doubts about certain details or note the skepticism of earlier hadith specialists. However, as long as the juridical tradition of Islamic legal scholarship was vibrant, there was always heated discussion about hadith. Even if one accepted reports in general, jurists had to assess what reports were applicable in various situations and what report should take precedent over others in case of contradiction.

In the modern period, even this discussion has been largely abandoned as Islamic jurisprudence itself has become stultified. The Wahhabi and Salafi movements, which became prevalent in the twentieth century, discarded juridical reasoning. They argued that a literal reading of hadith – without analysis of their origin or authenticity – could yield an authentically Islamic practice which should become the worldwide standard for all Muslims. In this environment, questioning hadith with the tools of classical Islamic scholarship became seen as heresy and Muslims increasingly shied away from the effort.

Hadith are often called "traditions." When taken individually they may each be susceptible to scrutiny and doubt, but when woven into a mutually supporting web they build into Tradition with a façade of unquestionability. The hadith manifest as a Tradition that is greater than any individual report and has great authority. In this sense, Tradition and family take analogous roles in defining the authority that rules over the lives of Muslims, and the activits interviewed for this study confront both. One can question individual actions or attitudes of one's own family, but the family as a whole still exerts an authority over one's life. The family is difficult to critique rationally, to repudiate, or to escape.

A scholar's critique of hadith and their authenticity is quite similar to someone's psychoanalytic critique of her or his parents and family. It is a critique that is quite difficult, as it brings up traumatic issues to which there is much emotional resistance, and it implies a questioning of authority that is discouraged by one's elders and tradition. Yet an individual's well-being depends on negotiating a reasonable critique of the family one inherits, just as the health of a religious community depends upon encouraging the reasonable and faith-based critique of customary attitudes and written sources that interweave to create tradition. For lesbian, transgender, and gay Muslims, the struggle with family and with religious tradition is linked, especially in the fraught field of arguing through hadith.

These two types of tradition – reports of the Prophet and the power of the family – overlap in intimidating ways. Both constitute the basis of authority in Muslim communities. To critique a particular hadith is often seen as rebelling against religious authority, disrespecting the Prophet, or rejecting one's elders.

The sociologist Andrew Yip, in his research on gay and lesbian Muslims in the U.K., has noted this close interweaving between written sources of authority and patriarchal obligations of family authority.[102] By their inherent disposition, such people challenge the parental authority that imposes heterosexual norms in the context of family, so it is not surprising that lesbian, transgender, and gay Muslims also challenge the scriptural authority of hadith that impose the same thing in the context of religious tradition.

As gay, lesbian, and transgender Muslims assess the authenticity of hadith that are used against them, they raise a wider theological question, one that is key to Islamic reform around any issue (not just sexual orientation and gender identity). Are Muslims bound by their faith to accept hadith? If they are skeptical of individual hadith or dismissive of the whole body of reports, do they repudiate the Prophet himself, whom the hadith intend to represent and whose example they purport to convey? Most Muslims would answer, "Yes, absolutely" – yet those Muslims open to reform would answer, "No, not necessarily." Do Muslims need hadith in order to practice their religion with integrity? That is a profound question that inspires endless debate, and it is too complex to decide here. However, it can be noted that the earliest generations of companions and followers lived exemplary lives as Muslims without an organized tradition of hadith. Indeed, many companions feared that hadith (even if authentically preserved and accurately interpreted) would get interjected into the Qur'an and confused with it, and therefore discouraged or even forbade Muslims to write down and spread reports about what the Prophet did or said.[103]

This seems like a real fear, for the Qur'an uses the term "hadith" sometimes to refer to the Qur'an while at other times it is used to refer to other people's talk or the Prophet's own sayings. One verse where this is quite clear is Surat al-Zumar – *God has sent down the very best speech [*ahsan al-hadith*] as a message, with matching similes, which makes those who fear their Lord shudder so that their hearts and bodies become receptive to the remembrance of God – this is the guidance of God with which God guides whomever God wills* (Q. 39:23). The Qur'an calls itself God's true discourse or speech (*hadith*), even asking whether believers will choose to follow other discourses afterwards and thereby fall into error.

When they confront the opposition of family and community who condemn them through hadith, lesbian, gay, and transgender Muslims can ask along with the Qur'an, *These are signs of God recited to you in truth, then to what other speech [*hadith*] apart from God and God's signs will they believe?* (Q. 45:6). Of course, it is a difficult issue that confronts the reason, trust, and conscience of each Muslim to decide which particular reports to believe, as the authentic may be mixed in confusingly with the fabricated or distorted.

More deeply, Muslims must also confront the question of whether they should place full faith in any other hadith, any other discourse or form of speech, beyond the Qur'an. Similarly, each person must ask to what extent she or he should abdicate the light of reason and insight of conscience in order to conform to norms of past generations which have accrued the patina of authority. Trusting hadith and conforming to family expectation derive from the same pressure to submit to the authority of other people, not necessarily to the authority of God. In its most radical pronouncements, the Qur'an demands that each person abandon reliance upon family tradition and step forward into complete reliance upon God alone. Such a path is not marked by convention and custom but rather is lit only, whether dimly or intensely, by the light of faith, trust, and hope.

Chapter 4

Assessing Fiqh: Islamic Legal Reasoning

> Listen to this famous story about a man being lashed in punishment. During the first ninety-nine lashes, he never let loose even one moan of pain, but when he was lashed with the final hundredth stroke, he moaned in deep agony. The people who had gathered around asked him about this strange behavior. The man replied, "During the first ninety-nine lashes, the beloved one for whose sake I have been lashed was present near me in the circle of onlookers; only when he turned away from me did I suddenly feel pain!"
>
> Ibn 'Ata' Allah al-Iskandari, *Kitab al-Tanwir*

In the story related above, a man is being lashed for the sake of his beloved, who is also a man. The narrator does not explain what his "crime" might have been or how the judge came to the decision that he must be lashed, for the story is told to illustrate the power of beauty to overcome pain.[1] Similar stories are often told in Sufi literature, about the inner strength of one's love enduring the outer trial of separation, judgment, and punishment.

However, the narrator of this tale, Ibn 'Ata' Allah al-Iskandari (died 1309), was not just a Sufi master; he was also the chief judge of Cairo and an accomplished jurist in the Maliki school of law. He knew that the man in the story was given one hundred lashes as an unmarried man who had had sexual intercourse with another man and that this punishment was a controversial subject of debate between competing Sunni legal schools. This unspoken background of legal debate served to highlight Ibn 'Ata' Allah's point that a real lover has courage to face public humiliation and legal punishment to be steadfast in love, knowing that seeing the face of one's lover would ease any pain the world might inflict. He had no doubt that the punishment was worldly whereas love is transcendental. Yet he also never questioned the need for Muslims to inflict corporal punishment in this world for bodily actions. Ibn Hazm agrees with Ibn 'Ata' Allah that "To love or be in love is one thing, perhaps even a noble thing (provided one does not let oneself go), but to act on it is another matter altogether."[2] This chapter will assess the legal decisions in *fiqh*, or Islamic law, as they apply to homosexuality. More specifically it will assess how Islamic law applies to male-with-male acts, which dominate the legal discourse, and to female-with-female acts, which are much less commonly discussed.

All Muslim jurists agree that God intends humanity to be governed by norms enforced by legal rules that require, in extreme cases, coercion and corporal punishment. All agree that such a system of rules should be based upon God's message in the Qur'an as understood through Muhammad's example as the Prophet of a distinct historical community, and all agree that Islamic law addresses only the deliberate and intentional acts of people who have free choice. After this, however, agreement blurs into the realm of conflicting principles and divergent rulings. It should come as no surprise that jurists discussed both male and female homosexual intercourse and arrived at very different rulings about it. We will consider in this chapter whether the fact that they drew conclusions without considering a concept of homosexuality as a part of the psychic constitution of certain people – as sexual orientation – limits the applicability of their rulings.

Contemporary Muslim activists who are gay, lesbian, or transgender are aware of these limitations, and those who are knowledgeable about legal matters face them squarely. I have conducted interviews with gay Muslim activists in the Netherlands who work with two different support groups. The Yoesuf Foundation advocates for the legal rights and social welfare of homosexuals, women, and youth in Muslim communities in the Netherlands. It is based in Utrecht and its founder is Omar Nahas, a Syrian intellectual who was trained in *shari'a* sciences before he emigrated to the Netherlands. "When the *fuqaha'* [Muslim jurists] speak about 'the deed of the Tribe of Lot' [sodomy], they are not referring to homosexual people as we understand that in the modern age ... The *fuqaha'* always speak of a person who is the victim and another who is perpetrator, one who does the act. There is always threat of violence ... There is [an imbalance of] power there."[3] Omar Nahas has written books on this topic, in both Arabic and Dutch, and his Yoesuf Foundation focuses on education and media intervention.[4] In contrast, a second support group grew in Amsterdam which is more immediately concerned with the social life and identity of vulnerable minorities. This is the Habibi Ana Foundation, a support group for lesbian, gay, and transgender people in the Middle Eastern and North African immigrant communities. One volunteer with this support group is Rasheed, a law student who grew up in the Netherlands as part of a Berber family from Morocco. When asked about the tensions between Dutch laws permitting homosexuality and what Muslims see as God's law in fiqh decisions, Rasheed answers, "I can be very clear about that ... The Qur'an says that you have to respect the government in the state that you are living in – the laws and rules of the state in the country where you are living. If there is a friction or distance in ideas between Islam and the Dutch laws, the Qur'an says to us that we have to respect the laws of the country in which we reside."[5] He gives a very nuanced answer about the legal obligations of Muslims living as minority citizens of a democratic state, an answer that is in accord with the view of moderate Muslim scholars like Tariq Ramadan.[6]

This chapter will explain the opinions of these activists in Europe, by assessing how Muslim jurists came to make their decisions, and whether their opinions create norms that should be followed in contemporary political situations. This chapter proceeds to address texts in their order of importance to Islamic jurisprudence: the Qur'an (*kitab*), the reports attributed to the Prophet Muhammad (*sunna*), legal reasoning by analogy (*qiyas*), and the consensus of jurists (*ijma'*). In many ways, this explication of four sources is idealistic – in practice they are tightly interwoven; Chapter 2 on the Qur'an has already noted that jurists were instrumental in interpreting the scripture while Chapter 3 on hadith has demonstrated how recording reports is not separate from legal reasoning. However, the delineation of four sources is a useful heuristic device, and I will use it to give some order to a complex problem. This chapter will focus on the last two sources, legal reasoning and juridical consensus, to show how they contributed to rulings on homosexuality in fiqh. By revealing the ambiguities and contradictions in these rulings and how they were made, the chapter suggests ways that Muslims can approach reforming the *shari'a* by reviving juridical thinking.

The Structure of Islamic Law

Fiqh literally means "understanding." It is the process of coming to decisions about practical acts based on divine guidance. Through the process of fiqh, Muslim jurists came to decisions upon which is based the *shari'a*. But is the *shari'a* best understood as Islamic law or as Muslim custom, as a code of rules or a constitution? In the modern period, there is great confusion and disagreement over this point because the answer involves political authority and the legitimacy of the ruler. The political implications of the question have intensified since the breakdown of autonomous Islamic government under European colonialism and such government's fragile and contested reassertion in in Muslim-majority nation states. The Islamic scholar Khaled Abou El Fadl, himself trained as a jurist, provides a succinct definition of *shari'a*: "Early Muslims debated and fought over who became the repository of legitimate authority after the Prophet. There were several candidates to receive this rather formidable authority ... By the eighth century CE, the most serious and formidable candidate had emerged as a coherent and systematic contender: the law of God, the *shari'a*, as constructed, articulated, and represented by a specialized body of professionals known as the *fuqaha'* (the jurists)."[7] This brief definition captures the tensions inherent in the term *shari'a*. It is a law "of God" but drawn up "by professionals" who claim a unique authority to understand (*fiqh*) and articulate divine will but do not have absolute authority to enforce it, depending as they do upon a government that they can influence by moral suasion but cannot control through direct power. It is not until the recent era of Islamic revolutions that Muslims have claimed that the *shari'a* should replace national constitutions, a role for which it is eminently unsuitable and which it never played in the past. This is a role that might, if forced upon it, distort the very principles of flexibility and comprehensiveness that are its classical hallmark.[8]

Muslim minorities living in secular democracies are seemingly buffered from this radical call for *shari'a* to replace secular constitutions. But in fact they are not. Even as residents or citizens of Western states, Muslims are affected by the rise of fundamentalist movements that advocate Islamic revolution. Therefore, many ask whether the Islamic law is sacred or profane. The confusing answer must be "both." It is a system of norms that guides ritual behavior in the arena of "sacred" acts of worship but also governs commercial and transactional behavior in the arena of "profane" acts of business. It represents the Muslim effort to order the world, in both sacred and profane behaviors, to bring human affairs into accord with God's will, inasmuch as God's intent can be ascertained by human knowledge. In this sense, the jurists who took it upon themselves to explicate God's will were both audaciously bold and humbly cautious. They were bold in asserting that every possible human act is governed by God's will and they were audacious in claiming that they, as a class, could use reason to interpret scripture to comprehend God's will in practical terms. Yet they were humble in acknowledging that their opinions were always provisional, and they were cautious in allowing other jurists to reasonably disagree. The feminist legal scholar Kecia Ali observes that most jurists would discuss a controversial point by stating all divergent opinions before pronouncing their own view; by closing their discussion with the provisional coda – "and God alone knows best" – they acknowledged that there could always be dissent or new perspectives that might reopen the discussion.[9]

For Muslims caught up in conflict, it is logical and necessary to ask whether the *shari'a* is an expression of God's will through revelation or is the product of human debate and social evolution. This is a question that arises in any discussion group of gay, lesbian, and transgender Muslims, as well as discussions of Muslim feminists or Muslim human rights activists. Many preachers and neo-traditionalist authorities claim that the *shari'a* is eternal and must not be questioned. In contemporary debates, the *shari'a* is presented as "a symbol of immutability" and this prevents practical discussion of how it is employed in historically grounded events.[10] Such Islamist ideologues have lost the classical jurist's training and abandoned their traditional humble caution, and end up using the *shari'a* as a rhetorical device to bolster their own authority. They transform the *shari'a* from an authoritative discourse into an authoritarian discourse, to buttress their own will to power, as documented insightfully by Abou El Fadl, who calls this behavior "usurping the Divine Will."[11] The abuse of *shari'a* for authoritarian ends must be resisted by all conscientious Muslims with a sensitivity to justice. The real question is whether *shari'a* expresses ethical values (which must be contextually applied to each circumstance with flexibility and self-reflective critique to the purpose of justice) or consists of rules and regulations (which must be obediently applied despite all circumstances with rigidity and self-abnegation to the purpose of fidelity).

Just as this book argued earlier that there is no such thing as a "literal" reading of the Qur'an or a "direct" transmission of the Prophet's example, so we argue here that there is no such thing as a "divine" legal system. It would be intellectually dishonest to obscure the human ingenuity and frailty that went into the creation of the Islamic legal system. Such a position would also be spiritually destructive, constituting an idolatry of a subtle kind. Rather, we should have the self-restraint to accept that the *shari'a* is just what its name literally means – "a broad pathway." In the Qur'an, the term *shari'a* is used only once: *Certainly we gave to the Tribes of Israel the message and the wisdom and prophethood ... and we gave them clear arguments in the affair, and they did not differ about it until after receiving knowledge out of ambition amongst themselves ... Then we made you [Muhammad] follow a pathway [*shari'a*] in this affair – so follow it and do not follow the selfish desires of those who have no knowledge* (Q. 45:16–18). Clearly, this single use by the Qur'an of the term *shari'a* does not technically denote a legal system. It means instead a pathway by which one can deal justly with *the affair* – which refers to the essential message of the Qur'an, the moral worth of life, the consequence of every action, the accounting before God, and the life after resurrection (Q. 45:14–15).

In Arabic, the term *shari'a* means a pathway such as that which an unruly herd of sheep might make as they were herded by a wise shepherd toward a source of water. It is not a narrow path, but rather a broad pathway. It is defined by individual tracks that converge and diverge as the sheep make their way, adjusting to local terrain, some moving in large clusters and others wandering in exploratory forays or venturing alone along previously uncharted courses. The shepherd keeps them within the limit of heading toward the source of water but does not insist that they travel single-file along a narrow path.[12] So too the *shari'a* as Islamic law allows for diversity and is based upon difference of opinion within the limits of shared sources and principles. Revealed scripture (*ayat*) provides divinely given signposts that mark the path, and the Prophet's example may give footprints to help distinguish it as a path that leads to life-sustaining water, which is the presence of God. But to say that the path is identical with the footsteps or signposts or the ultimate goal would be a mistake.

If God is present as the life-giving water that is the goal at the end of the path, then God's message constitutes the signposts. The Prophet is the one who first walked along the trajectory pointing out the signs. The jurists play the role of shepherd, for they claim to take up the responsibility to guide others, through argument and sometimes coercion. Jurists define the responsibilities of others because they cultivate the intellectual skill to read scripture and differentiate between what is a command and what is a suggestion, between what is an obligation and what is a recommendation, between what is an act incumbent upon the individual and what is delegated to the collective, between what is clearly determined and what is ambiguously allegorical. Ordinary Muslims delegate this authority to the jurists, assuming that they – as professional specialists and pious intellectuals – make their decisions contingent upon five qualities: honesty, diligence, comprehensiveness, reasonableness, and self-restraint.[13] Yet there has never been a formal committee to oversee the jurists' work or ascertain whether they have indeed operated within the limits imposed by these five qualities. Though jurists tussled with despots, sparred with philosophers, and jostled with Sufis (all of whom in one form or another were critics of the jurists), there was never any system of checks and balances or judicial review to pronounce whether the jurists' effort to build up the *shari'a* conformed to the demands of justice and needs of compassion.

Law as Executive Order: Rebellion, Apostasy, and Sodomy

In reality, a foundation for Islamic law was laid before jurists emerged as a cosmopolitan and educated class of specialists. When the Prophet Muhammad was alive, Muslims looked to the Qur'anic revelation to give them laws. However, only a few verses in the Qur'an are legislative in content. Muslims also looked to the Prophet himself to give rules for behavior, either explicitly based on the Qur'an (as interpretations or specifications) or based upon his own wisdom. Muslims revered the Prophet as a charismatic leader and accepted that God guided everything he did or said – as expressed by the Qur'an: *Those who obey you* [the Prophet] *are obeying God, for the hand of God is above their hands* (Q. 48:10). Commands based upon the Prophet's own wisdom may be intended to guide the behavior of Muslims or may simply express his personal opinion. That is, some things he said were pronounced in his role as conduit for divine guidance and some were said in his contingent role as a human being. All of these sayings are preserved by hadith scholars in reports, but it is up to jurists to decide which are intended as divine guidance and which are merely incidental.

Before either hadith scholars or jurists divided up these roles and responsibilities, the Prophet's followers were faced with crises and forced to act. As his death approached, the Prophet refused to name a successor. Upon his death, discord and violence broke out as different factions jockeyed for power, with very different claims to authority and theological conceptions of just rule. Some felt that the most noble Arab in lineage should rule, others felt that the closest male heir in the Prophet's own family should rule, and yet others felt that the most righteous believer should rule regardless of family, lineage, or ethnicity. In the chaos, a band of the Prophet's close followers recommended that his closest friend, the elder statesman Abu Bakr al-Siddiq, be elected as *khalifa* – as successor to the Prophet and ruler of the Muslim community. This set up a tradition of *khalifa* rule, which lasted only a generation. Elected by a council of tribal elders, the *khalifa* would succeed as vice-regent of the Prophet who had died. The *khalifa* would not inherit the Prophet's charismatic authority, for the revelation of the Qur'an ended with the Prophet's death, but he would inherit his political authority. The *khalifa* would collect taxes, direct military forces, conduct treaties, appoint administrators, and make laws. In this sense, the *khalifa* was a legislator by necessity through community delegation whereas the Prophet was a legislator through charisma by divine dispensation.

As the first *khalifa*, Abu Bakr was not easily accepted. Most Arabs in the three towns of Medina, Mecca, and Ta'if were persuaded to renew their pledge of allegiance (*bay'a*) to him, but Abu Bakr had to fight the Bedouin tribes throughout the Arabian Peninsula. His first few years of rule were marred by civil war, the so-called "Ridda Wars" against apostasy. It was in this context that the first punishment for sodomy was executed. Abu Bakr made the legal rulings out of his own sense of what was best after consulting his close colleagues, rather than based on any explicit command of the Qur'an, precedent of the Prophet, or verbal teaching from the Prophet.

When Abu Bakr became the first *khalifa*, many Arab tribes who had nominally pledged allegiance to the Prophet as Muslims renounced their allegiance when he died. Abu Bakr's first task, therefore, was to put down the rebellion and demand that these tribes uphold their religious and political commitment to remain Muslims. Their political rebellion against the authority of the vice-regent of the Prophet was seen as apostasy (*irtidad*), as addressed in the Qur'an – *O you who believe, if any from among you turns back from his religion, God will bring a people ... who are humble before believers but forceful against unbelievers, who will strive hard in God's way and not fear the censure of any critic* (Q. 5:54). Their desertion from the Muslim camp was seen as heresy, in which religious and political elements were fully fused. Abu Bakr sent the heroic and hot-blooded military commander Khalid ibn al-Walid (died 642) to lead the Muslim army and fight against the Arab tribes of Hawazin, Banu 'Amir, and Banu Salim in 633, to force them into submission and demand that they fulfill their pledge – which they had freely given to the Prophet – to be Muslims.

Abu Bakr ruled for only two years, but these two years were crucial in stabilizing the young Islamic community. He assigned Khalid ibn al-Walid to be the military commander during several important battles in Arabia and then Iraq. During these military campaigns, he wrote back to Abu Bakr in Medina "that he had found a man in some outlying region who does the act of the Tribe of Lot." This event was discussed in Chapter 3 for its relevance to critiquing hadith, as it illustrates how there were no hadith known to relate directly to the event. Here we will explore the event more fully and highlight its relevance to juridical decisions. Abu Bakr gathered his advisory council, consisting of leading companions of the Prophet, such as 'Umar al-Khattab (who was to the become the second *khalifa*), 'Uthman ibn 'Affan (who was to become the third *khalifa*), and 'Ali ibn Abi Talib (who was to become the fourth *khalifa* and whom the Shi'a regard as the first and only rightful ruler after the Prophet). These companions of the Prophet debated the issue, because it appears that none of them knew of a precedent for such a phenomenon. The Prophet had left no example to follow in this case; none of them quoted any hadith transmitting the Prophet's teaching or advice. In the end, 'Ali pronounced that "This is a sin that only one community practiced [the Tribe of Lot], and God did to them [a punishment] that you all know. I think that we should burn him with fire." In the Qur'an, God destroys the Tribe of Lot by raining down on them burning stones, so 'Ali suggested that Muslims should punish the man by burning him alive. The council consented to 'Ali's suggestion, and Abu Bakr ordered the Khalid ibn al-Walid to have the man burned. That was done.[14] This is a prime example of how the vice-regents to the Prophet in the first generation made law by executive order. There was no juridical debate, no mention of legal reasoning by analogy, and no need to base decisions upon hadith of the Prophet. The Prophet's successors were making law by command, based on their practical sense of what was best for the community in situations of crisis.

Jurists mention this as the first actual punishment of a man for "doing the acts of the Tribe of Lot." It set up a precedent for execution but also caused a controversy over the legality of burning as a punishment. The event leaves many questions open, questions that the jurists ignored: if this man were punished for homosexual intercourse, where are the eye-witnesses that the Qur'an insists present their evidence before anyone is found guilty of illicit sexual intercourse? Where is the man's partner if they were discovered having intercourse by others? Why did 'Ali suggest punishing him with burning rather than executing him by stoning as would have been the case for illicit heterosexual intercourse (*zina'*)? Some versions of this report preserve the name of the punished man as al-Fuja'a, but give no context to the event. His name provides a clue to discovering what really happened. In books of military history we find contextual information about the event which can answer these questions. It is a context that leads us to surprising conclusions.

There are two major historical chronicles of the early Islamic community and its expansion into an empire, written by al-Tabari and al-Waqidi. In al-Tabari's history, we find that the man named al-Fuja'a was a controversial military leader when Abu Bakr ordered the "Wars of Apostasy." Abu Bakr organized the Muslim Arabs in Medina, Ta'if, and Mecca into an army (joined by some of the semi-nomadic tribes of the Hijaz) to attack rebel tribes.[15] Some tribes had thrown off allegiance to Abu Bakr simply because they were proud of their independence and resented paying taxes to the nascent Islamic state. The rebellion was made more dangerous because other tribes opted to follow a local prophet who rose up to imitate and rival Muhammad.[16] The rest of the nomadic and semi-nomadic Arab tribes were divided between those openly hostile to the Muslims in Medina and those with a wait-and-see attitude, who were not willing to submit to any authority easily. The incident of "the act of the Tribe of Lot" occurred in the context of these wars against rebel Arab tribes and therefore has very political dimensions, our first hint that it may not have been so much about homosexual intercourse as rather about rebellion against Prophetic authority.

Khalid ibn al-Walid hesitated before punishing the man, and wrote back from the front for explicit instructions from the *khalifa*, Abu Bakr. Khalid was usually a bold and rash commander, but had been reprimanded before by the Prophet.[17] Khalid had previously been sent to fight against the Arab tribe of al-Jadhima when they resisted giving allegiance to the nascent Islamic state in Medina. He defeated them. However, because of their local dialect of Arabic, they did not say, "We submit to become Muslims" (*aslamna*), but rather, "We came out of one religion into another" (*sabana*). Khalid ignored this dialectical expression, and kept on killing or taking captive those who did not say, "We submit." He gave each Muslim soldier a captive and ordered each to kill his captive. However, the man who reported this incident, Ibn 'Umar, refused the order, saying, "By God, I shall not kill my captive and none of my companions shall kill his captive," because he understood that these Arabs had submitted and become Muslims again by expressing surrender in their own dialect. When they complained to the Prophet about Khalid's decision, the Prophet said, "O God, I am innocent of what Khalid ibn al-Walid has done," repeating this two more times.[18] Owing to earlier rebukes like this against his military decisions Khalid had become more cautious in the context of fighting Arab tribes to force them back to the Islam they had renounced.

So Khalid was cautious about punishing Fuja'a on his own initiative. If it had been a simple case of publicly witnessing homosexual intercourse that he considered illegal, there is little doubt that a rash military commander would have dispensed justice on the spot. Instead, he hesitated and sent word to Medina to ask for instructions. In al-Tabari's history, we find that Fuja'a was captured and sent back to Medina alive to face his punishment. Abu Bakr ordered him to be burned in the large open field used for communal prayers at holiday festivals.[19] The fact that the military commander hesitated before executing justice and that Abu Bakr personally oversaw his public punishment in the capital is our second clue that Fuja'a's crime was not same-sex intercourse.

The third clue we have about Fuja'a is his name. In Arabic, it refers to a surprise attack or sudden assault and is related to one of the many names for a pouncing lion.[20] It is a name fit for a warrior. In the history of al-Tabari, we find that he was indeed a warrior of the Arab tribe of Banu Salim. He was known by the nickname "al-Fuja'a" because of the ferocity of his sudden attacks, but his given name was Iyas ibn 'Abd Yalil.[21] His tribe had nominally converted to Islam while the Prophet Muhammad was alive, for material gain or political ambition – as the Qur'an comments about them, *The Arabs of the desert say, "We believe." Say to them, "You have not believed, so say rather 'We submit,' for faith has not yet entered your hearts. If you obey God and God's messenger you will lose no [benefit] from your deeds, for God is forgiving and merciful"* (Q. 49:14). When the Prophet Muhammad died, faith had not yet fully entered their hearts, and many of them retracted their offer of submission (*islam*). In their Bedouin logic, they were fully justified: the Prophet was dead so their political allegiance to him was no longer binding. But in Muslim logic, their retraction was an act of rebellion. In the view of Abu Bakr, their allegiance was to a religion, to God and God's messenger, such that even when the messenger was dead the religious community continued and its leader commanded allegiance.

In the eyes of the Muslims, the Arab tribes' retracting allegiance was religious heresy as well as political rebellion. The term "apostasy" combines these two dimensions. So Abu Bakr sent military expeditions against them, like that of Khalid ibn al-Walid. Under pressure of military attack, many of the tribes again agreed to become Muslims and owe allegiance to Medina. Having once rebelled, Fuja'a agreed to rejoin the Muslims, but he did this not from faith but for self-advancement. He saw that the Muslim forces were in need of military reinforcements, and offered to lead some of his tribe to fight on their behalf: "He presented his request to Abu Bakr, saying, 'Support me with weapons and send me against whomever you will from among the tribe of apostasy.' So he [Abu Bakr] gave him weapons and commanded him with his orders."[22] The Muslims accepted the offer of Fuja'a and armed his tribal band as a mercenary force.

Once armed, Fuja'a lived up to his predatory nickname. He made a sudden attack upon the hand that had armed him. Instead of fighting loyally for the Muslims, he fought against whoever stood in his way. He acted as a brigand, attacking Muslims and other tribes indiscriminately in order to gather wealth and power for himself.[23] His crimes included apostasy twice over, murder of Muslims, and highway robbery, as he could sustain a militia in the desert wastes only by preying on trade routes. In the course of his attacks, he may have perpetrated sexual assault as well against men or women – the history of al-Tabari does not mention sexual crimes, but in the context of his piratical lifestyle they are quite probable.

The political treachery of Fuja'a was more dangerous to the Muslims than his military attacks. He set a deadly precedent. If Fuja'a were allowed to continue, the Muslims would have a hard time controlling other Arab tribes who offered to re-ally themselves, and could not trust them with arms to join in the ongoing struggle. For this reason, Khalid ibn al-Walid turned quickly to capture Fuja'a, sending against him a contingent of warriors led by Turayfa ibn Hajiz. This contingent captured Fuja'a, and he was sent back to Medina for punishment, after Khalid ibn al-Walid had written to the *khalifa* Abu Bakr that the man was guilty of "doing the acts of the Tribe of Lot."

This is the key to the story. Fuja'a was executed for doing "the acts of the Tribe of Lot," but did that phrase mean homosexual intercourse? In these early days, did that phrase mean what jurists would later define as "sodomy" (*liwat*)? As we saw in Chapter 2, the Qur'anic narrative tells of many kinds of crimes perpetrated by the Tribe of Lot. It is probable that in the time of Abu Bakr, so close to the era of revelation, this phrase would be understood as an umbrella term for a whole constellation of acts that were named in the Qur'an. These various crimes were united in their intention, which was rebellion against the authority of the Prophet who was sent to them as a guide. From this perspective, we can understand why Fuja'a was accused of "the acts of the Tribe of Lot." It was because he had rebelled against the Prophet Muhammad's authority as delegated to his successors. In short, his major crime was apostasy and rebellion, his other kinds of assault being expressions of this intent.

Other evidence shows us that the early Muslim community applied burning as punishment for apostasy. The decision to burn Fuja'a was made by Abu Bakr, on the advice of 'Ali (a cousin of the Prophet). But it was a highly contentious decision. For example, one close follower of the Prophet, Ibn 'Abbas (who was also a cousin of the Prophet), apparently criticized this decision. His servant, 'Ikirma, reported "that 'Ali ordered to be burned some people who had rebelled against their former allegiance to Islam [*irtaddu 'an al-islam*]; when news of this reached Ibn 'Abbas, he said, 'I would not have burned them with fire for the Prophet of God has said, "Do not punish people with God's own punishment." Instead I would have killed them [by other means], according to the Prophet's statement, "Those who change their religion you should kill." This statement reached 'Ali, who said, "Woe be unto you, O son of my uncle, Ibn 'Abbas!"'"[24] Despite this criticism, Abu Bakr punished a man with burning in imitation of how God destroyed the Tribe of Lot, but his decision caused debate and dissent among the senior companions of the Prophet. One of them, Ibn 'Abbas, even suggested that 'Ali's decision was audacious in claiming to replicate God's destructive will in human decisions that transgressed the explicit teaching of the Prophet Muhammad, for al-Bukhari preserves a report in which the Prophet is remembered to have said, "Burning by fire is a punishment only given by God." This suggestion caused open disagreement between the companions, even those as close as Ibn 'Abbas and his relative 'Ali.

This chapter argues that this incident of apostasy and violent rebellion was, with the passing of time, mis-remembered. A man's punishment for treachery, rebellion against the Prophet's authority, highway robbery, murder, and assault that may have included rape (male-on-female or male-on-male) was remembered solely as an act of "sodomy." The phrase "the acts of the Tribe of Lot," which had covered a whole constellation of transgressions, with an underlying motive of violent infidelity, became limited to same-sex intercourse. We can observe this happening in the textual variations of this report. Some variants give the executed man's name not as Fuja'a but as "Fujjat," which is a term describing a man or animal with the thighs wide apart. It seems that Muslims remembered his name in a distortion that sexualized his crime, projecting upon him the quality of opening widely his thighs and make himself sexually available, with the hint of being penetrated anally. His character as preserved in historical accounts was such that, to the contrary, he was more likely to force open the thighs of others in sexual assault than to allow himself to be penetrated. But once he was captured and executed, later generations of Muslims distorted his name (whether with deliberate derogatory intent or spontaneously in a slippage of meaning) to accuse him of homosexual intercourse.

Once the Muslim armies put down the rebellion in which Fuja'a had participated, his punishment could be retold and remembered in ways that distorted his original crimes. It was remembered that Fuja'a was burned for doing "the act of the Tribe of Lot," but that phrase was narrowed in meaning to indicate only homosexual intercourse – in particular a man's anal penetration of another male. How did the phrase "act of the Tribe of Lot" (*'amal qawm lut*) get abbreviated into the more simple "sodomy" (*liwat*)? The term was taken over and shaped by Arab patriarchal values, in a manner parallel to how certain practices of women's public life were curtailed in the few decades of *khalifa* rule after the Prophet died. Fatima Mernissi has documented how 'Umar ibn al-Khattab, after being elected as the second *khalifa* after Abu Bakr died, ordered women's presence in public to be sharply curtailed. Measures taken in the Prophet's life which were specific to his wives or temporary in a political crisis were amplified and universalized to keep women out of public space, in ways that the Prophet Muhammad never intended.

When certain men with tribal ambitions used a public occasion to get close to the Prophet's wives in order to insult or influence him, a Qur'anic revelation commanded his wives to seclude themselves behind a curtain in a private space that non-family males were restricted from entering. Later, in a political crisis in Medina, some who wished to challenge the Prophet's authority hassled Muslim women on the street and later claimed that they mistook them for slave women who were sexually available. In that crisis, Muslim women were urged to cover their heads with cloaks when out of doors to distinguish themselves as protected persons and preserve their dignity. After the Prophet's death, these incidents were, by the *khalifa*'s command, expanded into rulings that Muslim women should always cover themselves or not leave home without their husband's permission.[25] As vice-regent, 'Umar also banned the institution of informal marriage (*mut'a*, also called "temporary marriage"), which potentially gave women much more flexibility in negotiating sexual and intimate relationships with men; this institution will be discussed in Chapter 5 on same-sex marriage.[26] In a similar way, an incident in which the Prophet banished an effeminate man (*mukhannath*) from his household for an ethical infraction gave rise in later generations to wholesale persecution of such people who were the exception to gender roles, as we noted in Chapter 3. Patriarchal values required the subordination of women, the marginalization of men who acted like women, and the suppression of men who questioned masculine norms by engaging in homosexual behavior. Patriarchal values inherent in Arab culture before Islam became strengthened after the Prophet's death and entrenched in the name of Islam.

This process was complex. It involved Arab patriarchal values that were evident before Islam and were upheld by the Quraysh Arabs who ruled Mecca before and during the Prophet's lifetime. Patriarchy is demonstrated most starkly by their practice of burying female infants alive, a practice that the Qur'an denounced and the Prophet outlawed. In many ways, the Prophet Muhammad challenged the patriarchal values of Arab tribal society, and in some ways, at the Qur'an's prompting, he compromised with them in order to create a workable social order in Medina. After his death, though, the forces that restrained patriarchy were removed, and Islamic norms were increasingly interpreted through the lens of Arab tribal values. Arab patriarchal values were reinforced by Judaic custom, which had been very strong in Medina, Yemen, and other areas where Muslims develped their early legal norms. As Muslims began to conceive of themselves as a new and distinct religious community that reestablished the legacy of Abraham without replicating Judaism, they distanced themselves from Jewish communities; through political and military maneuvers, the Jewish tribes in Medina were either killed or forced to leave. However, Judaic norms remained highly influential, as Muslims perceived themselves as both competing with Jews and surpassing them as upholders of monotheistic worship in Arabia. At the same time, some Jews converted to Islam and played important roles as scholars, folklorists, and transmitters of legal knowledge.

Judaic norms were increasingly absorbed into Muslim custom, and we find ample evidence of this in hadith and Qur'an interpretation. This study argues that Judaic customs were patriarchal and that the adoption of Judaic ritual and legal norms in Islamic communities led to a hardening of patriarchal norms among Muslims. This argument describes a historical evolution over many generations, in which Muslims rivalled Jewish communities but also looked to Judaic custom to inform their evolving ritual and legal norms. This argument does not amount to blaming Jews as people for Islamic patriarchy and should not be read as defamation of them.[27] Rather, early Muslims could no longer harken so easily back to the patriarchal values of their pre-Islamic Arab culture that was discredited as an "Age of Ignorance" (*jahiliyya*), yet they could refer to Judaic custom and precedent that were also patriarchal to inform their evolving religious practices, for Judaic sources were held in high esteem as conveying the teachings of the Prophets who came before Muhammad. The relationship of early Muslim scholars and jurists to the Judaic tradition was one of moral dismissal coupled with creative appropriation.

This process of interaction with Judaic scriptural interpretation and ritual custom hardened patriarchal norms among early Muslims. Examples of such norms are found in evaluations of sexual pleasure and women's status, as asserted by Mernissi, who writes that Islam was a "total revolution vis-à-vis the Judeo-Christian tradition and the pre-Islamic period with regard to women. However, very quickly the misogynistic trend reasserted itself among the *fuqaha'* [jurists] and gained the upper hand."[28] Judaic custom held that sex was only for procreation and not for pleasure – any sexual pleasure leading to ejaculation other than inside a woman's vagina is "destruction of seed," which was a crime against the Jewish tribes and against God. It constituted the "killing of one's children" and the Torah (in Genesis 38) records that God punished Onan for ejaculating on the ground to avoid impregnating his sexual partner.[29] A dominant strand of Judaic interpretation also asserted that women are inferior by nature because Eve was created from Adam's rib; this is a belief that was "remembered" as hadith of the Prophet and incorporated uncritically into scriptural exegesis although it contradicted the Qur'an.[30] Many Jewish scholars held that Eve was responsible for tempting Adam and for this she was especially punished with menstruation, which is polluting and brings bad luck.[31]

Such Judaic custom often accorded with pre-Islamic Arab custom, as they shared Semitic roots and a common cultural environment. This affinity often affected the "remembering" of hadith, such as the time Abu Hurayra reported that the Prophet Muhammad had said, "Three things bring bad luck – house, woman and horse." Upon hearing this, the Prophet's wife 'A'isha responded, "Abu Hurayra learned his lessons very badly. He came into our house when the Prophet was in the middle of a sentence. He only heard the end of it. What the Prophet said was, 'May God refute the Jews [who] say that three things bring bad luck: house, woman and horse.'"[32] On the issue of female impurity during menstruation, hadith that cited Judaic customs to refute them were cut or interrupted in order to have their meaning reversed, so that Muslims would revert to Judaic attitudes and behaviors. Although this time 'A'isha was present to contradict the mis-remembering, we can assume that in most instances she was not. Through hadith and jurists' decisions based upon them, Judaic and pre-Islamic attitudes crept back into Islam.

A similar process was at work considering the question of sex for pleasure and contraception. On many occasions, Muslim men in the early community practiced *'azl* (premature withdrawal, known in Western medical texts by the Latin *coitus interruptus*) as a means of enjoying sexual intercourse with a woman but not ejaculating inside her body so as to avoid pregnancy. One companion of the Prophet, Judhama ibn Wahb, reported, "I was there when the Prophet was with a group ... They asked him about *coitus interruptus*, and the Prophet answered, 'It is hidden infanticide.'" Here the Prophet appears to confirm the Judaic belief that for a man to ejaculate without using "his seed" for procreation amounts to a concealed way of killing his own children, which is a crime against his people and an abomination in the land. However, another hadith recalled by a different companion, Abu Sa'id, relates the same episode but says that someone said to the Prophet that "'The Jews say that *coitus interruptus* is minor infanticide,' and the Prophet answered, 'The Jews lie, for if God wanted to create something, no one can avert it.'"[33] In this incident the Prophet cited Judaic custom only to refute it, but some hadith transmitters recalled only that portion of the speech which cited the Judaic custom and deleted the refutation. This distorted report, for instance, led Ibn Hazm to declare contraception illegal in Islamic law, for he believed it meant killing an infant, in contradiction to the majority of other schools of jurisprudence which allowed it (but which debated whether the man had to have the explicit consent of his female partner in order to use a contraceptive technique, or it was his right to do so even without her consent). Despite this particular case, Ibn Hazm was generally critical of Muslim jurists who accepted Judaic custom or scriptural mandate, and he accused the Maliki legal school of being especially susceptible to such "Judaizing tendencies."[34] So it was that hadith often led to Judaic beliefs influencing Islamic law, especially when they confirmed patriarchal and masculine ascetic ideals.

Just as they affected heterosexual coupling, Judaic attitudes also affected how Muslim jurists understood same-sex intercourse. Male-with-male intercourse is prohibited in the Torah (Leviticus 18), along with a series of sexual and non-sexual acts. One scholar argues that they all involve the proper use of the semen of Jewish males: "What unifies all these acts is that they are considered affronts to procreation, either because they are sterile (homosexuality and bestiality), produce illegitimate progeny (adultery, incest), destroy progeny (sacrifice to Molech [an idol]), or represent rebellion against the source of one's own legitimacy (insulting one's parents)."[36] Others suggest that they prohibit mixing semen with defiling bodily fluids or transgressing status boundaries. In Judaic custom, as based on proscriptions in the Torah, idol worship and same-sex intercourse between men were blurred together, both being seen as rebellion against God and diabolical misuse of male semen.

It is impossible to know if this attitude was particularly Judaic or if it had affinity with pre-Islamic Arab custom. One suspects that the association of same-sex intercourse with idolatry and rebellion against the one God is particularly Judaic, since the Arab tribes were mainly idolatrous and polytheistic. This attitude is what drove early generations of Muslims to mis-remember the burning of Fuja'a the apostate and renegade. His rebellion against God and

God's messenger was labeled "the act of the Tribe of Lot" and 'Ali called his crimes "rebellion against God" (*ma'siya*) and recommended that he be burned. After Fuja'a was reduced to ash, it was conveniently possible to remember – under this same label of "sodomy" – that he was burned for same-sex intercourse. Later authors relate the incident by saying the man was found "having sexual intercourse with another man the way a woman has intercourse" rather than using the more authentic and ambiguous descriptive phrase "the act of the Tribe of Lot."[36] When citing this incident, most jurists intend to illustrate the first punishment for male-with-male intercourse and ignore the other crimes of which Fuja'a was guilty. The strategy is similar to citation of the narrative of the Tribe of Lot from the Qur'an, as discussed in Chapter 2.

During the first few generations of Muslims, the crime of heretical politics was displaced on to sexual acts. This was a convenient way of suppressing the memory of the wars of apostasy. This act of displacement was very strategic, for during these wars many Arabs rebelled but later acquiesced to become upstanding members of the Muslim community. They became front-line soldiers in the Islamic conquest of the neighboring Persian and Byzantine Empires. In the quickly evolving masculine ethic of the Islamic warrior, it was easy to displace complicity in apostasy and rebellion with persecution of same-sex sexuality. In these early generations, roughly the first century of Islam, the law of the community was based on local custom and the command of the ruler. Legal debate only gradually evolved as a specialist enterprise of jurists who hoped to create a system of rules to which all Muslims would adhere, despite their regional dispersion and against the command of rulers who were increasingly impious and imperious.

As the jurists debated, the precedent had already been set that same-sex intercourse should be punishment by death, but the fact that this was first done by burning a man alive was disquieting to the jurists. Rather than resolve the matter by inquiring whether the case of Fuja'a had really been one of apostasy, jurists resolved it by searching for opinions that recommended a more nuanced punishment in keeping with Islamic ethics. They recommended execution by stoning or other means rather than by burning. The jurists first found these opinions to have been held by members of the early Muslim community and later attributed them to the Prophet in the form of hadith.

As different schools of Islamic law took shape, they used different sources and principles to make legal rulings; depending on these differences they came to contradictory conclusions about homosexuality. This chapter now turns to analyze the decisions of each school of law and their legal rationale. The discussion will focus mainly on the issue of penetrative intercourse between men, because this is the issue about which jurists in all schools were most concerned.

However, we will also assess how their decisions framed sexual intercourse between two women and non-penetrative sexual acts, upon which jurists did not focus so intently. We will analyze and compare the legal reasoning of five major Sunni schools of law, beginning with those three – the Maliki, Shafi'i, and Hanbali schools – which were harshest in their decisions, and then turning to two others – the Hanafi and Zahiri schools – that came to more moderate and nuanced decisions. Each school's dominant trend of thought will be considered, though it should be admitted that there were always dissenting opinions and varied responses within any single school of law. It is beyond the scope of this study to delve into the detail of debates within any one school or to compare Sunni legal decisions with those of the Shi'i communities.

Needless to say, jurists focused upon evaluating actions – to declare whether they were forbidden, discouraged, allowed, recommended, or obligatory for Muslims. Jurists largely shied away from theological or philosophical discussion about human nature or personality and seldom inquired why an individual might act in a certain way. They felt that God is the ultimate judge of intentions – according to the Prophet's famous hadith that "Each act depends upon its intention, and each person will receive the consequence of his or her intention." But jurists asserted that they are delegated to judge the acts of others. We will explore the differences in how jurists judged homosexual acts as a way to assess whether one can assert what the *shari'a* says about homosexuality.

Law as Custom: The Maliki Approach

The earliest attempts to systematize the *shari'a* was to project the custom of Muslims as Islamic law. This reflected the organic growth of the community. It assumed that what the generation of one's fathers and grandfathers did is what Islam requires, because they were closer in time and social context to the Prophet's own community. In this way, the jurist Malik ibn Anas described Islamic law as the customary practice of the elders of Medina (*'amal ahl al-madina*). Jurists who followed Imam Malik's reasoning built the Maliki school of law, named after him. They adopted this approach to create an authoritative body of legal decisions that are still respected and often followed by Sunni Muslims across North and West Africa and among Muslim minorities in continental Europe who emigrated from these regions, as we saw in Chapter 1's focus on Morocco.

The execution of Fuja'a in Medina was in a highly politically charged environment and the reason behind the execution was ambiguous. It was for treachery and rebelling against Prophetic authority, combined with armed robbery and murder and possibly also rape, but the crime was labeled as "the act of the Tribe of Lot" and in later generations was remembered as a sexual crime – sodomy. Roughly a century later, Malik and the jurists who followed him conceived of sexual intercourse between two men as a special crime, sodomy, which was different from apostasy and was also distinct from heterosexual fornication. Malik argued that it was the custom of the Muslim community in Medina to execute both partners guilty of this act, without consideration of their age or status. However, execution by burning was seen as excluding the guilty person from the Islamic community, had no support in the Prophet's own personal example, and was criticized by some early followers. So Malik specified that stoning to death was the appropriate means of execution.

It is not just Malik's decision that is important but also his juridical method for arriving at the decision. The book that records his decisions, *al-Muwatta'*, is not exactly a book of law and is regarded by many scholars as one of the first comprehensive collections of hadith. Malik's legal book preserves many reports attributed to the Prophet and also reports attributed to his companions and followers. In an era before hadith scholarship codified reports and specified their chains of transmission, Malik assumed that the practice of the people of Medina organically reflected what the Prophet taught, since the Prophet lived in Medina.[37] In Malik's age, the concept of *sunna* had not been reduced to the example of the Prophet alone, but reflected the broad practice of the elders of Medina.

For instance, the man who recorded most reports that make up *al-Muwatta'* is Yahya, a follower of the jurist Malik. Yahya wrote down all that his teacher had said and heard about different topics, mostly on the authority of Ibn Shihab al-Zuhri (died 742), an esteemed Muslim elder in Medina.[38] Yahya records that "Malik told me that he [Malik] had asked Ibn Shihab about those who commit the act of the Tribe of Lot. Ibn Shihab said, 'He is to be stoned, whether he is married or unmarried.'"[39] This is the opinion upon which Maliki jurists base their decisions on same-sex intercourse. Notably, it does not involve any hadith attributed to the Prophet, but simply states what an esteemed elder of Medina said.[40] The Maliki legal method trusted that what elders reported as their community's custom had the force of law, and must reflect what the Prophet's intention had been. Malik raised the custom of the first generations of Muslims in Medina into the standard for universal Islamic law.

There was pressure to justify such decisions with the Qur'an. In the face of dissenting opinion, how did jurists defend the position that anal sex between men deserved capital punishment (by stoning or by other means)? To defend this decision, Imam Malik simply noted that God destroyed the Tribe of Lot by pelting them with stones as hard as baked brick (*sijjil*) that fell from heaven.

This is an argument by rhetorical association, not an argument by legal reasoning. However, it is a kind of argument that would prove very effective and seems to be based on early precedent among the companions of the Prophet but not on the example of the Prophet himself. The Prophet had ordered stoning as punishment for heterosexual adultery (fornication by a mature person already married). Malik raised the question of whether stoning to death as punishment for same-sex intercourse between two men was analogous to heterosexual adultery. Other jurists came to different conclusions about this – as we will see below. Hanafi jurists argued that heterosexual fornication is categorically different from homosexual intercourse whereas Shafi'i jurists arguied that heterosexual fornication and homosexual intercourse are objectively equivalent and require equal punishment.

Death by stoning was a punishment adopted from the Judaic tradition. There is no explicit command in the Qur'an to stone someone to death either for homosexual intercourse or for heterosexual fornication (*zina'*). For the latter, the Qur'an specifies lashing and possibly banishment (Q. 24:2, 15). However, some hadith depict the Prophet ordering stoning as the punishment for heterosexual fornication and adultery. It appears that his first order to this effect was to punish a man from the Jewish tribes in Medina who was found guilty of heterosexual fornication by his own community. The Jewish tribes had signed the "Constitution of Medina" accepting Muhammad as the political ruler of the city, with the understanding that they were free to worship God in their own way and that the Prophet Muhammad would enforce their own Judaic laws and customs when disputes arose in their community. When Muhammad inquired from Torah scholars what was the punishment in their scriptures for fornication he was told that God demanded stoning, so that is what he enforced. This punishment then seems to have been applied to Muslims guilty of heterosexual fornication or adultery, at the Prophet's command rather than by Qur'an's demand.

This ambivalent history of stoning as punishment illustrates the point discussed above, that Judaic custom had a profound influence on Islamic law from an early period, even during the lifetime of the Prophet Muhammad. This history was difficult for later authorities and jurists to rationalize, for it required acknowledgement of two controversial points. First, the Prophet demanded capital punishment by stoning for adultery, which was not specified in the Qur'an, and, second, this caused the punishment for adultery given in the Qur'an to be ignored (*manuskh*). This led jurists to theorize that the example of the Prophet is equal to the Qur'an's revelation and that the Prophet's actions could, in some cases, abrogate or overrule the Qur'an.

This theoretical resolution of the problem did not satisfy all Muslims, for it seemed to raise the Prophet's human decisions to the same level of authority as the Qur'an's divine voice. For this reason some early Muslims, like the second *khalifa* 'Umar, insisted that the Qur'an did in fact specify stoning as the punishment for adultery as a *hadd* crime, despite the fact that the Qur'an recited by most Muslims (and as written down today) did not include any words to this effect. A *hadd* is a crime that is explicitly defined in the Qur'an and for which specific punishment is demanded in the Qur'an. There are five crimes whose punishments are explicitly mentioned in the Qur'an: murder, highway robbery, theft, fornication between a man and a woman, and false accusation of fornication.

'Umar appears to have made this claim publicly after his final pilgrimage to Mecca, in his last years as *khalifa*, when he was preparing to die. Malik records 'Umar's claim in his legal decisions on fornication, and in this context Malik raises the issue of homosexual intercourse. It is instructive for us to examine the whole series of reports included in this particular chapter "on stoning" in Imam Malik's book, *al-Muwatta'*, as quoted in Chapter 3. Malik related the decisions of Yahya ibn Sa'id ibn Qays al-Ansari (died 760–61) and Sa'id ibn al-Musayyab (died 712), both elders of Medina. The whole series of reports by Malik begins with 'Umar ibn al-Khattab insisting that the punishment for heterosexual fornication by a mature person is death by stoning and that this punishment was explicitly commanded by the Qur'an. Malik related that 'Umar said, "By God whose hand holds my soul, had it not been that people might say that 'Umar ibn al-Khattab has added to the Book of God, I would have written, 'The full-grown man and the full-grown woman, stone them absolutely.' We have certainly recited that [as part of the Qur'an]." In a discussion of heterosexual fornication, Malik then points out that he heard the early jurist of Medina, Ibn Shihab, say that one who commits the act of the Tribe of Lot "is to be stoned whether he is married or unmarried."[41] 'Umar saw stoning as punishment for heterosexual fornication as integral to Islam, insisting it was part of God's message to believers, both in the Qur'an and in the Torah before it.[42]

Malik shied away from the controversial point of whether the Qur'an as currently recited was the authentic and complete Qur'an, and so will this chapter. Rather, Malik treated 'Umar's words as a binding legal decision, central to the custom of the people of Medina. Malik notes that 'Umar punished by stoning, and clarified that when he said "The full-grown man and the full-grown woman," he meant men and women who had already known legal sexual intercourse through marriage. Such men and women, if found guilty of fornication, were liable to be stoned. Malik suggests that a man or woman guilty of fornication who had not yet been legally married was not liable to be stoned, but rather should be lashed because they were considered not yet mature. In this way Malik and the jurists who followed him argued that the Prophet's example of stoning applies to mature people whereas the Qur'an's explicit command to lash applies to not-yet-mature people.[43] The potential conflict was resolved by allowing younger Muslims who may have erred to suffer a lesser punishment of lashing as a warning.

The punishment for heterosexual fornication elicited a subtle discussion but the punishment for homosexual intercourse did not. Tacked on to this series of reports is Malik's statement that he heard Ibn Shihab al-Zuhri say that those doing the act of the Tribe of Lot – by which he meant two men having anal penetrative intercourse – should both be stoned regardless of whether they were "full-grown" in having been married. By including this report in a series about heterosexual sex, the Maliki jurists were arguing that this punishment was related to the issue of fornication (both called for stoning) but also that it was worse than heterosexual fornication (for there is no concession for youth or those without sexual access to a legal partner through heterosexual marriage).

In this way, Maliki jurists held that sodomy was its own category of crime. In their eyes, it did not matter if the mode of punishment for sodomy was not based on the Qur'an or on the Prophet's practice. Rather, it was sufficient to note that Ibn Shihab al-Zuhri, an elder in Medina, said that this was the custom. The assumption was that if the elders of Medina did it this way, that was an authentic reflection of the Prophet's example. However, the historical story of Fuja'a allows us to pierce through this assumption. It reveals that execution for "sodomy" in this first case in Medina (whether conceived of as heretical treason, violent assault, same-sex intercourse, or a combination of these) was not an authentic reflection of the Prophet's example, but rather a decision of the *khalifa* and companions of the Prophet. The execution was by burning, not by stoning as later became the custom in Medina and which Malik and his sources validated.

Once Malik's decision validated stoning for both partners of homosexual intercourse regardless of maturity, it created a juridical precedent. Maliki jurists stuck to it despite the fact that jurists from other schools argued that it was not sufficient to base legal rulings on community practice but rather that each ruling must be based on Qur'an, hadith, or analogical reason extending one or the other of these sources. The Malikis were under pressure to justify their rulings and at first reacted with dogmatic denial. For example the Moravid dynasty in Morocco and Spain (in the eleventh and twelfth centuries) legitimized their rule by claiming to administer orthodox Maliki law; they ordered the books of Shafi'i jurists, like Imam al-Ghazali, in their realm to be collected and burned so as to suppress any criticism of their legal method. Coercive denial did not work, and some Malikis began to doubt the assumptions of their legal school. Ibn Hazm, for one, was raised as a Maliki in Cordoba but as an adult abandoned the consensus of Maliki jurists and adopted the more source-critical Shafi'i method; later he found that method also flawed and turned to the more radically critical Zahiri legal school, as we shall see. Some medieval jurists in Spain and North Africa did not abandon the Maliki school but did respond to pressure and argued that the Maliki rulings were actually justified by interpretation of the Qur'an.[44] We will observe below how Maliki rigidity in following the custom in Medina gave way slowly to pressure from other legal schools to justify rulings in reference to the Qur'an. But first let us examine how the other major Sunni legal schools derived their decisions.

Law as Analogy: The Shafi'i approach

During the era of Imam Malik, other jurists were at work. They were dissatisfied with having a special type of punishment for sodomy that argued it was a *hadd* crime even though the Qur'an does not speak of it in that way. They felt a more elegant resolution of the problem was to consider male-to-male anal penetration to be equivalent to illegal heterosexual fornication (*zina'*). This was the position of early jurists who held that in cases of male-to-male intercourse the mature man who had already been married should be stoned to death whereas the immature man who had not yet been married yet should be confined and disciplined (*yuhbasu wa yu'addabu*).[45] They further equalized the punishment between male homosexual penetrative intercourse and heterosexual adulterous intercourse by adjusting the punishment for a non-married partner to lashing rather than confinement and discipline. Some jurists of Basra and Kufa, like Sufyan al-Thawri, expressed the judgment in this way: "The *hadd* punishment for a sodomite [*luti*] is the *hadd* punishment for an adulterer [*zani*]."

This was the judgment supported by Imam al-Shafi'i and his legal school. They were dissatisfied with decisions based upon custom or rational deliberation. Against the Malikis, Imam al-Shafi'i argued that Islamic law is not just the accumulated practice of Muslims, even if they were those privileged to live in Medina, the city of the Prophet. Rather he asserted that all decisions must be based upon the Qur'an and the Prophet's actions, which he held to be divinely inspired.[46] Imam al-Shafi'i argued that the only way to know the Prophet's example (*sunna*) is through hadith attributed directly to him rather than through sayings of his companions or customs of his followers.[47] According to al-Shafi'i, jurists can use analogical reasoning based on the wording of Qur'an and Prophetic hadith to extend judgments from known cases and apply them to ambiguous ones for which no judgment is yet known. By this use of analogical reasoning, jurists can extend judgment based on divine will to cover all possible questions without human beings actually creating new laws by their own power. New rulings are deduced by jurists, but the rationale for them is given by the divine legislator, God.

In this way, Imam al-Shafi'i made Islamic law dependent upon hadith while not leaving their interpretation up to the hadith collectors, just at the time when hadith collections were being written down in earnest. He made acceptable the practice of juridical reason without abandoning the law wholesale to rationalists, just when Greek rationalism was being picked up and used by Muslim theologians. He argued that jurists must use reason limited to analogies based on syllogistic reason rather than free reasoning about the most expedient decision. His use of analogical reasoning (*qiyas*) is clear in his legal decision about same-sex penetrative intercourse. Al-Shafi'i said, "He [who commits same-sex penetrative intercourse] should be punished with the *hadd* penalty for fornication by reason of juridical analogy [*qiyas*]." The analogy is based on the fact that those engaged in heterosexual fornication and those engaged in same-sex intercourse have had penetrative sexual pleasure with a partner to whom they are not attached by a contract of marriage or other legal relation that is similar to a contract.

There is legal uncertainty about how to extend this analogy to sexual intercourse between two women or to non-penetrative sexual acts between two men because in these cases the analogy with "penetrating an illegal partner" breaks down. Such acts are often forbidden by the principle of "prevention of harm" or *sadd al-dhari'a*; according to this logic something that is possibly legal will be forbidden if it might lead to something that is illegal.[48] Such an interpretation would hold that same-sex partners' holding hands, kissing, or caressing might lead to penetrative intercourse, which is held to be forbidden, and therefore these prior acts should also be forbidden in order to prevent harm. Similar logic, however, could be applied to legalize non-penetrative sexual acts such as masturbation, known in Islamic legal sources as *istimna' bi'l-yad* or "sexual enjoyment by the hand." As an ambiguous practice, it was largely permitted in the *shari'a*, though al-Shafi'i himself wrote that masturbation is forbidden.[49] Jurists permitted masturbation on the grounds that it prevented a person with no legal sexual partner from engaging in fornication or sodomy.[50] Similarly, some Muslim women appear to have justified lesbian intercourse as a way to prevent the harm of pregnancy outside of marriage.[51] All jurists, including those who follow al-Shafi'i, encouraged heterosexual marriage as the primary way to enjoy sexual pleasure, and therefore masturbation was discouraged if it led a woman or man away from marriage – but general discouragement was not prohibition. Only the most ascetic minded, like the Shafi'i jurist al-Nawawi, absolutely prohibited masturbation as self-stimulation. Yet he was clear that the issue was its relation to marriage, for he and all other Shafi'i jurists allowed sexual pleasure by the hand of one's legal partner. The issue was not hand-to-genital pleasure or non-procreative ejaculation but rather whether sexual pleasure happened with a legal partner.

The Shafi'i legal school is highly influential, not so much in the number of its followers but rather because of its impact on legal theory.[52] This is especially true since al-Azhar has become increasingly recognized as the premier madrasa in the Sunni world; al-Azhar being located in Egypt, many top professors there specialize in Shafi'i legal theory. An example of the contemporary influence of Shafi'i legal thought is Shaykh Yusuf Qaradawi. He was trained in Islamic theology and law at al-Azhar and is a former member of the Islamic Brotherhood (al-Ikhwan al-Muslimin). From his base in Qatar, Shaykh Qaradawi projects his presence into Europe and North America through the media and Islamic minority organizations. From this vantage point, he has denounced the work of gay, lesbian, and transgender Muslim organizations. He illustrates how the Shafi'i school's use of analogy is used to extend the ruling against sodomy to apply to same-sex acts between two women. His speeches show how the decisions of traditional legal schools are often spliced into modern debates about sexuality and sexual orientation which were not in fact addressed by traditional jurists. In the early 1960s, he emigrated from Egypt to Qatar and became one of the foremost ideologues of the "Islamic Movement," thanks to his weekly television appearances on the al-Jazeera show *al-Shari'a wa'l-Hayat* (Shari'a and Life), a favorite among Arabic-speaking Muslims living in Europe. He helps direct the European Council for Fatwa and Research (al-Majlis al-Urubbi li'l-Ifta' wa'l-Buhuth), formed in London (in March 1997) as an initiative of the Federation of Islamic Organizations in Europe.[53]

Al-Jazeera's *Shari'a and Life* devoted a whole program (broadcast from Doha on June 8, 2006) to the issue of homosexuality and Islam. The journalist host, 'Abd al-Samad Nasr, interviewed Shaykh Qaradawi and asked him, "What is the punishment for someone who practices sodomy [*liwat*] or tribadism [*sihaq*]?" Shaykh Qaradawi answered from a Shafi'i perspective that had been hardened by Islamist ideology:

> The punishment of anyone who deviates sexually ... is the same punishment as the adulterous fornicator [*al-zani*]. The Qur'an calls adulterous fornication an "immorality" [*fahisha*] saying, *Do not approach adultery for it is an immoral and an evil way* (Q. 17:32). The Qur'an also calls the act of the Tribe of Lot an "immorality" [*fahisha*] saying, *Do you commit the immorality that no one in the wide world has done before you?* (Q. 7:80) and *Do you commit the immorality with eyes wide open?* (Q. 27:54). The immorality is

forbidden – *do not approach immoralities, those apparent and those hidden* (Q. 6:151). What is the punishment for it? The various schools of law have differed about its punishment. Some of them stipulate the same punishment as for the adulterer, distinguishing between one who is married and one is not married, male or female. Some of them stipulate that the punishment is the same for a married or unmarried person. Some say we should throw them from a deadly height the way our Lord did to the Tribe of Lot and after that, they say, we should burn them. Some say that because there are differences of opinion we can chose among these options depending on what is suitable in our time for protecting the common people of our country, because the common people of our country are under extenuating circumstances [*mukhafafat*] from the Islamic *shari'a* due to various tragedies or falling away from religion. The important question is whether we make this practice illegal. We must absolutely make it a crime. [Shaykh Qaradawi was then asked why the punishment should differ between male-with-male intercourse and female-with-female intercourse when both result from the same force of sexual attraction of a person to the same sex.] This is because the woman who is a tribade is, I mean, less weighty [*akhaff*] than a sodomite ... I mean, from a practical point of view. I mean, tribadism is not ... If we speak for example about the crime of adultery, there is adultery per se and then there are things that are a prelude to adultery [*muqaddamat li'l-zina*]. So tribadism is similar to the prelude to adulterous intercourse, you know what I mean. So therefore there is a difference, I mean, in punishment between these two things.[54]

Shaykh Qaradawi was about to say that tribadism or sexual rubbing between two women is not penetrative sex, but refrained from saying it. Without clearly saying what the punishment for sexual acts between two women actually is, he does clarify that it is less harsh than for two men who engage in penetrative sex. The assumption is that a woman cannot penetrate in the "active role" because she has no penis and that she would not betray her gender role by being penetrated, as in the "passive role." Same-sex intercourse among women, in Shaykh Qaradawi's view, is like foreplay that would lead to adultery in heterosexual intercourse, and should be punished by that analogy.

Even as he advocates the Shafi'i legal school's position that same-sex intercourse is equal to heterosexual fornication (*zina'*), Shaykh Qaradawi illustrates the limits of traditional juridical constructions. Jurists focus on acts alone, and do not comprehensively address the modern notion of homosexuality as a sexual orientation, a psychological disposition, or an identity. The interviewer reveals the tension between traditional notions of jurists and contemporary debates about homosexuality. He insists on using the terms by which jurists classify acts, using the terms "sodomy" for male-to-male anal intercourse (*liwat*) and "tribadism" for female-to-female "genital rubbing" (*sihaq*), even as he suggests that they are both expressions of a homosexual orientation. The interviewer pushed Shaykh Qaradawi to give a punishment for homosexual orientation. But, as a jurist, Shaykh Qaradawi insisted on discussing particular sexual acts. He illustrates clearly how Islamic law does not address homosexuality but only same-sex acts. Male-to-male intercourse is judged differently from female-to-female intercourse because women's gender role – determined by their lack of a penis – is considered "less weighty" than men's gender role. It is gender hierarchy that determines the traditional jurist's position and not a concept of homosexual orientation that is equally shared by gay men and lesbian women.

Law as Dogma: The Hanbali Approach

The Hanbali legal school is often counted as the "fourth Sunni school of law" though it has never had the popular appeal of other schools. Ahmad ibn Hanbal (died 855) traveled widely to collect hadith, before returning to Baghdad to study law under al-Shafi'i. He was more a hadith collector and ideological opponent of rationalist theology than a jurist, but his followers collected his scattered legal decisions, and later generations constructed from them a legal methodology. Ibn Hanbal threw himself into theological disputes and argued that influences of Greek philosophy should not be allowed to "distort" the original Islam, which can be known only through hadith.[55] In legal decisions, Ibn Hanbal basically followed the Shafi'i method, with more literalist adherence to hadith and less allowance for juridical reason. Therefore, Hanbalis consider homosexual penetrative intercourse between two men to be equivalent to fornication between a man and woman and stipulate a penalty of death by stoning for a mature, married perpetrator.

Although medieval Hanbalis counted among their number some extraordinary jurists, their school was always a minority and never came to dominate a particular region of the Islamic world. In general, Hanbalis were concerned with issues of dogmatic purity more than creative jurisprudence and focused most of their energy on defending the integrity of the hadith as the only way to know the personality of Muhammad and the will of God. The Hanbali school would have withered away if not for the modern reformer Muhammad ibn 'Abd al-Wahhab (died 1792), who founded the Wahhabi movement in Arabia. He rejected most of the Islamic theology and philosophy that he considered a heretical innovation. He preached a radical return to a puritanical version of Islam in which the only valid ruling was a literal reading of Qur'an and hadith. His reification of hadith and rejection of reason show his affinity with the Hanbali school though he formally rejected conformity with any legal school. Ibn ʿAbd al-Wahhab condemned any Muslim who did not follow him – namely all other Sunnis, Shiʿa, and especially Sufis – as infidels whose blood was licit to be spilled and whose property was liable to be confiscated.

It is primarily countries that follow the Hanbali legal method (or countries ruled by fundamentalists influenced by Hanbalism) that make a state policy of executing gay men. Hanbalis are a tiny minority in the Islamic world. Only Saudi Arabia is ostensibly an officially "Hanbali" state. The Saudi Kingdom was established by the Wahhabi movement, a fundamentalist movement advocating a strict application of rules derived directly from Qur'an and hadith. Since they reject legal reasoning and analogy, one can question whether the Wahhabis actually qualify as exponents of the Hanbali legal school in its classical form, with a bone fide juridical method. However, for political legitimacy and to claim leadership of the wider Sunni world, the Wahhabi kingdom emphasizes that it administers Hanbali law.

The Hanbali school became highly influential in the later twentieth century when it was exported in Wahhabi form funded by oil profits. It was adopted by fundamentalist regimes in Pakistan (under General Zia ul-Haqq) and Afghanistan (under the Taliban), which have been overtly influenced by Hanbali dogma despite ruling in a traditionally Hanafi region. Hanbalis follow Shafiʿi juridical positions in regard to anal intercourse between men, though they dismiss legal reasoning by analogy and advocate capital punishment as a "literal" reading of the Qur'an.[56] All these states argue that homosexual men are exclusively characterized by anal sex, which they claim is a crime with a *hadd* penalty. It is unclear whether any of these contemporary states actually apply the legal conditions that limit *hadd* cases, such as observation of the actual act of penetration by four adult male witnesses.

Intellectuals of the Salafi movement, who are also influenced by Hanbali thinking in its Wahhabi form, are much more influential than revolutionary fundamentalists like the Taliban. Though they maintain classical jurists' obsessive focus on anal intercourse in same-sex male couples, they show their modern ideological engagement by also attacking lesbian couplings. Whereas classical jurists tended to ignore same-sex female sexual activity or equate it with masturbation, modern Salafis influenced by Hanbali thinking equate female homosexual acts with male homosexual acts in innovative ways, though disguised as traditional "literal" interpretations of Qur'an and hadith.

Salafi intellectuals took leading roles in the Arab cultural renaissance of the early twentieth century. Pressure to justify their rulings by the Qur'an led to innovations among the Salafis, especially in regard to lesbian sex acts. There is no opportunity here for a full exposition of how the Hanbali school was usurped by the early modern Wahhabi movement, which then exerted influence upon modern Islamic fundamentalists, Salafi intellectuals, and neo-traditionalists. Such an analysis would certainly highlight Rashid Rida (1865–1935).[57] In his legalist Qur'an commentary *Tafsir al-Manar*, he asserted that the verse *for any two from among you who commit it [the immorality]* (Q. 4:15–16) refers to same-sex male and also same-sex female sexual intercourse and prohibits them both.[58] The ambiguities of this verse were discussed in Chapter 2. But Rida sees no ambiguity in it at all, despite classical and medieval jurists' offering contradictory opinions of its meaning. Rida writes that "the immorality" in the second verse means in particular sodomy, which is the sexual enjoyment of a man with a man; he specifies that "the immorality" in the verse before it refers to tribadism (*sihaq*), the sexual enjoyment of a woman with a woman.[59] He presents this novel interpretation as a "literal reading" of the verse. This is a hallmark of Wahhabi and Salafi thinking, which denies the role of human reason and imagination in interpreting scripture, which they feel must be read literally and merely implemented.

The Wahhabi movement's politicization of the Hanbali school had a great impact on fundamentalist ideologues like Sayyid Qutb in Egypt (1906–66).[60] His obsession with sexual purity became interwoven with his ideological interpretation of Islam and his militant rejection of secular societies (even Muslim-majority states with secular governments) as anti-Islamic systems.[61] His Islamist manifesto, *Milestones*, and his non-traditional interpretation of scripture, *In the Shade of the Qur'an*, were hugely influential. Qutb is a theoretical foundation of Islamic extremism, which finds its most forceful followers among Wahhabis and allied groups who declare all those who do not follow their ideological version of Islam to be non-Muslims, apostates, and therefore liable to be killed.[62] Qutb's writings in turn radicalized many within the Saudi Kingdom, whose official dogma is Hanbali and which exports its ideals internationally through books, politics, and students.[63]

Qutb and his followers let their rejection of modernity justify making innovations in Islamic interpretation and law. Qutb reads these same two verses (Q. 4:15–16) as commanding an explicit punishment for both same-sex female and same-sex male intercourse. Like Rida, he claims that the first reference to an immorality committed by women is to lesbian sex and that the next reference to an immorality committed by men is sodomy – "then later it chooses a single method of punishment for those women and those men also, and that is the *hadd* punishment for fornication [stoning to death for married adults]."[64] Qutb supports his claim with hadith, many of which discuss heterosexual fornication but which he applies to same-sex intercourse, and he does not mention the ambiguities or doubts in the chain of narrators or meaning of these reports which his sources – Ibn Hanbal and Abu Dawud – certainly did.[65] Such fine points of legal interpretation do not concern Sayyid Qutb. His opposition to secular liberalism and its sexual mores was such that he insisted the Qur'an must address in legal verses the issue of homosexuality.[66] He pictures homosexuality as part of the cultural depravity that Islam comes to purify. In this sense, Qutb and others like him adhere to the Hanbali legal school in only a superficial way as they break ranks with traditional legal thinking and adopt ideological politics.[67]

For Qutb, the most enduring characteristic of the anti-Islamic system is sexual perversion. "The first sign of the anti-Islamic system [*jahiliyya*] in every era – as we see in the present anti-Islamic system that has spread over the whole earth – is sexual chaos [*fawda jinsiyya*] and animalistic libertinism without restraint of ethics or law. This sexual chaos is considered to be an aspect of so-called personal freedom."[68] Sayyid Qutb's interpretation of the Qur'an exercises a pervasive influence over contemporary Muslim fundamentalists and neo-traditionalists. We can even observe his influence over those trained more deeply in Shafi'i law, like Shaykh Qaradawi, as discussed above. This is especially evident in Qutb's charge that homosexuals (Muslims and others) pervert the original human nature (*fitra*) created by God, rather than simply trespass beyond the bounds of proper behavior set by God and the Prophet. Qutb and those who share his mentality exercise a deep influence over Muslim minority communities in the West. The innovations disguised as literal readings of scripture advanced by Wahhabis and Salafis like Rida and Qutb have grave implications for lesbian, gay, and transgender Muslims.

Law as Reasonable Analysis: The Hanafi Approach

In the early Maliki school, male-to-male sexual intercourse was deemed a *hadd* crime whose punishment was harsher than that for heterosexual fornication. In the Shafi'i school and the traditional Hanbali school, it was considered a *hadd* crime whose punishment was exactly equal to that for heterosexual fornication, because the underlying rationale (*'illa*) was evaluated to be the same – sexual enjoyment by penetration with a partner who is not a legal spouse. However, not all early jurists agreed with these two positions. Imam Abu Hanifa (died 765) met Imam Malik but disagreed with him on fundamental issues of methodology and decision-making. Abu Hanifa did not consider same-sex anal intercourse to be equivalent to heterosexual fornication, and saw it as much less serious than that *hadd* crime. His followers in the Hanafi school of law were more open to the use of reason to determine the conditions of the problem and more restrained about extending the harsh and non-amendable punishment of a *hadd* crime. They upheld the importance of a hadith attributed to the Prophet which depicts him as saying, "Whoever applies a *hadd* [penalty] to an occasion that is not a *hadd* [crime] has transgressed the rights of others and committed injustice."[69]

Hanafi jurists held that *hadd* penalties are, by definition, those penalties described explicitly by the Qur'an itself, and jurists should not exercise legal reasoning and analogy in cases of *hadd* penalties. Influenced by al-Shafi'i, other jurists resorted to legal reasoning and analogy to argue that male-to-male anal penetration was like a *hadd* crime, since the language of the Qur'an is not explicit and exact in this case. Hanafi jurists differed with them and argued that anal sex between men could not justifiably be considered a *hadd* crime. "The punishment for adultery [*zina'*] is known [from the Qur'an explicitly]. Since this act [male-to-male anal penetration] is known to be different [in nature] from adultery, if should not be treated as a *hadd* crime equivalent to adultery ... This act is a kind of sexual intercourse in a bodily opening that has no relation to legal marriage and does not necessitate giving a dowry or determining parentage [as adultery does]. Therefore it has no relation to the *hadd* punishment for adultery."[70] Hanafi jurists accused other legal schools of applying a *hadd* penalty for an act that was not defined in the Qur'an as one, thereby committing a grave injustice.

In Hanafi analysis, same-sex acts are qualitatively different from illegal heterosexual acts that are related to marriage and procreation. Jurists determined that an Islamic marriage contract is only valid after the husband's penis penetrates the wife's vulva, thus anatomically sealing the contract with a bodily "offer and acceptance." In the view of Hanafi jurists, same-sex intercourse involves no penis-to-vulva penetration that can validate a marriage contract and no anatomical interaction that can possibly lead to procreation and legitimate offspring; it therefore falls into a different category of acts and cannot be compared to heterosexual penetrative intercourse. If the comparison is not valid, then the conclusion that it is equivalent to adultery (*zina'*) is also not valid and therefore the application of a *hadd* punishment of stoning to death or any other kind of execution is unjust. Same-sex penetrative intercourse should not be defined as "either marriage or fornication" as heterosexual intercourse is. Rather, it occupies an ambiguous "other" category. Hanafis hold that the punishment for same-sex intercourse, if done in public so that it causes a disturbance, is defined as *ta'zir* – its punishment should be set by the ruling authority in a form not to exceed what the Prophet stipulated for discretionary punishments (namely, a punishment not harsher than ten lashes in public). But it should never be punished with the *hadd* penalty as for heterosexual fornication.

In his commentary on the Qur'an, the Hanafi jurist Ahmad al-Jassas (died 981) addresses this issue. He argues that the Qur'an specifies a *hadd* punishment of death by stoning for adultery or fornication between a man and a woman. The punishment applies only to heterosexual fornication and not to anal sex between men or other types of sexual acts. He argues this position based on reason and logic, but also supports it with reference to a hadith attributed to the Prophet: "The blood of a Muslim is not liable to be shed, except in these three cases: adultery after marriage, infidelity after adopting Islam, and murdering an innocent person."[71] Al-Jassas acknowledges that certain hadith were in circulation, attributed to the Prophet Muhammad, that men found "doing the act of the people of Lot" should be killed. However, he notes that these reports have weak chains of transmission containing unreliable transmitters and therefore cannot form the basis for a juridical decision to put a Muslim to death.[72]

The Hanafi jurists mounted a strong case against the Malikis, Shafi'is, and Hanbalis (and also, implicitly, the Shi'a of the Ja'fari legal school) who all urged capital punishment by stoning to death for mature men who engaged in penetrative intercourse. In the Hanafi view, same-sex intercourse was a sin but not a major crime against God or a threat to the purity of the Muslim community. It necessitated disciplinary punishment but not execution. The Hanafi argument was persuasive to a huge expanse of the Muslim world, accounting for approximately forty-five percent of the world's Muslim population.[73]

Law as Critical Reassessment: The Zahiri Approach

As we review the opinions and approaches of the different Sunni schools of law, we can observe that clearly there was a hot argument among classical jurists on the issue of homosexual intercourse among men. There was no actual consensus on the nature of the act, the status of punishment for it, or the relation of punishment to the words of the Qur'an. Maliki jurists differed from Shafi'is in their method though both affirmed capital punishment. Hanafi jurists dissented from Maliki and Shafi'i decisions and affirmed a legal method based more on reason and less on custom or reports, which they found unreliable. Hanbalis reaffirmed capital punishment based upon hadith and attacked jurists who used reason to arrive at decisions. These disagreements often resulted in heated argument and sometimes degenerated into violence as jurists championed their legal school against others. The Hanbalis reverted to the mob to enforce ideas of orthodoxy. As riots based on legal school partisanship rocked Baghdad, some jurists dissented. Under the leadership of Dawud ibn Khalaf al-Zahiri (died 833–34) and his son, Muhammad ibn Dawud (died 909), they formed a new legal school. They claimed that their Zahiri legal school was based upon a method that could unite all jurists and overcome these disagreements.

Dawud al-Zahiri was deeply disturbed by the divergence of opinion of legal schools and the partisanship by which they coerced Muslims to follow their lead (*taqlid*). He argued that this was because their legal methodology was faulty. They ignored the apparent sense of the Qur'an and delved after hidden meanings that they claimed to extract by analogy or reason. They relied on hadith that were contentious or faulty and were led astray from the few reliable *mutawatir* reports about the Prophet. Al-Zahiri argued that believers should be Muslims first, before being Hanafis, Malikis, Shafi'is, or Hanbalis. They should adhere firmly to the apparent sense (*zahir*) of the Qur'an which was clear to anyone who knew Arabic, abiding by only those elements of *sunna* or Prophetic example which were confirmed as reliable by *mutawatir* narrative.[74]

Zahiris advocated zealous adherence to the minimum that is certain, without intricate analogies in order to "discern" rulings that covered ambiguous situations. In this sense, they were against the free use of reason, as were the Hanbalis. However, the Zahiris coupled this adherence to the literal sense of scripture and Prophetic example with optimistic trust that God revealed enough in clear language to practice Islam, and left everything else open to human negotiation. If a matter were not resolved by clear wording in scripture and prophetic example, then God intended it to be open to human reason and social evolution in the most liberal sense. The Zahiris were paradoxically "liberal literalists." They upheld the principle that everything not explicitly forbidden by a clear and authoritative text is allowed (*mubah*). In Ibn Hazm's words: "We know with absolute certainty that everything is originally allowed according to God's speech – *God has created for you everything in the entire earth* (Q. 2:29). Upon this foundation, everything is originally permitted [*halal*] until God reveals that it is forbidden [*haram*], for God says, *God has made plain to you what God has forbidden you* (Q. 6:119)."[75] Therefore Zahiris like Ibn Hazm resisted the effort of jurists from other legal schools to use analogical reasoning (*qiyas*) to "extend" God's commands from situations clearly described by the Qur'an and hadith to situations that were more ambiguously related.

The principles of Ibn Hazm and other Zahiri jurists are more valuable than their distinctive rulings. They upheld *ijtihad* as an individual responsibility and a devotional requirement. The Zahiris rejected imitation of one's parents, community elders, or exemplary jurists as sufficient grounds for Islamic behavior, and encouraged continual return to the scriptural sources (*usul*). They took a courageous stand against the authority of hadith, recognizing that many of them were mere hearsay. For example, Ibn Hazm rejected any hadith with single narration (*ahad*) as unreliable, even if attributed to the Prophet; such reports could not lead to certainty and should not be allowed to compete with Qur'anic verses that had explicit meaning or a hadith that had multiple and mutually confirming chains of narration (*mutawatir*). This severely limited the scope of legal decision-making and challenged the theoretical system set up by Imam al-Shafi'i. The Zahris charged that jurists could not claim to "discern" God's will but only to "clarify" it through reference to the literal meaning of explicit sacred texts, but such strictness in interpretation left wide areas open for social change and cultural negotiation.

How did Zahiri jurists evaluate homosexual acts? Ibn Hazm believed that homosexual intercourse (defined as anal penetration between two men) is a forbidden act, but he totally disagreed with other Muslim jurists about the reason behind this or the rationale for its penalties. He asserts that punishment for homosexual acts is not based upon the Qur'an, refuting those jurists who argue that execution by burning or stoning is the command of the Qur'an, based upon the story of Lot. Rather, he argues, the Tribe of Lot was punished by God "not for their abomination alone but also for their unbelief [*kufr*]."[76] He concludes that perpetrators of sodomy should not be executed or punished with the *hadd* for adultery (which is stoning for a married person or lashing for an unmarried person), for neither the Qur'an nor the Prophet makes this obligatory. In Ibn Hazm's view, the status of one who commits sodomy "is that of someone who had committed a forbidden act [*munkar*] and the Messenger of God has ordered that such people be subjected to correction in addition to the *ta'zir* punishment." This punishment he specifies as no more than ten lashes, based on the Prophet's example for other *ta'zir* misdeeds.[77] He supports his view with a verse of the Qur'an which describes the servants of the merciful One as those *who do not call upon another deity besides God and do not kill another person, which God has forbidden except for one who justly deserves it, and who do not commit adultery, for the one who does this will get the consequence of sin* (Q. 25:68). Ibn Hazm specifies that the Prophet forbade killing except in cases of heterosexual adultery after marriage (*zina'*), disbelief after belief (*irtidad*), and homicide (*qatl*). Homosexual intercourse was not mentioned by name in this list of capital offenses, so it should not be included with them.

Ibn Hazm asserts that the Qur'an does not stipulate execution for sodomy, in contradiction to the rulings of other legal schools. But he does believe that it describes "the act of the Tribe of Lot" as sodomy or anal penetrative sex between men. If Ibn Hazm had perceived an alternative interpretation of the Qur'anic narrative of Lot which emphasizes that his Tribe's crime was rape rather than consensual intercourse between men, then his decision that this sexual act constitutes a crime would also change. This is because he bases that judgment solely upon the Qur'an while dismissing hadith that discuss the act of the Tribe of Lot as weak or fabricated. Ibn Hazm's detailed and boldly critical discussion of homosexuality in his legal text *al-Muhalla* raises the vital question of whether there ever was juridical consensus (*ijma'*) on the issue.[78]

Ibn Hazm is one of the few Muslim jurists to give deep consideration to same-sex acts between women and to ask by what rationale they are comparable to anal intercourse between men. He is highly critical of Maliki jurists who execute men for same-sex intercourse but stipulate one hundred lashes for women's same-sex intercourse. He argues that this difference goes against logic, for those who apply stoning for male-to-male intercourse should do the same for female-to-female intercourse, as "they are both cases of genital contact in a way that is not allowed."[79] He charges the Maliki jurists with ignoring the demands of analogical reasoning and basing their decision simply on the statements of Ibn Shihab al-Zuhri, the jurist who taught Imam Malik. Ibn Hazm refutes them by arguing, "One must not follow the words of anyone except the messenger of God. Now, neither *sahq* [genital rubbing between two women] nor *raf'a* [a woman's 'mounting' another] constitute *zina* [heterosexual penis–vulva penetration with an illegal partner]. If neither of them is a form of *zina* then the *hadd* punishment for *zina* does not apply to them. It is not for anyone to distinguish between more and less serious acts according to his personal opinion."[80] Again in the case of same-sex acts among women, Ibn Hazm does not simply break a consensus that obtained among prior jurists, but demonstrates forcefully that consensus never really existed among jurists as a whole.

Because previous discussions have focused more upon sodomy among men, it is instructive to quote here the detailed argument Ibn Hazm offers about same-sex acts among women. In *al-Muhalla*, he writes,

> The jurists have differed about two women's sexual rubbing [*sihaq*]. One group has said each of the women is to be lashed with one hundred stripes; this has been said by Humam (related from Ibn Mufarraj from Ibn al-A'rabi from al-Dubari from 'Abd al-Razzaq from Ibn Jurayj) who reported that Ibn Shihab [al-Zuhri] said, "I know that our learned scholars say that when a woman does it with another woman from above or anything similar, both women should be lashed with a hundred stripes, both the one who does it and the one it is done to [*al-fa'ila wa'l-maf'ul bi-ha*]." A similar command was transmitted by 'Abd al-Razzaq from Ma'mar from Ibn Shihab. Another group permitted this for women; as transmitted by Humam (from Ibn Mufarraj from Ibn al-A'rabi from al-Dubari from 'Abd al-Razzaq from Ibn Jurayj) who reported that "Someone who is trustworthy said that al-Hasan

al-Basri did not see anything wrong with any action of a woman which kept her away from adultery [*zina'*]." Yet others have said it [sexual rubbing of two women] is forbidden but does not constitute a definitive crime [*hadd*] but is rather punished by discretionary punishment [*ta'zir*]. Ibn Hazm says, "Because people of knowledge have differed about this ruling as we have mentioned above, it is incumbent upon us to examine the issue closely. We have examined the statement of [Ibn Shihab] al-Zuhri and have not found in it any definitive proof except that somebody said so, just has he asserted that the act of the Tribe of Lot is worse than heterosexual fornication [*zina'*] and ruled for it a punishment more onerous than the scripturally mandated punishment [*hadd*] for heterosexual fornication; by the same logic he says this [two women's sexual rubbing] is less than heterosexual fornicaton and has ruled for it a punishment less than the scripturally mandated punishment for heterosexual fornication." [Ibn Hazm] says, "This legal analogy is obligatory upon those who have ruled that stoning is the punishment for those who do act of the Tribe of Lot [sodomy] because [of their reasoning] that it is worse than heterosexual fornication. They cannot get out of this analogy at all. They must be consistent and conclude that same-sex female intercourse is also worse than heterosexual fornication, just as [they claim about] the act of the Tribe of Lot [sodomy or same-sex male intercourse]. They are obliged by consistent logic to order stoning to death [for same-sex female intercourse] just as they order stoning for the act of the Tribe of Lot. This is required of them, since both acts are logically equal: they both involve relinquishing the sexual orifice [*farj*] to one who is not legally entitled to it in any way. But the jurists do not make legal analogies justly and do not know how to draw proof from sources [*istidlal*]; they do not fully examine their statements from all sides, do not follow fully their own analogical reasoning and do not make their statements dependent fully on authoritative sources [*nusus*]. In this matter, they related only what [Ibn Shihab] al-Zuhri said, without relating the authority of those before him from the companions of the Prophet or the greatest followers! One can only make this ruling by what is related from these [earliest] sources. We do not know anyone who can contradict this from among those who hold this opinion. They claim that this act is forbidden by their word, as they cite the earliest authorities when it accords with their already established opinion ... As for us, we [Ibn Hazm and his followers among the Zahiris] believe that such analogy is null and void. We are not obliged to follow the opinion of anyone but the Messenger of God. Therefore, women's sexual rubbing [*sihaq*] and mounting [*raf'a*] is not heterosexual fornication [*zina'*]. Since it is not heterosexual fornication, then the two who commit it are not to be punished with the proscribed

> punishment for fornication [*hadd al-zina'*]. There is nobody with the authority to say that it is greater or lesser according to his own opinion and adjust the proscribed punishments [*hudud*] according to such subjective assessments. One cannot adjust these to suit one's whim, but is rather constrained by the punishments bounded by God. To do otherwise would be to make rulings obligatory in religion which are not allowed by God, who says *[These are the limits of God] and those who go beyond the limits of God do injustice to their own souls* (Q. 65:1). Indeed, [this warning of God] applies to those who know this absolutely definitive proof but still persist in their errors out of mere partisanship for advocating blind following of their legal school. It is clear that the Qur'an says nothing like what [Ibn Shihab] al-Zuhri asserts, and neither does any authentic report of the Prophet [*sunna sahiha*] ... so there is no proscribed punishment for this act at all, and God alone gives success. Someone might cite the report recorded by Ahmad [ibn Hanbal] ... that the Prophet said, "Same-sex female rubbing [*sihaq*] is the fornication [*zina'*] of women amongst themselves," but this report is not genuinely applicable.[81] It is narrated on the authority of Baqiya [ibn al-Walid] and Baqiya is weak in narration [*da'if*]. Another person in the chain of narration, Makhul, is an unknown personality. The founding person in this chain of narration is Walitha [ibn al-Asqa'] after whom some narrators are missing before it is attributed to the Prophet. Even if it were genuine, there is nothing in it that commands the application of the proscribed penalty [*hadd*] for fornication, for the Prophet defined what constitutes fornication requiring the proscribed penalty in a hadith report about al-Aslami: in it he defined adultery as a man's penetration of a woman who is forbidden to him and has not been recognized as permitted to him by his community ... So it is true that there is only fornication between a man and woman with the act of penetration, which is the male penis [*dhakar*] inserted in the female vulva [*farj*] through which children are birthed, and nothing other than this.[82]

Ibn Hazm does not try to ban homosexual intercourse through a comparison to heterosexual fornication and adultery, a strategy he thinks is flawed both intellectually and morally. Rather, Ibn Hazm says that homosexual penetrative intercourse is illegal because of a Qur'anic verse that says, *Successful are the believers ... who guard their genital openings [*furuj*], except before their spouses or those whom their right hands possess, for they are surely not held to blame; but those who seek to go beyond that are surely exceeding the limits* (Q. 23:1–7). Based on this verse, Ibn Hazm argues that women should guard their sexual opening (vulva and vagina) and not let anything enter that is not sexual penetration by her spouse (or material to absorb menstrual bleeding, which is allowed). According to him, anything other than this is rebellion (*ma'siya*) against the limits set by God. "Since it is established that a woman engaging in sexual rubbing with another woman [which involves penetration of her genitalia in a way analogous to penile penetration in heterosexual coupling] is rebelling, so she is guilty of a reprehensible action [*munkir*] and so it is obligatory to change her behavior by force ... and she is liable to discretionary punishment [*ta'zir*]."[83]

However, Ibn Hazm is able to nuance his decision based on a realistic assessment of the ambiguities of what might constitute "penetration." In the mind of a male jurist, discussion of same-sex acts among women blurs inevitably into a discussion of masturbation, since such acts are more difficult to define as penetrative sexual acts than are same-sex acts between two men. Ibn Hazm rules that,

> If a woman presents to her genitalia anything that does not reach the point of penetrating into it, this is discouraged but does not constitute any sin [*ithm*]. This is also the ruling on masturbation, which is equivalent to that of men. A man's touching his penis with his left hand is allowed [*mubah*] and a woman's touching her genitals is just the same – allowed – by consensus of all authorities in the Muslim community. There is nothing in this phenomenon [of masturbation] more than what is permitted [touching the genitals], except the further intention to experience orgasm and ejaculate, and that is not forbidden in itself. This is true because God has said, *God has made plain to you what God has forbidden you* (Q. 6:119), and there is nothing involved here that God has explicitly forbidden. Therefore it is permitted, according to God's saying, *God has created for you everything in the entire earth* (Q. 2:29). However, we disapprove of this act, because it does not express the most noble of ethical virtues or most exemplary conduct. Jurists have discussed this issue [masturbation] and one group has declared it disapproved and another group declared it allowed ... [It is reported that] a man said to Ibn 'Abbas, "I play with my penis until I ejaculate" to which he [Ibn 'Abbas] said, "Awful! Community-approved marriage is better than this, but this is better than adulterous fornication."[84]

Ibn Hazm then considers the possibility of a woman playing with her fingers in the genitalia of another woman. He concludes that there are no reports about this from the Prophet, but there are reports from followers of the Prophet which state that a woman who inserts her fingers into the genitalia of another women must pay her an amount equal to the dowry (*sadaq*), implying that this action deflowers her and therefore demands compensation. There are reports about a boy who inserted his fingers into a girl's genitalia and had to pay a fee equivalent to her dowry in compensation. The issue here is about breaking her hymen and ruining evidence of her virginity, thereby lessening her value for heterosexual marriage. The issue is not discussed in terms of homosexual desire or pleasure.[85]

But Ibn Hazm contests any ruling based upon these reports. "It is not permissible to judge that one must give the other dowry because this interaction has nothing to do with marriage and dowry has no meaning outside a contract of marriage. There is no authoritative text in the Qur'an and no consensus among the Prophet's companions about dowry payment being obligatory to any except one engaged in a marriage contract. So regardless of whether it is a man or woman who inserts fingers [into a woman's genitalia], there is no penalty incumbent upon him or her in any way, since God has not placed upon us obligation for any fee nor has God's messenger."[86] Again, Ibn Hazm argues that any man or women who inserts fingers into another woman's genitalia, or inserts any other object there, has done a reprehensible act but not one that is regulated by explicit ruling of the Qur'an and the Prophet's example; therefore their behavior should be changed and they are liable to penalization by discretionary punishment (*ta'zir*). "Nobody that we know of says that any action like this equals [heterosexual] adultery or necessitates any proscribed punishment from among those explicitly called for by God [*hudud*]. This action is like any other action that does not necessitate a proscribed punishment because no explicit scriptural or prophetic order [*nass*] that is authentic and reliable refers to it. With God is all success."[87]

Ibn Hazm is important not just for his innovative legal rulings on discrete issues. He might be right or wrong just like any other *mujtahid* – or one qualified for creative reasoning about religious and legal issues. Ibn Hazm accepted that the Qur'an depicts Lot chastising his community for male-to-male intercourse, but he did not see Lot's admonition as a legal ruling for the Muslim community. He disagreed with other jurists about what kind of punishment should be applied in cases of homosexual penetrative intercourse, just as he differs from them in his legal theory about how to justify punishment. Moreover, in regulating female-to-female intercourse, he appealed to more general verses about sex being permissible only with a partner with whom one shares a contractual relationship. His arguments are subtle and can teach us much about how contested were hadith and how varied the opinions of the early generations of Muslims. However, Ibn Hazm's arguments are important for another deeper reason. He shows that there was no consensus among Muslim jurists about same-sex acts between two men or between two women. If there was no consensus in the tenth century when Ibn Hazm lived, there is surely no consensus in the present day, and therefore the issues under discussion are open to scrutiny and revision.

The Jurists' Consensus or *Ijma'*: Absolute or Conditional Authority?

According to Islamic legal theory, there are four sources of law that shape the *shari'a*. They are the Qur'an, the hadith of the Prophet, the operations of legal reasoning, and the consensus of the jurists. We have seen above how the first three sources are agreed upon in theory but defined differently in practice by each legal school. The final source – consensus of the jurists – is the most difficult to define. It exists as a weighty authority in theory although there is no institution to enforce it, for Muslims have no Papacy as Catholics have or church councils as Protestants have. Definition of what constitutes consensus differs widely among different legal schools: in terms of the number of jurists, in what generation, and exercising what authority.

In Ibn Hazm's legal method, the only consensus that carried weight was the consensus of all the companions of the Prophet. If they all agreed to a matter, it was binding upon all Muslims, but if they did not agree, their opinions were not binding. The consensus of jurists in later generations, after the legal schools were established, was not binding on Muslims at all. The decisions of the founders of legal schools or consensus of their followers were not a source of binding authority in the view of Ibn Hazm and the Zahiri legal school. The jurists offered opinions that could be criticized, and it was the duty of all Muslims with knowledge to critique and assess such opinions. *Ijtihad* was not an option but a religious duty, and Ibn Hazm engaged in it with a passion that led him to be ostracized, attacked, and exiled by his juridical and political opponents.

This position was highly controversial, and Ibn Hazm wrote a whole book to assess on what points there was binding consensus: *Levels of Consensus* (*Maratib al-Ijma'*). He defines legally binding consensus in this way:

> We have found consensus to be of two kinds ... One kind of consensus covers issues upon which all scholars agree that they are obligatory or forbidden or permitted – that is, neither obligatory nor forbidden – and thus we call this type consensus of necessary belief [*al-ijma' al-lazim*]. The other kind of consensus covers those acts upon which all scholars agree that anyone who commits them or avoids them should be punished – for doing it or refraining from doing it – and thus we call this type consensus on reward-or-punishment [*al-ijma' al-jazi*] ... Between these two extremes [upon which there is total consensus] there are many issues that some scholars say are forbidden while others say they are not forbidden but rather permitted. About these issues some scholars say they are obligatory while others say these are

> not obligatory but rather permitted; some scholars judge such issues as disapproved while other scholars say they are to be encouraged. It is impossible to arrive at real consensus about such issues in legal matters and ritual norms. No consensus is possible about them as a class nor about them as individual issues ... [The only real consensus] is a true opinion established by proof of scriptural text [*burhan sam'i*] or by proof of reason [*burhan 'aqli*]. If these two conditions are met by all types of research and investigation which agree in comprehensiveness and trustworthiness and soundness, only then does it constitute a consensus of the real jurists about a particular issue which is real consensus, to which one can refer and take as a guide in disagreements ... These are the several dimensions of legally binding consensus. Other than this, there is no other consensus and without such proof no statement of consensus is ever valid ... and all other opinions about consensus are corrupt![88]

Ibn Hazm insists that Muslim jurists have not even come to consensus about the definition and extent of the concept of consensus itself. It is not surprising, then, that jurists differ over individual issues, including homosexual acts.

For Ibn Hazm, the best definition of consensus is that which is narrowest and upon which all Muslims can agree, as he explains in the passage above. When he applies that definition to the issue of same-sex acts, he sums up the extant consensus of the jurists quite concisely, with the strongest binding decision signified by "they come to consensus [*ajma'u*]" and the less binding accord signaled by "they agree [*ittafiqu*]."[89] Ibn Hazm writes, "The jurists all agree that a mature man penetrating another man [*wat' al-rajal al-rajal*] is a crime. They all agree that a woman rubbing another woman [*sahq al-mar'a li'l-mar'a*] is forbidden [if it involves genital penetration]. They differ over the issue of sexual pleasure by cleaving together [*lizq*] or manipulation with the hand [*istimna'*], differing over whether it is forbidden or discouraged or permitted and under which conditions.[90] They differ over what punishment is required for one who penetrates in anal intercourse [*luti*], for one who sexually penetrates an animal [*wati' al-bahima*], for one who is penetrated [*mankuh*] and also for the animal that is penetrated; on these issues they disagree in such a way that there is no possibility of consensus on punishment [*ijma' jazi*] or on the form of punishment."[91] In Ibn Hazm's evaluation, very little comes under the rule of consensus and much falls in the zone of ambiguity and is therefore open to debate.

The consensus that Ibn Hazm sees is based primarily upon the Qur'an. In this view, sodomy is criminal because of the story of Lot, and tribadism is criminal because a woman must not have penetrative sex with anyone but her contractual spouse. Only secondarily is it based upon the Prophet's example, because Ibn

Hazm rejects most hadith about the subject as unreliable (weak in narration or patently fabricated). He relies only on reports about bathing, seeing or touching others who are naked, or about men who behave like women. He sums up his position when assessing the consensus about marriage: "The jurists have all agreed that is it forbidden for a man to sexually penetrate anyone other than his spouse or slave who are licit for him."[92] Ibn Hazm is explicit about the issue of consensus which most jurists would like to keep implicit; jurists of other schools would like to keep *ijma'* as a rhetorical authority rather than as an honest assessment of their actual differences. Ibn Hazm is honest about the severe limitations of consensus because he is critical of the jurists of other legal schools, even as he maintains respect for the founders of the schools. This is because he feels that the legal schools discourage *ijtihad*, or independent legal reasoning, whereas the founders of each school depended upon it and encouraged it.

In his book on legal decisions, *al-Muhalla*, Ibn Hazm includes decisions from the three earliest founders of the Sunni schools: the Imams Malik, Abu Hanifa, and al-Shafi'i and more rarely Ahmad ibn Hanbal. Ibn Hazm said, "Abu Hanifa, Malik and Ahmad [ibn Hanbal] advised their followers not to imitate them blindly, and al-Shafi'i was even stronger than the others in forbidding his followers to follow him blindly. Al-Shafi'i, may God have mercy on him, was most eloquent in affirming that one should follow only the most authentic of traditions and adhere only to what is proved by them of necessity ... and keep clear of following the decisions of others even if they are a majority. He said so openly, may God let us benefit by his example and grant him ample reward! For his example is the cause of much good."[93] After Ibn Hazm's death in exile, the Zahiri legal school that he championed faded away. Although his legal method (along with that of prior Zahiri jurists in Iraq) is well preserved in his many books, he had few followers to carry his decisions into practice.

Ibn Hazm's writings are left to us as silent testimony to the possibility of alternatives that were ignored by the majority of Muslims, possibilities that may still be open for us to build upon if we take up Ibn Hazm's courageous example. The scholar Camilla Adang studied in depth three issues of Ibn Hazm's source-critical approach – to same-sex acts, women's access to public space, and the position of non-Muslims under Islamic rule – and concluded that Ibn Hazm's legal methodology led him to conclusions that differed greatly from Maliki jurists (and other legal schools) in ways that seem "liberal" to modern observers.[94]

How did jurists from other legal schools react to Ibn Hazm's bold critique of their methods and his assertion that there is no consensus about punishment for same-sex acts? Although the Maliki legal method prevailed in Andalusia and North Africa, Maliki jurists continued to argue with Ibn Hazm even long after his death. They admitted that the Zahiris had challenged their decisions, even as they insisted their decisions carried binding consensus that gave them executive force. For instance, the eminent scholar of Cordoba Muhammad ibn Ahmad al-Qurtubi (died 1273) was a Maliki jurist who lived approximately two centuries after Ibn Hazm. He wrote a commentary on the Qur'an to justify Maliki decisions in reference to scripture, which is proof that Zahiri critiques and competition from the Shafi'i school of law had an impact upon Maliki jurists. Al-Qurtubi's concern was not to give a semantic or thematic analysis of Qur'anic discourse, as this book has strived to do in Chapter 2. As a jurist, he was concerned with acts rather than intentions. In al-Qurtubi's commentary on the Qur'an, he argued that anal sex between men was a *hadd* crime requiring capital punishment, even if this is not explicitly stated in the Qur'an, since this act is the legal equivalent of *zina*.

To make this argument, al-Qurtubi lines up a series of assertions, all of which are open to question. In the Qur'an, Lot says to his community, *Do you approach the immorality [*a ta'tuna al-fahisha*]?* In the commentary on this verse, al-Qurtubi gives a classic example of interpretation by substitution. He is unconcerned with the semantic range of the term *fahisha* or whether it is related to wider themes. Rather, he defines the word *fahisha* in juridical terms, by substituting it with a phrase that is explicit. "*Do you approach the immorality* means 'sexually entering males' [*idkhal al-rijal*]. God mentions this act with the term *the immorality* in order to make it clear that this act is adultery [*zina'*]. It is just like God's statement in another verse, *Do not approach adultery* [zina'] *for it is an immorality* (Q. 7:80–84)."[95] In the Shafi'i legal school, the *hadd* punishment for adultery is either lashing (if the person is unmarried) or stoning to death (if the person is already married). This is the punishment that al-Qurtubi argues should apply to men who have anal sex with a man. By offering a definition (substituting "entering males" for "transgression") and an analogy (sexual penetration of an unmarried man by a man is equal to sexual penetration of an unmarried woman by a man), al-Qurtubi argues that this juridical decision is in reality nothing but a simple "reading" of the Qur'an.

Al-Qurtubi ignores the fact that the Qur'an often uses the term "immoralities" (*fawahish*) in the plural in the narrative sections about Lot. This suggests that "immorality" is a general category including many different specific kinds of acts; one could speak of a particular immorality by specifying an act or one could speak of immorality in general to imply a whole range of acts that transgress the boundary of decency, righteousness, or legality. Not every term mentioned as "immorality" would be equivalent, morally or legally or punitively. One would have to ignore grammar and narrative context to draw the one-for-one equivalence that al-Qurtubi has done.

Nonetheless, al-Qurtubi insists that he knows God's intention in using particular terms. But he cannot deny that other jurists have read the same passage and come to different conclusions. He admits, "Jurists have differed amongst themselves over the exact punishment for this [anal sex between men] after they have come to consensus on forbidding it."[96] Early Maliki jurists insist that anal sex between men is a *hadd* crime punishable by death, whereas Shafi'i and Hanbali jurists nuance this by arguing that it is equivalent to heterosexual adultery and therefore constitutes a *hadd* crime. This contradicts the Hanafi and Zahiri jurists, who argue that although it is an immoral act it does not qualify as a *hadd* crime. Jurists from both these schools insist that there should be no execution and rather allow that government authorities can punish the act as they think suitable (up to but not exceeding ten lashes in public). Al-Qurtubi quotes Imam Malik, for whom two contradictory judgments have been recorded: one says, "He should be stoned [to death] whether he is married or unmarried," and the other says, "He should be stoned if he is married and disciplined if he is unmarried." The second opinion clearly parallels the Shafi'i decisions about male-to-male intercourse, and this is the one that al-Qurtubi upholds.

Jurists like al-Qurtubi faced opposition from commentators who read the Qur'an as a narrative of ethical exhortation rather than as a legal text, as well as from other jurists who argued that the Qur'an's narrative about Lot does not provide legal prohibitions for Muslims. When al-Qurtubi argued that the Prophet Lot's conflict with his community was about forbidding anal sex between men and that this justified capital punishment against those men found doing this, he recognized at least two possible objections to his interpretation, both based on ethical readings of the same Qur'anic narrative. The first objection is that "the Tribe of Lot were punished because of their disbelief in God and their calling their Prophet a liar just like the rest of the ancient communities that were destroyed by God." The second objection is that "the young children and old people of Lot's Tribe were included with the mature men in being punished, and that proves that their actions should not be considered a *hadd* crime [for it was not primarily sexual intercourse]."[97] He states that these objections come from an anonymous critic, but in reality it was Ibn Hazm in Cordoba and his Zahiri colleagues who had raised them. Al-Qurtubi states these objections only to dismiss them, but this cannot be construed as indicating consensus among the jurists on the legal status of homosexual acts.

There cannot be any consensus among the jurists when Zahiri and Hanafi legal schools deny that same-sex intercourse is a *hadd* crime calling for capital punishment of any kind. Zahiris point out clearly how previous rulings in Islamic law are not based on explicit commands of the Qur'an or on authentic hadith of the Prophet. Hanafis point out how same-sex intercourse differs in practical consequence from heterosexual intercourse and thereby justify why punishments for same-sex intercourse should be different from the *hadd* penalty for adultery. In both Zahiri and Hanafi analysis, same-sex acts should be punished by *ta'zir* or mild preventation as determined by the ruler.

There is lack of consensus about the issue in the classical tradition of Islamic law, and this leaves open the question of whether homosexual acts are criminal or sinful. As the question is open to new deliberation, we should also introduce into the discussion new facts of research and critical reflections on new social conditions with no precedent in the classical Islamic period. Confronting the lack of meaningful consensus in the past, Muslims face an ethical choice. They can turn away from the challenge and falsely assert that the *shari'a* is univocal, claiming like neo-traditionalists that the *shari'a* condemns with death not only all homosexual acts but also homosexual feelings and those who build an identity upon honest acceptance of them. Or, conversely, Muslims can embrace the challenge with a progressive approach, seeing homosexuality as just one of many phenomena that confront traditional notions in Islam and challenge Muslims to rise above the limitations of their classical tradition and discover ways to make Islam relevant to new possibilities.

Progressive Reform of *Shari'a*

Theoretical justification for progressive reform of *shari'a* has existed for a long time. In tenth-century Andalusia, Ibn Hazm advocated continual *ijtihad* by returning to the fundamental texts of Islam in order to expound more flexible or liberal legal decisions. Many jurists in the Maliki tradition which dominated Andalusia rejected Ibn Hazm's ideas and hardened their opinions, as we saw in al-Qurtub's rulings on homosexual intercourse. However, other Malikis in Andalusia had a more creative response to Ibn Hazm's call for reform of *shari'a*. Abu Ishaq al-Shatibi was a Maliki jurist in Granada (died 1388) whose theory of *shari'a* allows for continual adaptation and change. Though his ideals were largely ignored in the past, they are currently attracting much attention and their potential has not yet been fulfilled.

As al-Shatibi faced the bewildering variety of rulings and conflicting decisions promulgated by the various competing schools of law (as documented by Ibn Hazm), he felt they could be reconciled. He was dismayed by the authoritarian interpretations of each school, which fostered partisan arrogance and pictured the *shari'a* as statically inscribed in scriptural texts. He therefore identified the fundamental principles that the *shari'a* intends to promote. These he called the intended goals (*maqasid*) of the *shari'a* and equated them with wisdom (*hikma*), which the Qur'an says God sends along with the revealed Qur'anic message (*kitab*).

The contemporary legal scholar and practicing jurist Muhammad Khalid Masud calls these principles "the objectives of the law." He explains, "Al-Shatibi concluded that the shari'a law aimed to protect five basic human interests: religion, life, reproduction, property and reason."[98] Shari'a aims to protect these five interests because they are essential to achieve felicity (*sa'ada*), which is both happiness in this world and salvation in the next. Religion (*din*) means the preservation of belief in God, the soul, and moral conduct in Islam (as in other revealed religions). Life (*nafs*) means the preservation of the individual against murder, disease, imprisonment, or other constraints that remove the possibility of thriving. Reason (*'aql*) means preservation of intellect, discernment, and judgment so that moral agents are free from coercion or deprivation to bear responsibility for their decisions. Property (*mal*) means preservation of norms of ownership that are the basis of economic livelihood free from theft, confiscation, and corruption. Finally reproduction (*nasl*) means the preservation of lineage so that parents bear responsibility for their children in maintenance, upbringing, and inheritance.

These five principles address both individual existence and social cohesion. Al-Shatibi professed that they were the essential objectives that Qur'anic revelation and the Prophet's regulations aimed to embody. By articulating these principles, al-Shatibi returned to the essential sources of Islam without getting bogged down in texts and arguments about their authenticity as Ibn Hazm did. Al-Shatibi formulated a philosophy of legal norms rooted in the Prophet's leadership of the early Islamic community but not limited by it. "Al-Shatibi examined the Qur'anic laws by situating them in history. He found them to be closely related to local practices. He distinguished the laws revealed in Medina from those revealed in Mecca. The Meccan verses refer to the universal or basic norms and constitute the objectives of Islamic law. The Medinese verses refer to substantive laws. They are local applications of the Meccan universals in detail ... Islamic law faced serious problems when the jurists overlooked the Meccan universal principles and ignored the inductive method in dealing with new cultures."[99] In al-Shatibi's view, the *shari'a* could flexibly expand and self-critically adapt to new circumstances; jurists could examine particular issues of social concern in the light of these principles to gauge whether particular rulings actively promoted these five essential objectives. If they did, the decisions were just and in accord with God's will, and if not, then particular rulings should be changed to promote better these five objectives and secure human welfare (*maslaha*).

Al-Shatibi's contemporaries attacked him for articulating this wider vision of a flexible *shari'a*. He lamented, "I found myself a stranger among the majority of my contemporaries."[100] But over the long term al-Shatibi was not alone in arguing that the *shari'a* should be assessed according to how well it furthers these essential objectives. In other regions and schools of law, Muslim jurists in the medieval period closely echoed al-Shatibi's formulation. In Egypt, the jurist Ibn Nujaym (died 1563) articulated similar ideas from within the Hanafi school of law and in accord with Sufi ethics. He strived to identify the "universal principles" (*qawa'id kulliya*) that particular decisions of jurists must manifest in order for them to be justly considered an expression of divine will in the *shari'a*. Ibn Nujaym's ideas were central to the Ottoman efforts in the late nineteenth century to simplify, systematize, and modernize the *shari'a*. They felt that the *shari'a* must be reformed to accord with modern issues so that it would not be displaced by European codes of positive law.[101]

There is a rationalist orientation in all these efforts that effectively redefines what it means to "follow the Prophet." For these reformist jurists, following the Prophet means being attentive to justice, social welfare, and human need while preserving basic practices of Islamic worship. In their view, the Qur'an and hadith give indications of a general movement toward justice but do not define the final form that justice should take. Following the Prophet does not mean literally trying to replicate what the Prophet did in Mecca or Medina. This rationalist argument for continual renewal and reform opposed those jurists who reified hadith, argued for imitation of past legal decisions, and argued that "the gate of *ijtihad*" was effectively closed.

Many Muslim reformist scholars in the twentieth century adopted al-Shatibi's insights. Muhammad Abduh and Rashid Rida among others encouraged the study of al-Shatibi's legal philosophy as the key for renewing the *shari'a* in modern conditions. They felt that the *shari'a* authorized operations that could reform it from within when it lost relevance to modern conditions or when its traditional decisions led to injustice or incoherence. We will examine below such operations, like *istislah* (deciding an issue in favor of human welfare) and *istihsan* (abandoning an established decision on an issue in favor of an alternative that gives a more beneficial result) which together can secure human welfare when the *shari'a*'s past norms clash with contemporary needs.

However, Muslims largely ignored these reformist jurists' call for renewal. In the wake of European colonialism, many Muslims trusted secular nationalism to secure their interests. Yet as nationalism increasingly failed in its utopian promises, many turned in desperation to Islamism and religious fundamentalism. In the later twentieth century, modernist reformers made more extreme suggestions. Fazlur Rahman argued that Islamic law should be based upon the spirit of the Qur'an and not limited to its discrete pronouncements that are historically contingent on the early community in Medina. "Whereas the spirit of the Qur'anic legislation exhibits an obvious direction toward the progressive embodiment of the fundamental human values of freedom and responsibility in fresh legislation, nevertheless the actual legislation of the Qur'an had partly to accept the then existing society as a term of reference. This clearly means that the actual legislation of the Qur'an cannot have been meant to be literally eternal by the Qur'an itself."[102] Rahman argues that if Muslims do not reform the legal norms based upon the Medina experiment and update them to meet the needs of modern conditions, then they must confront the possibility that these legal norms were not intended for eternal application and might need to be abandoned.[103]

Even more radical were the reformist ideals of Ustad Mahmoud Taha of Sudan. Echoing Fazlur Rahman, he asserted that the Qur'an contains two types of messages. The first articulates universal ethical principles, rituals of worship, and moral values; these are contained in verses revealed in Mecca, when the Prophet was a religious leader living under persecution. The second type of message contains detailed commands, rules, and laws for establishing a social order as a discrete expression of those universal principles, and these were conveyed in verses revealed in Medina, when the Prophet was the leader of a polity. But jurists who developed the *shari'a* argued that earlier verses are abrogated or nullified (*mansukh*) by later verses or later decisions by the Prophet. In this way, the *shari'a* was an extension of the Medina experiment, the jurists taking over the function of the Prophet as lawgiver to create a social order.

Ustad Mahmoud Taha's radical assertion is that the jurists' notion of abrogation (*naskh*) is backward.[104] He asserts that the earlier verses of the Qur'an are universal and eternal, whereas the later verses (which give concrete rulings on social order, warfare, government, marriage, and gender relations) are particular and contingent. These rules and norms were intended for the early Muslims in Medina, or at most the Islamic state with its capital in Medina. As social conditions change, Taha argues, these verses lose their relevance and authoritativeness, leaving Muslims with the eternal principles and universal values that were first revealed.

A few generations after the Prophet Muhammad's death the Islamic community degenerated into dynastic kingship, with the role of *khalifa* reduced to a mere pawn and empty token of legitimacy. In the early twentieth century even the *khalifa*'s formal vestiges in the Ottoman Empire were abolished. Therefore, Taha concluded, in the modern period there is no authentically Islamic state (even among Muslim-majority countries like his native Sudan). For this reason, Taha asserts that the "second message" of the Qur'an is abrogated, nullified, and invalid, meaning that the *shari'a* as elaborated by medieval jurists is no longer authoritative. Muslims are providentially free to create nation states that are democratic republics. This endeavor returns them effectively to the universal principles of the original revelation, which preached individual accountability, moral responsibility, and absolute egalitarianism. According to Taha, Muslims can order their society in any way that best expresses these eternal principles and moral values in their changing situations. His was a total challenge to an Islamic *shari'a* based upon tradition – that is, upon hadith and past jurists' consensus. For this reason, his reformist ideal sparked major controversy and he faced grave persecution.[105]

Faced with such examples of persecution, contemporary reformists are more circumspect. One prominent contemporary Muslim reformer, Tariq Ramadan, called for an international voluntary moratorium on applying the death penalty in the name of Islam. This call certainly involves *shari'a* decisions about homosexual acts, though Tariq Ramadan did not address this specific issue.[106] His proposal is an example of *istihsan istithna'i*, an operation by which jurists opt not to enforce a *shari'a* ruling if, under exceptional conditions, it leads to results that are unjust.[107] As proof of its authenticity, jurists cite the Qur'an, in which God says, *Give good tidings to my servants who listen to the word and follow the best of it ... and follow the most beneficial of what is revealed by your Lord* (Q. 39:17–18, 55). Opting to not enforce a *shari'a* ruling if it leads to injustice is a recognized operation in Islamic jurisprudence though it is disavowed by neo-traditionalists. A moratorium on applying the death penalty in the name of Islam would be a first step toward reforming *shari'a*, but perhaps a faltering one. It advocates alteration of practice without actual reform. Tariq Ramadan's proposed moratorium shies away from addressing the deeper issues of Qur'an interpretation, hadith authentification, and assessment of the *shari'a* inherited from the past to see if they meet the requirements of justice, conscience, and reason.[108]

Though Muslim authorities in Western democracies display intransigence and refusal to assess the theory and rulings of the *shari'a* from their existential position as citizens of a non-Islamic state, many Muslims in response have openly rejected the *shari'a*. Some gay, lesbian, and transgender Muslims refuse the *shari'a* on religious grounds, claiming that it is a product of human minds which may have provided just rulings, based on what was known of God's will in the classical era, but which is distorted and unjust if applied directly in present conditions. Neither the mainstream Muslim community nor its homosexual members seem prepared to take up the challenge of reforming the *shari'a* in the interest of justice, public welfare, and humane benevolence, which are its guiding principles. However, the *shari'a* does contain resources to promote flexibility and gradual reform.

Reforming *Shari'a* to Accommodate Homosexual and Transgender Believers

The issue for many Muslims today is whether to reform the *shari'a* or not, rather than the more subtle question of how to reform it. But if one were committed to a *shari'a* that can change and adapt, what are the mechanisms by which it can grow flexibly while staying true to its noblest principles? Can it in fact accommodate homosexual and transgender believers who wish to live as Muslims, to live as fellow believers within Muslim communities with more dignity than is granted to them by a simple moratorium on the death penalty? These are questions that only the future will answer. But for now we can point out the tools and operations by which the *shari'a* might change if Muslim communities put their collective will, faith, and intelligence into the wide project of reform, not just issue by issue but at the deeper level of theory and principle.

Even as Muslim jurists in the classical period laid down rules drawn by analogy from scriptural texts, they realized that application of rules did not always lead to justice. Under some conditions, strict application of scriptural texts or logical deduction by analogy led to rules that were harsh, unreasonable, or injurious to public welfare. They understood that particular rulings in the *shari'a* sometimes were not in harmony with the fundamental principles that the *shari'a* was to promote, as made explicit in the five principles of al-Shatibi. In such cases, many jurists argued, the ruling that led to unjust or harmful consequences should be set aside in favor of a new ruling that explicitly promoted social welfare (*maslaha*). The Prophet himself served as their model for this operation, since he allowed Muslims to adopt certain practices that were necessary for beneficial trade but which might have been outlawed by a strict and logical extension of the prohibition on usury. Another example is the second vice-regent 'Umar, who opted in times of famine not to apply the *hadd* punishment for theft. Both are examples of laying aside a clear ruling based on scripture, which would lead to injustice and hardship, in favor of enacting a more subtle or innovative ruling that promoted justice and social benefit.

The jurist Abu Hanifa gave a technical term to such juridical operations: *istihsan* or deciding in favor of what one considers most beneficial. He defined it as an essential principle of Islamic jurisprudence. It means abandoning a decision based upon a scriptural text "in favor of what is deemed to be easier and more accommodating to the people."[109] He saw it as a necessary corrective, for analogical reasoning makes sure that a ruling is rooted in a scriptural text but does not examine its consequences in practice; in contrast, *istihsan* looks to the consequences of a ruling to see if it promotes justice and fairness, and, if not, overrides the ruling even if it is clearly based on a scriptural text. Abu Hanifa considered this principle to be based in the Qur'an: *God intends ease for you, and does not intend to put you to hardship* (Q. 2:185). Usually, the jurist enacting *istihsan* lays aside a clear and established ruling in favor of adopting one that is rooted in the people's custom (*'urf*) or adjusted to social need (*darura*) or based on a more subtle analogy (*qiyas khafi*). Abu Hanifa found this operation to be so central to achieving fairness in Islamic law that he allowed a jurist to override a ruling purely on the basis of personal insight, conscience, or intuition about harm that might come from strict or literalist interpretations.

The jurist Malik also promoted this type of flexibility in adopting legal rulings but gave it a different technical name – *istislah* or choosing a course that seems best to promote welfare. He advocated that jurists should not only understand the scriptural sources of the law but also comprehend the social context in which legal rulings get enacted, so they can adjust their rulings to make sure that they protect social welfare and promote justice. So expansive was his sense of public welfare (*maslaha*) that Maliki jurists hold that legal rulings can be incorporated into the *shari'a* based solely on the fact that they are needed, even if they do not have scriptural mandate or are not based on hadith. Maliki jurists called this kind of juridical operation *maslaha mursala* or ruling based on public welfare and common good attributed to the intent of the divine lawgiver even in the absence of scriptural text (*nass*). This broad mandate for Muslims to order their society based on a concept of the common good justifies non-*shari'a* legislation in Muslim-majority societies that have democratically elected parliaments, constitutional norms, and secular law.

Al-Shatibi compared the Maliki and Hanafi conceptions of ruling in favor of what is good and useful, and discovered that they shared a common principle. Both assert that the *shari'a* is not good in and of itself but rather is good because it protects certain human interests and promotes social welfare. These he defined as the five essential principles (*maqasid*). The juridical operations of *istihasan* and *istislah* were crucial for him "as an instrument of consolidation between *usul al-fiqh* [deriving rulings based on scripture] and the *maqasid* [essential principles] ... to secure justice, benefit and *ihsan* [benevolence] and to find ways of removing and eliminating hardship, as well as accommodating the exigencies of necessity and *'urf* [custom]."[110] Al-Shatibi's insights are also crucial for Muslims living as minority communities, for he found that these basic principles of *shari'a* were universally recognized among other nations as basic principles of legal order and good government.[111]

How do we apply this notion of reform from within the *shari'a* to rulings about homosexual acts? What is the social good promoted and the harm avoided? From our overview of how jurists in the classical period constructed the *shari'a*, we learn that they addressed sexual acts rather than sexual orientation. From Ibn Hazm's Zahiri legal analysis we understand that there is no consensus on the punishment for same-sex penetrative intercourse, the sexual act that jurists most closely discussed. Ibn Hazm showed that jurists agreed that same-sex intercourse is a crime but did not agree on whether punishment should be based upon the Qur'anic story of the Tribe of Lot or rather on hadith that are varied and contradictory. Ibn Hazm observed that all hadith used by jurists to justify their rulings on the punishment of homosexual intercourse are reports with only single chains of narratation, and further judged all of them to be weak, flawed, or fabricated. Ibn Hazm further points out how the jurists' decisions on punishment for same-sex intercourse cannot be logically or literally based upon the story of the Tribe of Lot. He concludes that the punishment can only be considered *ta'zir* punishment, one that is not scripturally mandated but is dependent upon the ruler's discretion (and can be no more than ten lashes). In this conclusion, he is in accord with Hanafi jurists.

Although this conclusion is comparatively mild (in contrast to the Maliki, Shafi'i, and Hanbali decisions), it cannot be called "liberal." Ibn Hazm's legal method is not open to progressive and rational methods of reform. His legal method constitutes an insightful critique of other legal schools but does not embrace reasoning about what is just or observations about social welfare. In large part, the Hanafi school agrees with Ibn Hazm's analysis of the sources but is based more on rational analysis of the social conditions and is more open to progressive revision and reform than is the Zahiri position. Hanafis argued that the punishment for same-sex intercourse should be left to the discretion of the ruler. In this sense, Hanafis accept that as social and governmental conditions change, so too the punishment for same-sex intercourse can change. Although Malikis held that punishment for same-sex intercourse was fixed by consensus of the practice of the authorities of Medina, they did hold more generally that rulings should be altered to protect justice and promote social welfare. The Maliki and Hanafi positions are brought together in al-Shatibi's theory of the principles of the *shari'a* which guide every ruling.

A progressive reform of *shari'a* is possible if we examine the issue of homosexual intercourse from the view of the underlying principles of the *shari'a* as enunciated by al-Shatibi. What would such an examination look like? We first have to define the phenomenon and analyze its social context. We observe that homosexuality is a natural part of human diversity and find that the Qur'an does not directly denounce homosexual orientation, as explained in Chapter 2, and contains some hints of acceptance of same-sex oriented members of the Muslim community. The Qur'an does denounce sexual coercion in the story of Lot and his struggle against his tribe. In contrast, Muslim jurists by and large did not differentiate between coerced sex or consensual sex, between sex as a weapon of domination and sex as an expression of one's inner disposition. In secular democracies, the context is one in which same-sex intercourse is not a crime, in which homosexuality is not defined as a mental illness by health professionals, and in which same-sex couples have the same legal rights as heterosexual couples to partnership or even marriage. In this context, it is in the interest of justice and welfare of Muslims for Muslims to stop viewing homosexual members of their community as sinners and to cease viewing consensual homosexual intercourse as criminal. This reassessment is based upon the possibility of an interpretation of Qur'an that sees the Prophet Lot not specifying homosexuality or same-sex acts as moral degradation, but rather condemning rape and sexual abuse of the vulnerable.

What is the social good promoted by such a reform? It separates rape and sexual abuse from sex acts that are performed between two consenting, mature, and responsible adults, rather than allowing these issues to be juxtaposed confusingly in the terms "sodomy" (*liwat*) or "tribadism" (*sihaq*). This is a social good that helps not only lesbian and gay Muslims, but also heterosexual Muslims. It focuses attention on rape as a manifest social ill and crime, rulings about which are not well grounded in classical Islamic law. It focuses attention on the fact that consent from both parties is crucial in sex, even within a marriage. This is a just reform, for the classical *shari'a* posits a husband's unrestricted right to sexual pleasure without asking for his spouse's consent. In classical *shari'a* the wife has little or no scope to refuse sexual intercourse with her husband or specify conditions for intercourse, and this is an aspect of heterosexual marriage that is changing in modern conditions.[112] The reform that removes stigma from consensual homosexual sex strengthens the right of heterosexual women to refuse intercourse if it is not in their best interest. In this age of dangerous sexually transmitted diseases, this reform is essential to the well-being of women, and all other people (children, youth, captives, and other dependents) who are vulnerable to sexual abuse, rape, or other kinds of coercion.

What is the harm that is avoided? Friction over the issue of homosexuality often causes Muslims to be seen as uncivil and can even lead to Muslims breaking the law of their country or transgressing against the constitutional rights of homosexuals. The reform of *shari'a* proposed above eliminates an issue of social and legal friction between Muslim and non-Muslim citizens of constitutional democracies. Eliminating this friction will promote integration and greater cooperation on meaningful issues of political, social, and ethical importance for society as a whole. More specifically, the Muslim community's treatment of its gay, lesbian, or transgender members often causes them great harm. Suppression can cause them psychological distress, social alienation, and inability to worship in congregation, and persecution can cause bodily harm and loss of job or housing. At its worst, Muslim community attitudes can lead to honor killings and execution in the name of *shari'a* punishment. More often they can indirectly cause gay, transgender, or lesbian Muslims to commit suicide because they feel so alienated.

Such harm certainly infringes against the basic principles of *shari'a* as outlined by al-Shatibi. The principle of protection of life (*nafs*) is violated by actual execution, killing of a family member for the sake of "honor," or alienating someone until she or he commits suicide. Further, the principle includes the promotion of life, which means that *shari'a* rulings should actively support a Muslim's right to basic welfare, including health, housing, and economic livelihood, all of which are threatened when Muslims who are lesbian, gay, or transgender face persecution in their communities. The prevalence of suicide among gay and lesbian Muslims, especially those who are young and vulnerable, raises another principle – that of protection of reason (*'aql*). The way Muslim communities treat their lesbian, gay, and transgender members often destroys their clarity of reason and freedom to choose, even when it does not drive them over the edge to suicide. Treatment that violates the principle of protection of reason includes harmful electroshock or other "aversion therapy," especially when administered under coercion, accusations of insanity, or allegations that someone is possessed by evil spirits (*jinn* or *shayatin*). Such treatment can distort one's sense of reality, perception, and self-worth, which are the prerequisites for reasoned deliberation and free choice. In a more subtle way, Muslim communities rhetorically uphold the death penalty against gay, lesbian, and transgender Muslims or condemn them as the contemporary embodiment of the Tribe of Lot, leading the community to ostracize them. This amounts to driving believers away from the faith and thereby violating the principle of preservation of religion (*din*).

Community pressure to marry and family goading to procreate in a heterosexual union, which go against the inner disposition of many gay and lesbian Muslims, often lead to nervous breakdown. The principle of preserving progeny (*nasl*) is often used against them by families who claim that it is their duty to marry and produce children. However, procreation should be understood as a community obligation (*fard kifaya*) and not an obligation upon every individual (*fard 'ayn*).[113] A heterosexual Muslim who does not produce children is no less a Muslim and even the Prophet's favorite wife, 'A'isha, never gave birth to a child. 'A'isha was jealous of the Prophet's first wife, Khadija, who had died before he married 'A'isha and who had born him children, but her own status as a non-procreating wife did not diminish 'A'isha's status in the Prophet's eyes or in the view of the Islamic community, which admired her as a learned teacher and politically influential woman. The principle of preserving progeny is not about forcing people to marry and procreate, but rather about promoting the well-being of those who choose to have children and protecting the rights of children to legitimacy, maintenance, inheritance, and welfare. Forcing lesbian or gay Muslims into heterosexual marriage not only violates their rights but also infringes the rights of the spouse (who often does not know of the real condition and desires of her or his partner) and the rights of any children born of such a marriage. The principle of preservation of progeny should protect children from being born to a parent who does not actually want them or the marriage that produced them. Forced marriages often produce children under duress but then quickly lead to divorce which damages the welfare of the children.

For these reasons of promoting benefit and removing harm, the *shari'a* rulings by which Muslims condemn homosexual intercourse should be changed. But what are the legal means to create this change? The juridical procedure of *istislah* can be invoked, to choose not to enforce *shari'a* rulings in a context in which they cause harm to Muslims. The broadest means of reform is to invoke the principle of *maslaha mursala*, or welfare of Muslims in general, which can be used to change *shari'a* rulings even without appealing to legal sources in Qur'an, hadith, or consensus. However, such an operation is often unsettling to Muslims who are not trained in jurisprudence and who suspect that such changes are merely "secularization" or corruption of religion. For this reason, it is useful to seek a more subtle legal instrument of change that has specific reference to religious sources.

We have such an operation in *istihsan qiyasi.* This an operation that seeks to change a particular ruling by shifting from one legal analogy (*'illa*) to a different one that, though less commonly accepted, would result in a more beneficial outcome for the lived reality of Muslims. In the case of punishment for same-sex intercourse, the accepted legal analogy varies. The Maliki school implicitly holds that same-sex intercourse (especially between two men) is analogous to apostasy and therefore should be punished by killing (*qatl*). The Shafi'i and Hanbali schools hold that it is analogous to heterosexual fornication and should therefore by punished by stoning to death for an already married person or one hundred lashes for a non-married person. The Hanafi and Zahiri schools hold that it is not analogous to heterosexual fornication but rather is a crime to be punished by discretion of the judge or government, based on the analogy that it was forbidden by the Prophet Lot. The legal operation of *istihsan qiyasi* would abandon these analogies in favor of an alternative analogy that would enact a more beneficial result, even if it may be less obvious or less commonly accepted.

What would be the new legal analogy (*'illa*) that would govern a new ruling? In Islamic law, the legal analogy can change as a result of new information about the phenomenon or about scriptural sources that address the phenomenon. New information includes the whole range of medical, psychological, and sociological analyzes that see homosexuality as a sexual orientation that is part of one's inner disposition and is not subject to choice or change. New information includes an unprecedented legal context in which homosexuals are protected as individual citizens with inalienable rights that are equal to those of heterosexual citizens. New information includes a plausible interpretation of the Qur'an, as presented in Chapter 2, which makes sense of its literal discourse about the Prophet Lot without contending that he came to prohibit same-sex intercourse but rather asserts that he condemned his tribe for using sex as a weapon, for abuse and rape (along with other crimes against the vulnerable under their control). They did all these acts to drive out the Prophet who was sent to them to preach monotheism and an ethic of care. New information would include the continuing scrutiny of hadith to assess their authenticity, as Chapter 3 did and found that most hadith used to secure the condemning legal analogies are single unconfirmed reports, many of which of weak and some of which are fabricated.

In the face of such new information, we can specify a new legal analogy. Sexual intercourse between consenting adult homosexual Muslims is analogous to sexual acts that do not have the potential to create pregnancy and illegitimate children between consenting adult heterosexual Muslims. There should be a fundamental equality in legal assessment between homosexual and heterosexual intercourse, with the exception that homosexual intercourse does not produce unwanted children of uncertain parentage which endangers the couple or threatens society. Unwanted pregnancy poses a threat to the mother, who might undergo an abortion that could injure her physical or psychological health. Unwanted pregnancy could pressure a couple to marry even if it were not suitable or desirable for them. Children born of uncertain parentage create tensions and conflicts among a couple and their extended families, with a negative impact on the health of marriages in the whole society. The presence of illegitimate children also raises conflicts in inheritance. It is for these reasons that heterosexual fornication and adultery are so harshly punished in the *shari'a*, based upon the explicit wording of the Qur'an. Homosexual intercourse, in contrast, is less harmful to society at large. It does not infringe upon the Qur'an's explicit command to prevent the procreation of illegitimate children (known generally as "orphans") who will be vulnerable to abuse and neglect.

If we take this as the new legal analogy (*'illa*) guiding our rulings on homosexual intercourse, we arrive at a result that is more beneficial and less harmful for those Muslims – both homosexual and heterosexual – who live as minorities in democratic nations. With this new legal analogy, the issue is not whether to lash or stone or imprison or burn lesbian and gay Muslims. Rather, the issue becomes whether there are means by which they can have sexual intercourse within the framework of a contractual relationship, as heterosexual Muslims can enjoy through marriage. Increasingly, this is the case in the law of the secular democracies in which Muslims are citizens. The question is whether same-sex marriage and civil unions can be assimilated into the *shari'a* in the practice of these Muslim minorities. That is a question of specific and technical *ijtihad* which will be the subject of the next chapter.

If gay and lesbian Muslims can live in partnerships ordered in a contract (whether called "marriage" or civil union), then the final legal analogy that condemns them can also be left aside. The analogy upheld by Ibn Hazm is that same-sex intercourse is a crime because it constitutes sexual penetration of a person who is not related to one by contract or possession. Addressing this point with *ijtihad* about whether it is permissible for same-sex partners to marry or forge a contract of domestic partnership or civil union – not just under secular law but under the *shari'a* – would collapse the final barrier against integrating lesbians and gays into the wider Muslim community as equal and respected members.

Conclusion

If Muslims do not adapt to new circumstances by changing some rulings of the *shari'a*, then increasingly many will opt for secular solutions. They may hold that the *shari'a* need not be followed outside of the field of ritual norms for worship, or they may leave Islam altogether in frustration to place their faith in secular humanist values and the politics of human rights. In fact, these two fields of ethical debate – the Islamic *shari'a* and secular human rights – are potentially compatible. There are resources in the *shari'a*, which have been latent and undeveloped by its medieval elaborators, which are in accord with the secular notion of inalienable human rights.

It is especially in the legal thinking of Abu Hanifa that one finds a notion of essential rights that inhere in one's very "humanness" (*adamiyya*). The Turkish scholar Recep Senturk explains, "I am therefore I have rights ... universal human rights are granted by birth to every one, Muslim and non-Muslim, equally and by virtue of being a human. They are not conditional, contingent, divisible or reciprocal. All human beings and communities are charged to protect their own rights and the rights of others as a legal, moral and religious duty ... Protection of universal human rights is the common ground and the objective of all legal systems, secular and religious, even if they are characterized by different ways of legitimizing rights ... I derive this view from a major strand in the classical Islamic law, originating from Abu Hanifa's doctrine on the axiomatic relationship between *'isma* and *adamiyya.*"[114] *'Isma* literally means "sanctity" in the sense of inviolability, and Abu Hanifa uses the term to mean the irreducible and basic rights that accrue to each person simply because of her or his being a human person. He argues that sanctity of rights inheres in all people purely for the sake of their humanity (*al-'isma bi'l-adamiyya*), including protection of life, property, religion, mind, honor, and family against any intrusion by individuals, communities, and states.

Jurists who followed Abu Hanifa advocated granting basic human rights universally, long before the more secular doctrine of human rights was fully elaborated and institutionalized in the West. This Islamic root of a doctrine of inalienable human rights allows Muslims in democratic states to argue that the secular human rights doctrine is not foreign to the Islamic tradition. This insight can serve as a catalyst for corrective reform of the *shari'a.* The concept of sanctity of person is an essential reinforcement of al-Shatibi's exposition of the principles of the *shari'a* (*maqasid*) which limit dogmatic literalism by rational understanding of social welfare. Both approaches are essential tools for reform of the *shari'a* and they are much needed in contemporary discussions.

Some Muslim readers will find the proposals above to be utopian. But what begins as an unrealistic idea often gathers momentum until, after several generations, it is accepted as common sense. This is the way that the *shari'a* originally grew. Jurists debated contradictory proposals until some of them found a following; once popular, such proposals were incorporated into authoritative legal texts and then were accepted as the consensus opinion. There is reason for optimism that these reformist proposals about homosexual intercourse will gain approval by some Muslims. This is because the proposal addresses points that are of common concern to women and youth even if they are heterosexual. They demand that the *shari'a* be reformed in a way that protects the individual Muslim from abuse, rape, and sexual assault while granting to each an inviolable dignity in the intimate, even sexual, expression of her or his humanity.

Even if this proposal is not taken up by a broad consensus of Muslims in the West, a small minority of lesbian, gay, and transgender Muslims can adopt it to guide their own practice and strengthen their faith. Individual believers cannot wait for the slow process of evolution to change their community's perception. Issues like finding peace within one's own conscience, acceptance in one's family, and loving relationships with one's partners cannot wait for slow evolution over many generations. Indeed, we find individual Muslims acting upon reformist notions of the *shari'a* to guide their own conduct, even without the approval of their wider community. This is especially apparent when we turn to the issue of same-sex partnerships and marriage. The next chapter will focus on this issue in the context of support groups in the U.S. and Canada, where some lesbian and gay Muslims have formed partnerships and engaged in marriage rituals. After that, this study will examine the issue of same-sex marriage and partnership from the point of view of Islamic norms, as a case example of how the *shari'a* might be reformed to better meet the requirements of justice and conscience.

Chapter 5

Reforming *Shari'a*: Islamic Ethics of Same-Sex Marriage

Blessed indeed are these two loving friends
They sleep through the night in an embrace without end
Their two souls become one soul, and then
That one soul lies in the two loving men
Those two don't quarrel – they avoid any strife
They guard their love as more precious than life

Abu Nuwas, *The Lovers*

The prolific and provocative Arab poet known as Abu Nuwas wrote this beautiful description of two lovers who consider themselves one soul. His name means "He with the Curling Forelocks" and his love poems depict primarily homoerotic love.[1] Though they are usually ribald, the poem quoted above depicts two men in a loving partnership as if they were married. It shows that Abu Nuwas (died 815 in Baghdad), like other Muslims in the 'Abbasid era, was not blind to the possibilities of homoerotic pairing despite the fact that Islamic law left no option for same-sex partnerships or marriages to be consummated legally.

In the *shari'a* that Muslims have inherited from that classical period, issues of procreation, legitimacy, and patriarchal privilege limit notions of what a marriage is and could be. The *shari'a* defined marriage in a way that is demeaning most immediately for women, is damaging for same-sex couples (whether they are two men or two women), and is limiting even for straight men who are the immediate beneficiaries of the system. This is because the issues of love, care, reciprocity, and mutual consent are not adequately addressed by the *shari'a*'s codifying marriage as a contract that gives a man dominion over a woman's sexual organs.[2]

In Chapter 4, we addressed the need to assess the fiqh decisions of Islamic law. There we encountered the urgency of continuous *ijtihad* or independent juridical thinking both within and beyond the established schools of Islamic law. This chapter will promote *ijtihad* around one issue of social concern – the possibility of Muslims engaging in same-sex marriage or partnership. There is an urgent need to extend the rulings of *shari'a* to regulate issues that never arose in the past, upon which science has shined the light of new information not accessible by jurists in the past, or about which political progress has created new opportunities not experienced by Muslims of the past. Same-sex marriage is one of those issues. It is an issue that contemporary Muslims confront, especially those living in secular democracies.

This chapter addresses the possibility of extending the ethics of partnership through same-sex marriage. In preparation for writing this book, I interviewed gay, lesbian, and transgender Muslims who have set up support groups in South Africa, the Netherlands, the United Kingdom, Canada, and the United States. In all the countries where they reside, there are legal same-sex unions of some form, and this creates the possibility for Muslim citizens of these nations to consider the possibility of accepting same-sex marriage among members of their religious community. The Netherlands was the first to legalize such relationships, same-sex civil unions being legalized in 1998 and marriages allowed in 2001. Canada legalized civil unions and allowed same-sex marriage in 2005, after several years of their being accepted in some provinces but disallowed in others. The United Kingdom legalized civil unions for same-sex couples in 2004 and allowed marriages at the end of 2005. South Africa legalized same-sex marriage in 2006 without adopting the piecemeal approach of first recognizing civil unions before debating marriage. Of all nations that have legalized marriage, only Canada and South Africa specifically grant absolutely equal rights to same-sex and opposite-sex married couples without distinction.[3]

That leaves the U.S. It lags behind these other democracies and has avoided real debate at the federal level. Several states have legalized same-sex civil unions, prompting more conservative states to ban them by defining marriage as always and only between a woman and a man. This disparate approach will most likely result in a court cases that will force the U.S. Supreme Court to address the issue, though it has so far declared it a matter of states' rights, allowing each state to define its own norms of marriage (just as racial segregation was unofficially tolerated by the federal government as a matter of states' rights). In 1996, Congress passed the Federal Defense of Marriage Act (D.O.M.A.) and President Bill Clinton signed it into law. The Act declares that no state of the

U.S. need acknowldge same-sex marriages as legally binding even if another state does acknowledge them; it also states that the federal government will not acknowledge same-sex marriages even if individual states pass laws that legalize them. So the only federal decision has been to pass ruling on the legality of same-sex marriages back to the individual states and to isolate states that do recognize such marriages' legality.

Since then a few states have legalized same-sex marriage but many more states have passed state consitutional ammendments to prevent any such legal recognition. The U.S. and Canada are fascinating to compare, since Canada has moved rapidly in a path parallel to European Union states that have legalized same-sex marriage, whereas the U.S. languishes in moralistic debate and some conservative politcians flirt with banning same-sex marriages through a federal constitutional amendment. This chapter will therefore focus on case examples from the U.S. and Canada.

Between Love and Law

Abu Nuwas, the poet quoted at the head of this chapter, felt that love was far more powerful than the law and he openly flaunted the jurists' proscriptions. The more cautious Ibn Hazm upheld a reformed version of Islamic law but also admitted that love was a powerful force that slipped beyond the grasp of law. In his anthology of love poems, *The Neck-Ring of the Dove*, Ibn Hazm states, "Love is neither disapproved by religion nor prohibited by the law, for every heart is in God's hands."[4] Love as a passionate emotion cannot be constrained by the law, even if sexual acts can be, and Ibn Hazm includes in his poetic anthology love poems about both heterosexual and homosexual love. He hardly distinguishes between them, for "to him all love is psychologically one and the same."[5] However, Ibn Hazm urges anyone who cannot legally join with his or her partner in marriage to remain chaste in love. But why would God create passionate love between two persons who cannot find the legal means to consummate their love in a partnership? Ibn Hazm observes that God does create such love, between two women or two men, but does not ask whether the *shari'a* might create legal means for their consummation.

Ibn Hazm accepts that some men and women are homosexual by nature in their innermost disposition. The earlier spokesman of his Zahiri legal school, Muhammad ibn Dawud of Baghdad (died 910), accepted the existence of homosexual love based on the Platonic model. He suggested that all human souls were originally spherical. In coming into the material world, each split into two. Each half yearns to be reintegrated, in great completion and increasing joy, through uniting emotional and sexually with its sundered half. This explains the force and effect of love in our worldly lives. Muhammad ibn Dawud wholeheartedly accepted this model of two becoming one, a pair forming a whole, that he finds in harmony with the Qur'an's suggestions about love. *From among God's signs is that* [*God*] *created for you from among yourselves mates that you might live with them in tranquillity and generated between you love and compassion* ... (Q. 30:21). Muhammad ibn Dawud was the first to write a collection of Arabic love poetry in which homosexual and heterosexual love were depicted side by side, setting the precedent for Ibn Hazm and a host of others. He saw both hetero- and homosexual love as equivalent expressions of the same emotion. He believed that God inspires love in each person to spur the soul to seek its mate and give itself over to another as a means of spiritual ascension and fulfillment.

Plato sets out this vision of love as the quest of each of their lost half in the speech of Aristophanes in his *Symposium*. "Human beings were once round and whole – but now, cut in half for their over ambitiousness, they feel a sense of lost wholeness and run about searching for their 'other half.' There are ... three types of search corresponding to three original species of human beings. There are males whose 'other half' is male, females whose 'other half' is female and people whose 'other half' is of the opposite sex. The speech describes the feelings of intimacy and joy with which the lost 'other halves' greet one another and the activity of sexual intercourse as a joyful attempt to be restored to the lost unity of their original natures. This is so not less for the same-sex than for the opposite-sex couples: in all cases, lovemaking expresses a deep inner need coming from nature, and in all cases the couples, so uniting, have the potential to make a valuable civic contribution."[6] Muslim theologians appreciated Platonic philosophy long before European Christians rediscovered such works. They accepted the Platonic scheme of love, for it explained the mysterious workings of passion and the force of attraction that draws people together into a couple. But they did not accept Plato's assertion that same-sex love played a vital civic role – especially of a mature man for a younger man. Muslim theologians accepted that such love, like all varieties of love, played a crucial spiritual role but did not assert that it should be channeled into legal forms of partnership or marriage.

In this sense, the Arab and Persian Muslims who found congruence between Hellenic ideals and Islam also neglected important dimensions of Greek insights into homosexuality. Plato's dialogues picture same-sex love as completely natural and as civilly moral. Same-sex love was expected to be sexual and was not complete until expressed in intercourse. The partnerships formed of such emotional attachments were long lasting, and though they were not formalized as marriages they were seen as just as important to the continuity and morality of civic life as marriage between man and woman. Plato, through the speech of Aristophanes, "situates same-sex longings deep in nature, describes intercourse as a way of being restored to a natural wholeness and unity, and argues for the civic benefits of male–male love in particular," argues the American legal scholar Margaret Nussbaum. She bases her analysis of the legal standing of same-sex relationships, intercourse, and partnerships upon this classical Greek heritage, which so deeply shaped Christian Europe and America, as it did the Islamic world. "There is absolutely no doubt that lovers of all three types are envisaged as engaging in intercourse – intercourse indeed is a central topic of the speech. Although the speech does recognize the distinction between the *erastes* (lover) and *eromenos* (beloved), it is remarkable for its suggestion of mutual desire and pleasure: Both partners feel 'friendly love and intimacy and passionate love' and the younger 'halves' of original male–male 'wholes' are said to enjoy 'lying with and being embraced by men.' … Relationships between 'other halves' are said to endure throughout life … Custom may force such male–male couples to marry [heterosexual partners], but they 'do not turn their thoughts to marriage and begetting of children by nature … but it is enough for them to live unmarried with one another.'"[7] Since in the Hellenic world marriage was instituted more for procreation than for emotional fulfillment, same-sex bonds were not necessarily conceived as marriage. But this did not lessen their social, emotional, and civic importance and they were seen as an institution central to the moral fiber of society.

Islamic society perpetuated this Hellenic sense of love that encompassed same-sex attraction, but Muslim jurists formed a hetero-exclusive system of marriage.[8] For most Muslims in the classical period, same-sex attraction was seen as useful if it led to friendship or love but was condemned if it led to sexual acts, especially penetrative intercourse. This is the position of Ibn Hazm, a position determined by his patriarchal cultural context and affirmed through his own jurisprudence. He questioned the reliance of his predecessor, Muhammad ibn Dawud, on Plato's philosophy even as he affirmed the psychological and spiritual importance of love in whatever form it might take. He was concerned to root this conception of love in specifically Islamic sources, like the Qur'an and the hadith of the Prophet. In the preface of his collection of love poetry, Ibn Hazm explains, "I consider love as a conjunction between scattered parts of souls that have become divided in this physical universe, a union effected within the substance of their original sublime element … We know the secret of commingling and separation in created things to be simply a process of union and disassociation; every form always cries out for its corresponding form; like is ever at rest with like."[9] Ibn Hazm finds that through love the human soul, "whose constituent principle is so disposed as to be intensely sensitive to harmony and inclination, yearning and aversion, passionate desire and antipathy," finds its wholeness by associating with another in whom it recognizes a primordial sameness. "My theory is further proved by the fact that you will never find two persons in love with one another without there being some likeness and agreement of natural attributes between them ... The Messenger of God confirmed the matter when he said, 'Spirits are regimented battalions: those which know one another associate familiarly together while those which do not know one another remain at variance.' ... For the same reason Hippocrates was not distressed when he was told of a man deficient in virtue who was in love with him. The matter being remarked upon, he said, 'He would not have fallen in love with me if I had not accorded with him in some aspect of my character.'"[10]

In Ibn Hazm's view, love is essential because it leads us from a fragmentary individuality into a more fulfilling harmony with others. It goads us into finding those with whom we can voluntarily enter a partnership with the goal of perfecting our character. It is neither merely about pairing man and woman to ensure procreation nor simply a matter of limiting sexual intercourse to legal spouses to prevent fornication. It is about setting up a structure through which one can enter into caring partnerships with others who accord with one's personality, comfort one in distress, and challenge one to rise above one's baser instincts. A marital partner is a social, sexual, and emotional mate to promote the perfection of one's character through love for another.

As Ibn Hazm observes with his subtle citation of the story about Hippocrates (a Greek philosopher much admired by Muslims), same-sex love can serve the same essential function as heterosexual love. Both lead one to search for a like-minded and similar-hearted partner with whom to share life with all its burdens and joys. The American Muslim gay activist, scholar, and lawyer Daayiee Abdullah calls this "family that is beyond the blood-plan." He notes, "We need to let our [Islamic] community know that out of necessity we gay people create our own families ... to let them know that once we are outside of their particular plan, their 'blood-plan', that doesn't mean that we still do not seek family. That's another part of human nature, to seek family."[11] Daayiee acts as imam for those who join Al-Fatiha Foundation. Though he has formal degrees in Middle East studies and law, with experience in family counseling, that is not what makes him an imam. Daayiee reflects on the informal process of becoming an imam when he explains, "I think that once I began associating with al-Fatiha [Foundation] and then writing about homosexual and positive interpretation from the Qur'an ... just through that process people have turned to me for guidance." If people in the community turn to you for guidance, you are their imam – literally, "one who stands in front." As an imam, he has helped same-sex couples to marry, as we will see.

The question for Muslims is whether they will grant the moral dignity and legal sanction to partnerships of same-sex couples who establish between themselves love, care, and sharing that is equivalent to that between heterosexual pairs. For Muslims to do this requires that they reflect deeply on what the Qur'an intends by marriage and to reject the neo-traditionalist notion that marriage is solely or primarily for procreation. Though the idea that marriage for procreation is gaining strong support in fundamentalist and Islamist movements, it is not well supported by classical Islamic conceptions of marriage.

Pairing and Mating in the Qur'an

The Qur'an challenges each person to find a suitable mate or partner. The term for "partner," *zawj*, is ambiguously gendered: it is a masculine noun grammatically even when describing a female person. In this sense, the word *zawj* mirrors the term *nafs* for "person" or "soul," which is grammatically feminine even when describing a male person. The Qur'an does not differentiate between a male or female person as *nafs* or between the person's female or male partner as *zawj*. Homosexual pairs could also, within this wide and varied framework, be considered mates. This is because the Qur'anic language is suitably abstract: *From among God's signs is that [God] created for you mates from amongst yourselves that you might live with them in tranquility, and generated between you love and compassion, for surely in this are clear signs for those who ponder!* (Q. 30:21).

This pronouncement with its abstraction traces the universal pattern, and the story of Adam and Eve as the primordial mates is a specific instance of the general truth. The Qur'an describes this first pair, saying, *It is God who created you all from a single self and made of it a mate, that one might take repose in the other* (Q. 7:189). In this specific case, the Qur'an talks of male and female being a pair. But it does not do so in a prescriptive way, for the Qur'an also talks of night and day being a pair, of light and dark or soul and body being a pair. God creates for each person a mate or mates "of it" or of the same pattern and suitable for the two to join together, in love and compassion, to reach a greater emotional and ethical completion. The purpose is for us each to overcome self-centered pride and through loving another to realize that God created us all, all of humanity, *from a single self.*

Discussing the permissibility of same-sex marriage in Islam is complicated, because it rests on our perception of human nature, our acceptance of social norms, and our understanding of God's intent. Clearly, the Qur'an values the pairing of Muslims in loving partnerships and hints that this is a fulfillment of the intention for which God created human beings. The Qur'an says, *The creator of the heavens and the earth has made you pairs from among yourselves*

(Q. 42:11). But what kind of pair is this? The Qur'an encourages pairing, urging Muslims to see erotic desire and mating instincts as a good, as a path toward moral responsibility and spiritual maturity. It is as if by finding a partner (or partners), we act in harmony with our original nature in which we were created (*fitra*). Such universal verses are often gender neutral. They use terms, like *nafs* or *zawj*, that do not clearly depict one human gender as opposed to the other. In this sense, the universal Qur'anic verses apply to same-sex couples as well as heterosexual couples.

The Qur'an evokes the Platonic idea that all souls, when they enter the world of material manifestation, are split from their original unity. In this fragmented state, each soul feels attraction to another soul in whom it find hints of its lost half; this is the Platonic explanation of passionate love, psychological attraction, and erotic desire. Medieval Muslim philosophers like Ibn Hazm found these Platonic ideas to be in harmony with the Qur'anic depiction of how God created humanity from a single soul and from each individual created a mate. Many Muslim Sufis elaborated on this idea, seeing human love of a partner to be a bridge to the higher reality of human love for God.[12]

Despite some Muslims' acceptance of same-sex attraction and love as natural and even spiritually beneficial, Muslim jurists did not allow marriage or legal contracts between same-sex partners. However, the Qur'an talks about sexual pairing and partnerships in ways that are much deeper than the rulings of Islamic law, and the Qur'an should be the starting place for a reconsideration of homosexuality among Muslims. Now that some constitutional democracies are allowing same-sex partners to have the same legal and moral standing as heterosexual married couples, there is a new opportunity to hear the Qur'an speak in a voice that may have been ignored in the past. The Qur'an says, *Glory be to the One who creates the mates, all of them, in what grows upon the earth and from themselves and from what you do not even know!* (Q. 36:35). In this verse, the voice of God invokes pairs and partners in ways too complex to be reduced to a heterosexual pairing of man and woman. Certainly, Adam and Eve are termed "a pair" who mate at God's direction to provide each other with rest and tranquillity. In the Qur'an, all life is created through pairs, "male and female," to ensure reproduction and growth among animals and fruits and plants. However, the Qur'an does not limit the mysterious principle of growth to gendered pairs, but extends it to all pairs. In recognition of this, classical interpreters of the Qur'an have considered the soul in intimate harmony with the body it animates to be a pair of mates.

The Qur'an does address pairs of people who come together in a partnership. Within such a pair, sexual intercourse and intimacy are part of this ethical training and spiritual refinement. Islam does not condemn sexual pleasure in favor of ascetic renunciation and does not limit sex to procreation.[13] The Qur'an is clear that sexual pleasure, though good in itself, should be pursued within ethical limits. Partners should establish between themselves a contract or agreement (*'aqd*), through which they acknowledge their legal, financial, and ethical obligations to each other. These obligations include comfort and care, keeping secrets, upholding the other's dignity, preserving the other's physical health, and safeguarding the other's psychological well-being. Interactions with others outside the purview of a contract should be conducted within accepted norms of modesty. The Qur'an enjoins both men and women to wear modest clothing, speak respectfully, and lower the gaze to prevent lascivious looking at others.[14] In general, the Qur'an announces a principle of avoiding objectifying others in a sexual way, in order to uphold our common humanity. It permits pleasure bounded by care and enjoins reciprocity of rights and pleasures within a relationship.

This basis of sexual ethics applies to men as well as women. In a pluralistic Islamic community, it would apply to homosexual couples as well as to heterosexual ones. The purposes of finding one's mate are the same for hetero- and homosexual couples, so the ethical guidelines to establishing relationships should also be the same, if the rulings on marriage (*nikah*) can be extended by *ijtihad* or creative legal reasoning from the example of heterosexual pairing to that of homosexual pairing.

The Qur'an's most universal verses often seem to apply to same-gender couples as well as heterosexual couples. However, the Qur'an also addresses the subject of pairing in more specific language, as it defines norms that regulate sexual activity and define legal unions in the public sphere. These verses seem to address heterosexual couples only, for they have always been – and will always be – the vast majority in any society. The Qur'an explicitly speaks to heterosexual couples about marriage, but addresses only implicitly same-sex couples. Through *ijtihad* in scriptural interpretation and legal reasoning, Muslims can draw out the implicit meaning from the explicit words of revelation; it is our responsibility as ethical believers to do so, and this chapter describes how some lesbian, gay, and transgender Muslims are doing this and reflects theologically upon their endeavors. Before we can achieve this drawing out of the possibility of same-sex marriage and partnership from the implicit meaning of the Qur'an, we have to examine in detail the form and intent of marriage in Islam and assess whether it is a secular or sacred institution. This is necessary because many Muslims contend that the Qur'an explicitly speaks about heterosexual couples alone because God intends and allows sexual contact between a male and female only, which is a sacred duty.

The Qur'an speaks about marriage in later verses that were revealed in Medina, when Muslims were building a new society. Their forms of marriage continued from pre-Islamic custom with some reform, in both positive and negative aspects. The Qur'an forbids certain aspects of marriage that were common in pre-Islamic Arab society.[15] These negative aspects are supplemented by positive injunctions. The Qur'an urges spouses to live together rather than maintain separate households, as was common in the pre-Islamic times (Q. 65:6–7). It enjoins Muslim men to marry believers in the one God (Q. 2:221) and, more specifically, allows them to marry women from other monotheistic religions, known as the "people of scripture" or *ahl al-kitab* (Q. 5:5). It demands that husbands provide for their wives and children (Q. 4:34), in return for which husbands can expect sexual intimacy and pleasure (Q. 2:223) except when this is a hardship for the wife, like during menstruation (Q. 2:222). The wife is entitled to own her own property (Q. 4:4, 20). Based upon this, Islamic law allows women to make business contracts on their own and has defined marriage in such a way that wives are obliged to provide only sexual pleasure and social comfort for the husband and he cannot demand that she work in the home or outside it.[16] In general, the Qur'an enjoins Muslims to view marriage as a *mithaq ghaliz* or firm covenant (Q. 4:21).

The question that faces us is why the Qur'an speaks specifically to a man's marriage with a woman. There are three possibilities. First, the Qur'an might address heterosexual couples because God intends only their couplings; this is the option that many neo-traditionalists uphold. Second, it may be that because heterosexual couplings are the statistical majority God addresses the most common social situation. Third, it may be that because only heterosexual couplings produce children God intends legal marriage to create family structures that will ensure protection and identity for children (in terms of parentage, financial support, and inheritance). This study favors the second and third possibilities, which are compatible with each other. It asserts that a just and compassionate God would not create people with homosexual orientation and yearnings and then subsequently will them into heterosexual bonds, forbid them from finding emotional fulfillment in a homosexual relationship, and punish them for expressing this emotional fulfillment though sexual contact. However, it is not unjust for God to speak in explicitly legal terms to the majority while leaving the minority to infer from these words an ethical standard that is equivalent but suitable to their own existential position. It makes sense that God would speak explicitly to regulate heterosexual coupling, because such negative social consequences for children result from reckless heterosexual intercourse and failed heterosexual marriages. In stark contrast to this, neo-traditionalists like Shaykh Qaradawi assert the first possibility as the only possibility, even though their assertion is based upon preconceptions about natural law rather than specifically upon the Qur'an.

In the same al-Jazeera TV interview quoted in Chapter 4, Shaykh Qaradawi says, "God the glorious and mighty has made procreation the result of man and woman, male meeting female ... If every man were to be content with a man like him and every woman content with a woman like her, this is against nature. This is because God the glorious and mighty created man and woman in their bodily formation with the intent that each should complete the other."[17] Shaykh Qaradawi's explanation narrows the subtle creation of God into an exclusive binary and reduces the human personality to anatomy. He sees procreation as the purpose of sex. "What would happen if all the people decided to [be] content with his own kind and dispenses with the other [sex] or the opposite gender, then what would be the result? The human race would end after a generation or two! This is because God the glorious and mighty has made procreation the result of man and woman, male meeting female." Neo-traditionalists like Shaykh Qaradawi have strayed far from the subtle intellectual vision of Muslim thinkers like Ibn Hazm. The latter perceived that pairing happened owing to love, which ignited when two souls found harmony between each other such that they formed an integral whole. Shaykh Qaradawi leaves no room for love or personality – in his explanation pairing happens when male and female sexual organs come together, like a plug in an electric socket.

Shaykh Qaradawi's view fails to live up to the human complexity revealed by science. Human complexity is also revealed by the inimitable subtlety of God's speech in the Qur'an, such as *God is the first and the last, the outer apparent and the inner hidden, and God is the knower of every thing ... God knows everything that moves on earth and that emerges from it, and knows everything that descends from the sky and ascends into it. Thus God is with you wherever you may be, and God is the seer of all that you do* (Q. 57:3–4). The Qur'an describes God as both outer and inner, both apparent and hidden, so we might understand that human beings created by God have these qualities reflected in them. We are not just an outer form but also an inner soul. We are not merely our anatomy but also our psyche. We consist not only of our observable actions but also of our invisible intentions.

Neo-traditionalists like Shaykh Qaradawi greatly reduce our God-given subtlety when they declare that sex is a matter of anatomy leading to procreation. Human sexuality is complex. Gender identity is not limited to reproductive anatomy. Sexuality is not defined by friction between sexual organs. When the Qur'an declares that *God is with you wherever you may be, and God is the seer of all that you do*, it reveals that God sees not only our outer actions but also our inner intention that shapes and drives our actions. God judges the moral worth of any action by its intention, and we should try to live up to this standard to the best of our limited ability.

Our legal judgment about sexual acts should be cognizant of the intention – colored by psychology and deepened by faith – that shapes such acts. This is why the contract of marriage is so important, for it makes apparent to the public one's intention in the private matter of sexual relations. For this reason many lesbian, gay, and transgender Muslims desire to enter into a marriage contract with their chosen partners just as heterosexual Muslims do. Before we can envision how they might enter into same-sex marriage as an Islamic *nikah*, we have to understand fully the construction of heterosexual marriage contracts in Islamic custom.

The Marriage Contract: Forms and Intentions

We have seen above how the Qur'an discusses marriage as a *mithaq ghaliz* or firm covenant (Q. 4:21). Its verses on marriage specifically speak to men about their obligations and privileges in marriage contracts with women. From these verses, Muslim jurists specified the details of formal marriage contract (*'aqd al-nikah*), based upon the model of a business contract. "Islamic marriage is a contract of exchange that involves a sort of ownership. In exchange for some money or valuables the men pay women, they gain an exclusive right of sexual union. All schools of Islamic law consider marriage to be a contract, an *'aqd.* This contractual exchange that lies at the heart of a Muslim marriage legitimizes it in the eyes of law and religion."[18] But there is some slippage in the status of women, for jurists' formulation of the marriage contract only exaggerated the inequality in status between male and female spouse. Islamic law was progressive in recognizing the wife as an independent legal entity rather than property, for she receives the money of the bride-price (*mahr* or *sadaq*) rather than her father or male guardian. The woman must consent to the marriage, though in practice she is sometimes under coercion by family and cannot refuse if her family has arranged the marriage. As a free agent, the woman surrenders some of her freedom by entering into a contract of marriage. In exchange for money and protection, she gives the right of access to her sexual organs, which are granted to the husband as his dominion (*milk*) but not his property (*mulk*). Access to her sexual organs – and by extension her physical and social being – are restricted by this contract to her husband alone. He has dominion over her sexuality and therefore has the right to forbid her access to other men outside the family's circle of close relatives or servants. By extension, he can restrict her movement outside the home and demand obedience, at least inasmuch as it involves exposure to other men (which covers almost any transaction in public). Although the wife theoretically retains legal autonomy over her property and can make business contracts with others, she practically gives up the right to act upon this legal autonomy without her husband's permission.

After the marriage, there is a hierarchy of power within the home between heterosexual partners. The contract gives a husband sexual access to his wife at any time or manner of his choosing, without adequately addressing consent or mutuality in the giving and receiving of sexual pleasure. Although Muslim jurists assert that each spouse must satisfy the other's sexual needs, they assign only to men the power to determine how this is accomplished. In addition, men are given the right to initiate divorce, which is not granted to women (except for exceptional circumstances such as a husband who is insane or has contracted an infectious disease). Jurists also give men the right to marry several times concurrently whereas women are allowed to be married to only a single man at any given time.

The jurists' solution to the problem of marriage is both admirable and problematic. It is admirable in judging marriage to be a contract by two free independent people. But it is problematic because women are assumed to be lesser than men, and it allows or even enforces fundamental inequalities in the marriage bond. Is the Islamic legal framework of marriage an adequate response to the Qur'anic challenge? In addressing heterosexual couples, the Qur'an clearly meshes several different interests, as it promotes a stable family unit and a caring and sexually fulfilling intimate life, protects the legitimacy of children, and limits sex outside of contractual relationships.

This is the formal marriage contract designed for heterosexual couples, addressed in the Qur'an and systematized by Muslim jurists in the *shari'a*. Is it a suitable model for lesbian, transgender, and gay Muslims? Can it be extended by analogy to same-sex couples? If it can be extended, by operations of *ijtihad*, should it be extended without addressing the gender-differentiated roles that are central to it? These are not easy questions to answer. Currently, some Muslim women doubt whether this system of formal marriage is a good model for heterosexual couples and whether it can be reformed to accommodate a more gender-egalitarian distribution of rights and privileges. Both homosexual Muslims and feminist Muslims (whether female or male) address the same core issues when dealing with the conventional marriage contract as formalized in the *shari'a*. The changes in emphasis that homosexual Muslims require in order to use this model of marriage are the same changes that feminists are proposing to make the model work for contemporary heterosexual couples with more egalitarian gender relations. We will return to this crucial point.

The hierarchical difference in power between the male and the female within the marriage contract owes to the possibility of procreation. In sexual intercourse between a woman and man, there is usually the possibility of conception and pregnancy, especially in societies where contraceptive techniques were far from reliable (as in all pre-modern Islamic societies) or not available or accepted (as in some contemporary Islamic societies). Even though the Islamic tradition, in general, values sexual pleasure as good in itself and allows contraceptive measures, the possibility of pregnancy has always loomed large. The Qur'an discourages any practice that might lead to illegitimate children or create doubt about their parentage, leading as that does to orphans, neglected young, or parents who deny their financial and emotional responsibilities to care for their offspring. The Qur'anic concern to protect the vulnerable explains its harsh penalties for heterosexual adultery and fornication (*zina'*). It also explains some – but not all – of the hierarchical difference of power between women and men in marriage.[19] When lesbian and gay Muslims contemplate marriage, their relationships are different from those of heterosexual married couples not only because both partners are of the same gender but also because their intercourse does not result in procreation.

When confronted with the possibility of same-sex marriage, many neo-traditionalist Muslims counter that marriage is only for heterosexual couples because the sole purpose of sex is procreation. They have adopted this argument mainly from Christians, including fundamentalist Protestants and conservative Catholics. This argument does not arise from within the Islamic tradition itself, because most Muslims in the past did not limit the purpose of sexual pleasure to procreation even if they valued procreation very highly.[20] The Prophet encouraged Muslims to have active sex lives and cultivate reciprocal relationships of pleasure and trust; he never taught that the only purpose of sex was procreation.[21] He enjoyed sexual pleasure with his wives even when they did not produce children, whether that was by choice or by fiat of reproductive biology. He married many women who were older – they had been widowed or divorced and had already borne children from previous marriages – so the purpose of these marriages was clearly not procreation.

Though valuing sexual pleasure as a good in itself, the Prophet taught that it is necessary to channel sexual pleasure through relationships that are based on a contract, so that both partners recognize their rights and obligations toward each other. Accordingly, the Prophet recognized several ways for Muslims to have legitimate sexual relationships. Besides formal marriage (*nikah*), the Prophet recognized temporary marriage (*mut'a*) and servitude (*riqq*) as legal arrangements that permitted sexual intercourse.

The Prophet himself had female sexual partners who were not formal wives but rather were servants or slaves. We might call them concubines if their primary purpose were sexual enjoyment rather than other kinds of labor; he acquired them as the spoils of war, in accordance with pre-modern and pre-Islamic practices of slavery. The Prophet himself did not enter into a temporary marriage, but did permit his companions to do so when they could not or did not want to enter into a formal marriage. This raises the possibility of "non-marital sexual relations" that are legal and accepted in Muslim communities, as discussed insightfully by Kecia Ali.[22] The practice of informal temporary marriage is controversial and contested, based upon conflicting reports about the Prophet's actions. Shi'i jurists allege that temporary marriage was a pre-Islamic Arab custom that the Prophet allowed to continue, though it was later outlawed by the second caliph, 'Umar ibn al-Khattab. But because the Shi'a do not view 'Umar as a legitimate *khalifa*, they dismiss his rulings and view the institution of temporary marriage as still valid. For most Sunni jurists, the fact that 'Umar outlawed temporary marriage is enough for them to consider it forbidden.

The practice became a flashpoint of conflict between Sunnis and Shi'a, forcing Sunni jurists to refine their position. They have taken debate about temporary marriage to a deeper level by pointing to hadith that report that the Prophet Muhammad outlawed the custom. Shi'i jurists counter that he may have outlawed it in a specific sitaution, but later allowed the practice to continue during his lifetime, such that the forbidding is "specific" to a particular circumstance whereas the permitting is "general" and remains in force after the Prophet's death. The controversy illustrates the difficulty of working with hadith as the basis for legal rulings, and it is beyond the scope of this study to document all the details of the controversy. For our purposes, it is enough to note that temporary marriage is legal in the major Shi'i school of law (the Ja'fari school of the Twelver Shi'i community) and is still practiced in contemporary Shi'i communities, most notably in Iran. All Sunni schools of law forbid the practice and judge it to be like prostitution. Yet some few Sunnis consider that, because it is legal in at least one legitimate school of law – namely the Twelver Shi'i school – temporary marriage can be adopted strategically by Sunnis in situations of necessity and benefit. Though few Sunnis are learned enough or bold enough to step outside their own legal school to adopt the ruling of another, such a practice is juridically acceptable.[23]

Therefore, putting aside the sectarian debate between Sunnis and Shi'a, it is beneficial for Muslim sexuality minorities to consider these alternative forms of sexual relationship that are outside the bounds of formal marriage. These forms of contractual relationship do not have the high social status of formal marriage, but gay, lesbian, and transgender Muslims can consider them as alternative models. The difference between them has to with the kind of contract of exchange upon which they are based. Formal marriage is based upon a contract of sale (*bay*ʿ), in which the wife surrenders ownership or access to her sexual organs for a term considered permanent as long as the contract holds. Temporary marriage is based upon a contract of lease (*ijara*) in which the wife gives access to her sexual organs for a specified time without the limitations of ownership being transferred. Slavery or concubinage is based on a contract of ownership (*tamlik*) in which the whole woman is owned in all her parts and potentials.

Many Muslims today do not understand the contractual nature of marriage in Islam. As they get married, they leave it to jurists and family elders to work out the terms of the exchange. Many families postpone the actual exchange of money or goods until after the wedding, in order to conceal the nature of the transaction. Often they postpone the transfer of money forever, if both sides agree to that. However, legally, the marriage contract is not valid unless the amount to be paid is specified, whether it is actually passed over immediately or postponed to a later time.[24] In contrast to the technical understanding of jurists, many Muslims consider formal marriage to be a sacred duty more than a legal contract. This is an opinion popularly supported by a hadith that depicts the Prophet saying, "Marriage is half of one's religious obligation." Most Muslim families make heterosexual marriage a religious duty because it is so important to them as a way of generating security, making social connections, securing wealth or prestige, and of course continuing the family lineage through procreation. However, no matter how important marriage is, it is not a rite of worship (*ʿibada*) between believers and God; rather it is a transaction (*muʿamala*) between two persons and their families and communities. For the earliest Muslims, marriage was an institution inherited from pre-Islamic Arab society; as the Qur'an discussed some points relating to it and the Prophet guided them, they reformed their marriage practices to further accord with Islamic values. The Qur'an and the Prophet were interested in reforming an already existing secular institution of marriage, formalizing it, and restricting whom a Muslim might marry and under what conditions. Muslim jurists have modeled the standard marriage (*nikah*) for heterosexual couples on a business contract, further revealing that it is, in essence, a secular institution. As a human–human interaction rather than a God–human interaction, marriage's rules can change in accord with the internal principles of fiqh and under pressure from the practices of the surrounding society and the norms of government.

In form and substance, Islamic marriage is quite similar to the secular "civil union" that is increasingly being adopted by Western democracies. Heterosexual Muslims living as citizens of Western countries register their marriages as civil unions, even if they have a religious ceremony to mark the occasion. Legally, this is no different from homosexual unions under governments that allow same-sex marriage (such as Canada, Britain, the Netherlands, South Africa, and many other European Union states) and same-sex civil partnerships (like some states in the U.S.). In these places, homosexual Muslims can form unions of same-sex partners which have legal status equal to heterosexual marriage partners. Would Muslim citizens of such nations recognize the legality and validity of same-sex marriage contracts even if they found them morally questionable or even repugnant? Increasingly, Muslims living in secular democracies have to confront this reality. Yet sadly online fatwas and television talk shows document how neo-traditionalists fail to live up to the challenge.

Reasoning by Analogy: Same-Sex Marriage for Muslims

Will Muslims engage in reasoning by analogy to reform the *shari'a* in ways that will approve of same-sex marriages? It seems like a utopian suggestion in the current climate, when legal reasoning seems stalled in Muslim communities and ideology overshadows legal thinking. However, it may not appear so utopian when we realize that most Muslims are more than happy to alter their understanding of the *shari'a* where heterosexuality is concerned. Owning slaves and concubines was perfectly legal under the *shari'a* as inherited from the classical period, but the vast majority of Muslims no longer recognize these practices as morally allowable in Islam. These practices that are supported by *shari'a* rulings have been quietly abandoned in favor of a more bourgeois conception of marriage and family. Another example is the presence of eunuchs. Castrated formerly male servants were once ubiquitous in aristocratic Islamic homes, royal courts, and even at the Prophet's tomb in Medina. Rulings about these "males made non-men" are found in the *shari'a*, but most contemporary Muslims are horrified by the idea of castration and the resulting gender ambivalence. Another example is gender equality between men and women. This is increasingly accepted by Muslims in the workplace and home, despite the fact that the marriage contract inscribes highly differentiated rights and privileges for men and women; many contemporary Muslim women are shocked to discover the real nature of their marriage in *shari'a* terms and its underlying legal rationale as a contract of sale.

Beyond the immediate sphere of gender and sexuality, most Muslims are quite willing to innovate in matters of finance, banking, trade, transport, dress, and government in order to harmonize their religious ideals with modernity's social changes and technological innovations. The *shari'a*, for instance, presumes government by a king, emperor, or military autocrat, but most Muslims are happy to adjust their conception of legitimate governance and citizenship to conform to democratic and parliamentary norms. Most simply ignore the dissonance between the rulings of the *shari'a* as inherited and their own current practices. The educated few try to confront the contradictions and urge reform of the *shari'a* based upon its inherent principles of flexibility, potential growth, and gradual accommodation to changing circumstances, as we saw in Chapter 4. The question is whether the heterosexual majority of Muslims will allow the same liberality and progressive change for their gay and lesbian fellow believers as they apply to themselves.

Although classical Islamic law generally forbids same-sex acts, there was no juridical consensus (*ijma'*) as to why, under what conditions, and with what punishment. Thus the subject should still be discussed and, in the light of new evidence and under unprecedented social conditions, be open to revision through *ijtihad*. Classical Islamic law forbade same-sex penetrative acts but did not address same-sex relationships. This allows us to ask whether, if there could be legal contracts of marriage or civic union between same-sex partners, the sex acts would still be illegal or immoral. Jurists outlawed same-sex acts on the basis of hadith not the Qur'an, for the verses about the Prophet Lot (even if they are interpreted as being about homosexuality) do not have legal specificity to govern rulings in the *shari'a*. Some of the relevant hadith are of questionable authenticity and all of them have single-transmission chains that, in Islamic legal theory, can lead to speculative opinion but not to obligating certainty. From within the sources of *shari'a*, there is room for doubt that the decisions of past jurists are comprehensive or immutable. From outside the *shari'a*, changing social conditions and scientific knowledge have created the situation that decisions of the past are no longer adequate to address with justice contemporary realities. This is another indication that reform is not just possible but necessary.

Can the *shari'a* be adapted to a more pluralistic ethic that celebrates sexuality and embraces sexual diversity? These are not utopian questions but rather intensely practical ones, and are being worked through slowly and tentatively by gay and lesbian Muslim support groups. The support groups are informed by the insight that sexual orientation is inherent in one's personality, an insight that is increasingly supported by psychologists and sociologists and was not available to jurists of the classical era. The support groups are enlivened by the legal expansion of individual liberties enshrined in the notion of universal human rights and constitutional safeguards (which is present in the classical *shari'a* in the notion of *adamiyya* or human inviolability but was not fully developed by those who crafted the classical *shari'a*). They are empowered by the political ascendancy of democratic governance and the breakdown of authoritarian regimes based upon patriarchal, imperial, or racist ideologies. Under pressure from these forces, the *shari'a* must either flex while expanding upon its essential principles, or it will break. Breakdown will lead to increased family trauma, cognitive dissonance, and social violence among Muslims. The symptoms of such breakdown are visible in contemporary Muslim-minority communities, as elders and spokesmen resist necessary reform and some men of a younger generation are drawn toward extremist violence, and many avoid the mosque or leave the religion disillusioned.

Reforming the Norms of Marriage

After asking whether Muslims will address reform and if reform is justified, the question is how to carry out reform. Gay and lesbian Muslims take the lead at this point and indicate out how Islamic norms guide their own relationships whether sanctified as *nikah* marriage or other forms of contractual agreements. Same-sex couples can model their own marriages and partnerships on the Qur'anic statements about marriage, even though these are phrased in language that addresses heterosexual couples. Great wisdom is available in the Qur'an for same-sex partners if they can extract general principles from beneath the specifically gendered terms it uses. For instance, the Qur'an says, *Your women are garments for you [men] and you [men] and garments for them [women]* (Q. 2:187). This metaphor of marital partners being "garments" is very rich. Like clothing, a marital partner is both very private and very public. Clothing is very intimate to us because it is the object that is closest to us, like a second skin. This is the inner dimension of clothing: we wear something that feels good against the skin, fits comfortably, and moves with us fluently.

This Qur'anic verse about spouses as "garments" for each other invites deeper analysis. There is also an outer dimension to clothing. One wears something that expresses one's personality to the public, knowing that people see clothing and associate it with the inner self that is not visible. In this way, a marital partner is like the clothing we wear. She or he is very intimate to us, sexually, emotionally, and logistically. "Covering" is always a metaphor for having sexual intercourse, which is easily conjured up by clothing (the Qur'anic verse quoted above speaks about partners as "garments" of each other in the context of permitting sexual relations after sunset during days of fasting). But one's marital partner, whether in a heterosexual or homosexual couple, is also part of one's public persona. The public knows one through one's partner and not just as an individual. By using the metaphor of clothing to speak of the benefits of marriage, the Qur'an explicates a principle that is deeper than its surface-level use of pronouns to indicate a male and female couple. Both homosexual and heterosexual Muslims derive the same benefit from wearing clothing, and they can experience the same comfort in clothing themselves in the intimacy of a legally married partner.

The formalities and conditions of an Islamic marriage are not complicated. The question is whether they are applicable to a non-patriarchal social system and adaptable for a same-sex marriage. The conventional *nikah* for heterosexual couples has several structural elements (*arkan*) that must be fulfilled in order to be a legally valid union. The contract (*'aqd*) consists of a verbal act of offer and a response of acceptance made on the same occasion. Normally the woman will make an "offer" by saying a set formula and the man will make an "acceptance" by saying a set formula. This oral offer and acceptance constitutes the contract, which is then written down and signed by witnesses and the marriage partners. The contract is sealed by an exchange of value known as the marriage payment (*mahr*, often called "bride-price" in English), which is specified in the contract and is paid by the man to the woman. "In exchange, the husband gains a legitimate ownership right over the object of sale, which in this case is his wife's sexual and reproductive organs. Essentially an economic transaction ... it [also] signifies a woman's and her family's status and prestige in the community."[25] The exchange might be immediate or postponed, but its value (whether great or small) must be specified for the contract to be valid, because the exchange legitimates sexual intercourse. The bride's acceptance of the valuables signifies her allowing the husband to have sexual relations with her in exclusion of other men and obliges her to obey her husband in matters that impact her sexual availability to him and sexual restraint with others. This is summed up in the juristic maxim, "Intercourse invokes either payment or punishment."[26] It is required that the offer, acceptance, and exchange of some object of value be witnessed by adult, sane Muslims who sign the contract to ensure its validity and truthfulness.

In conventional marriage as defined in the *shari'a*, there are conditions that both partners must meet before they can make a marriage contract. Both partners must meet standards of maturity, sanity, and morality. In addition, they must have confessional compatibility (*mahal*): in classical *shari'a* this means that a Muslim man can marry a woman who is from a monotheistic faith (whether Muslim, Christian, Jew – or possibly other faiths by analogy), but a Muslim woman can marry only a Muslim man. Because the *shari'a* specifies that a child belongs to the biological father in identity, name, and religion, this ensures that the child of the marriage will be considered a Muslim even if the mother is not. It is a matter of controversy whether a woman needs the permission of her male guardian (*wali*) in order to contract her first marriage.[27]

Once signed and witnessed, the marriage must be consummated before it can be considered legally binding in all aspects. The marriage contract, ceremony, and celebrations are only a precursor to the real event, which is sexual intercourse now made legally permissible. In Arabic the term for marriage – *nikah* – also means sexual intercourse and the two meanings are entirely enmeshed. If the husband and wife do not have penetrative sexual intercourse, the marriage contract is not considered fully binding. Once consummated, the consequences of a marriage contract are many and varied. The husband is legally responsible for spending of his own wealth (*nifaqa*) to support his wife economically; in return, she is obliged to offer him sexual pleasure (*tamattu'*). The wife is entitled to companionship and sexual satisfaction, though in a completely unequal manner to the husband's right to sexual satisfaction with her.[28] The husband is responsible for maintaining any children born of the marriage and the wife is entitled to inherit from his wealth in the event of his death. The marriage, like any contractual agreement, can come to an end – by divorce, dissolution, or annulment.[29]

These technicalities, conditions, and consequences can be adapted to same-sex couples without compromising the integrity of the Islamic contract. The specific features that would need to be altered are exactly those features that Muslim feminists are trying to reform in the heterosexual marriage contract. These are the features that establish a hierarchy of power between the two partners based upon gender, entrenching male superiority and compromising female autonomy. In a non-patriarchal social environment, the marriage contract could be altered to assume an egalitarian parity between two partners. The reforms needed to ensure equality between man and woman in a heterosexual *nikah* are the same reforms needed to extend the right to marry to a homosexual couple in a same-sex *nikah*. In considering the possibility of reform of the marriage contract in Islam, this book refines the conclusion of Kecia Ali, the first Muslim scholar to consider seriously the permissibility of same-sex marriage in Islamic law. She concluded, "Same-sex marriage fundamentally challenges the basic structural premises of marriage as a contract."[30] What she meant is that same-sex marriage challenges the premises of the traditional model of Muslim marriage as defined in classical Islamic legal texts, which is built on analogies to sale and assumes strongly differentiated gender roles. This definition of marriage cannot accommodate same-sex marriage, just as it cannot accommodate egalitarian heterosexual marriages.

This book argues that same-sex marriage challenges some of the structural premises of the marriage contract that has been modeled on a contract of sale. Modeling marriage on a contract of sale is fundamentally limited and limiting, not only to same-sex couples but also to heterosexual couples who have an egalitarian relationship. The possibility of same-sex marriage challenges the marriage contract that jurists traditionally defined in a fundamentally patriarchal and hierarchical way. It does not challenge the basic concept of marriage as a contract, but rather challenges the conception of marriage as a contract of sale.

Before we consider these deeper issues, let us examine the commonalities between contracts for heterosexual marriage and contracts for same-sex marriage. A same-sex *nikah* should have the same fundamental structural elements that define a legally valid union for heterosexual couples. The basis of the contract (*'aqd*) is the verbal offer and acceptance: the bride would initiate by saying, "I marry myself to you in accordance with the message of God and the example of God's Prophet (may God bless him and grant him peace) for the specified marriage payment. Those present bear witness to this and God is the best of witnesses." To this offer, the groom will reply, "I accept marriage to you in accordance with the message of God and the example of God's Prophet (may God bless him and grant him peace) for the specified marriage payment. Those present bear witness to this and God is the best of witnesses." These words can be said in any language understandable by the two partners and witnesses, though some Muslims feel that they should be said also in Arabic. If pronounced in English, a same-sex couple can say this formula of offer and acceptance exactly as a heterosexual couple, as the pronouns "I" and "you" are not limited by gender (such is the case in most other European languages and also in Urdu and Persian); no alteration of the words or meaning is necessary. In Arabic, the pronoun for "you" is gendered (such that "you" for a female is slightly different than the "you" for a male), so a slight alteration in the pronouns would be required for a woman to offer to marry female partner or a man to marry a male partner.[31]

It is not really in the actual words of the Islamic marriage vow that differences arise for a same-sex couple. After the oral vow and written record, the contract is sealed by an exchange of value (*mahr*). In heterosexual *nikah*, the man pays the woman, reflecting a patriarchal assumption that the man earns money outside the home and is expected to support his wife. The partner who is more economically independent could take on this role and offer something of value to the one who is not earning outside the home (or not earning as much). If the couple does not want there to be a hierarchical difference of economic status between them, one could give *mahr* to the other in order to seal the contract, and the other could respond with an equivalent gift as a token of esteem. One partner's acceptance of the valuables from the other signifies one's allowing the partner to have exclusive sexual access and obliges one to consult honestly in matters that impact sexual availability with the partner and sexual restraint with others. As in a heterosexual *nikah*, the witnesses sign the contract.[32]

Other conditions apply to same-sex couples who wish to marry. Both partners must meet standards of maturity, sanity, and morality, just as heterosexual partners must. In addition, same-sex couples should also have confessional compatibility (*mahal*) so as to ensure religious harmony in their marriage. Determining compatibility in a same-sex couple requires some alteration of the conventional norms, because the classical *shari'a* enshrines a gender hierarchy in this condition. In a same-sex marriage, reproduction is not an important issue, so the condition that the two spouses' religious allegiance is compatible can be altered (a condition intended to ensure that children of a Muslim man will be raised Muslim). Both partners in a same-sex *nikah* can take on the empowered role reserved for the man in conventional heterosexual *nikah*. That is, a Muslim in a same-sex *nikah* can marry a partner who is also a Muslim or belongs to a related monotheistic religion. This is a reform that many feminist Muslims are pushing for in heterosexual *nikah*. They argue that in a non-patriarchal social system it is not realistic to assume that a child "belongs" solely to the father, and therefore there is no need for a Muslim woman to be limited to marrying only a Muslim man. In modern social systems that are moving beyond patriarchy, religious identity and faith are not given by a father to his children, but are rather a matter of conscience that children as autonomous individuals must adopt free of coercion. Before marriage, both partners should deliberately discuss the issue of religious compatibility and agree on how children might be raised if the marriage results in children. This is important also for same-sex marriages, as partners (especially women) may be caring for children born from a previous heterosexual marriage, about which they may not have had full conscientious choice.

In a same-sex *nikah*, both partners can give themselves in marriage as long as they are legally adult. On this issue, advocates of same-sex *nikah* agree with feminist Muslims that it is not required to have permission of a male guardian (*wali*) if one is mature and sane. They assert that an adult has her or his own independent legal agency to initiate a contract of marriage. This is an important condition, because many lesbian, gay, and transgender Muslims do not have their parents' or family's support to marry in a same-sex *nikah*. In taking this position, they follow the decision of Hanafi jurists that a woman who is mature and sane does not need a male guardian to contract her marriage for her.[33]

For same-sex couples as for heterosexual couples, the exchange and contract make licit their sexual intercourse, and the contract is fully binding with legal consequences only after consummation. It is in the couple's lived reality that a same-sex *nikah* is most different from a conventional heterosexual one. This is because the two partners are not differentiated by gender. In conventional marriage, the husband is responsible for supporting his wife and she offers him sexual pleasure in return. For a same-sex couple, these roles would be mutual and shared; both would be expected to contribute economically to the household in accord with their capacity, and each would offer sexual satisfaction to the other as a shared obligation. While each contributes to support the household, each can also hold property in her or his own name without sacrificing that right upon entering a marriage. If there are children in the marriage, secular law would define their parentage, and that would determine responsibility for maintenance and inheritance. In the event of the death of one of the partners, the other would be entitled to inherit from her or him.

The possibility of divorce is an integral part of any Islamic marriage contract. A same-sex *nikah* may end in dissolution, mutual separation, or annulment, but here too there are technical differences from heterosexual *nikah*, owing to the fact that the couple's roles are not determined by gender difference. Because both partners (whether both male or both female) are considered independent and autonomous legal agents, there is no possibility of a one-sided pronouncement of divorce (*talaq*) with the right to take the other back even against her or his will. This is a right of men in heterosexual *nikah*, as it was elaborated in a patriarchal environment. Muslim feminists lobby to have this kind of divorce renounced by Muslims, and national codes of law in Muslim-majority countries increasingly restrict the right of men to such unilateral divorce. Many Muslims in modern societies see this kind of divorce as injurious to women and encouraging irresponsible abuse by some men. For this reason alone, same-sex Muslim couples should renounce the practice of unilateral divorce and stipulate that in their *nikah* contract. In contrast, a same-sex *nikah* can end in a more limited dissolution of marriage (*khul'*). Dissolution of the marriage would be enacted with the consent of both partners, but in extraordinary cases – such as a partner's insanity or contagious illness – it can be unilateral. In either case, the value of the *mahr* must be returned to the partner who gave it in order for the partners to be released from contractual obligations. Mutual separation (*mubarat*) is also possible if both partners feel irreconcilable dislike for each other, and some portion of the *mahr* must be returned to symbolize the end of the contract. Alternatively, either partner can initiate an annulment if any details of the marriage contract are fraudulent or faulty.

In summarizing these small adjustments, we can observe that the two partners of a same-sex *nikah* are treated as equals legally and morally. This is required by the fact they are of the same gender. This is as true when both partners are women as when both partners are men, because they are acting as independent and autonomous moral agents, the role assigned only to the male partner in a conventional heterosexual *nikah*. Muslim feminists strive for the same adjustments in their proposed reform of Islamic marriage law, because in increasingly non-patriarchal societies women are recognized as legally and morally equal to men. Thus we can see that the adjustments to the *nikah* contract envisioned by lesbian, gay, and transgender Muslims are analogous to those envisioned by feminists who focus more exclusively on women's rights. If Islamic marriages consisted of partnerships that were not differentiated by gender inequality, then they would be more open to the possibility of same-sex couples engaging in marriage. The underlying obstacle to the full participation of gay and lesbian believers in marriage is the inequality in gender roles that patriarchy enforces, rather than specifically the issue of sexual orientation. The relationship between sexual orientation and gender identity is a theme that has emerged repeatedly in this study, and the next chapter on transgender issues will focus exclusively upon it.

It is one thing to propose reforms to Islamic marriage customs and another thing to justify the reform Islamically. Many Muslims would respond with horror to the reforms and adjustments proposed above, claiming that the conventional customs of marriage are enshrined in the *shari'a* which represents the immutable will of God. But in fact these customs are based on juridical analogy and not on the will of God as articulated in the Qur'an. The Qur'an calls marriage a "firm contract," but it was jurists who imagined that contract to be based upon a contract of sale. This was the firmest and legally most simple kind of contract, so jurists elaborated the details of marriage between a man and woman on the analogy of the woman "selling" access to her sexual organs to the man, who thus attained sole proprietorship in exchange for monetary value. Just when and how Muslim jurists decided that a marriage contract should be based upon a sale contract is not clear.[34]

The reforms suggested above can be justified Islamically if the marriage contract were to be articulated in analogy to a different kind of contract. Islamic law recognizes many kinds of contracts: in addition to contracts of sale there are those of rent, deposit, or partnership. In choosing to base the law of marriage on a contract of sale, early Muslim jurists reverted to patriarchal values in which women were considered property, despite the Qur'anic imperative to assert women's moral and legal agency. Contemporary jurists can alternatively conceive of marriage as based by analogy upon a contract of partnership (*musharaka*) rather than one of sale (*bay'*). Partnership is an economic exchange in which two or more persons entrust some objects of value to a common venture, to be under the custodianship of another for a period of time. A contract of partnership witnesses this exchange, establishes its conditions and limitations, and serves to regulate its future consequence. The person specified as custodian of the partnership's objects of value is offered some money or object of value with respect to his or her role as manager. It is thus different from a contract of sale, in which ownership of the object of value is completely given over to the dominion and control of another in exchange for a monetary amount or other valuable considered its equivalent in worth. In an interaction of partnership, dominion is retained by the original owner but certain rights are granted to the one entrusted with custodianship to deal with the objects of value so as to protect, cultivate, or enjoy them for the allotted period; however, these rights are limited by the understanding that the object of value not be damaged or endangered, so that it can be ultimately returned intact (or with increased value) to its original owner at some future date. In a partnership, risk is shared among those entering into the contract and the fruits of profit are also shared, without total dominion being assigned to any one member of the partnership.

What would an Islamic marriage look like if it were based on a contract of partnership rather than one of sale? In a conventional marriage, the bride "sells" access to her sexual organs to the husband's exclusive dominion. If marriage were based upon a contract of partnership, each partner would entrust access to his or her sexual organs to the other partner's custodianship and enjoyment, without giving over complete dominion to the other. A partnership implies shared responsibility. Sexual access is granted to the partner under the condition that the partner protects and cultivates one's sexuality while enjoying it, such that the partner can ultimately "return" it intact and undamaged if the contract were to come to a close. Basing marriage upon a contract of partnership would entail that each partner enjoy access to the other's sexuality and sex organs while also protecting them from harm – this means both physical harm (such as sexually transmitted disease) and also psychological harm (such as sexual abuse or coercion). It also means that one partner does not surrender "ownership" of an integral part of herself to the dominion and complete control of the other. Neither would have to take on conventional gender roles that are inherently unequal.

This last issue is a crucial distinction, for conventional Islamic marriage rests upon the disturbing notion that a woman's sex organs can be separated from her personhood, such that she can "sell" access to her organs for the control and pleasure of her husband. But this is simply a notion, a supposition upon which are based the legal rulings governing marriage. In real life, a woman cannot separate her sexual organs from her personhood. This fact justifies her husband's right – according to classical *shari'a* – to survey and control her movements and interactions outside the home and with all other people. He is granted this authority in order to exercise his dominion over what he rightly owns – namely, access to her sexual organs and the pleasures associated with them.

In contrast, basing marriage upon a contract of partnership would emphasize the mutual trust necessary for both partners. Entrusting something of value to the custodianship and protection of another requires trust to be established between them and to be reinforced periodically. Some level of scrutiny and questioning of one partner by the other is allowed by such a contract, but one partner's inherent legal autonomy is not surrendered to the dominion and full control of the other. This requirement of mutual trust is further strengthened if both partners in a marriage entrust their sexual organs and associated pleasures to each other, in a partnership of risk and benefit shared by both sides.

It is possible to adjust Islamic legal reasoning to base marriage upon a contract of partnership rather than upon a contract of sale. The Qur'an calls marriage a firm contract and notes that it involves an exchange of value, but does not specify an analogy to a specific kind of contract. This leaves it open for jurists and the community they represent to decide upon what kind of contract to base the norms of marriage. Jurists in the classical period chose an analogy based on sale, much to the detriment of women. The jurists' choice was dictated not by the Qur'an but rather by their patriarchal assumptions about women's human worth, moral agency, and legal capacity. If contemporary jurists were to decide that the marriage contract is better conceived through analogy to a partnership, the detailed adjustments suggested above would be suitable and justifiable. Such a shift of legal rulings might even better fulfill the Qur'anic vision of what marriage should be. It is the force of precedent, the comfort of habit, and patriarchal authority that prevent Muslims from reconceiving marriage in this way.

Such a shift of legal ruling is possible within the framework of the *shari'a*, as we saw in reference to the principles articulated by al-Shatibi in the previous chapter. According to al-Shatibi, the jurist must reason about how shifting legal rationale to embrace an innovative ruling will be effective in removing harm and ensuring benefit. Just because an alternative ruling is possible does not mean that it is to be adopted and the *shari'a* adapted to it. Let us first consider what would be the benefit to heterosexual couples, for they are the statistical majority in Muslim communities. Reconceiving marriage as a contract analogous to that of a partnership would greatly benefit heterosexual couples. It would enhance the rights of women within marriage by making them comparable to those of the men (especially in the controversial area of divorce). It would emphasize complementarity and reciprocal obligation between the two partners, bringing marital norms closer to the Qur'anic ideal of gender equality. It would also have the consequence of forcing men to forgo the custom of polygyny (marriage to several women at once), thereby dispelling a source of mistrust and insecurity for women. More subtly, it would acknowledge that women possess a unique sexuality and experience of sexual pleasure that are of worth in themselves and are not simply defined as the husband's penetration.

Male medical doctors are only slowly acknowledging what women knew all along – that men's pleasure in penetration does not always lead to women's sexual fulfillment. If marriage were conceived as a contract based upon partnership, both partners would entrust access to their sexual organs to the other in all their unique specificity; each can therefore expect (or demand) sexual fulfillment according to the unique configuration of her or his body, psyche, and sexuality. This would promote more fulfilling marital bonds, eliminate potential causes of divorce, and reduce the likeliness of infidelity.

Such a shift in the legal construction of marriage would benefit women directly, and the male partners of women would also benefit from women's increased security, trust, and sexual fulfillment. This reform would remove many types of harm that affect both men and women in heterosexual marriages. Next let us consider how it would benefit homosexual couples. The same adjustments that would make heterosexual marriages more egalitarian and reciprocal would constitute the groundwork upon which the right to marriage could be extended to same-sex couples. Both depend upon rejecting the hierarchal gender roles that patriarchy promotes. The first step would be to view men and women as equal in their reciprocal rights and privileges within the heterosexual marriage contract. The second step would be to see same-sex couples as having a relationship that is equal to that of heterosexual couples, for it fulfills the inherent needs, desires, and emotional drives of their sexual orientation. From this perspective a committed homosexual relationship is based upon the same social principles, human urgency, and moral worth as a committed heterosexual relationship. If that second step is made, then Muslims can extend the privilege of marriage to homosexual couples, allowing the Qur'anic verses that were explicitly articulated for heterosexual couples to implicitly guide homosexual couples. If the same principles are at work in both cases, then the same rulings should be constructed to guide them both.

Same-Sex Marriage in Practice

Although many contemporary Muslims are gingerly taking this first step toward a greater gender equality, there is no guarantee that Muslim communities will collectively take the second step toward allowing same-sex Muslim partners to marry. While they hesitate, constitutional democracies are rapidly coming to acknowledge and legalize same-sex civil unions and marriages. This values gap creates a great danger for Muslims living as minorities in such democratic states. For some conservative Muslims, the government's legalizing same-sex unions or marriages seems like an assault on their religious integrity, causing them to retreat from civic engagement or denounce democratic values.

In some democratic states, like the Netherlands, one's civic loyalty is almost defined by one's vocal acceptance of the rights of minorities such as lesbians and gays, and Muslims are often suspected of civic treason or incompatibility with national values when they say that homosexuals should not be allowed to marry.

When Muslim minorities are facing such civic trials, many ask why gay and lesbian Muslim activists push same-sex marriage. The activists provide several answers . The first is that it is a matter of justice and compassion, which are not subject to negotiation, dilution, or postponement. If transgender, gay, and lesbian Muslims are citizens with rights, then they deserve the right to enter into civil unions or marriages that are recognized by the state, just as do all other citizens regardless of their religious faith, sexual orientation, or gender identity. There are practical financial, logistical, and social benefits to being in a civil union or marriage and it is discriminatory to bar people from these because of sexual orientation. Further, there is great emotional satisfaction in getting state or community recognition as a committed partnership, and this helps couples to stay together when so many other forces conspire to break couples apart. Finally, life is short, and when one finds a partner with whom to share love, joy, pain, and sorrow, no consideration of gradual social change or political strategy can justify delaying the urge to seal one's commitment.

Skeptics will continue to ask, if civil unions are legally available to same-sex couples, why do activists push for marriage? Many constitutional democracies experimented with first allowing same-sex unions – the equivalent of the state recognizing heterosexual couples who choose to share a household or start a family without being formally married – without calling such unions "marriages." After years of continual advocacy by activists, such states (like the Netherlands, the U.K., and Canada) later legalized same-sex marriages that are fully equivalent to heterosexual marriage in legal consequence and in name. The name "marriage" itself if very powerful, loaded as it is with symbolic power, legal authority, and religious significance. Many religious communities strongly resist the term "marriage" being appropriated by same-sex couples to describe their commitment to each other.

For example, in 2006, the constitutional court in South Africa ruled that it was discriminatory that same-sex couples had no legal way to formalize their commitment and ordered the government to eliminate this discrimination that infringed upon inalienable rights enshrined in the constitution. The government, controlled by the ruling African National Congress (A.N.C.), proposed amending the laws to allow same-sex marriage. This sparked vociferous protest by religious communities – mainly Protestant, Catholic, and Muslim – who charged that offering same-sex couples the ability to marry infringed on their religious values and their freedom to worship without state interference. The government initiated a series of public meetings where legislators could listen to the public voice their opinions in open-microphone sessions in town halls. When I attended one such session in Cape Town, conservative Muslims and Christians argued that same-sex couples should be given the right to civil unions but not to "marriage," for "marriage" is a religious term that symbolizes legitimacy in the eyes of God. Eventually, the government rejected that argument as a "separate but equal" solution that is discrimination under the constitution. The government of South Africa legalized same-sex marriage in December 2006 without enacting intermediate legislation to allow civil unions that are legal but devoid of the symbolic power of the term "marriage." However, the public uproar and debate reveal the emotional weight of the term "marriage" for religious communities.

The question remains whether Muslims who are citizens of constitutional democracies that have legalized same-sex marriage are to consider it like a civil union under secular law or a *nikah* under religious custom. Does it make a difference whether a marriage is secular or sacred? To many interviewed for this book, it makes a huge difference – as we will see in the coming interviews with activists involved in same-sex marriage. Skeptics may continue to query why, even when same-sex marriage is legalized under secular law, activists attempt to justify same-sex marriage in terms of Islam as a faith. Why not just consider it a civil union under secular law and leave religion out of the picture? Such skeptics may include many gay, lesbian, and transgender Muslims who see getting religion involved as only complicating what is already a very complicated business. Many conservative Muslims might find it easier to tolerate the presence of lesbians and gays in their society if they did not lay claim to Islam in any way. But many of those Muslims who enter into same-sex unions and marriages also desire an element of religious ceremony or even a full *nikah* contract, though that is separate from the government-mandated legal proceedings. What makes a civil union or same-sex marriage recognized by the state equivalent to an Islamic *nikah*? It is the sense among participants – most importantly the couple coming into a union but also the witnesses and audience – that the union is consummated under the watchful observation of God and in accord with God's standards. It differs from a civil union or marriage under secular law because it involves the recitation of Qur'an and the deep symbolism of that seemingly simple act.

Same-Sex Muslim Marriages in Practice: Case Studies

Some of the lesbian and gay Muslims activists interviewed for this book have reflected deeply on the issue of marriage as it impacts their own lives and loves.

I interviewed Tamsila, one of the organizers of the Safra Project, a support group for lesbian and bisexual women based in London. At the time of this interview, she was planning to marry her lesbian partner who is also a Muslim, and both were determined to have a religious *nikah* ceremony in addition to the secular marriage. She was encouraged in her planning by the example of Daayiee Abdullah in the U.S., who has officiated as the imam in several same-sex *nikah* ceremonies (which in the U.S. do not entail legal consequence in the view of the state, which has not legalized same-sex marriage). Like Daayiee, Tamsila has personally tried to distill principles from the Qur'anic pronouncements on marriage that are relevant to guiding lesbian Muslims. She explains, "I look at it from a Qur'anic perspective, and ask what is the purpose of marriage in the Qur'an. I think that it is quite clear that in Islam marriage is not just about procreation. Marriage is about making a declaration of commitment between people, a commitment that is open toward the community and the family. It is not something that is hidden. It should be recognized by community and family, and they recognize the responsibilities of the people involved. That is the purpose of marriage: that responsibilities are upheld and kept, in a way that encourages the *iman* [faith] of the people involved, to promote it between themselves and amongst the community."[35] The primary purpose of marriage is to uphold the faith of two partners who share resources, build family, provide emotional comfort, and share sexual intimacy. In her view, whether children result from the marriage is a secondary factor; marriage should provide a stable base for raising children, but its essential purpose is wider and deeper than mere procreation. Lack of children (whether on purpose or forced by circumstance) does not invalidate a marriage for heterosexual couples in Islamic law and so this should not be presented as an obstacle to same-sex couples seeking to marry.

If the issue of procreation is set aside, the essential purpose of marriage is the same for heterosexual and homosexual couples. Tamsila observes that the form of the Islamic marriage is the same for both kinds of couple. "For me, marriage or *nikah* is not limited to heterosexual couples, but can also be open to homosexual couples ... The *nikah* vows are not gender-specific ... I think that opens up the possibility of same-sex couples having a *nikah* and introduces that possibility. Personally, I feel that if you are going to have a ceremony and public declaration of your commitment with somebody, it might as well be a *nikah*, as a Muslim. The purpose of it is the same ... The idea behind a *nikah* is the same if you were having a civil union. But as a person of faith, it would add more to the relationship to have it [a *nikah*] than without it, because it would include the *suras* of the Qur'an. From a very personal point of view, I would say that this adds to the day, to the event, to the ceremony ... For me, the Qur'an is not about specific [sexual] acts but rather it is about the meaning behind it, about the purpose and intention behind it." The actual words of the vow witnessed to in the contract are the same for a man and woman in a conventional, heterosexual *nikah*. Therefore, they can be pronounced with no change by a same-sex couple. The structure and legality of the *nikah* contract is equivalent to a civil union under secular law (and Tamsila is speaking in the context of the U.K., where same-sex marriages are legal and fully equal to heterosexual marriages). However, the *nikah* has a ritual dimension that is above and beyond the issue of contractual legality. The recitation of Qur'an during the ceremony of exchanging vows, signing the contract, and having witnesses confirm it gives the *nikah* a symbolic force. It is God who also witnesses the acts and judges the intentions of the couple, and God's presence is made palpable in the recitation of Qur'an, which is God's speech to humankind. It is this moral force, rather than mere legality, which has the power to keep a couple together through thick and thin.

Tamsila also observes that this adaptability of the *nikah* contract is not merely theoretical. It is possible in practice. She mentions that Daayiee Abdullah in the U.S. has conducted same-sex marriage on the model of a *nikah*, a *nikah* whose form need only be minimally adjusted to accommodate its innovative use for same-sex couples. In the U.K., there has not been the opportunity to conduct such a ceremony, but Tamsila mentions that several people are qualified and willing to forge ahead with such *ijtihad*. "Two of the people who work in Safra Project have a legal *shari'a* background. They've had to write *nikah* [contracts] before as part of their course. They have not done one for same-sex couple, but they are more than willing to write up a *nikah* for a same-sex couple." Several months after this interview, Tamsila entered into a *nikah* with her lesbian Muslim partner, witnessed by friends and some family members. The strength of their conviction and the sincerity of their intent were strong enough to overcome caution about the potential controversy this might raise in their extended families and the wider Muslim community.

In the U.S., Daayiee has officiated at several *nikah* ceremonies for unconventional Muslim couples. At the time of his interview (November 2005), he had officiated at two same-sex *nikah* ceremonies involving lesbian partners, at least one involving a transgender partner (who was denied marriage by other imams despite the fact that the couple consisted, at the time of the ceremony, of a male and a female partner), and six heterosexual couples who wanted a progressive and open imam. He has had five gay male couples seek counseling as they consider marriage, but none of them had undertaken the ceremony yet. Echoing what Tamsila says about the importance of the symbolic and ritual elements of marriage to Muslims who are lesbian, gay, and transgender, Daayiee explains, "Because of their closeness within their family – they were raised as

Muslims or as religious people in general – they want to satisfy their inner understanding, their religious understanding, that marriage is the appropriate way to wed [create a sexual union] in their faith. So they want to fulfill that, so they can have a sense of moral standing within their community in which they live." Daayiee is very careful to keep confidential the identity of the couples to allow them full control over publicity about their marriages. But he is very open in discussing how he conducts these marriages in terms of ritual norms, legal technicalities, and pastoral counseling. Issues he has addressed in practice include: who qualifies as an imam, how the imam is authorized by the state to conduct a marriage, to what extent the wording of the contract can be adjusted to reflect the individuality of couples, and in what ways the contract can be adjusted to contemporary realities of gender equality and secular citizenship.

In terms of who qualifies as an imam, Daayiee asserts the most radical and original simplicity of Islam. There are no clergy, no formal hierarchy of believers, and no ecclesiastical bureaucracy. Anyone with knowledge, moral probity, and community recognition can serve as imam in a *nikah*, though conventionally the imam is a male elder of the community and is sometimes required to have government license to play this role in a wedding. The minimum knowledge is sufficient Islamic training to understand the Qur'an and the legal formalities of the contract in Arabic. "Moral probity" means that the imam is known for honesty, fairness, and self-restraint so that no aspect of the contract will be tilted to the advantage of some and injustice toward others. "Community recognition" means that the couple approaches him as an Islamic authority and that the adult, sane, Muslim witnesses testify that he functions as the imam, along with a community that looks up to him to fulfill this function. The imam who conducts a marriage ceremony is often the formal prayer leader of a mosque, but this is not a requirement. Daayiee points out that his legal training in secular American law and social training as a marriage counselor actually make him more qualified to conduct Islamic marriages than most mosque leaders in the U.S.; they usually lack professional training in fields outside religion which necessarily impact the marriage couple.

In the U.S., the imam is delegated by the state to conduct a marriage, just like a Catholic priest, Protestant minister, or Jewish rabbi. However, the imam does not need authorization by a congregation or theological council in order to play this role. Some Islamic organizations in the U.S. would like to standardize this procedure in order to dominate the sphere of religious authority, but currently no organization is specified by the U.S. government or individual states to play this role, to the great advantage of Muslim believers. Daayiee explains how he proceeds: "In some states, you do [need government permission]. The person has to go and register as an imam. If I performed a marriage here in

Washington, D.C., for instance, I would have to go and register as the imam. In some other states, you don't have to be registered. But because the couple has to go to the state government for a blood test and other official things, their [Islamic] marriage is still considered a [legal] marriage even if it is not Christian marriage."

The couple must submit to blood tests in order to qualify to be married, under U.S. state laws. This is mainly to determine whether one has a communicable disease that could be sexually transmitted to the detriment of the other partner. It is also useful in alleviating medical emergencies and determining the parentage of children who might be born out the union. The blood test brings up the issue of whether the couple has had sexual intercourse (with the partner or with others) before marriage. Daayiee always raises this issue during the pre-marriage counseling that he insists upon before agreeing to marry any heterosexual or same-sex couple. "Most of the people I have dealt with have actually decided not to have sex before they get married ... But I asked them [as part of counseling] whether they had sexual relations and they answered that, up to that point, they had not ... I tell them that within twelve months, you should be able to decide that you would like to move into a *nikah*, after that period of time, or at least establish that that is what you are going to do and make it known. Because it often makes a difference how you are known within the wider community. If you let it be known in the wider community that you are a couple, then that gives you standing, and you can make it official after that. With other couples I've had – heterosexual couples – five of the six were older people who had been previously married ... So it was not like they were not accustomed to it, and they were waiting to establish their sexual relationship until after the marriage ceremony."

The counseling that Daayiee offers those considering marriage involves not just their personal relationship as a couple but also dealing with parents and wider family members. They are part of the marriage process, whether they support it or denounce it. A marriage brings the whole family and wider community into the relationship, in ways that a more personal and less public relationship does not. Daayiee explains, "In the counseling I've done with parents of gay, lesbian, and transgender people I've worked with, I try to tell parents that they cannot live the lives of their children. The children have grown up under their tutelage, and the child is going to take the best of what they taught him or her and will try to move forward with that. That is why the child is trying to get the parent involved in it [the marriage or partnership]. Though the parents may not agree that the child is marrying a person of the same sex, they should be at least willing to accept the respect that the children are extending to them and should keep the lines of communication open. They don't have to agree, but at least they should try to listen and understand the reasoning of why the child is doing this." Whether because of the couple's persistence or because of the mediation offered by Daayiee as a counselor, some parents who initially resist and denounce find ways to back away from their hurt and disappointment to see the wider picture. "A lot of times, when the parents step back and stop demanding and just listen, they tend to become more accepting, saying, 'I don't understand it all, but I see that the partner seems to be a good person with my child, and I just have to let it play out and see what happens.' This tends to be easier for mothers than for fathers! But I have found, in a couple of instances, fathers who are more understanding and accepting than their wives. It is hard to predict."

Daayiee's approach to marriage counseling is both flexible and comprehensive, because of the many intertwined issues encountered by same-sex couples or couples involving transgender people. He brings to it his skills in theology and pastoral care, family counseling and social work, and legal advising. It is quite common in the U.S. for a Muslim to desire marriage with a non-Muslim partner, so Daayiee often focuses on mediating a deep discussion between partners on their religious differences and how this might impact their relationship years down the road, even if they love each other. He makes this discussion and resolution of any outstanding confessional issues a requirement before going ahead to act as imam in their marriage. In practice, he does not discriminate between a male Muslim marrying a non-Muslim partner or a female Muslim marrying a non-Muslim partner, thereby laying aside the gender inequality enshrined in the classical *shari'a.* He finds that religious difference can be an issue even if both partners are Muslim, because of the wide variation in doctrinal beliefs, sectarian loyalties, and ethnic customs of Muslims in the U.S.

In this pre-marriage counseling, dialogue about religious differences leads to issues of child-rearing. He obliges the prospective marital partners to discuss whether they want children, how that decision might be made in the future, and whether religious differences between them as parents will affect how they raise children. His concern is not necessarily to guarantee that the child is raised Muslim, but rather to ensure that the couple is in accord over how to deal with the issue in the long term and whether they will agree to give the child some fair exposure to and training in Islam so that he or she can make a conscientious choice upon reaching maturity. He notes with some satisfaction that those who go through his pre-marital counseling, whether heterosexual or homosexual or transgender, get a deeper, more rigorous, practical, and caring preparation for marriage than conventional Muslim couples who get married within family custom at the local mosque. Heterosexual couples usually receive no advice, have no mediated sessions about potential problems, and are not encouraged to have heart-to-heart discussion about their intentions in getting married.

Alternatives to Formal Marriage: The *Mut'a* Model

Most Muslims today assume that Islam sanctions marriage between a man and a woman, a contract meant to be a life-long bond that ensures procreation and support for children. This is the discourse on marriage that fits into modern Western conceptions of morality and family. And indeed most Muslim marriages are of this kind, solemnized by a *nikah* or formal marriage contract. But during the lifetime of the Prophet there were several ways that heterosexual Muslims had "legalized sexual intercourse," which is the original meaning of the Arabic term *nikah*. I mentioned above that temporary informal marriage (*mut'a*) and concubinage (*riqq*) were also ways that Muslims enjoyed legally and religiously sanctioned sexual relationships. *Mut'a* offers a model that is especially interesting for contemporary lesbian, gay, and transgender Muslims as an alternative to formal marriage. Daayiee has discussed it with some same-sex couples as a possible first step toward *nikah* or formal marriage.

Mut'a or temporary marriage is a very controversial topic among Muslims and has been since the second decade after the Prophet died. It is a form of marriage that pre-dates Islam in Arabian custom, reflecting the simplicity and necessary flexibility of nomadic life. If a couple felt attraction and love between them, the partners could make an oral pact to be married for a stated period of time. The contract would require the man to give an object of value to the woman in exchange for her company and sexual intimacy. He would have to support her financially during that period of time, but did not have to set her up in an independent household. The intention of the *mut'a* marriage is legal sexual pleasure and companionship rather than setting up an independent household or bearing children.

As Muslims adapted this practice to their new religion, they saw *mut'a* as a contract just as moral and legal as a *nikah* or permanent formal marriage. However, as an oral contract *mut'a* did not require a written document, witnesses, public announcement, or family celebration. To be valid, the contract had to specify the length of time the marriage would last (from one day to ninety-nine years) and the value of the object exchanged. Inheritance and paternity issues were not involved because procreation was not the intention of such a marriage. Divorce was also not possible, because the marriage would end after a set time as stipulated in the contract. After the termination of such a marriage, the couple could make another temporary marriage contract and continue their relationship. If not, the female partner was required to wait for a set period (*'idda*) to ascertain that she was not pregnant from her former marriage before she could marry again; this is the same norm as occurs after a divorce, separation, or annulment of a permanent formal marriage. As Muslim jurists in later centuries worked out the norms of both *nikah* and *mut'a*, they came up with the following analogies. *Nikah* as permanent formal marriage was modeled upon a contract of sale (*bay'*) in which a woman hands over total dominion over her sexual capacities to her husband (with expectation of life-long maintenance, sharing a household, and probably reproductive activity). In contrast, *mut'a* as temporary informal marriage was modeled upon a contract of lease (*ijara*), in which a woman grants conditional use of her sexual capacities to her partner for a set duration (with expectation of temporary maintenance and companionship only). If a woman became pregnant while in a temporary informal marriage, her situation was complicated and difficult.[36]

The issue of *mut'a* is further complicated by the fact that the majority of Muslims, especially those of Sunni allegiance, denounce it as illegal and akin to prostitution (*bigha'*). Though the Prophet never personally had sexual relations with a woman through temporary informal marriage, there is evidence from hadith that some of his close companions did take wives through *mut'a*. Later generations argued heatedly over whether the practice was explicitly permitted by the Prophet, whether it was eventually outlawed by him after it had been practiced for some time, or whether he kept silent about it even as his companions engaged in it. Several decades after the Prophet's death, the early Meccan jurist 'Ata' ibn Abi Rabah circulated the opinion that *mut'a* was forbidden (we saw in Chapter 4 that he was influential in supporting the stoning to death penalty for sodomy). 'Ata' reports that "he thought *mut'a* was forbidden, but others disagreed with him. They went to see Ibn 'Abbas who said, 'Yes [that is permitted].' He ['Ata'] was still concerned about it, and asked Jabir ibn 'Abdallah, who said 'Yes [that is permitted]. We practiced it in the lifetime of the Messenger of God, of Abu Bakr and of 'Umar until – at the end of 'Umar's caliphate ... he was afraid that this could ultimately lead to degeneration of morals [and for this reason prohibited it].'"[37] In this report, the jurist consults Ibn 'Abbas, the cousin of the Prophet and source of many hadith, and Jabir ibn 'Abdallah, the Prophet's long-time companion, both of whom we met in Chapter 3 as alleged sources of hadith. Both of them contradicted his opinion, reporting that Muslims engaged in *mut'a* while the Prophet was alive without his criticism. Jabir further specified that the practice was banned by the second *khalifa*, 'Umar ibn al-Khattab. Despite the fact that the Prophet had allowed it, 'Umar felt that it might devolve into "degeneration of morals," apparently meaning that it would be used as a cover for prostitution. It was common for the early *khalifas* to appropriate for themselves such legal authority, and Sunni schools of law accept 'Umar's decision as binding.

However, not all Muslims accept that a *khalifa* could make such legal decisions on matters that had already been decided by the Prophet. Ibn 'Abbas is reported to have held the opinion that not only did the Prophet allow *mut'a* but that it is also mentioned in the Qur'an as allowed. This debate centers upon a verse in Surat al-Nisa', which comes after the specifications for what women a man can formally marry – *Allowed for you are women besides those, as long as you seek them by means of your wealth as men in marital bonds* [muhsinin] *not in fornication* [musafihin]. *Then in accord with the pleasure you enjoy with the women* [istamta'tum bihi min-hunna], *give them the monies* [ujur] *due to them as a duty. There is no blame upon you in giving more as you mutually agree beyond what you give as a duty, for God is a knowing One, One most wise* (Q. 4:24). The legal term *mut'a* for a temporary marriage is derived from this Qur'anic phrase "the pleasure you enjoy" (*istimta'*), which can be interpreted as different from the sexual exchange of formal marriage (*nikah*). Only the minority group of Shi'a Muslims have historically accepted the practice as legal in Islamic law.[38] As Shi'a, they do not accept the first three *khalifa*s, including 'Umar, as legitimate rulers or as juridical authorities who can override the Qur'an and the Prophet's example. Therefore, as their Ja'fari legal school developed in ways parallel to the Sunni legal schools, this Shi'a community formalized the standards of *mut'a* as an acceptable practice with legal norms comparable to the more common *nikah*. Some even argued that *mut'a* carried positive merit, since it had been practiced by some of the revered Shi'i imams who should be emulated.

In a climate of sectarian conflict that often erupted into violence, the issue of *mut'a* often became a rhetorical battlefield instead of a private arena for sexual relations. After the Iranian Revolution in 1978 and debilitating war with Iraq, Ayatollah Khomeini revived the practice of *mut'a*, encouraging Iranian youth to see in it a step toward the more expensive and difficult *nikah* marriage, and as a way for younger heterosexual couples to legal satisfy sexual desires while avoiding prostitution or fornication. His pronouncements brought the practice of *mut'a* back to global Muslim attention, though many Iranian Shi'a still frown upon it as antiquated, low class, overly pious, or injurious to women, as illustrated by the anthropologist Shahla Haeri in *The Law of Desire*.

Despite continuing Sunni–Shi'a sectarian tensions at the level of political rhetoric, Sunnis respect the Shi'i school of law at the level of jurisprudence. This school is called the Ja'fari School of law, and Sunni jurists grant it legitimacy as an Islamic expression of the *shari'a* on a par with their four major legal schools. Their decisions may differ, but all the schools of law (including the Shi'a school) refer to the same basic sources and adopt comparable legal principles. Thus a Sunni trained in Islamic law may consider a particular issue and opt to follow the decisions of another school of law, such as the Ja'fari school practiced by Shi'a, if that decision is more conducive to promoting benefit and reducing harm. I personally know of several cases in South Africa and the U.S. where

Sunni Muslim heterosexual couples engage in *mut'a* as a legal and moral way of enjoying conjugal relations without the publicity or expense of *nikah*.

As some lesbian, gay, and transgender Muslims consider marriage and look for Islamic means to form and legitimate their relationships, they do examine *mut'a* as a possible model. Youth from Sunni communities may only have heard of the practice in rhetorical denunciations of the Shi'a. However, Sunni Muslims like Daayiee, with legal training and knowledge of the *shari'a*, can consider the merits of *mut'a* as a marriage practice that is more flexible in its informality and therefore perhaps suited to the needs of same-sex couples, albeit there is no known case from classical Islamic history of *mut'a* between a same-sex couple just as there is no known case of *nikah* between such a couple. Most Muslims are not well enough educated about Islamic law to really know about *mut'a*, but if they are innovating in considering the possibility of same-sex marriage, they ought to consider all the available models. Daayiee explains that "I know that people and their libidos are different, and so the younger they tend to be [and therefore less able to restrain their libido], the more I move toward the concept of *mut'a*: that they have an [informal] contract between them and that they've known each other beyond a period of thirty to sixty days so that their relationship is beyond the simple lust stage, and therefore they've decided they like this person a lot and are spending time together and go places together, that is the stage at which they can really make a decision that they will be together sexually." *Mut'a* as an informal temporary contract of marriage allows people to be together both socially, intimately, or sexually without it being considered fornication (*zina'*) and morally punishable.

Daayiee counsels abstinence as two people in a same-sex couple get to know one another, feel attraction, and possibly fall in love. If they feel drawn toward each other and their sexual energy or libido drives them to the point that they are unwilling or unable to remain chaste, he advises them to consider a *mut'a* arrangement adjusted for same-sex couples. "I tell them that after they have known each other for a period of time and have moved beyond the stage of lust – because when you first meet a person there is always infatuation – but once you've gotten to know a person for thirty to sixty days, you know if you like the person and whether you want to try to make this thing happen [to become a couple]. At that point, you've upheld a standard even higher than what heterosexual couples do in a *mut'a*. So then you have abstained to the point that you know whether you really like this person. I tell them that, if you want to follow the *mut'a* model, if you're hot and bothered, to make a contract between the two of you, that this is your purpose and that you would like to have a *mut'a* relationship that should lead into marriage [formal permanent *nikah*]."

Like earlier Muslim jurists upon whom Sunnis relied, Daayiee perceives that *mut'a* is an ambiguous practice that does not have the high social status or religious sanction of formal marriage, for it can be abused to become like prostitution. Therefore, he recommends it to same-sex couples only once they feel that they would actually like a formal marriage, as a kind of pre-marital trial period. "I see it [*mut'a*] as a precursor to marriage – it should lead toward *nikah*." But it may also be very beneficial for same-sex couples, because they often lack the family support, economic independence, or autonomy to have a full-blown marriage with its concomitant publicity and the expectation of creating a joint household. Whether as a step toward formal marriage or as an end in itself, *mut'a* offers some lesbian, gay, or transgender Muslims an opportunity to sanctify their bond as a couple before God and enjoy intimacy without public scrutiny or formality. Yet it requires a degree of reformist flexibility and innovation for Sunni Muslims to adopt the practice and to adjust it for same-sex couples.

Reforming the *Shari'a*: Removing Harm and Ensuring Benefit

According to al-Shatibi, Muslim jurists can choose reformist or innovative interpretations of Islamic law, as long as their legal reasoning is principled and the new ruling removes harm and ensures public benefit. It is clear from the discussion above that for Muslims to allow and respect same-sex unions and marriages will be a long-delayed benefit for lesbian, gay, and transgender people within their community. Respecting such marriages will also be beneficial for heterosexual Muslims. First, it will provoke deep discussion within Muslim communities of the true meaning of marriage and help clarify for mainstream Muslims why and how they enter into marriages, which can only strengthen the institution. Second, such discussion will raise important issues of gender inequality that are inherent in the classical definition of marriage as *nikah*, inequalities that are detrimental to heterosexual women and are in need of reform if Muslims are to live in democracies based upon equal citizenship, individual liberties, and inalienable rights. Third, the discussion provoked by same-sex marriage will highlight the importance of love, trust, and mutual reciprocity in any marriage, especially since these virtues are sometimes lost in heterosexual Muslim marriages.

Benefit must be weighed against harm. Despite these potential social benefits, would there be any harmful consequences to accepting same-sex marriage? Despite the potential benefits described above, many Muslims will oppose same-sex marriage when it comes up for political discussion. They charge that legalizing such marriages in secular law or in religious custom would lead to destructive consequences. In an opportunistic alliance with conservative Christians and Jews (whom they will in other contexts disparage), conservative Muslims charge that accepting same-sex marriage will destroy conventional heterosexual marriage. For the reasons noted above, the reality may be the opposite: a dispassionate discussion of same-sex marriage might in fact help heterosexual couples refine their own approach to and commitment to marriage.

Neo-traditionalist Muslims oppose same-sex marriage with the rhetorical charge that accepting it will constitute a threat to procreation. They contend that continuation of the human race is part of God's will and that same-sex marriage is the final step in acknowledging and tolerating homosexuality, which will terminate procreative sexual activity and violate God's will for humanity. Above we read part of an interview with Shaykh Qaradawi in which he was asked to respond to the fact that some Western nations and some Christian denominations have accepted and legalized same-sex marriage. Shaykh Qaradawi answered, "What would be the result? The human race would end after a generation or two!" Decades before Shaykh Qaradawi's rise to media fame on al-Jazeera TV, a Deobandi scholar in India, Mufti Zafeeruddin, wrote a book in Urdu against homosexuality entitled *Nasl-Kushi* (*Killing the Lineage*). His viewpoint was that homosexuality amounts to "murdering" one's own children and the following generations that would have resulted if one had followed God's will and engaged in "natural" heterosexual procreative intercourse. Some even contend that the Qur'an accuses the Tribe of Lot of this very crime when Lot chastises them for *qat' al-sabil* or "cutting the path" (Q. 29:29). Most classical interpreters note that this phrase is an Arabic metaphor for highway robbery – to cut the path is to stop people who are traveling in caravans in order to steal their goods. With their Cities on the Plain (including Sodom and Gomorrah) strategically situated on important desert trade routes, the Tribe of Lot were in a commanding position to rob passing merchants, hold them for ransom, or demand from them unjust tolls.

Yet neo-traditionalists who are obsessed with finding homosexuality in the story of Lot suggest that this phrase has a far more tenuous interpretation, as "cutting the path" of procreation, an interpretation that is not supported by Arabic grammar or rhetoric.[39] The Qur'an uses the word *sabil* in many ways to mean a path – as a literal road, a metaphorical direction (as in the "paths of peace"), or rhetorically "a purposeful direction" (as in sacrificing one's life or wealth in the "path of God"). But it never uses *sabil* to indicate a path of nature consisting of procreation, raising offspring, or fostering succeeding generations. Although it is undoubtedly a collective duty (*fard kifaya*) for Muslims to ensure that children are born and raised to take responsibility in the next generation, that is clearly not an individual duty (*fard 'ayn*). It does no damage to that collective effort if some members of society do not procreate, whether because of infertility, rational choice, or as a consequence of their sexual orientation. In fact, those freed of the responsibility to care for their own few children can and do play socially beneficial roles assisting others, by teaching, nurturing, serving, healing, or pursuing artistic or scientific goals that are directly beneficial to the next generations. It is certainly hysterical to shout that if homosexuals are allowed to live in peace as partners, the human race will be extinguished in two generations.

Continuing our search for potential harm, we hear neo-traditionalist Muslims charge that accepting same-sex marriage means "promoting" homosexuality and causing it to spread. The metaphor they use is that of a virus. The underlying psychological connection is that sex is linked to disease. We can refer again to the television interview with Shaykh Qaradawi. When asked about homosexuality being openly discussed in society (as happens with the legalization of same-sex marriage), he answered, "This is a great calamity for all societies. It [homosexuality] is a kind of rebellion against religion and morality that is not so injurious to society as long as people cover it up. In that case, it is a matter that society isolates and limits so it does not manifest openly. However, it becomes the plague [*balwa*] afflicting everyone whenever it gets out from under secrecy and enters public knowledge, from the narrow confines to the wide-open space, where it is flaunted ... The Qur'an says, *Those who love that immoral scandal should circulate among those who believe shall have a grievous chastisement* (Q. 24:19). So spreading scandalous immorality is the great danger ... Whoever is afflicted with this has a disease that we must certainly cure. But we must not expand upon this. We must not consider this to be a natural phenomenon [*amr tabi'i*]. We must not ... open any doors for them ... and if not ... then our society is destroyed." In Shaykh Qaradawi's imagination, homosexuality is like a plague virus and same-sex marriage is like a huge sneeze in public. He contends that when same-sex marriage is legalized then homosexuality spreads, infecting the bodies of people who were previously healthily resistant or unexposed to it.

This viewpoint totally misdiagnoses the reality of homosexuality. It is not a contagious disease but rather an element of certain people's personalities such that they form a minority subculture. The struggle for lesbian and gay people is to find others like them and bond with them; it is not to convert heterosexual people into what they are not. The real social harm is in silencing and marginalizing gay and lesbian people. Legalizing and supporting same-sex marriage would help prevent forced marriages of homosexual men to heterosexual women or of lesbian women to heterosexual men, which often leads to marital unhappiness, depression, or infidelity. Such side effects force the man into unsafe sex practices that can spread sexually transmitted diseases – from a man to other men or from a man to his wife, who may get a disease while having marital sex with her husband. Sexually transmitted diseases are a real threat to all sexually active people, and are not exclusively associated with gay men, despite much negative publicity from the early years of the H.I.V./A.I.D.S. pandemic.[40] The same sexually transmitted diseases are transmitted by heterosexual and homosexual penetrative intercourse. According to global statistics, H.I.V./A.I.D.S. is more frequently transmitted in heterosexual intercourse, and heterosexual women are most vulnerable. For homosexual couples, legalized same-sex unions and marriages encourage commitment to an exclusive sexual relationship and also reduce the number of gay men coerced into heterosexual marriages in which they cannot be satisfied and faithful.[41] From the point of view of public health, allowing same-sex marriage will help limit the spread of disease rather than being akin to a disease in itself.

The social harm that neo-traditionalists claim will ensue from legalizing same-sex marriage is an illusion. Their visions of catastrophe, plague, and termination of the human race are fevered figments of their imagination, fueled by deep-seated fear and hatred of lesbian and gay people. They actually fear a stereotype of such people rather than fearing the actual people, whose nature they do not recognize and with whom they refuse to dialogue. Their concerns are not rooted in a factual analysis of those societies that have already legalized same-sex unions or marriages. Nor do they address the lived realities of the lesbian and gay people, including Muslims, who may benefit from such marriages. The benefits to Muslims in acknowledging and supporting same-sex marriage are many, as are the harms avoided by doing so. There is good reason for Muslims – both jurists and ordinary believers – to support both secular legislation for same-sex marriage and also to advocate for *shari'a* reforms that would allow these bonds to be sanctified as *nikah*.

Some Muslims perceive as a grave harm in their community opposing the legalization of same-sex unions and marriages. These progressive Muslims see a political danger in Muslims, as a minority community that often feels marginalized or threatened, refusing to stand up and support the human rights of another minority community, that of lesbian, gay, or transgender fellow citizens. For instance, in 2005 the Canadian Justice Minister proposed legislation that redefined marriage to include same-sex partners, against much opposition from the conservative political parties. The Justice Minister urged other minority groups in Canada – and specifically included Muslims in his call – to support the legislation as a sign of solidarity for another marginalized minority within their nation. However, most Muslims in Canada opposed the move and drifted toward the conservative parties, despite the latter's track record after 9/11 of suspecting Canadian Muslims of support for terrorism and extremism. Yet many dissenting voices were raised in the Muslim community. For example, the Muslim Canadian Congress (M.C.C.) – a Toronto-based grassroots organization – announced in a press conference in Ottawa that its members, as Muslim Canadians, welcomed the proposed legislation to legalize same-sex partnerships as marriage. Rizwana Jafri, President of the M.C.C., said, "It is incumbent upon us, as a minority, to stand up in solidarity with Canada's gays and lesbians despite the fact that many in our community believe our religion does not condone homosexuality ... This legislation is not about religion; it is about fundamental and universal human rights that are a guarantee that all Canadians, irrespective of their religious or ethnic background, feel part of the same family. While, within this family, we may agree to disagree we must respect each other and treat others with dignity that is a hallmark of civil society."[42]

In the U.S., some Muslims also point out the potential political harm that can come from their community's opposing human and legal rights of another minority and touting such opposition as a genuine and necessary expression of their religious faith. Such debates that involve political values just as much as religious beliefs are being played out in the U.S. on a more individual level. As noted above, the issue of same-sex unions and marriages is not being addressed in the U.S. at the federal level but rather at the state level. As states propose to either legalize or constitutionally bar same-sex legalized partnerships, some Muslims are speaking out in support of lesbian, gay, and transgender rights. Those few who speak out see this as a matter of human rights, legal justice, and political betterment for the Muslim minority as a whole. For example, Washington State, with support of its Governor, passed legislation that adds the category of sexual orientation to the state law banning discrimination in housing, employment, insurance, and credit (though it does not go so far as to grant same-sex partners civil unions or marriage).[43] This prompted conservatives to organize Referendum 65 to repeal the legislation, in the name of protecting religious faith and family values. In response to the conservatives' use of religion to garner support, progressive clergy of many different religious communities organized simultaneous prayer services in eight cities across the state to "thank God for creating and loving all persons just as we are" and bolster support for the legislation. Christian, Jewish, Buddhist, and Muslim clergy took part in the prayer service. Representing Islam was a Muslim chaplain, Nayer Taheri, who challenged traditional religious leaders who have "closed their eyes to the beauty of all people," including gay, lesbian, and transgender persons.[44] More than five hundred people, including clergy, lay-people, and the

Governor herself, took part in the interfaith prayer service organized by the Religious Coalition for Equality (R.C.E.), an interfaith association committed to educating Washington State citizens about civil rights and advocating marriage equality for all couples. Beginning in 2005, the R.C.E. turned the popular Saint Valentine's Day holiday (which celebrates love and commitment) into "Equality Day" for a public rally by people of all faiths to support equal rights for all regardless of gender identity or sexual orientation. In 2006, clergy from many faith traditions, including Rev. Jamal Rahman, spoke at the rally to encourage members of the Muslim community to support politically the human rights of all fellow citizens, including marital rights.

Despite outspoken support by such Muslim clergy and other religious leaders, the U.S. public seems to veer increasingly toward the conservatives' goal of banning same-sex unions and marriages (along with other legal rights for sexuality and gender minorities). In the November 2006 elections for state representatives, local government officials, and legal policies, the voters of nine different states considered referendums to ban same-sex marriage and civil unions in their state constitution. Wisconsin was one such state, where voters were confronted with a referendum reading, "Shall section 13 of article XIII of the Constitution be created to provide that only a marriage between one man and one woman shall be valid or recognized as a marriage in this state and that a legal status identical or substantially similar to that of marriage for unmarried individuals shall not be valid or recognized in this state?" Voters were asked to respond yes or no to this question, which would amend the state constitution. In the weeks before voting, some Muslim citizens spoke out against the referendum and its goals. One Muslim who supports civil liberties of all citizens as an expression of his Islamic faith worked with the community organization Fair Wisconsin to campaign against the referendum. He worked as a Legal Assistant for the American Civil Liberties Union and wrote, "This was my commitment to social justice, as a Muslim, as an Indian-American, as a person who believes in human rights. This was my desire to prevent the government from dictating the expression of faith and sexuality. Although I believe that homosexual acts are not permissible in Islam, I do not want the government to espouse or express these religious views. Such entanglement with religion is dangerous ... It is not strange for a practicing Muslim to support gay rights in this country. Such activism does not perpetuate homosexuality; it simply expresses our devotion to legal equity for all. Islam has a commitment to justice and as practicing Muslims we must be consistent in exercising it ... As members of this society, it is our duty to hold the government to these standards [that the equality and dignity of all individuals are protected under its constitution] regarding people of all religions, genders, ages, ethnicities, sexual orientations, and economic status."[45] He saw that protecting the rights of lesbian and gay fellow citizens was a way of protecting the rights of his own Muslim community. In his Islamically inflected vision of progressive politics, justice that excludes some is not the justice required by God, whom the Qur'an names *al-'adl* or the Just One. Despite the hard campaigning of this conscientious Muslim and many other citizens, the Wisconsin public voted to support the referendum and thereby curtail the ability of legislators or judges to protect and promote the civic rights of gender and sexuality minorities.

As of 2006, the public in eight of the nine states facing such referendums also voted to support them and ban same-sex marraige. Citizens of the U.S., of all faiths and beliefs, can expect this dynamic to continue until the federal government (mostly likely through the Supreme Court) addresses the issue. Allowing issues of fundamental civic inequalities for a minority to be decided as "states' rights" will replay the conflict over racial segregation that wracked the U.S. half a century ago.

Conclusion

Some heterosexual Muslims with a progressive approach to politics may support moves toward legalization of same-sex unions or even marriage. However, for many Muslims in minorities living in secular democracies, issues of religious fidelity (like personal morals, ritual duties, and theological imperatives) are weightier than coalition politics. Many will not support the rights of lesbian, transgender, and gay citizens because they view them as morally depraved or psychologically sick individuals rather than as a minority group. It is imperative therefore to examine closely Islam as a religion, as this study attempts to do. Secular politics is not the answer to the deep issue – it is only one piece of the solution. It is unlikely that Muslims will support civil rights for an abstract "gay community" when they suppress or reject members of their own faith, mosques, and family who are gay, lesbian, or transgender.

A potent combination of patriarchal custom and theological belief keeps many Muslims from seeing their lesbian, gay, and transgender fellow citizens as fully human and therefore deserving compassion and demanding justice. What is required is a deep reform of Islamic belief and action, not just a secular invitation to progressive political coalition-building. We must be honest in acknowledging that patriarchy existed before the Qur'anic revelation, persisted in the early Islamic community, and continued to exist centuries later during the formative period of Islamic law. The Qur'anic revelation and the Prophet Muhammad's creation of a new community challenged many of the patriarchal practices that were routine in Arab societies. The young community often did not live up to the initial challenge, especially after the death of Muhammad. It fell back on patriarchal norms in hopes of social stability and in the creation of a new Islamic elite ruling class.[46] With the advent of modernity, perceptions of human nature and social organization have changed, and the practice of religion changes with them. This is not just a reality; it is an ethical challenge and is also potentially a blessing. Modernity gives Muslims the chance of thinking differently and freeing ourselves from the shackles of patriarchal power.

For most of the history of Islam, Muslims assumed that the Qur'an demanded the political rule of a monarch, whether conceived as a *khalifa*, sultan, or king. This was true despite evidence of dissent in the earliest community, as many early followers of the Prophet rejected authoritarian rule.[47] Monarchal rule of an all-powerful male is one facet of patriarchy that is deeply woven into Islamic society and religion, even though the Qur'an does not explicitly sanction monarchy. In previous centuries, it was almost unthinkable to be a Muslim who questioned the right of monarchs to rule. If one rebelled against monarchs, one would be branded an apostate. Today, most Muslims do not live under monarchies, and most Muslims think this is a good thing. Their Islam is not less faithful because they live without monarchies; in fact it might be stronger for that reason.

For most of the history of Islam, Muslims took for granted that slavery was a legal and useful social institution. Islamic law adapted to the practice of owning human beings as slaves, a practice that existed before Islam and continued after Islam's advent. A wealthy male's right of ownership is one facet of patriarchy that is deeply woven into Islamic society and religion. This was true despite the Qur'anic emphasis on freeing slaves and the Prophet's example in this matter. Yet today most Muslims do not own and sell fellow human beings. Most Muslims would consider this a good thing and consider slavery a form of oppression.

For most of the history of Islam, Muslims have assumed women to be inferior to men. Some might limit this inferiority to realms of physical constitution and legal privilege, whereas others would extend the inferiority to piety and even rationality. The presumed superiority of gendered males is one facet of patriarchy that is deeply woven into Islamic society and religion, despite the Qur'an's empowerment of women in many fields. Islamic law adapted to this basic assumption of patriarchy and encoded it in all manner of legal norms and authoritative interpretations. Yet many Muslims today assert the fundamental equality between women and men in economic, social, religious, educational, and political spheres of life. Their Islam is not less faithful because they live without gender segregation and tribal honor codes; in fact their Islam might be stronger for their commitment to gender justice.

In many democratic nations, homosexual Muslims can now form legal unions with same-sex partners, unions that have equal legal status to those of their heterosexual neighbors. Will Muslim citizens of such nations recognize the legality and validity of same-sex marriage contracts, even if they find them morally questionable or even repugnant? Increasingly, Muslims living in the West will have to confront this reality, and the answer Muslims give may determine whether they are seen as citizens who accept the laws and values upon which the nation rests or rather as outsiders who are a threat. If Muslims insist that civil unions or marriages can only be between a man and a woman, they may find themselves in a troubling alliance with right-wing parties who wish to coopt them as religious conservatives while disparaging them as ethnic and religious minorities.

The issue of same-sex marriage depends upon Muslims' conception not just of sexual orientation but also more deeply of gender. If gender is dimorphic and the world is divided between male and female (with the male defining what it means to be human and controlling relations of power), then there is little scope for acceptance of same-sex marriage. This leads us to consider, in the next and final chapter, the issue of gender identity in a more direct way. Contesting dimorphic concepts of gender has been implicit throughout our discussion of sexual orientation. Muslims mainly oppose homosexuality because they think it amounts to a man giving up masculinity to act like a women, or involves a woman rebelling against her assigned gender to act like a man. For some people, however, it is not so clear who is a woman or what makes a man. In the experience of some people, the issue of gender is ambiguous, deceptive, or transitional. To take seriously their experiences, which are rooted in biology and genetics but are also psychologically complex, is to question the dimorphic definition of gender at its very heart. It is to this issue that we turn to reflect theologically upon the experience of transgender Muslims and the activists who speak up for them.

Chapter 6

Reviving Spirit: Islamic Approaches to Transgender Experience

> The human being has a manifest dimension and a non-manifest dimension. In other words, the human being has a body and a spirit. The spirit is truly simple and cannot be divided into parts ... The body is compound and can be divided into parts ... Every compound thing has within itself manyness and parts. When a thing has manyness and parts, each of its attributes and acts is singled out for one of its parts and organs ... The human spirit, which is truly simple, is living, knowing, hearing, seeing, and speaking. Its attributes do not resemble the attributes of the bodily frame, since the frame hears from one place, sees from another place, and speaks from another place. But the human spirit [is not like this] ... for its attributes and acts have no instruments and organs. This is the meaning of the saying, "God created Adam in [God's] form."
>
> Aziz al-Din Nasafi, *Kashf al-Haqa'iq*

The spirit is truly simple, indivisible, not bounded by space or corroded by time. The body is not simple – it belongs to the created world of material objects and is compound, divisible, limited by space, and corroded by time. The spirit is that which is of God present in every person. Each person is a unique individual and therefore limited by the body's materiality, yet each person also expresses the universal spirit and contains that which is of God. Resolving this paradox is the key to living an ethical life and understanding how God can be both everywhere and nowhere, both far and near, such that God can say *I am closer to human beings than their own jugular vein* (Q. 50:16). Muslim theologians have struggled to understand this paradox, but Sufis – Muslim mystics – have most deeply explored it.

The explanation given above in the epigraph is from Nasafi, a Sufi master and prolific author of Persian Sufi texts (died 1295). His writings helped to popularize Ibn 'Arabi, the daring theologian and profound Sufi thinker (died 1240). Ibn 'Arabi sought to explain the Qur'an's teaching about the interface between God and humanity, in ways that challenged patriarchal assumptions about gender and sexuality.[1] For Ibn 'Arabi and his followers, maleness is the force of spirit that takes an active creative role, whereas femaleness is the force of spirit that takes a passive receptive role. Acting together, these forces create effects in the material world, which are likened to "children" born from the intimacy and friction between these two forces. For these Sufis, maleness and femaleness represent kinds of forces or positions in the creative unfolding of the spirit in the midst of the material world. For them, male and female are not primarily biological descriptions of persons and do not limit the character of actual male or female individuals.

This chapter on gender identity takes Sufis like Ibn 'Arabi as its guide, since our previous guide to theology, Ibn Hazm, did not reflect so intensely upon the issue of gender. But Ibn 'Arabi admired Ibn Hazm greatly. He lived in Andalusia and adopted from Ibn Hazm the courage to assert highly unconventional Islamic interpretations. Ibn 'Arabi accepted many of the Zahiri scholar's critical insights into Islamic law. He saw in Ibn Hazm the very iconoclastic spirit of the Prophet Muhammad, who had the guts to confront all the idols of his era. Ibn 'Arabi, in his monumental book *al-Futuhat al-Makkiyya* (The Meccan Openings), records a dream vision he had of the Prophet. He said, "I saw the Prophet, may peace and blessings be upon him, in my sleep. The Prophet was embracing Ibn Hazm, the hadith scholar, such that the one disappeared into the other and I could see them as only one person, and that was the Prophet of God, peace and blessings be upon him. This is the most utmost kind of union."[2] In such dream visions, Sufis saw the soul as clearly as we routinely see the body, such that two could unite into one in an embrace of union if their souls were in perfect harmony.

According to such Sufis, the spirit was "blown into" the body of Adam, Eve, and all of their children by God's merciful breath, sparking life within the inert human body. Between the spirit and the body is an ambiguous force called the "soul." The soul can be imagined as the body's consciousness of its own life-force, which lets it breathe, think, act, reflect, and comprehend its mortal finitude. Or the soul can be imagined as the spirit's awareness of its being "trapped" in the body, that it is prior to the body, transcending the body, and persisting long after the body even as it bears the moral consequences of the body's actions. Either way one imagines it – from the perspective of the spirit confined to the body or from the perspective of the body animated by the spirit – the soul bridges the vast difference between ephemeral body and eternal spirit.

It is the goal of Sufis to highlight this vast difference between body and spirit and to encourage the Muslim believer to explore the spirit, to desist from identifying solely with the body, to leave behind the limitations of its appetites, drives, and obsessions. Sufis encourage Muslims to focus on the heart more than on the other limbs and organs of the body, for the heart is the place where the body interfaces with the unlimited spirit, which blows through the body yet is always in the presence of God. In this sense, the heart – above and beyond all other parts of the body – is the dwelling place of the spirit and is the seat of the soul.

The soul is an awareness more than a substance. It is a consciousness rather than a thing. It is the identity of the person who is animated by the spirit of God's merciful breath of creation. As an identity, it is self-reflexive – it is that part of our personality that says "I" and bears all the scars of such egoism. As an identity, it recognizes a name, perceives an individuality, and accepts culpability for the actions of the body. It organizes the parts of the body into a single being, a self. In that sense, the soul as an identity can be said to have gender. The soul, reflecting on the body, perceives itself to be female or male, or possibly both-male-and-female or neither-male-nor-female. No matter where a person, deep in his or her soul, situates the self in this duality between male and female, gender is a part of the human condition reflecting our partialness, incompleteness, and quality of being mired in duality.

In this sense, understanding how we are shaped by gender is essential, because through it we struggle to comprehend God. Human beings are sunk deeply into gender duality, but God is free of gender. It is a basic part of Islamic teachings that God is absolutely non-dual and has none of the limitations or conditions that characterize human existence. The Qur'an commands us to say, *God is a singular One, the eternal One, never begetting and never begotten, to whom no other bears comparison* (Q. 112:1–4). Not being ever born, God's existence is not based upon duality. Not ever begetting, God's creative nature is not limited by the maleness and femaleness that shape our understanding of reproduction. God created us in and through the gender differences that we feel so deeply, but God is above gender as the Qur'an reveals: *By the night when it falls, by the day when it breaks, by what has made the male and the female – you strive toward diverse ends!* (Q. 92:1–7).[3] This is true even if many Muslim theologians and ordinary believers assert that God is more like a masculine person than a feminine person, a flawed assertion that is the foundation of the patriarchal social order.[4]

The Qur'an both invokes gender differences – the male and the female – and also challenges our generalizations about them. This chapter will discuss in detail how the Qur'an uses gendered terms and images. However, before that we have to understand the variety, ambiguity, and flexibility of human gender identity. For as the spirit animates the inert body, the human soul takes shape. The soul is an identity and organizes the parts of the body into a cohesive self. In that sense, the soul as an identity can be said to have gender. Gender is not inherent in the body, but is rather a part of the personality which reflects upon the body. A body's anatomical parts do not determine the gender of the person who inhabits it. Rather gender is a component of the human personality; it is an identity that is learned through experience with the body. This identity may or may not be "in accord" with the body's apparent anatomical structures, as we will analyze in detail below. We will adopt the perspective of modern sociological and sexological research about gender identity before returning again to a theological perspective based upon the revealed words of the Qur'an.

Gender Identity and Sexuality

Muslim communities, like many communities shaped by patriachy, often confuse sexual orientation with gender identity. In interviews with gay Muslim men it is evident that when they come out, their families often understand them to be acting like or thinking like women. Similarly, Muslim families and communities often understand lesbians to be thinking or acting like men. The Islamic tradition has developed a complex understanding of gender – the differentiation between women and men – but it has not developed an equally nuanced notion of sexual orientation. Often matters of sexuality are treated by Muslim families and communities as problems of gender behavior or identity, much to the detriment of lesbian or gay Muslims who understand themselves as women who love other women or men or who love other men.[5] Yet there are others whose difference is not a matter of sexual orientation but rather of gender itself. That is, there are Muslims who feel like women even though their body and social status is deemed by others to be "male," as if one were a woman trapped in man's body; also there are those who feel that they are men even though others understand their body and social status to be "female," as if one were a man trapped in the body of a woman. There are others whose sense of gender is ambiguous, who feel that they are neither "male" nor "female" but rather both or neither. Such persons can be said to have "gender dysphoria" or anxiety arising from disharmony between their assigned gender (as imposed by others) and their own gender identity (as perceived by the self).[6]

We use the newly coined terms "transgender," "transsexual," and "intersex" to describe such people and their complex identities. The subtle but important differences between these terms will be discussed in detail below. These people ask not be judged by appearance, for outward appearance is not the same as inward identity and does not determine one's destiny in life. A person who may appear like a woman to observers – whether family, medical doctors, or people on the street – may identify as a man and feel like a man inside; further, this person may ardently desire to be seen by others as a man, to such an extent as to alter their appearance, dress the part, or even elect for hormone therapy and sexual realignment surgery to become biologically male. They also entreat others not to judge them too quickly without first considering their experiences, feelings, and intuitions from a perspective informed by medical knowledge, moral restraint, and heartfelt compassion.

Consciousness of being constantly watched by God is the key experience of Islam, and the watchful judgment of God is a double-edged sword. It restrains one from acting rashly and holds one tightly to a norm of ethical conduct. But it also frees one from being overly concerned with the shallow judgment of others, because one is deeply aware that only God judges one's soul and the worth of one's action. If one sinks profoundly into this Islamic consciousness, how can one bother with the snap judgments of others, based as they are all too often on shallow appearance or egoistic self-righteousness?

Transgender Muslims need the confidence that such belief provides even more than others, for their identities are difficult to hide. Gays and lesbians can, if need be, pass as conventional men or women. But transgender people have a more difficult time in families and in public. Their identities and experiences call into question the very notion of dimorphic gender, which in many ways is more basic than sexual orientation to our assumptions about what constitutes being human. For the sake of clear analysis, we have to distinguish between three different terms, though in popular usage they blur together or are juxtaposed: "sex," "gender," and "sexuality." "Sex" refers to one's anatomical genitalia, through which one is classified as male or female. "Gender" refers to one's expression of social behavior organized by gender norms, through which one is classified as masculine or feminine. Sexuality refers to one's consciousness of sexual desire and expression of intimacy and pleasure, which includes not just one's sexual orientation (whether one desires sexual contact with an opposite-sex or a same-sex partner) but also more subtle issues of degree of sexual desire (whether one experiences sexual desire at all, for instance), its intensity, and its focus. Finally, it should be noted that all these terms of analysis – "sex," "gender," and "sexuality" – are free of any assumption about specific acts of a sexual nature; one should never assume that stereotyped associations of certain sex acts with certain kinds of people actually accord with the lived experience of those people. These three terms help us to clarify the diverse ways in which gender and sexuality manifest in different people's lives. One could belong to a minority in terms of sexual orientation, if one were a man who desires sexual pleasure with another man or if one were a woman who desires the same with another woman. One could be a minority in terms of gender identity, if one were a man in sex anatomy but felt like a woman and behaved socially in feminine ways, or if one were a woman who felt like a man and behaved socially in masculine ways.

We can call the latter kind of people "transgender," meaning that they manifest the identity and behavior of the opposite gender from that which, in accordance with their anatomical sex organs, they were socialized to be. Transgender means a person has "moved across" from the gender into which they were socialized to the gender with which they identify. If such a transgender person actually acts to alter physique, hormonal balance, or sex organs to match their inner psychic gender identity, we can call her or him a "transsexual person." "Transsexual" refers to a person who has "moved across" from the sex organs with which they were born to the sex organs with which they feel comfortable as the organs that accord with their gender identity. One can be a transgender person without becoming a transsexual, if one chooses not to use hormone therapy and/or sex-realignment surgery to alter the body to conform to one's gender identity. In this sense, all transsexual individuals were at first transgender, meaning that they felt like a person of the other gender even before they acted to change their body to conform to that internal feeling and identity.

Both transgender and transsexual people are distinct from "hermaphrodites." A hermaphrodite is a person who bears both male and female anatomical features (in regard to genitalia or secondary sex features that develop with puberty).[7] However, natural hermaphrodites share similar struggles with transgender people, in that they are not easy to categorize and often suffer stigma, marginalization, or violence for this reason. Many hermaphrodites undergo surgery (either by choice or often by imposition in infancy) in order to become either male or female, since society offers no ambiguous middle ground. Some transgender people deliberately inhabit this ambiguous middle ground even if society punishes them for it; they choose to retain in one person features commonly identified as both male and female. Such people identify as "intersex" – inhabiting a social space and bodily presentation that is between the two sexes; some transgender people who have begun medical therapy to alter the body but have not completely changed into a "passable" male or female appearance also identify as intersex. Such are the variable positions that unconventional people can take with regard to gender as an internal identity manifested in bodily appearance. All these terms – "transgender," "transsexual," and "intersex" – are clearly distinguished from "transvestites," who are simply men who enjoy dressing in women's clothing or women who dress in men's clothing (without this behavior indicating anything about their deep gender identity or their sexual orientation). Most men who engage in transvestite behavior are heterosexual, though this behavioral pattern is often projected on to gay men as a stereotype. Similarly, lesbians are often stereotyped as women who dress as men, although in fact this sexual orientation may have nothing to do with dress patterns.

These complex terms help us to describe the highly variable patterns of gender identity and mutability with much-needed precision. The terms are relatively recent inventions of the modern disciplines of sociology, sexology, and clinical medicine, which have been spurred on to greater specificity by transgender activists and human rights groups who have taken up their cause. New terms are necessary especially as hormone therapy and sex-realignment surgery techniques are invented and improved, allowing physical alteration of the body in ways never possible only a generation ago. However, these new terms are not popularly known or used in the West in general, let alone in Muslim communities. Though the terms are new, the patterns of identity and behavior they describe may have existed long before.

Muslims may be more familiar with indigenous terms from their own local culture for people who do not conform to a binary division between male and female. Islamic history has witnessed at least three classifications of gender-ambiguous people: the eunuch, the *mukhannath*, and the hijra. We discuss these categories in more detail below, but it is important to define them here, especially because these pre-modern categories often interfere with how Muslims perceive lesbian, gay, and transgender members of their communities. The eunuch (*khasi* in Arabic) is a person who was born with male sex organs and raised as a boy until enslaved and castrated (usually by cutting off the testicles, though it is not clear whether sometimes the penis was also removed). Eunuchs did not become female, but rather inhabited an in-between position and were legally and socially of neither gender.[8] In contrast, a *mukhannath* is a person born with male sex organs and raised as a boy but who displays effeminate behavior in speech, gesture, gait, or dress. The term does not explicitly describe sexual organs, sexual behaviors, or sexual orientation but rather describes feminine behavior on the part of one who is socially known to be male; it describes transgender behavior or transvestite display rather than implying any homosexual orientation or same-sex intercourse. However, in medieval times and later, the term came to be associated with men who accepted the passive role in anal intercourse, an association not essential to the category's definition.[9] A parallel category of *mutarrajjulat* existed for women who behaved like men in speech, gesture, gait, or dress. Many concubines in the royal court during certain periods of the Abbasid era took on this gender-inverting performance as a matter of fashion, without this interfering in their very heterosexual roles at court as entertainers and sexual partners of aristocratic men. Chronicles that describe their behavior do not imply that these "emmasculine women" had a homosexual orientation or engaged in same-sex intercourse, demonstrating the distinction between gender ambiguity and sexual orientation.[10]

Finally, a third indigenous category was acknowledged in Islamic societies in South Asia (Pakistan, India, and Bangladesh) – that of the hijra. The hijra is a person born with male sex organs and raised as a boy who, after the onset of puberty, increasingly identifies as a woman. He abandons the category "man" for good, taking on female behavior, name, and dress, and voluntarily undergoes a ritual castration to remove both testicles and penis. Once transformed, society conceived of the hijra as neither-man-nor-woman but rather as inhabiting an acknowledged "third gender" that is "neither-nor" and therefore "in-between." Hijras leave their families and communities to form subcultures of their own, often in highly structured clans that have developed their own dialects of speech.[11] Contemporary observers in South Asia often mistakenly call them "eunuchs" because of the superficial similarity that both have undergone some kind of castration. However, it is clear that the psychological motivation of a hijra (who voluntarily undergoes castration after maturity through a ritual and with initiation into a subculture) is completely different from that of a eunuch; the hijra's status and social role are therefore distinct from that of eunuchs in pre-modern society.

Because the hijra feels like a woman in the body of a man, the hijra comes closest to transgender experience as described in modern terms. In pre-modern times without contemporary medical therapies or reconstructive surgery, the hijra could not physically alter the body to become a woman. All the hijra could do was remove the sex organs associated with men and take on the performative features associated with women, like growing long hair, wearing women's clothes, and adopting female names. Their patriarchal society did not acknowledge any parallel category of people born with female sex organs and raised as girls who could opt to remove outward organs and take on the gender performance of men. So, though there is some experiential overlap between contemporary transgender people and categories already established in Islamic societies in the pre-modern period, there is no easy equivalence.

The modern category of transgender describes both men who feel that they are women and strive to become women and also women who feel that they are men and strive to become men. This category depends upon the new reality that medical techniques can actually engineer the transformation, such that the transgender person can actually become transsexual, often to the point that one is no longer recognizable as belonging to the former and somehow mistaken gender in which one was originally socialized. This new reality opens up new possibilities for people who, for whatever reason, suffer from "gender dysphoria," the clinical name for persistent and profound discomfort and existential unhappiness with one's gender as it is perceived by others and imposed by their perception. This new reality also raises a profound challenge to all religions that were formed and formalized in patriarchal societies.

In such religions – including Islam but not unique to it – the immutable difference between man and woman was seen as not just natural but also socially necessary, legally normative, and divinely mandated. As Muslims encounter this new challenge, in the form of transgender members of the Islamic community, they turn to the Qur'an for guidance. Whether Muslims are simply conservative, ideologically neo-traditional, modernist, or progressive, they all turn to the same Qur'an to ground their arguments and positions. This chapter now asks whether the Qur'anic revelation can encourage a progressive interpretation that offers a dignified and protected place for transgender Muslims.

Gender Polarity in the Qur'an

God has no gender, even if the human languages through which we speak about God are highly gendered. As God speaks to us through the Qur'an, the revealed message is filtered through a human language – Arabic – that is highly gendered. This gives some listeners the impression that God has a gender and is like a male being. However, God has no gender in any way comparable to human gender, and that is central to the Qur'anic teaching about God's absolute oneness. Although the proper name Allah ("the God") is rendered into the pronoun *huwa* (he/it) in Arabic, as any masculine being is, this does not mean that God can be said to have a gender. That the proper noun "God" is conventionally replaced by the pronoun *huwa* only means that Arabic is a binary-gendered language. In Arabic, every noun – whether referring to an animate being, an inanimate object, or an abstract concept – is rendered in pronoun as either "he" or "she," for there is no neuter pronoun in Arabic like the English "it." Thus, the noun "sun" (*shams*) is grammatically feminine, whereas the noun "moon" (*qamar*) is grammatically masculine; in Arabic, neither the sun nor the moon can be described as "it." Despite this strict binary gender differentiation of pronouns in the language, the moon is not a man and is not compared to a being with human masculine qualities, just as the sun is not a woman and is not compared to a being with feminine qualities. The great Sufi scholar 'Abd al-Rahman al-Sulami (died 1021) noted this insight when, after writing the biographies of famous Sufi women, he wrote the following couplet:

> If all women were like the ones I've mentioned, before women all men would pale
> For there's no blame for the sun to be called feminine and no pride for the moon to be called male.[12]

We have observed above how gender among human beings is a condition of duality that is specific to creatures, and human beings in particular are concious of gender and construct around it social roles based upon biological function and anatomical difference. The Qur'an cautions us against projecting on to God qualities that are human, like anatomical features, biological functions, or social roles. God is not a father or a mother and has no relationship to people through metaphors of reproductive biology. God may have qualities that we humans, through the filter of our patriarchal cultures, commonly associate with men (such as strength, authority, and might) as well as qualities that we associate with women (such as care, nurture, and gentleness). However, these qualities do not make God a gendered being in any way comparable to male or female human beings.

Accepting that the assignment of gender in language is merely conventional, one might reasonably ask why God is assigned a masculine grammatical gender rather than a feminine grammatical gender. The answer to that vexing question lies in the fact that there is an oppositional tension between God and the human soul (*nafs*). In Arabic, "soul" has a feminine grammatical gender, regardless of whether the body animated by the soul is male or female with regard to reproductive anatomy and masculine or feminine with regard to social roles. This feminine gender assignment reflects the soul's close association with the body, which the Qur'an describes as made of clay and earth (*ard*), which is also of feminine gender. Body and soul are joined by the spirit (*ruh*) that bridges the vast distance between divine nature and human nature, for in the Qur'an God says, *I shaped and breathed into [the human being] some of my spirit* (Q. 15:29).[13] "Spirit" is one of the only Arabic nouns that can be either masculine or feminine in gender, just as its ambiguous nature partakes of both lofty divinity and corporeal humanity by infusing the body with life and the soul with awareness.

The Qur'an often talks about the natural world being divided into pairs, through which it replicates, grows, and evolves. It is the interaction of contrasting pairs that perpetuates the dynamism of the natural universe as an expression of God's creative will. The Qur'an often refers to human genders – female and male – as a kind of pairing through which God's will plays out in the world.

But in highlighting their contrast and pairing is the Qur'an describing or prescribing? Does the Qur'an simply assume that most people clearly belong to one gender or the other and come together in heterosexual pairs, and use this metaphor to describe the natural world? Or does the Qur'an rather prescribe that all human beings be clearly defined as either male or female, and judge any ambiguity, alteration, or indeterminate status as forbidden deviation from the pattern of nature as willed by God?

This is certainly a deep question, and any answer tendered should humbly express tentativeness in the face of nature's complexity and God's inscrutability. However, when faced with this question, many neo-traditionalists assert that God ordered not only humanity but the whole cosmos into gendered pairs that are clearly, eternally, and unambiguously dual. In his TV interview, Shaykh Qaradawi was asked by a journalist, "What are the sources that define the original human nature or *fitra* [created by God] before it is affect by any alteration [*tabdil*] or deviance [*tahrif*]?" He answered,

> The word "nature" [*fitra*] is derived from the term for creation [*al-fatr*], as in the verse *All praise be to God, the One who brings into being* [fatir] *the heavens and earth* (Q. 35:1) ... It refers to the original nature with which each person is born, that is not acquired or learned or attained, each and every person has it without entering school or being taught by parents or being affected by environment. Such things are natural things ... The human being is created with innate disposition to feel attraction to the other sex, with man attracted to woman and woman attracted [to man] ... I mean, this is a matter of biology [*amr tabi'i*] ... Such things are matters given to us by nature ... The religion of Islam came to preserve the original human nature not to oppose this nature by rebelling against nature ... Look, God most glorified and mighty created the human being as male and female ... So natural attraction is between the two sexes, because the Qur'an mentions that this cosmos is based upon pairing [*izdiwaj*], not based upon sameness [*mithliya*]. The principle of mating [*zawjiya*] is the principle of the cosmos ... This is based upon the behavior of positive and negative, to the extent that it is a basic principle of existence even in atoms. The atom is formed of electron and proton, isn't it?[14]

Shaykh Qaradawi here expresses an ideology of gender that is shared by most Muslims who are raised in a patriarchal society and perpetuate it through their cultural assumptions. Patriarchy rests upon a definition of gender in which male is clearly and immutably separate from female, such that male mates only with female and that male needs to control female. What makes Shaykh Qaradawi's presentation neo-traditionalist rather than simply conservative is that he does not simply assume this gender ideology, but rather actively asserts it, in this case through appeals to biology and physics.

However, the Shaykh's knowledge of biology and physics is outdated. Modern biology has discovered that mating behavior in many animal species is far more complex than patriarchal dichotomies between male and female can explain. In some species, an individual actually lives for a while as a male before transforming into a female, so that each individual effectively lives as both genders for a time. In other species, a single individual can be both male and female at the same time.[15] Modern physics, too, has moved far beyond facile dualities between proton and electron. There are of course neutrons, which the Shaykh conveniently ignores, and all these elementary particles that make up each atom are in turn complex composites of more basic energy particles like quarks, with qualities that are so varied and subtle that they cannot easily fit into the boxes of patriarchal metaphors.

These subtleties discovered by modern physics and biology do not discount the Qur'an. Rather, they add richness to our interpretation of the Qur'an if we have open ears to hear it speak from beyond our patriarchal preconceptions. We can take as an example the Qur'an's chapter Surat al-Fatir or "The Creator," which Shaykh Qaradawi cites in his interview. He stopped reciting its opening verse after the first phrase, but had he continued he would have found that the Qur'an not only describes procreation through the meeting and mating of pairs but also reveals that God intends also ambiguities that are beyond simple pairs. *All praise be to God the creator, the One who brings into being the heavens and earth, the One who makes angels messengers on wings two, three or four, who multiplies in creation according to divine will, for God is capable of all things* (Q. 35:1). To say that God devises the law of nature always to create in strict pairs is therefore simplistic, for God multiplies in creation according to divine will on patterns – of two, three, four, or more – that are subtle beyond our simple observation.

"The Creator" is a hymn to the creative ingenuity of God that bewilders our preconceptions and dazzles our reason. It is deeply relevant to a critical examination of gender identity. *God created you all from dust then from a spermazoid then made you all as pairs. No female carries her pregnancy or gives birth except with God's knowledge, and nobody's life span is extended or shortened except as is recorded, as that is easy for God* (Q. 35:11). Clearly, that God "made you all as pairs" refers to fetal development within the womb, but it is not clear that it refers to gender. It could refer to how the fertilized egg-and-sperm create a new cell (called a zygote), which grows by dividing itself into pairs. However, the pairing and dividing quickly grows so complex that tissues form and organs differentiate in patterns that are more complex than simplistic notions of pairing that distinguish females from males. We know that as the sexual organs develop in the human fetus, there is no easy distinction between male and female but rather an amazing ambiguity. Penis or clitoris, which in patriarchal cultures are imagined to be opposites that provide the anatomical basis for distinct gender roles, grow from the same fetal tissues in similar patterns, as is true also of the testes and ovaries that will later provide the hormonal stimulation for a child's secondary sex characteristics. We know that sometimes in a fetus there are persistent ambiguities in the development of these tissues such that the visible sex organ develops as male though the chromosomal patterns are female or while internally ovaries develop that release hormones that are more characteristic of a female. Sometimes the opposite happens and no penis develops but internally gonads develop that stimulate male hormonal patterns. Modern sexological studies have amply documented all these natural varieties of human development.[16]

The Qur'an implies that God's creation of the cosmos and human beings includes both a manifest differentiation of female/male as well as a subtle ambiguity of moments or phenomena that are betwixt and between this bifurcation. "The Creator" includes a beautiful verse about the sun (which is grammatically feminine in Arabic) and the moon (which is grammatically masculine). *God makes night merge into day and makes day merge into night, and controls the movement of the sun and the moon with each coursing for an appointed time. That One is God, your sustainer who has total dominion and the others you invoke except God control not even a speck* (Q. 35:13). The feminine sun and the masculine moon run their courses, but their effect in the ambiguity of our routine life is not so clear; there is no neat division between day and night, between the sun's presence or its absence. God merges day into night in a spectrum of shades from light to dark, and merges again night into day.

Likewise, the division of human beings into dimorphic gender is both clear and ambiguous at the same time. It is a division that is certainly persistent in most people, but not totally clear in all people. It is based upon a division of anatomical tissues and reproductive roles that are vital for the continuation of the species, but in any particular person the tissues and roles may not neatly match, as they are mediated by genetic forces, hormone circulation, and psychological identity that are very subtle and vary from person to person. These variations are the "colors" of the human personality (*alwan*) which are far deeper than mere skin tone, as discussed in Chapter 2 in relation to sexuality. The Qur'an celebrates the power of God to create diversity within any category of being. *Do you not observe that God sends down water from the sky and by it we bring forth fruits of varying colors? And how in the mountains there are streaks of white and red in different shades along with rocks jet-black? Human beings and beasts and livestock are likewise of diverse colors. Indeed, those who have knowledge from among God's servants revere God, for God is the empowering One, the One who forgives* (Q. 35:27–28).

Although this verse is certainly a powerful lens through which to understand race and to critique the political hierarchies of color that most societies (including Islamic societies) have established, it would be limiting to think that "different colors" in this verse means only skin tone or appearance. Rather, the verse challenges us to observe and to get knowledge in order truly to hold God in awe. The verse equates the diversity of human "color" to the varieties of minerals, plants, and animals that derive from deeper structures of chemistry and biology. It is scientific knowledge and medical research that can reveal to us the deeper patterns of God's creation. This is the pattern of God's behavior (*sunnat allah*) to which the Qur'an says, *You will not find any change in the pattern of God's behavior* (Q. 35:43). This creation is far subtler than to place every human being into an easily definable box of either male or female.

New discoveries in biology, physics, and other sciences goad us into a deeper interpretation of the Qur'anic metaphors of gendered pairs. A more nuanced reading of the Qur'an can in turn goad us into a more sensitive attention to the lives of real people. In every society, there are people whose gender identity falls outside the normative distinction between male and female upon which patriarchy is based. Their lived experience is one of constant struggle against their families' and communities' most deep-seated cultural assumptions. Their stories can be very moving and also very disconcerting for others, for they call into question what most of us never consider: how do males become boys then men and how do females become girls then women? What if the process is not completely natural and inevitable? What if nature is actually more complex than our culture allows? What if the reality of God's creation, as expressed in nature's complexity, is wider and deeper than conceived by our religious traditions as they were formalized through the cultural assumptions of an earlier era? The voices of real Muslims struggling with the experience of transgender identity are very important for other Muslims to hear; without their voices which reveal their deep introspection and painful choices, the theological discussion presented here will remain abstract and devoid of living spirit. In-depth interviews with activists who identify as transgender Muslims have informed this theological reflection, but there is no scope in this book to present their words and personalities. It is hoped that readers will turn to my separate forthcoming volume of interviews to read about their experiences in their own words.

Each of the Muslim activists interviewed there has struggled against notions of a strict gender binary that is enforced in their Islamic communities. To cross the line of gender distinction is to risk losing one's family, one's children, and one's standing in the community. Indeed, transgender Muslims often suffer more overt persecution than lesbian or gay Muslims, because their unconventional gender identity is visible to others in their appearance in ways that sexual orientation is not visible. Confronting their experiences of persecution, it is not enough to investigate what the Qur'an as scripture indicates about gender identity and norms, for Muslim communities usually refer to the *shari'a* to regulate the behavior of its members, rather than to the Qur'an. Therefore, we must consider the question, "What does the Islamic *shari'a* say about transgender behavior?"

We have seen that the Qur'an expresses God's speech in a profoundly complex interplay of genders, citing masculine and feminine while leaving room between them for ambiguity. It simplifies the complexity of God's poetic speech to hold that the Qur'an asserts simply that men should act like men and women should act like women, despite the fact that most Muslim interpreters assume this and some outspoken ideologues like Shaykh Qaradawi express it in simplistic terms. Yet the *shari'a* is built upon much more than the Qur'an. The *shari'a* is based upon the Prophet's example, as preserved in hadith by later generations of Muslims. It is further shaped by the judgments and consensus of later scholars and jurists, as expressed in fiqh decisions. This chapter should therefore proceed systematically and carefully – in contrast to the rash and simplistic method of neo-traditionalist ideologues – to examine transgender behavior and identity in the light of Qur'an, hadith, and fiqh before offering conclusions on what the *shari'a* says or could say about these phenomena.

Hadith and the Prophet's Example

Having looked at the Qur'an, we now turn to hadith and oral stories about the Prophet Muhammad's example. We observed in Chapters 3 and 4 that the Islamic tradition offers us no concrete evidence that the Prophet Muhammad ever adjudicated a case involving homosexual intercourse, such that the jurists based their fiqh judgments on the opinions of the Prophet's companions or later generations of moralists. But when we shift our focus to transgender behavior, we are faced with a markedly contrasting case. Unlike the case of homosexual intercourse, we do know that the Prophet himself met and interacted with gender-ambiguous individuals during his lifetime in Medina.

Reports attributed to the Prophet's wives and companions portray him interacting with both *mukhannath* or effeminate men and also eunuchs. We might expect, then, that the *shari'a* would offer much clearer policy in regard to gender ambiguity than it did with homosexuality. Indeed, we find that the classical *shari'a* offers more resources for contemporary jurists to deal with transgender behavior in a creative way, though not all decisions in contemporary cases have shown creativity or compassion. It is apparent that both *mukhannath* and eunuchs were part of the Prophet's extended household and he must have had routine dealings with them in Medina. The two categories of gender ambiguous men were quite distinct, even if in medieval times the distinction was blurred. We also saw in Chapter 3 that hadith show that the Prophet's wives were regularly visited by *mukhannath* or effeminate men inside their rooms in the Prophet's household; the hadith about Umm Salama were reviewed in detail, but other wives such as 'A'isha also had intimate dealings with them. *Mukhannath* were a regular feature of pre-Islamic culture in Mecca and Medina, and persisted in the Islamic community. In contrast, eunuchs appear to have been a new phenomenon in the early Islamic community in Medina.

The first eunuch to be noted was a castrated servant of Marya (died 637), an Egyptian woman of Coptic Christian background whom the Prophet maintained as a concubine. Whether she was later freed and married is a disputed point, but Marya was originally sent to the Prophet as a "gift" from the Byzantine Patriarch who governed Egypt, named Cyrus (in Arabic, al-Muqawqas). As a slave woman of high status, Marya was sent along with her sister attended by a personal servant, a eunuch who was presumably castrated in Egypt and may have been Egyptian or Ethiopian. Eunuchs were castrated in order to better serve and protect such a high-status woman without compromising her chastity.[17] The Prophet Muhammad said that Muslims should not castrate their male slaves; Marya's eunuch had not been castrated by Muslims, the operation having been done before he moved with Marya into an Islamic environment.

Hadith clearly state that Marya continued to have the eunuch live with her after she became the Prophet's concubine. This novel luxury led to turmoil in the household and envy among the Prophet's other wives, who hated Marya. They were unhappy that the Prophet accepted this gift of a beautiful young slave girl. They were threatened by her foreign, sophisticated Egyptian habits and were incensed that she retained her Christian religion and refused to convert to Islam – at least initially. The Prophet's sexual relationship with Marya led to a crisis in the Prophet's household in which two of his wives – 'A'isha and Hafsa – conspired against him, leading the Prophet to threaten to divorce all his wives.[18] This crisis was deep enough for 'Umar ibn al-Khattab to intervene and censure the wives – who included his daughter, Hafsa. The crisis was so deep and its political ramifications so dire for the young Islamic community that the Qur'an also addressed the wives' behavior directly (Q. 33:28–29, 66:1–5).

Perhaps owing to this upheaval in his household, the Prophet kept Marya in separate quarters, unlike all his other wives and women, who lived in rooms of one household (which adjoined the community's mosque). Marya lived in an apartment on the northern limits of Medina, attended by her eunuch servant, and the Prophet visited her there frequently. She became pregnant and gave birth to a boy, whom the Prophet named Ibrahim (Abraham). This was the Prophet's only living son, and his more powerful wives like 'A'isha, Hafsa, and Zaynab bint Jahsh had not become pregnant. This elevated the status of Marya and increased the jealousy of the other wives, as the Prophet began to address Marya as "Mother of the Believers" like all the legal wives and urged her to segregate herself from other men as his wives had to do, behavior that differentiated them from other Muslim free women (who veiled their heads when in public) and from slave women (who did not have to veil).

This resentment against her came to be expressed as anger against the presence of Marya's eunuch inside her chambers. Others saw the eunuch as a "man" even if Marya – in accord with the aristocratic norms of Roman, Byzantine, and Persian custom – saw him as an "unman." The Prophet Muhammad must have originally agreed with Marya that the eunuch as an "unman" posed no threat of sexual attraction or gender discord within his household, for he had let the eunuch stay in Marya's chambers. The status of the eunuch certainly became a public issue when Marya swelled with pregnancy. Some in Medina who resented the Prophet began to gossip that the eunuch was a "man" who had sexual access to Marya; they said, "an infidel man has access to an infidel woman."[19] Such malicious gossip would have been amplified by the jealousy of the other wives, until the Prophet himself was afflicted with doubts. He sent his most trusted relative, 'Ali ibn Abi Talib, to investigate the accusations. "When 'Ali, sword in hand, approached the Copt [the Egyptian eunuch], the man was either sitting on a date palm and threw his clothes away, or he climbed up on a date palm and his garment slipped off. In either case, 'Ali saw him to be without genitals, 'without penis or testicles.'"[20] 'Ali had been sent to "investigate," but the report infers that if he had found the eunuch to be a "real man" then he would have attacked or even killed him. But seeing his anatomical situation, 'Ali did not attack the eunuch but rather returned to the Prophet to ask whether it was right to disobey his order if one found that the situation was not what it was assumed to be. The Prophet assured him that he had acted correctly. It appears that this eye-witness of the man's eunuch status mollified the Prophet, and we have no evidence that the eunuch was otherwise harassed or forbidden from living with Marya to carry out his duties. Another hadith claims that when Marya bore her son, the angel Gabriel greeted the Prophet by saying, "Peace be with you, O father of Ibrahim!" Thus divine intervention seems to have finally settled any lingering doubts the Prophet might have had about the paternity of his son, and indirectly confirmed the special status of the eunuch as an unman. After this, the Prophet supposedly freed Marya, raising her to the status of a free wife rather than a kept concubine.[21]

This conflict had more to do with jealousy between the Prophet's wives than it did with the eunuch's gender ambiguity. The conflict did not lead to any long-term ban on eunuchs in the early Islamic community. In fact, it seems to have confirmed their legality, usefulness, and potential to be righteous members of the community. Some reports assert that the Marya's eunuch servant was in fact "her brother." It is not clear whether some narrators believed this to be literally true, or whether the term "brother" was applied to him to clarify his non-sexual intimacy with a woman. In any case, eunuchs continued to play the role in Islamic society that they played in Byzantine and other earlier Middle Eastern and Mediterranean societies, that of "bed-keeper" (the term eunuch is derived from Greek *eure* for "bed" plus *ekhein* for "keeper"). They would prepare high-status owners for bed, help them dress, bathe, and groom, and cut their hair or nails. In subsequent centuries, eunuchs were easily assimilated into the Islamic culture of the ruling class, especially as Muslims built a rich empire that took over the lands and customs of the Byzantine Romans and Zoroastrian Persians. To have eunuchs as household slaves and in particular as guards to the women's quarters of aristocratic houses was a mark of high status; the overtly patriarchal jurists accepted them as easily as concubines and Islamic law was compiled with their presence firmly entrenched.

Muslim jurists show no discomfort in making decisions about the social role of eunuchs. In their view, eunuchs are to occupy a "neither-nor" gender position between men and women; their ambiguous status simply reinforces the separation between more routine groupings of men and women who must not mix freely. Jurists do show discomfort with the idea of believing Muslim men being castrated, so it was assumed that only young men captured in war or sold into slavery from non-Muslim populations would be castrated. Jurists also expressed qualms about believing Muslims castrating others, so it was assumed that the operation was done by non-Muslim slave-holders before the eunuchs were sold to Muslims as household servants. Once sold into Muslim households, the assumption was that they would become Muslim themselves and adopt the same moral duties as others believers. Hence eunuchs were expected to be present in communal prayer and were directed to stand in a row behind the men but before the women. Their presence acted as a sort of human veil between the two genders, even in the mosque.

The *mukhannath* were not so easily accommodated into the new Islamic society. When we assess the *shari'a*, eunuchs are not a good analogue to contemporary transgender Muslims. Although eunuchs did display a kind of gender ambiguity, it was imposed by society upon them without their consent. Their gender ambiguity was the result of violence against them, not the result of inherent personality traits or inner disposition as contemporary transgender persons assert about themselves. As a result, eunuchs served to demarcate the boundary between two rigidly defined genders without actually transgressing the boundary in their own personalities. They never willfully chose to act as a woman despite being born male or being raised as masculine. Moreover, there is no role for women that is parallel to the eunuch – eunuchs were uniquely unmen who were manufactured through cutting off the male sexual organs, promoting a subsequent deficiency of testes-produced hormones, and whose resulting gender ambiguity was used to reinforce the separation between empowered men and disempowered women.

The *mukhannath* offer a much better analogue to contemporary transgender people. This is true despite the cases of *mukhannath* – men who willingly gave up the masculine social role in favor of behaving like women – and despite the fact that there was no parallel role for emmasculine women in the early Islamic community. In other words, in the patriarchal environment of early Islam, it was possible for those born male to give up their gender roles as men and become *mukhannath* and be identified as "not-male-but-like-female," yet it was not possible for those born female to adopt a more masculine gender identity. In a patriarchal environment, men could move "down" the scale of status to become like women, but women could not in general move "up" to become like men; the barrier against gender ambivalence is much more rigid for women.

It is important that most early Muslims recognized that the *mukhannath* acted in gender-ambiguous ways because of their innate disposition and that this was not in and of itself blameworthy. We noted in Chapter 3 that, according to various hadith, the Prophet banished a *mukhannath* who frequented his household when he overstepped ethical norms (specifically using knowledge of women's affairs to incite heterosexual men to be immorally involved with women to whom they were not married). Early Muslim authorities did not define the *mukhannath* according to sexual acts or sexual orientation, but rather solely defined them according to gender identity as performed in behavior (speech, gesture, gait, and clothing). According to Ibn Habib (died 852), a *mukhannath* is "an effeminate man, even if he is not known to be guilty of immoral acts, the derivation being based on the idea of languidness of gait and in other ways [resembling women's behavior]."[22] Other commentators make subtle distinctions between a man who acts effeminately by inherent nature (*khilqi*) and one who affects such behavior for ulterior motives (*takallufi*), only the latter kind of behavior being blameworthy. They acknowledged that for some rare individuals this behavior was a natural expression of their gender identity, in a phenomenon that we would in today's clinical terminology call "transgender" identity. This was not blameworthy; but Islamic moralists found men affecting such behavior to be blameworthy if their behavior did not express their innate internal disposition.

Who became a *mukhannath* in Medina during the lifetime of the Prophet and subsequent generations? Why would a person raised as male self-consciously imitate a woman in dress and manner in the early Islamic community if it were not an expression of innate disposition? *Mukhannath* were given special roles in Medina and the early Islamic society that spread from it, and a publicly recognized effeminate man had some unusual advantages. It meant one was beyond the routine sexual economy of desire and had a uniquely flexible role in the separation of genders. A *mukhannath* had access to the private homes of women from which normal men were barred, but could also circulate in the public domain where men dominated and women were not welcome. Some *mukhannath* took on roles as entertainers, singers, and comedians through which they profited by their unique gender identity. This was especially so when Medina became a wealthy and luxurious capital of a world empire in the decades after the Prophet died. In early Islamic times, most musicians and singers were women, and the only way someone raised as a man could excel in music was to embrace *mukhannath* identity, abandoning patriarchal manhood to become an effeminate with all the privileges and dangers of that identity. However, such advantages could be abused, and some *mukhannath* were accused of facilitating romantic trysts or adulterous affairs between heterosexual couples. This dynamic was illustrated by the story of Hit, as discussed in Chapter 3. The Prophet banished this *mukhannath* for helping incite heterosexual lust. Later rulers of the Umayyad Empire in the century after the Prophet died sometimes punished *mukhannath* for actual or alleged facilitation of heterosexual adultery, not because of their unusual gender identity.

Literary sources from the early centuries of the Islamic community preserve many stories about *mukhannath*, such as the *Book of Songs* (*Kitab al-Aghani*) by al-Isfahani (died 967). The scholar of Arabic literature Everrett Rowson has documented how *mukhannath* often used their unusual gender identity and role as entertainers to poke fun at government authorities. They spoke out against Umayyad rulers, who had usurped power to rule as kings, in ways that other Muslims could not; their unusual gender identity allowed them to act as buffoons or comedians to deflate the egoistic claims of rulers whose legitimacy was highly questionable. One story about a *mukhannath* named Find illustrates this dynamic. The Umayyad King Mu'awiya (died 685) often rotated the governorship of Medina. Two governors of Medina, Marwan ibn al-Hakam (died 685) and his brother, Yahya, were largely responsible for state persecution of *mukhannath.* Marwan suspected a *mukhannath* named Find of facilitating adulterous liaisons between men and women, based on a poet's verses that boasted of his amorous affairs. Once, during a period when he was removed from the governorship, Marwan met Find in the street and "accused him of immorality and threatened him. Find turned coolly and replied, 'Yes, you're right about me! But praise God, what an ugly ex-governor you are!' Marwan laughed, but added, 'Enjoy while you can! It won't be long before you see what I have in store for you!'"[23] Find not only insulted the former governor's looks and pointed out his removal from power, but got away with it in the short term by forcing the strongman to laugh at his own condition.

As a *mukhannath,* Find could talk back to those in power, using their threats of punishment to raise his own public status as a comedian. However, Marwan's threat against the *mukhannath* became reality. In the early eighth century, an Umayyad governor of Medina ordered all singers (*mukhannath* and ordinary men who had taken up music) to be castrated. In al-Isfahani's version of the story, the governor was angered that his slave girl to whom he was attracted ignored him for a moment to listen to a distant man's voice singing, and so the governor ordered this man castrated out of jealousy, along with all male singers and *mukhannath* as well. The inclusion of *mukhannath* in the castration order, which is particularly cruel considering that they were publicly considered not to be real men, may have been to appease Islamic moralists and distract attention from his real intent, the emasculation of a heterosexual rival. Several *mukhannath* were castrated, having their testicles and penises cut off. Sources portray the *mukhannath* facing this brutality with sarcastic humor, saying, "This is simply a circumcision which we must undergo again," or "We have been spared the trouble of carrying around a spout for urine," or "What would we do with an unused weapon, anyway?"[24] After this persecution, sources rarely mention *mukhannath* in Medina and Mecca. Most likely they were driven out, to resurface much later in Baghdad during its heyday as capital of the 'Abbasid Empire. By then the Islamic discourse on gender and sexuality had changed greatly, and male homosexuality become the focus rather than male-to-female transgender behavior. It is in this totally changed environment that jurists from the Sunni legal schools made their fiqh decisions upon which the *shari'a* is understood to depend.

Jurists and Their Fiqh

Starting in the Umayyad period, and continuing through the Abbasid period, Muslim perceptions of *mukhannath* changed drastically. Jurists began their work of building a body of legal decisions and promulgating social norms. As they did so, they juxtaposed issues of gender identity with issues of sexual orientation, so that the distinction between these different phenomena became blurred. Medieval commentators reveal that, gradually, effeminate men became assumed to be those who enacted a passive role in anal intercourse with other men, rather than being distinctive in their gender identity alone. Rowson's survey of the commentary on hadith about them concludes that this shift in perception happened as early as the ninth century, more than a century and half after the Prophet's death.[25] He concludes, "Increased public awareness of homosexuality [in the 'Abbasid period from 750 to 950], which was to persist through the following centuries, seems to have altered perceptions of gender in such a way that 'effeminacy,' while continuing to be distinguished from (passive) homosexuality or desire, was no longer seen as independent from it; and the stigma attached to the latter seems correspondingly to have been directed at the former as well."[26] This means that in fiqh decisions formulated in the classical period transgender behavior was seen as a side effect of same-sex desire.

Jurists did not allow that a "real man" could be sexually attracted to another fully masculine man, so they assumed one of the partners acted as a woman. Either one partner was male-but-not-yet-fully-man (a boy or youth) or one was male-but-acting-as-woman (a man who accepted penetration in sexual intercourse). Transgender behavior was not seen as an independent phenomenon. Rather jurists saw it as behavior display to advertise acceptance of the "passive role" in homosexual male couplings. Similarly, jurists saw the transgender behavior of a woman adopting male behaviors (in speech, gesture, gait, or dress) as assertion of the "active role" of penetrator in homosexual female couplings. Except for the eunuchs, who were assumed not to have sex, and hermaphrodites, who were assumed to have a gender that could not be fully determined, any other gender ambiguity was perceived as a code for homosexual acts. Forbidding transgender behaviors was seen as a necessary means (*sadd al-dhara'i'*) to forbidding homosexual acts and was assimilated to this judgment.

Medieval jurists recognized that gender ambiguity did occur naturally if infrequently in natural hermaphrodites. However, they focused solely upon anatomical features and did not develop a concept of gender identity to deepen their analysis of the issues. Paula Sanders has analyzed Muslim jurists' thought in a stimulating article in which she summarizes their legal opinions about children who possess traces of both male and female sexual anatomy. Jurists ruled that such a child should be raised as either male or female, based on the assumption that either the male or female sexual organs must predominate. Predominance was determined by observing whether urine passed out of genital structures identified as male or female. A jurist's judgment about the child's sexual anatomy and consequent gender was unalterable; "once the sex of the person had been established, that judgment was irreversible, regardless of any evidence that might be produced to the contrary."[27] Such evidence might include changes in puberty due to hormones, such as "secondary sex characteristics" like maturation of genital organs, change in voice, onset of facial and body hair, or growth of breasts; such changes were not accepted as grounds to change the assigned gender of the young person. However, such later development of bodily character could be appealed to if observation of urinary patterns remained ambiguous – "If the sex of the child could not be determined by these conventional methods, it remained in a state of dubiousness [*ishtibah*] or ambiguity [*ishkal*] until the onset of puberty."[28] In this sense, Muslim jurists unwittingly allowed that gender identity could conflict with one's apparent anatomical sex. However, jurists always saw this as a problem that needed to be fixed as early as possible, based upon anatomical observation rather than upon an individual's own assertion of gender identity. Islamic law could allow children to exist in a state of gender ambiguity, but at the onset of puberty (when the person become sexually and legally mature) their gender had to be assigned based upon observation of the body.

In these legal decisions, jurists did not mean to uphold gender ambiguity as a real element of human variation or as an expression of God's creative will. Rather, they allowed gender ambiguity in order to preserve the patriarchal order of medieval Islamic society. The specification that hermaphrodites or gender-ambiguous persons could pray in an intermediate position between men and women was so that they "neither threatened the superior status of men nor was it threatened with an inferior position. Should it turn out to be a man, he would simply constitute the last row of men; should it turn out to be a woman, she would be the first row of women."[29] However, in cases involving inheritance, when such persons might endanger the status of fully gendered men, they were categorized as female. "What was important was that access to the higher status of men be successfully protected. The rules assured that no hermaphrodite would attain the status accorded to men unless it could be demonstrated that he was, indeed, a man."[30] It is this legacy that contemporary Muslims have inherited from the classical *shari'a.* Does it give us resources in the contemporary period to face new ethical challenges?

Shari'a and the Ethics of Sex-Change Operations

It is clear that the Prophet himself distinguished between various kinds of personalities based upon gender identity and display. He differentiated between transgender men (who identified with and behaved like women) and eunuchs (castrated men). He also upheld the subtle distinction between men who were transgender based upon their sincere internal disposition (thereby not having sexual attraction to or carnal knowledge of women) and those who merely acted this part for ulterior motives. However, by the time hadith scholars were preserving oral reports and Muslim jurists were making decisions based upon legal reasoning, this subtle differentiation was obscured. By the end of the classical period, the *shari'a* constructed by these experts dealt with gender ambiguity only in terms of preserving patriarchal male privilege and perceived gender identity in terms of sexual orientation. This chapter urges contemporary Muslims to recover the Prophet's own subtle understanding of gender identity and question the medieval construct of the *shari'a.*

In contemporary times, there are two factors that impel Muslims to challenge this heritage of the classical *shari'a.* The first is mounting sociological evidence that gender identity is a psychological reality that is not always determined by anatomy. The second is accelerating medical technology that now allows people to alter the body to accord with their perceived gender identity. Neither this psychology nor technology was available to medieval jurists. However, some contemporary Muslim jurists display attentiveness to the new reality and show a willingness to rethink the issue through *ijtihad.*

Recent decisions from Islamic authorities in Egypt, Saudi Arabia, and Iran have demonstrated that Muslim jurists can allow sex-realignment surgery to "fix" people, and can even advocate this technique as approved by Islamic teachings, and these cases have received the attention of progressive Muslims in the West, like Rusmir Musić and Kecia Ali.[31] Though such cases might empower transgender people to proceed with hormone therapy and surgery despite resistance from Muslim relatives, we must question whether contemporary Islamic societies' apparent acceptance of sex-change operations is really progressive. Such decisions are not necessarily progressive if they simply reinforce gender apartheid and mask a very punishing approach to transgender people (who do not actually undergo surgery to alter their anatomy) or gender-ambiguous people who may appear like effeminate men or masculine women whose behavior goes against the norms of their local societies.[32]

Reports about current medical practice with regard to gender ambiguity in Saudi Arabia present a case where Muslim doctors do not confront the issue but rather rely on the classical *shari'a* concept – the patriarchal assertion that determination of gender resides in the functionality of male sexual anatomy, especially the penis. Two Saudi medical researchers, Taha and Magbool, have surveyed patterns of gender ambiguity and medical attempts to fix what they term intersex "disorders." They conclude that in contemporary Saudi Arabia "the single most important factor for female gender assignment [is] phallic inadequacy."[33] If a doctor examines an infant and determines, through cursory observation and stereotyped notions of genital normalcy, that the child does not have an "adequate penis" then the prevailing practice is to discount the child as male and declare the gender to be female. Female gender category is the default position if penile adequacy is missing or suspect, regardless of the possibility of the child growing up feeling "male" inside, having residual testes, or going through puberty with secondary sexual changes that might resemble male patterns. The doctors note that most patients who were classified as "female" under this penis-focused regime later felt internal conflict with the assigned gender and often, later in life, requested reassignment to the male gender, based upon internal feeling (whether linked to bodily changes in puberty or deriving solely from psychological identity). Though acknowledging the existence of this "disorder," the Saudi doctors discouraged gender reassignment later in life, despite the disabling effects of this condition upon the patient and the availability of medical procedures to address them. The Saudi doctors cite the "complexity of surgical operations involved, the associated psychosocial problems to patients and parents of a late gender reassignment, and the cosmetically and functionally unsatisfactory nature of the resulting small penis" to justify the policy of discouraging sex-change operations.[34] In their view, society's judgment is more valid than that of the patient: the change will be traumatic to family and community and the surgery will only produce a penis that society judges as small, inadequate, and fake. They do not value the patients' own sense of oppression at being forced by family and community to live in the wrong gender, or the patients' sense of liberation and tranquillity should they gain a body that accords with their internal gender identity, even if the genital structures are not large or functional by patriarchal standards. This report shows that Saudi medical policies continue to uphold patriarchal notions that were embedded in the classical *shari'a* – in which the jurists' observation of genitalia overrode a subject's internal sense of gender identity and in which female gender assignment was the default position in order to preserve male social privilege.

Saudi Arabia is an exceptional case because it is one of the few Muslim-majority countries in which a version of the classical *shari'a* is asserted by the government as national law. Therefore patriarchal concepts embedded in the *shari'a* have a uniquely perpetuated force in this country, and other developments – in medical practice, clinical psychology, or human rights politics – are marginalized. A more typical case is that of Egypt, a country where aspirations toward modernization and adherence to Islam exist in a tense balance. In Egypt, the government does not enforce a version of the *shari'a* as national law even though the Muslim majority there often looks to *shari'a* (or Islamic norms more broadly construed) for guidance on social and ethical issues. Accordingly, the al-Azhar Academy – the most prestigious Sunni institution of Islamic learning and decree – makes rulings on Islam outside the official structure of the government (but with a wary eye toward not contradicting the secular authoritarian regime). Al-Azhar has recently dealt with a high-profile case of a transgender student and has made official decisions about sex-change operations and the resulting status of transsexual Muslims. Most Sunnis worldwide (especially in Muslim minority communities in the West) look to al-Azhar's decisions about reconciling Islam and modernity rather than to authorities in Saudi Arabia.

In the 1980s, a student named Sayyid registered to study at al-Azhar as a male. In the course of his studies, Sayyid acknowledged feelings of gender ambiguity and increasingly identified as a woman who was trapped in a man's body. Sayyid altered the personal name to Sally and opted for sex-realignment treatment. In 1988, after sex-change surgery, Sally – now possessing female genitalia – applied for readmission to al-Azhar to complete her studies as a female student. The academy denied readmission and claimed that Sally's gender ambiguity violated its policy of strict separation between men and women, based upon concepts of gender differentiation enshrined in the *shari'a.* One scholar who has studied this case in detail, Jakob Skovgaard-Petersen, asserts that the al-Azhar authorities held that "God has created mankind in pairs and His [sic] Revelation makes it clear that the distinction between the sexes (as well as the one between believer and unbeliever) is the fundamental distinction whereupon society is founded. Their interaction may pose a threat to the social order, and this threat (which mainly emanates from the woman) must be contained."[35] Beyond reasserting that men and women must be clearly defined and should not mix, al-Azhar's authorities discounted Sally's own gender identity and asserted that this claim by a man that he was in fact a woman was a surreptitious way of legitimizing sexual intercourse with other men. Al-Azhar's decision fell back upon the dominant patterns of the medieval jurists who formulated the *shari'a* as they saw the issue of gender identity as primarily a question of forbidding homosexual intercourse. The initial reaction by al-Azhar denied that a man like Sayyid could become a woman – Sally – solely because of an interior sense of gender identity, and insisted that this disorder was actually a case of homosexual attraction disguised as transgender behavior, a phenomenon that threatened their institution with *fitna* or social disruption. They judged that after surgery the student in question was neither fully male nor authentically female, but had mutilated the body in order to justify homosexual intercourse.

The case of Sally received wide publicity in Egypt. Eventually Shaykh al-Tantawi, the Grand Mufti of Egypt and the highest juridical authority at al-Azhar, was forced to make a more in-depth investigation. He issued a fatwa or legal opinion that allowed Sally to be considered a woman for readmission to the academy and also went far beyond the actual case to address the issue in its complexity from an Islamic position. Skovgaard-Petersen has translated the fatwa, in which Shaykh al-Tantawi pronounces, "It is permissible to perform the [genital reassignment] operation in order to reveal what was hidden of male or female organs. Indeed, it is obligatory to do so on the grounds that it must be considered a treatment, when a trustworthy doctor advises it. It is, however, not permissible to do it at the mere wish to change sex from woman to man, or vice versa."[36] Shaykh al-Tantawi legalizes gender-realignment surgery under certain conditions, based upon the motivation of the subject. The surgery is obligatory when there is ambiguity in the genital structure; in this case medical treatment is to "reveal what was hidden," acknowledging that bodies sometimes naturally contain ambiguities that do not conform to God's will that each individual have a clear gender displayed by one's genital organs.

According to Shaykh al-Tantawi, if nature fails to be fully clear, then human agency is required to intervene and medical techniques can alter the body to reveal structures that were present in latent form but hidden in the organic growth of the body. Modern medical therapy can clarify the intent of God, and this is fully Islamic. But medical therapy should never contradict the intent of God, and his fatwa continues to forbid an individual from undergoing gender realignment therapy "at the mere wish to change sex." The Shaykh denigrates as mere whim (*wahm* in Arabic, a term that connotes selfish lust and satanic delusion) the feeling of being trapped in the wrong body if there is no anatomical ambiguity as the cause of such a feeling. Only in anatomy can he find evidence of God's will, and he relegates all other cases to human lust which modern medicine should never empower.

In his analysis of this fatwa, Skovagaard-Petersen insightfully characterizes the logic behind this decision. "One might say that far from legalizing a sex-change operation, Tantawi's fatwa denied the possibility of performing one altogether."[37] One cannot change one's God-given gender, but one can discover through experience that one's bodily structures are ambiguous and one can uncover through medical intervention a more clearly gendered anatomy so that one can live in accord with God's will. On the surface, it appears that Shaykh al-Tantawi's decision is in harmony with contemporary transgender people, who do not see themselves as wanting to "change sex" out of whim, personal choice, or ulterior motive. Rather they see themselves as wanting "genital realignment" because they are convinced they were born with the wrong body and raised as the wrong gender; their urge to realign their bodies with their inherent gender identity is to live with greater integrity, in harmony with what they feel is their God-given destiny, and at peace with the formal requirements of their religion.

However, beneath the surface of Shaykh al-Tantawi's fatwa there lurk deep problems. Though many transgender Muslims welcomed this decision and see it as legal precedent for their right to have gender realignment therapy, the decision shies away from explicitly acknowledging the experience of most transgender persons by insisting on a hermaphrodite model of gender ambiguity. Shaykh al-Tantawi assesses positively only transgender persons who suffer from a "corporeal disease which cannot be removed, except by this operation," and hence speaks of medical therapy as a means to uncover a person's real sexual organs that may have been buried or covered by one's body in a strange riddle of God's will.[38]

But in what sense can a person have genital anatomy that is buried or obscured by the body? One Muslim activist interviewed for this study expressed the idea that he is transgender not because of any anatomical ambiguity but rather because of the psychological reality of feeling like a man trapped in a woman's body. This is the case for the vast majority of transgender people who desire medical treatment to adjust their bodies to be in harmony with their minds and/or souls. But even as Shaykh al-Tantawi insists on talking about anatomical ambiguity to acknowledge gender ambiguity, his language in other parts of the fatwa is more open-ended. He relies on Islamic theological concepts to makes a distinction between outward appearance (*zahir*) and an inward essence (*batin*).[39] One's outward appearance may be deceptive, but one's inner essence is always true. This essence can be hidden by clothing or obscured by one's apparent genitalia, but once one discovers one's personal essence through experience, one should endeavor to live with integrity by displaying that essence socially and conforming to religious and moral expectations. If one needs to realign one's name, clothing, or genitalia in order to live with sincerity by the essence God has given in the form of the soul, then these external markers can be adjusted to conform to the needs of the essential person. By using these terms – appearance and essence – which are taken from Islamic theology and deepened by use in Sufism, Shaykh al-Tantawi gives his fatwa an open-ended potential that goes far beyond his initial pronouncement that is limited to anatomical considerations. This potential is reason for optimism for transgender Muslims.

After a long trial and nearly two years after her surgery, Sally was granted a certificate formally declaring her a woman. Yet this did not fully resolve her dispute with al-Azhar. The Academy refuses to acknowledge her gender realignment even with legal certification; it claims that Sally "had been a man, and was still a man, but now less so, because she had been bereft of her male sexual organs and been attributed with artificial (and 'imperfect') female ones. She was not a full man, definitely not a woman, and not a true hermaphrodite."[40] In this language, al-Azhar asserts that Sally is something like a voluntary eunuch; the institution sees her surgery as mere castration. By this operation, she relinquished privileged status as a whole and functional male, but cannot claim to be an authentic woman. It asserts, against the spirit of Shaykh al-Tantawi's fatwa, that Sally has no gender – Sally is "not a full man and definitely not a woman." It is also not willing to acknowledge Sally as a "third gender" (on the model of Islamic societies in South Asia who accept hijras as "neither man nor woman but someone else in between") to whom social status and certain rights must be given.

In Egypt, a fatwa even from the highest juridical authority at al-Azhar is not legally binding upon the government or other institutions. This partially accounts for the halfway measures of Egyptian cases. The open-ended pronouncement of Shaykh al-Tantawi is not fully accepted by many institutions and families, though it may empower individuals to seek medical treatment and embolden medical professionals to provide such treatment. In contrast, the Republic of Iran seems to have fully accepted sex-change operations as Islamic, and in Iran the pronouncements of Shi'i jurists have governmental backing as national law. This is because, since the revolution in 1978, certain provisions from the classical *shari'a* have been imposed as national law in tense coexistence with parliament and preexisting constitution.

Although this book focuses mainly upon Sunni cases and legal theology, at this point a comparison with Iran is very instructive. A full discussion of how Shi'i theology and legal schools treat sexual orientation and gender identity cannot be pursued here, as it is a rich and complex subject that deserves its own book. It is sufficient here to note that Shi'i communities developed the Ja'fari legal school in parallel to the Sunni legal schools and based upon similar principles. The Ja'fari legal school as enforced in Iran exhibits patterns of legal reasoning and decisions similar to the Shafi'i school among Sunnis. Accordingly, Shi'i scholars in Iran insist that Islam forbids homosexuality and cross-dressing, such that men should dress and have sex like men, and women should dress and have sex like women.[41]

However, Shi'i scholars in Iran are open to philosophical debate – based upon reason and aiming toward *ijtihad* – far more than their Sunni colleagues. In Shi'i Iran, the study of Islamic law has never been divorced from the study of dialectical logic and philosophy, and this remains true today. Also, Shi'i communities have preserved the institution of the *marji'a*, or authoritatively creative jurists, who though limited in number are authorized to give innovative legal decisions in reaction to new situations (an institution that most Sunni legal schools forswear). Drawing on this intellectual background, some contemporary Shi'i scholars assert that neither sexual orientation nor cross-dressing is equivalent to the transgender issue. For example, Hojatulislam Kariminia wrote his doctoral thesis on the implications of sex-change operations for Islamic law in Iran. He asserts that Ayatollah Khomeini wrote about new medical issues like transsexuality: "I believe he was the first Islamic scientist in the world of Islam who raised the issue of sex change ... I want to suggest that the right of transsexuals to change their gender is a human right ... I am trying to introduce transsexuals to the people through my work and in fact remove the stigma or the insults that sometimes attach to these people."[42] This theological and legal discourse, though it happens at the elite level of scholars, does have practical effects for the general population. Iran's leading sex-change surgeon, Dr. Mirjalali, reports that he has performed 320 sex-change operations in the last 12 years in Iran (whereas he claims in Europe a surgeon would do about 40 sex-change operations in a decade).[43] Shi'i scholars who are government employees now recommend that people with gender dysphoria undergo hormone treatment and surgery, and in some cases the government pays for the procedure. In addition, Iranian law allowed a transsexual to receive a new birth certificate validating her or his new gender identity, and to receive a passport specifying the new gender category, long before many European or American countries have allowed such legal recognition of medical treatment.

Such innovative decisions were the result of one transsexual's efforts to convince Shi'i jurists of the reality of gender identity. Fereydoon Molkara was born in 1950 in a body with male sex organs and was raised as a boy, but always felt like a woman who was romantically and sexually attracted to men. She was aware that before the Islamic Revolution sex-change operations were allowed if one had enough money; but after the revolution the new Islamic government classified transsexuals and transvestites along with homosexuals who were to be punished with lashing or execution. While still perceived to be a man, Fereydoon participated in the Iran–Iraq War: "When the war started, I did voluntary nursing work near the front line. When I bandaged wounded men, they sometimes felt as though a woman was doing it because I was more gentle and I overheard them wondering what kind of person I was."[44] One of these patients was connected with officials in the Islamic government, and thus Fereydoon gained interviews with high-level jurists. In 1987, she was granted an interview with Ayatollah Khomeini. In just a half an hour, she was granted a decision – "Khomeini decided then that it was a religious obligation for me to have the sex change because a person needs a clear sexual identity in order to carry out their religious duties. He said that because of my feelings, I should observe all the rites specific to women, including the way they dress." It took many more years for Fereydoon to overcome her family's opposition, find a hospital where she could undergo treatment, and pay for costly surgery. But finally she has transformed her body into that of a woman named Maryam Khatoon Molkara, having persuaded a state-affiliated religious charity, the Imam Khomeini Relief Committee, to pay for the procedure both for herself and for future transsexuals.

Recent court cases in Iran and Egypt demonstrate that Muslim jurists can advocate sex-realignment surgery to "fix" people who suffer from gender dysphoria. However, the theological approach of such decisions reifies the assumed division of society into "masculine males" and "feminine females" without addressing the deeper ambiguities in gender identity and its complex relationship to sexual orientation. Such an approach does not acknowledge that both are diverse within any society, including Muslim societies. At a popular level, many Muslims interpret all forms of homosexuality as "men who think they are women" or "women who think they are men." The fact is that most lesbian women think of themselves as women and are happy to stay that way in order to seek sexual pleasure and intimacy with another woman, just as most gay men think of themselves as men. However, some people who at first feel attracted to a same-sex partner (and may initially identity as lesbian or gay owing to that experience) later discover that this sexual attraction owes to the fact that they identify as men despite having been raised in a feminine role and having female sexual anatomy (or they identity as women despite having been raised in a masculine role and having male sexual anatomy). That is, an initial feeling of homosexual orientation may, upon deeper introspection and wider experience, turn out to be a transgender identity.

These recent juridical decisions in Egypt and Iran focus on the medical technique of sex-realignment surgery and the subsequent gender fit of those who undergo its ardors. They are concerned mainly with the stability of gender-binary Islamic society and give little or no consideration to the human being who suffered before the operation and may continue to endure stigma and marginalization after it. Without openly and compassionately acknowledging that gender identity exists independently of anatomy and sexual orientation, Muslim jurists will never do justice to the experience of transgender Muslims. Self-knowledge and clear identity do not come easily to transgender people, who are oppressed or punished for homosexuality before coming to a deeper realization that their profound feeling of disharmony owes to gender identity rather than sexual orientation. As long as Muslim societies withhold compassion and understanding from lesbians and gays in their communities, then transgender persons will also suffer and have a harder time coming to a clear understanding of their own existential reality.

Conclusion

Despite their limitations, recent decisions of the Islamic authorities in Egypt and Iran give some optimistic signs for the future. They are signs that *ijtihad* is not dead, either among Sunnis or among Shi'a. This is true even if the *ijtihad* so far exerted by Islamic authorities around questions of transgender experience is partial and selective, with a view to reinforcing gender binaries in society rather than to ameliorating the suffering of transgender people themselves. These tentative steps of *ijtihad* will remain unjust if they are enacted in an environment of increasing denunciation of lesbian and gay Muslims. Often jurists accept gender realignment as a diversionary tactic to justify their refusal to reexamine with compassion the issues of lesbian and gay Muslims. It is seen as a way to get confused or wayward Muslims to "properly enact their gender roles" within a heterosexist and patriarchal framework, rather than to more deeply examine the fundamental assumptions of that framework which are vigorously and often violently asserted as "natural."

But when we really observe nature with humility, as the Qur'an urges us to do, how facile we find our simple notions of what is natural! Often we find the order that we assume is "nature" is in fact our human projection of a simple and rigid notion upon the complex and ambiguous reality that is nature. As a conclusion to this chapter, the reader is reminded of the pronouncement of Shaykh Qaradawi about nature and gender. Confronted with questions of sexual orientation and gender identity, he said, "Look, God most glorified and mighty created the human being as male and female ... So natural attraction is between the two sexes ... This is based upon the behavior of positive and negative ... The atom is formed of electron and proton, isn't it?"[45] The Shaykh simply articulates what most Muslims assume, from scholars to local imams to authorities with the family. The natural world is simple, and its simplicity reinforces our social categories and moral values – there are electrons and protons that make up physical matter, so there are male and female genders that make up social matter, and both are decreed by God. However, the Shaykh's boldness in making such assertions cannot cover up the fact that he is wrong – about both physics and gender.

The more we observe nature, the less we find it conforms to our simplistic notions. This is true whether we look at matters of physics or matters of gender. Our Muslim ancestors were great astronomers and they asserted with full certainty that there were five planets in our solar system (corresponding, along with the moon and the sun, to the seven heavenly spheres mentioned in the Qur'an), but now with increasingly powerful means of observation we assert that there are nine planets. Even this school curriculum truism is not exactly true, for contemporary astrophysicists cannot agree on which material bodies circling our sun are planets and which are not. One of the astrophysicists deeply involved in the debate over whether Pluto is really a planet gives us this summary of our confrontation with nature: "Nature is much richer than our imagination. Life is tough, life is complicated. Get over it."[46]

If assessing Pluto is difficult, one might assume that assessing our moon would be easier, since it is so much closer to us, has been scrutinized longer, and was even visited by us. We presume that the moon is spherical and orbits the earth in circles so regular that we Muslims can set our calendar by its phases, but none of our idealist projections about the moon turns out to be true. Astrophysicists are still discovering surprising facts about the moon: "The moon is moving away from the earth and slowing down ... each year the moon is another 3.8 cm from the earth ... If the moon were sliced in half along its equator, the cross-section would not be a circle, but more of an oblong shape."[47] The moon is not a sphere and its orbit is not perfectly regular; it has a much more complex personality than we project upon it. People read the Qur'an with assumptions about the moon that limit the way we imagine the moon. In fact, our observations, especially those that go against common sense, give us a much more tantalizing moon in all its imperfections.

A realistic assessment of the moon or the planets does not contradict the Qur'an. It enriches our reading of the Qur'an, if only we jettison our presumptions and common-sense illusions in favor of observing carefully what is real. We must confront the unexpected richness and endless variation of nature, as the Qur'an urges us to examine God's signs *on the horizons and within the selves* (Q. 41:53). When our presumptions about what is natural fail to account for the reality that confronts us, a challenge opens up before our egoistic pretense. We can either accept our fallibility with humility and look for wisdom in our own weakness, or we can divert our gaze from the reality with which God confronts us and narrow our minds in order to preserve our egoistic self-aggrandizement.

If we confront nature's baffling complexity, we discover opportunities to return to the Qur'an with new insight. Listen to how the Qur'an swears by the planets: *When the sun is covered, when the stars darken ... when the female infant buried alive is asked for what sin she was killed ... every soul will know what is has prepared – Nay, I swear by the planets that run their course and hide themselves, this is the word of an honorable messenger* (Q. 81:1–18). The planets are sometimes evident to our observation as they run their course, and they are sometimes hidden from our sight and understanding. Never should we assume we know fully the secrets of the planets and always we should keenly observe to learn more. As the Qur'an swears by the planets and the stars, it also forces our attention toward gender in speaking of the infant girls unjustly oppressed and killed because their society assumed that boys are valuable and girls are a burden. So sure were the pre-Islamic Arabs that they knew natural and immutable truths about gender that they had no moral qualms about killing their girl children.

Muslims are proud that they, armed with the Qur'an, ended the practice of female infanticide. But should we rest there? Have we really understood the Qur'an's discussion of female infants to its fullest meaning? Until we return to reexamine our assumptions about gender – not only with regard to those born with "female anatomy" but also those who are born with female psyches in bodies with "male anatomy" – we cannot claim to have listened intently to the Qur'an and felt its full resonance. How many girls and boys are being "buried" from infancy under stereotyped and inflexible notions of gender? How many are suffocated by family and community who impose upon them a gender identity that their own psyches reject? How long must they endure this burial under defamation in the name of fidelity to Islam which gives their personal experience and existential struggle only the shallowest regard?

Conclusion: Embracing Islamic Humanism

Many Muslims today cannot imagine that Islam could be a religion that acknowledges and respects diversity in sexuality and sexual orientation, even to the point of allowing same-sex couples to marry. They may not even recognize the aspects of patriarchy that oppress those characterized by same-sex erotic desire or gender-ambiguous behavior. But these kinds of oppression, though often hidden from public view, are no less unjust than other forms of prejudice that Muslims in the past have struggled to change with jihad and *ijtihad*. Muslims have overcome many kinds of prejudice with positive results for our understanding of our faith. Why do we contemporary Muslims focus our sense of justice as demanded by radical *tawhid* on the fields of political organization or economic ownership and just stop there? Why not continue to extend this challenging focus on justice into the more private spaces of our intimate lives with regard to gender identity and sexual orientation, in order to think more clearly about how our erotic lives intersect with our spiritual lives?

Some Muslims who are transgender, lesbian, or gay have begun this long process of discovering how Islamic *tawhid* can help them integrate their lives, despite conflict with other Muslims over whether they are acceptable members of the religious community. They, too, have challenged injustice with both jihad and *ijtihad*. Their jihad is evident in their life stories as they struggle to overcome alienation and persecution, create communities, and build support groups to look after their own welfare. Collecting those life stories through interviews was an integral part of researching this book, though they are not presented here. It is hoped that a companion volume to this one will be published that presents and analyzes the life stories and struggles of those Muslim activists. This book, in contrast, focuses on their *ijtihad*; it presents a composite picture of their inner struggle to understand the message of Muhummad with all the intellectual, ethical, and spiritual resources at their disposal. It is hoped that their ideas and insights will help others to come to a better understanding of the ambiguity of gender identity and sexual orientation, the complexity of the Islamic tradition, and the flexibility that is demanded when the two things are held together.

The dimensions of gender identity and sexual orientation are integral parts of our humanity. Conflicts and complications in these dimensions are an unavoidable part of being human. We Muslims boast that Islam is a religion in accord with the needs of human nature (*islam din al-fitra*), but too often we use our religion as a shield to deflect the existential challenge to look squarely at human nature in all its complexities, with intellectual clarity, faithful resolve, and humane compassion. Our present condition as Muslims in the early twenty-first century makes this challenge all the more formidable. Whether we are Muslims in minority communities in "the West" or Muslims in Muslim-majority nations in Africa, Asia, or the Middle East, we live our Islam in a situation rife with conflict and violence. Whether we like it or not, we have inherited the twentieth century's identity politics that have profoundly altered the way we practice and articulate our faith. Seeing Islam through the lens of identity politics has become especially dominant under the influence of Islamism (so called Islamic fundamentalism or extremism), whose movements and organizations highlight the ideological aspects of Islamic belief and belonging, to the complete detriment of nuanced psychological understandings of human personality and ethical insights into humanness.

Such Islamist movements stress conformity to narrow norms, which they project as both "natural" and also scriptural. They demand conformity to ideological participation in a politicized Islamic community that stands against the outsider (variously construed as colonialism, Christianity, Zionism, communist atheism, or secular modernity). In taking up the oppositional stand against "outsiders" who threaten Islam, these Islamist movements disguise their own ambiguous and contingent historical development; they claim that by adopting the pose of "defending Islam" they have some unquestionable Islamic authenticity, such that anyone who opposes their movement or its representation of the religion must be un-Islamic. In terms of individual psychology, such Islamist movements demand conformist obedience and see all other responses as traitorous hypocrisy.

However, human nature is more complex than Islamism can allow for. This is why Islamist movements – like all ideological movements – will fail in the end to hold the loyalty and imagination of Muslims. Islamism cannot offer a method for the creative embrace of life, and can only shout utopian slogans while breeding disenchantment over the long term. This is because human nature is wider, deeper, and more beautifully varied than Islamist movements can admit. Human nature cannot be captured, harnessed, or limited by the framework that Islamism imposes. When we focus our attention on the erotic dimension of life, Islamism's psychological shallowness is clearly revealed. This is so because love – with its non-rational urges, its power over our emotional and spiritual life, and its undeniable expression of human diversity – threatens the fragile order that Islamists assert so forcefully. Ironically, it is the experience of gay, lesbian, and transgender Muslims who are outspoken activists that may offer a path toward redemption for the greater Muslim community, if and when they choose to face the complex reality of love.

What are our resources in the search for an Islam that embraces love in harmony with justice? European colonialism has largely destroyed the resources – political, educational, and spiritual – that we Muslims inherited from our ancestors. The independence movements in Africa, Asia, and the Middle East which opposed colonialism and Western domination have largely bred authoritarian regimes that either use Islam as a tool to prop up their own power or suppress Islam as a threat to their power. In the aftermath, we Muslims have lost our classical theological training, jettisoned philosophical inquiry, and allowed Sufism to be eclipsed. When Sufism or Islamic mysticism remained an integral part of Islam, there were mechanisms in place for Muslims to balance the rational and non-rational dimensions of the human personality, to balance erotic urges toward rapture with ascetic impulses toward self-control. It must be the goal of a revived "Islamic humanism" to counter the destruction wrought by both colonial domination and Islamist ideological reactions. Islamic humanism must recover the insights formerly provided by Sufi communities and Muslim philosophical circles. It must also encourage reform of Islamic law as a framework for ethical living in creative engagement with modern conditions. Upholding the dignity of each individual is an essential component of all these developments.

Islamic humanism must strongly assert that God has not created individuals in order for them to fit into an ideological and communal regime. Rather God imparts to us the responsibility to alter any social order to foster the ultimate goal of human flourishing (*sa'ada*). Human flourishing means that the small rewards of pleasure in this world – pleasure for oneself and also pleasure in helping others to overcome obstacles to their own fulfillment – can lead us to an attitude of reverence for God who gave this world to us in stewardship. The small pleasures can lead us to give thanks for blessings received, to help others receive the blessings they too deserve, to see these blessings as subtle signs pointing to the enduring rewards of the life to come if we sacrifice our self-interest to uphold the equality of all and stand for their justice and dignity. Without an ethical practice of Islamic humanism, we cannot achieve this state of social development toward which the Qur'an calls us.

Law by itself cannot achieve such social development. Law can impose order but cannot foster development of a truly ethical society. An ethical society is based on the decentralized actions of networks of people and depends upon their individual motivations, their subtle psychological states, and their spiritual awareness. Law is a crutch that can help a society maintain some order while it is unhealthy; but, like a person depending so much on a crutch that it becomes a fetish, a society that deifies law can never foster healthy ethical development. If Muslims allow their Islamic faith to be narrow and shallow – to believe that the Qur'an and Prophet's example are only to establish a code of rules or to be focused solely on application of the *shari'a* – then we will never achieve peace with justice or establish faith-based communities that foster love and compassion.

Some lesbian, transgender, and gay Muslims who read this study will support the challenge articulated above. However, many will wonder whether any purpose is served by focusing on classical jurists and Qur'an commentators. They may feel that holding on to a personal belief in God and a loving respect for the Prophet Muhammad is the best they can do, and any discussion of interpretation, Islamic law, or hadith traditions will be turned quickly against them, based on the deeply held stereotypes in their Muslim community more than on the contents of their religion. Can there be any rapprochement with the *shari'a* and the authorities that support it? Is any discussion of the *shari'a* a capitulation to authority that is hopelessly prejudiced against the very possibility of thinking that same-sex orientation or transgender identity is anything but misplaced lust? These are crucial questions.

The Islamic legal scholar Abdullahi Ahmed an-Na'im has addressed these questions directly in their widest form. He asks whether there is any possibility of "reforming" the *shari'a* in contemporary times to revive its underlying principles so that it protects civil liberties and human rights rather than suppressing them. He concludes that this is possible, but it is complicated by the neo-colonial struggles of nations inhabited by Muslims for the long-deferred promises of political and cultural self-determination. "We have Muslim demands for self-determination by the application of Islamic law in public life. Yet such Islamic law cannot possibly be *shari'a* as historically established. The only way to reconcile these competing imperatives for change in the public law of Muslim countries is to develop a version of public law which is compatible with modern standards of constitutionalism, criminal justice, international law and human rights ... We can then proceed to resolve the conflict and tension within the framework of Islam as a whole, albeit not necessarily within the framework of the historical *shari'a*."[1] An-Na'im argues for the disengagement of the *shari'a* (as historically formed) from Islam as a whole. The *shari'a* in its historical development is not divinely ordained. Rather it is the creation of many generations of commentators, jurists, and hadith scholars who lived long after the Prophet Muhammad died and in a completely different political and cultural milieu. Radical *tawhid* demands that Muslims let nothing created by human beings stand in for Allah, the God who is the single and unique One.[2] From a critical point of view, it is a type of icon worship to imagine the *shari'a* to be infallible, unchanging, or somehow divine. Just as building the *shari'a* was an historical process, the creation of fallible human minds, hands, and hearts, so the *shari'a* should be open to continual reform and re-creation.

A renewed and evolving *shari'a* is a politically and religiously necessary project. It would offer Muslim-majority nation states a way of resolving many of the contradictions created by European colonialism's imposition of modernity through violence and domination, without having to destroy the nation state or reject some of the more valuable innovations of modernism. It would offer immigrant or indigenous Muslim communities that are minorities (in North America, Europe, and South Africa) a way to reconcile their religious faith and community aspirations with the reality of living as citizens of states that enshrine secular legal traditions and cultural values.

An-Na'im has pointed out that the central questions to be addressed in this reformation of the *shari'a* are those of international law, human rights, and civil liberties. Under the rubric of rights and civil liberties come concerns about women's equality and vulnerability, to which an-Na'im is very attentive, having learned much from generations of Muslim feminist scholars and activists. However, as argued in this study, the effect of asserting women's rights will never be limited to the realm of women. It will necessarily change the way men behave and the way both women and men perceive sexuality. As feminism opens sexuality as a topic for discussion, homosexuality will inevitably come up as a challenge to all Muslims with a keen sense of justice.

At the end of the day, many Muslims will respond that it is too much for lesbian and gay Muslims to ask for Islam to change to accommodate them. However, this is not really what we are asking for. In reality, we assert that Islam must change to grow, to continue growing as it had in the past, confident that in facing new challenges with a keen sense of justice Muslims will renew the roots of their faith. Lesbian, transgender, and gay Muslims assert that we may be agents in this slow but necessary change, along with women, youth, and other disempowered groups. But that is only because of God's granting us a pivotal place in the diversity of humanity – at the edge, a place of both danger and insight.

We ask only to be treated as fully human and insist on being recognized, if not embraced, as equals in faith. As for the details of which interpretation is right and who is wrong, we can answer in the humble but powerful way that all classical Muslim scholars finished their debates: "And in the end, only God knows best." For in the end, whatever position one takes on crucial issues of the day, it is to God that we all return – with no exception in regard to gender identity or sexual orientation. At the end of this life, we are responsible before God through God's Prophet, rather than to any other authority. We know that God will ask us whom we have injured in being homosexual or transgender and will also ask who has committed injustice against us. We can answer with words the Prophet conveyed in Surat al-Saba (Q. 34:50):

> If I err, I err only against my own soul
> and if I follow a right direction
> it is because of what my lord reveals to me
> for God is surely One who hears, an intimate One

Notes

Preface

1. Abou El Fadl, *Speaking in God's Name*, p. 10 note 8.

Acknowledgements

1. Kecia Ali takes seriously the possibility of new interpretations of the Qur'anic narratives about the Prophet Lot – seriously enough to disagree with my interpretation in several details in her own book, *Sexual Ethics and Islam*, pp. 63–96. I thank her for offering guidance on the details of marriage contracts – including the possibility of same-sex Islamic marriages – but the discussion of same-sex marriages in Islam expresses my own opinions and their shortcomings are mine alone.
2. Wadud, *Inside the Gender Jihad*, pp. xvii, 85–86, 238, 271 note 36. Dr. Wadud pleads for more women to write not just about gender issues but also about female sexuality. Though arguing about gender is slowly being recognized as legitimate in public discourse, at present women still take great risks if they talk about sexuality, especially in ways that affirm women's distinctive sexuality over and against that perceived by men. Lesbian women face even greater risks. But some women have stepped forward to speak and be heard, to write and be read, to demand respect and be acknowledged. Some of these women are lesbian Muslims, like Khalida, who has published an autobiographical essay in Abdul-Ghafur, *Living Islam Out Loud.*
3. This reputed hadith in Arabic is "al-khalq 'ayyal allah fa-ahabb al-khalq ila allah man ahsana ila 'ayyali-hi." All translations from Arabic and other non-English texts are by the author of this study, unless otherwise noted.

Introduction

1. Kugle, "Sexuality, Diversity and Ethics," pp. 190–234.

2. For definitions of *ijtihad*, see Abou El Fadl, *Speaking in God's Name*, p. 9 and Khaddouri, *al-Shafi'i's Risala*, p. 31.
3. Abou El Fadl, *The Place of Tolerance in Islam*, pp. 15–16.
4. Translations of Qur'an are by the author, with gratitude to previous translators for their guidance, like N.J. Dawood, M.H. Shakir, A'isha and Abd al-Haqq Bewley, and Michael Sells. I follow the insights of Sells in refusing to use gendered pronouns (he and his) to refer to God, for God created gender as a characteristic of created beings and God is far above such divisions.
5. Kugle, "Sexual Diversity in Islam," tries to explain how I am a Muslim, as a non-sectarian Sunni with a progressive approach to Islam, a reformist within the Hanafi legal method that values rational assessment of traditional sources, and an admirer of Ibn Hazm, who upheld the primacy of the Qur'an's poetic subtlety. Some have accused me of insincerity or heresy; I will not name these critics, some of whom are Muslim academics in universities and others of whom are Muslim intellectuals in other professions. I hope their critiques of me have led to improvements in this current work.
6. Al-Maturidi, *Kitab al-Tawhid*, p. 10. Al-Maturidi is a Sunni theologian who articulated an intermediate position between the traditionalist Ash'arites and the rationalist Mu'tazilites, and offers a creative way to negotiate between the divisive theological debates within Sunni communities; al-Maturidi worked primarily within the Hanafi legal school and he, along with Ibn Hazm, offers inspiration for this study.
7. The interviews had the following diversity in terms of gender: four were with lesbian women, twelve were with gay men, and two were with transgender persons (one transitioning female-to-male and one identifying as male-to-female). They were diverse in terms of ethnicity: eight are South Asian, four are Arab, one is Berber, one is African–American, and four identify as "mixed ethnicity" (or in South Africa as "coloured").
8. Wadud, *Inside the Gender Jihad*, p. 238, states this most explicitly: "the Qur'an itself, as well as the shari'a, is founded upon male sexual experience." If the Qur'an as well as classical Islamic texts are founded exclusively upon male sexual experience, then it is difficult if not impossible to formulate an Islamic liberation theology for heterosexual women, gay men, lesbian women, and transgender people, all of whose experience differs in drastic ways from that of heterosexual men. I feel that there is some room to negotiate even as we acknowledge that most Islamic texts, based upon the Qur'an itself, have an inherent bias toward heterosexual and patriarchal male experience. It is too early to dismiss the Qur'an as inherently and inalterably patriarchal. I accept Wadud's warning that reference to the Qur'an and normative Islamic texts (hadith, fiqh, and moralistic literature) must be balanced with attention to the ethical and spiritual struggle of actual believers who are not patriarchal and heterosexual men. This study tries to balance between allegiance to the Islamic tradition, criticism of its past lapses, and new exploration of its founding sources.

9. There are eunuchs or celibates who do not conform to patriarchal expectations of sexuality and gender; these categories come up in the analysis but are not the focus of this book.
10. El-Rouayheb, *Before Homosexuality in the Arab–Islamic World*, pp. 5–12 and chapter 1; Schmitt and Sofer, *Sexuality and Eroticism among Males in Moslem Societies*; Murray and Roscoe, *Islamic Homosexualities.*
11. Nahas, *Al-Junusiyya*, pp. 30–31. In later writings, Nahas has nuanced this stance, stating that God condemned the Tribe of Lot not because they acted in bisexual ways but rather because they used sex as a tool of coercion in opposition to their Prophet.
12. Kugle, "Sexuality, Diversity and Ethics," pp. 199–200.

Chapter One

1. Written testimony presented at the United States Department of Justice Immigration Court, Arlington, Virginia; in all quotes from this document, identifying information is withheld to protect the anonymity of those involved in the trial.
2. Kugle, "Framed, Blamed and Renamed."
3. Written testimony presented at the I.N.S. Court – see above.
4. Written affidavit presented at the I.N.S. Court. The author quoted uses the term "orders of Islam" to mean Islamic sects, legal schools, or confessional groupings.
5. Sakr, *Matrimonial Education in Islam*, pp. 33–34.
6. Doi, *Shariah*, pp. 241–242. Professor Doi was a Muslim scholar with a Ph.D. from the University of Cambridge, with interests in Islamic education and Islamic society in Africa.
7. There is a basic division of Muslim believers into two sects. "Sunni" refers to the majority of Muslims who call themselves the "People of Custom and Community" (Ahl al-Sunna wa'l-Jama'a), who believe that the Prophet allowed his community to decide by consensus upon their leader after his death. "Shi'i" refers to the minority group of Muslims (who form a national majority in Iran and Iraq, an influential group in Lebanon, and a minority in some Gulf Arab states, Afghanistan, Pakistan, and India) who call themselves "Partisans of 'Ali" (Shi'a 'Ali) and believe that the Prophet appointed his closest male relative, 'Ali ibn Abi Talib, to lead the community after he died. Based upon this political disagreement, both sects developed their own theology, traditions, and legal system. This book will focus mainly on Sunni discourses, but will mention Shi'i similarities and differences when relevant.
8. Classical jurists fully believed in the teaching that "Difference of opinion is a mercy to my community" – attributed by many to the Prophet Muhammad, though Ibn Hazm disputed its authenticity; see Abou El Fadl, *Speaking in God's Name*, p. 10.
9. Ibn Hazm, *Al-Usul wa'l-Furu'*, vol. 2, pp. 275–276. See also Maribel Fierro,

"Women as Prophets in Islam," who argues (contrary to this study) that Ibn Hazm was not concerned with asserting women's equality but rather with defending a theological position on the integrity of Prophets' reception of revelation.

10. Abu Laylah, *In Pursuit of Virtue*, p. 30. Also Ibn Hazm, *Ring of the Dove*, pp. 21–32.
11. Rowson and Wright, *Homoeroticism in Classical Arabic Literature*, describe the subtleties and controversies around "pederasty."
12. Abu Laylah, *In Pursuit of Virtue*, p. 30.
13. Written testimony of a staff member from I.G.L.H.R.C.'s program for Africa and South-West Asia (the "Middle East") presented at the I.N.S. Court hearing.
14. Masterclass with Fatima Mernissi, November 5, 2004, organized by Stichtung Praemium Erasianum, the Research Institute for Culture and History, and the Netherlands Research School of Women's Studies at Utrecht University.
15. Moroccan intellectuals stress that their national culture is part of the Mediterranean world, in which they participate intimately through the legacy of Andalusia, via centuries of trade and owing to contemporary migration of Moroccan workers and professionals to nations of the European Union. They imagine their allegiance to Islam to be perfectly compatible with modernity and emphasize that Morocco is far more "liberal" than other Arab nations of the Middle East. Yet recent events call this self-image into question, as several Moroccans resident in Europe have been indicted in terrorism trials, and the Casablanca bombings (of May 16, 2003) involved 14 suicide bombers inpired by al-Qa'ida. Moroccan immigrants or children of immigrants have been indicted in Germany for supporting the cell that carried out the 9/11 attacks, in Spain for the Madrid train bombings, and in the Netherlands for a political assassination.
16. President Mubarak accepts how fundamentalists in Egypt have targeted gay men; his government has used special courts set up under emergency law for prosecuting fundamentalists to instead prosecute those accused of homosexual acts or relationships, under the accusation of "contempt against religion" or "propagating extremist ideas" because Egyptian law does not explicitly criminalize homosexuality.
17. The newspaper *al-Ittihad al-Ishiraki* and many others in Morocco publicized the "Queen Boat" controversy, in which police raided a Cairo nightclub known to be a gay meeting place in 2001, arrested 52 men, and prosecuted them for "habitual debauchery" and/or "contempt of religion" in special courts set up to combat fundamentalists.

Chapter Two

1. Yunus Kemp, staff reporter, *Cape Argus*, <www.iol.co.za>.
2. All quotations from Muhsin Hendrix here and subsequently are from an interview with S. Kugle in Johannesburg (November 1, 2005), unless otherwise specified.

3. Qur'an 34:31–34 explains that those with power, wealth, and status set themselves and their own interests up as a god, demanding that others worship it. But the weak and vulnerable see the hypocrisy of the system and are faced with a challenge: they can either accept being victims by saying, "If not for you, the powerful, we could have believed," or they can embrace the Prophet's call to rise up against those who render them weak, worship the true God, and reject the system of oppression.
4. As the Qur'an 7:137 states: *Therefore we inflicted retribution on them [*the Egyptians*] and drowned them in the sea, because they rejected our signs and were heedless. Thus we made the people who were oppressed inherit the land, from east to west, the land we had blessed. Thus the good promise of your Lord was brought to fulfillment in the Tribes of Israel because they bore with patience such suffering and we brought to ruin all the Pharaoh had wrought.*
5. Farid Esack found inspiration in earlier Muslim theologians, especially in South Asia where he studied. The South Asian Muslim intellectual and reformer Mawlana Abul Kalam Azad pioneered an Islamic liberation theology approach when he participated with Gandhi in the Indian National Congress, and recorded his insights in a powerful interpretation of the Qur'an, his *Tarjuman al-Qur'an* (first published in 1930). Azad's Islamic liberation theology was further developed and popularized in South Asia by Mawlana Wahid al-Din Khan and Asghar Ali Engineer, who both published numerous books on the subject; see for example Engineer, *Islam and Liberation Theology.*
6. Shaikh, "Gender Justice."
7. There was a movement earlier in the twentieth century called "Progressive" among Muslims in South Asia, but it was largely a literary and philosophical movement that was secular in outlook, emphasizing modernist existentialism and socialist politics.
8. Such activists participate in the broader movement of Progressive Muslims because their identity has multiple dimensions. They participate not only as homosexual or transgender people but are also simultaneously engaged in human rights advocacy, feminist politics, youth empowerment, the protection of racial and ethnic minorities, and the promotion of non-violent conflict resolution within families and between nations.
9. Abou El Fadl, *Speaking in God's Name*, p. 24.
10. Kugle, "Sexuality, Diversity and Ethics."
11. Consultation is sadly lacking in Islamic communities, in which elites effectively forbid the knowledge necessary for interpretation to Muslims who are not male and heterosexual. Patriarchal authorities arrogate to themselves the sole voice to "speak in God's name." The Qur'an does not authorize this power dynamic that creates a priestly class. Rather, it encourages all believers to ask questions, to make inquiries, to search for an understanding of God's speech *on the horizons and in the selves* (Q. 41:53). It commands all Muslims – male and female, elite and common, rich and poor, Arab and others – to search for knowledge, to read, to think, and to interpret.

12. On the link between humanity (*adamiyya*) and moral–legal sanctity (*'isma*) in the Islamic legal tradition, see Recep Senturk, "'I Am Therefore I Have Rights'."
13. The Qur'an provides humanity with guidelines that we must apply with our own God-given agency (through reason, experience, and spiritual insight) in ways that promote justice for all. It is an expression of God's wisdom that the Qur'an does not impose a legal order but rather asserts ethical principles. Solutions to moral quandaries are left to us to discover as we interpret the Qur'an and apply its principles, and that application must change with changing circumstances if justice is to be achieved.
14. Muslims believe that the Qur'an is God's speech, communicated through the Prophet Muhammad and preserved by succeeding generations of Muslims (who memorized it, wrote it down, and argued among themselves from the beginning over its meaning). Its form is Arabic speech but its meaning overflows and it is accessible to speakers of any other language. There is no "literal" reading of the Qur'an that is not an interpretation involving the reader's personal assumptions, prejudices, and experiences, which both enable and limit the understanding she or he has of the Qur'an.
15. If our interpretation of the Qur'an becomes obsessed with legal details and becomes reduced to discussions of *fiqh*, we lose sight of the higher goals of the Qur'an, especially the promotion of loving and harmonious relationships at all levels of society. This does not mean dismissing *fiqh*, but it requires that we temper rules with justice's demands and balance them against love's aspiration.
16. Esack, *The Qur'an*, provides an overview of tools of *tafsir*.
17. This point expands upon insights of the Zahiri legal school, based on the maxim that "everything is allowed unless specifically and explicitly forbidden."
18. *Tafsir* from the classic age did not affirm the integrity and wholeness of the Qur'an consistently. Modern Muslim interpreters offer this tool to complement and correct details of the interpretive tradition we have inherited.
19. Muslim interpreters have always asked how the meaning is shaped by contexts of revelation (*asbab al-nuzul*), whether the verse was revealed in Mecca or Medina (in very different social and political contexts), whether it was revealed to address a specific person or crisis or rather to address particular audiences. Does the verse use language in a metaphoric way or definitive way? Finally and most importantly, does the verse intend to have a legal application? If so, does the wording of command allow any ambiguity, require any conditionality, or suggest any limitations? Such tools of traditional Islamic interpretation are of vital importance, even though ideological interprets in recent decades have sometimes abandoned them or diluted their use.
20. The Qur'an encourages us to embrace the world in all its bewildering diversity, to see it as the means through which God challenges us to live up to the highest ethical principles rather than to adopt a negative, pessimistic, and world-rejecting stance that sees the world as only a place of trials. A pessimistic attitude often equates the world (as a place of trials) with women (as embodiment

of temptation) and sex (as a polluting threat to morality), thereby supporting patriarchal assumptions, misogynistic assertions, and authoritarian politics.

21. Wadud, *Qur'an and Woman*, pp. 23–29, and Barlas, *Believing Women*, pp. 133–139.
22. The Qur'an uses "colors" to speak of the varieties of plants that grow on the earth (Q. 16:13), of food crops (Q. 39:21), of fruits and soils (Q. 35:27), of the diverse hues and tastes of medicinal honey (Q. 16:69), as well the diverse natures of humankind, beasts of burden, and animals of the fields (Q. 35:28).
23. See the scientific research of Hamer et al., "A Linkage between DNA Markers on the X Chromosome and Male Sexual Orientation," and Le Vay, "Difference in Hypothalamic Structure between Heterosexual and Homosexual Men." See also the socio-cultural studies by Boswell, "Concepts, Experience and Sexuality," and Roughgarden, *Evolution's Rainbow.*
24. Brooten, *Love Between Women*, pp. 115–142 documents astrological theories of pre-determined sexual orientation common in Greek, Roman, and Early Christian contexts.
25. Kugle, "Sexual Diversity in Islam," elaborates upon these four layers of personality as revealed in the Qur'an as the basis for rethinking Islamic spirituality.
26. This essential teaching is repeated in Q. 2:233, 6:152, 7:42, 23:62.
27. Al-Bukhari, *Sahih*, "Kitab al-Wahi," book 1, chapter 1, report 1. For citation from al-Bukhari and other hadith compilations see Chapter 3, note 1.
28. Razi, *Mafatih al-Ghayb*, vol. 2, p. 383.
29. For the use of "desire" in descriptions of heaven, see Q. 21:2, 41:31, 43:71, 16:57, 56:21, 77:42. For the use of "desire" the fulfillment of which is absent in hell, see Q. 34:54.
30. See Q. 19:59, where sensual desire and egoistic desire are juxtaposed to describe why people have perverted the Prophetic teachings that came before Islam.
31. Desiring egoistic aggrandizement (*bagha*) that transgresses ethical limits is more dangerous than desiring bodily pleasure (*shahwa*), for it leads to organized activities that are more harmful for society at large, such as political corruption, organized crime, and rivalry based on ethnicity or tribe. In Arabic, the legal terms for prostitutes (*baghaya*) and violent rebels (*bugha*) are derived from the linguistic root for desiring aggrandizement (*bagha*).
32. See Kugle, *The Book of Illumination*, pp. 161–177.
33. In the medieval period, Arabic grammarians obscured the fact that the term *liwat* is a juristic invention, by claiming that it is not derived from the non-Arabic name for the Prophet Lut but rather is derived from the Arabic verb *lata.* That verb means "adhere" – it literally refers to making plaster or mud adhere to a wall and figuratively describes how a person or thing adheres to one's heart if one loves it; in this usage the verb appears in hadith and Arabic poetry but not in the Qur'an. The discrepancy was plastered over by grammarians who claimed that in anal intercourse the men of Lot's tribe "adhered" to each other front-to-back. For discussion of the verb *lata* and its early uses, none of them about sex acts, see Lane, *Arabic–English Lexicon*, pp. 2681–2682.

34. Ibn Hazm, *Al-Muhalla*, vol. 1, p. 393 (part 12 on "the act of the Tribe of Lot").
35. Ibid., p. 397.
36. The Qur'an does not specify exactly how Lot's wife betrayed him; it says only that she was "under him," meaning within his protected household and obliged to obey him, but that despite this she betrayed him. Commentators have provided details from non-Qur'anic sources saying that she used to alert men in her tribe if Lot were protecting and hosting strangers in his home, so that the men of his tribe could deny him this opportunity to offer hospitality, a way in which he expressed his ethical authority over their cities.
37. Al-Tabari, *Tafsir*, vol. 3, p. 163.
38. Jamel, "The Story of Lut."
39. See Kugle, "Sexuality, Diversity and Ethics," pp. 203–219, where the interpretive assumptions of al-Tabari and al-Qurtubi are discussed in detail.
40. See for instance Abdullah Yousef Ali's translation of Q. 29:28–35, in which he translates *al-fahisha* as "lewdness" and then in a footnote defines the special crime of the people of Lot as anal sex between men in public. Yousef Ali is more honest than many other translators in using footnotes to make these definitions, rather than inserting them into the translation itself.
41. The other verses that tell Lot's story are Q. 6:86, 11:77–81, 15:61–72, 21:71–75, 26:161–174, 27:54–57, 37:133–134.
42. Ibn Hazm, *Al-Ihkam fi Usul al-Ahkam*, vol. 5, p. 764.
43. It is a persistent pattern in Islamic law that Qur'anic verses that critique and limit patriarchy are systematically ignored or distorted to allow men's exertion of power: jurists allowed polygyny though the Qur'an warns against it, legalized concubines though the Qur'an urges believers to free slaves, and enforced seclusion upon women alone though the Qur'an enjoins both men and women to uphold modesty and fidelity. This is what Leila Ahmed identifies as the "ethical egalitarian voice" of the Qur'an which is often lost in classical interpretation and legal elaboration; see Ahmed, *Women and Gender in Islam*, pp. 64–66.
44. Lot is mentioned in the Torah because he was known to the Israelite tribes, having been related to Abraham's family and lived in Abraham's time; in contrast, Salih is a Prophet not mentioned in the Torah, for he belonged to the other Semitic tribes who were the ancestors of the Arabs.
45. The narrative of Salih sent as a Prophet to the people of Thamud is told in Q. 7:73, 9:70, 11:61–95, 91:13, and many other verses. The tribes of Thamud carved cities into the rocks of cliffs (Q. 89:9), perhaps at the city of Petra, whose ruins are located in Jordan.
46. Ibn Hazm, *Al-Muhalla*, vol. 11, p. 384. For a discussion of this point, see Adang, "Ibn Hazm on Homosexuality," p. 20. Ibn Hazm taunts traditionalists by saying they must follow their own logic fully, thus burning to death those who unfairly weigh merchandise because God destroyed with fire the tribes of the Prophet Shu'ayb for unfair trading practices.

47. Al-Tabari, *Tafsir*, vol. 3, p. 465, makes clear that the Qur'an always narrates Lot's story in the context of other Prophets' stories.
48. Ibn Hazm, *Al-Ihkam fi Usul al-Ahkam*, vol. 5, p. 728–729.
49. Ibn Hazm, *Kitab fi Ma'rifat al-Nasikh wa'l-Mansukh.*
50. Ibn Hazm, *Al-Ihkam fi Usul al-Ahkam*, vol. 5, p. 764.
51. Musallam, *Sex and Society in Islam.*
52. Juynboll, "Sihak," pp. 565–566. See also Ali, *Sexual Ethics and Islam*, pp. 81–82.
53. Jamel, "The Story of Lut."
54. Q. 25:38 and 50:12 mention the People of Rass but never specifies the cause of their destruction.
55. An example of diversion from the intended meaning is how male jurists interpret the verse allowing plural marriages for men. Although the Qur'an does say to men, *marry those of the women that appear good for you – two, three or four* (Q. 4:3), it says this in the context of protecting orphans and warning the men who act as their guardians not to consume unjustly the wealth entrusted to them as the orphans' inheritance. The whole verse reads, *Give to the orphans their wealth without exchanging what is good for what is spoiled. Do not consume their wealth as part of your own wealth, for that is a profound outrage. If you fear that you cannot deal justly with the orphans, then marry those of the women that are good for you – two, three or four. But if you fear that you cannot act justly, then just one.* The ethical context is clearly the command to treat orphans justly and manage their wealth without fraud; the license to marry the women among these vulnerable people (as a way of ensuring them logistical and financial support) is given as a last resort if one cannot live up to the expectation of financial care. Yet male jurists took it out of context to justify plural marriages as a social norm for the wealthy elite.
56. For an intelligent presentation of this argument as it relates to U.S. politics and conservative Christianity, see Jakobsen and Pellegrini, *Love the Sin*, pp. 4–7.
57. The word *'aqim* literally means "not reproducing" or not fecund; the Qur'an uses it in several metaphorical ways. It describes a dry wind that makes the land barren. It describes Sarah, the wife of Ibrahim, who laughs at the angel's announcement that she will bear a son because she believes herself to be an old woman beyond reproducing.
58. Once the Prophet Muhammad's young wife, 'A'isha, was left in the desert after his caravan took off, but she was rescued by a handsome young man who brought her back to Medina, leading many of the Prophet's closest followers to accuse her of adultery. 'A'isha used this term, *husur*, to describe the young man, Safwan al-Mu'attal, to mean he does not sexually desire women owing to his wary abstention and is therefore righteous.
59. Some modern commentators deliberately ignore this possibility. Sayyid Qutb, for instance, says those without *irba* "are those without desire for women for one of many possible reasons, such as impotence, imbecility or insanity or other such things that prevent a man from desiring a woman." Qutb, *Fi Zilal al-Qur'an*, vol. 6, p. 97.

60. Wadud, *Inside the Gender Jihad*, p. 193, addresses this verse and challenges the idea that post-menopausal women are devoid of sexual desire.
61. The ideas that homosexuals are sinful and sick are often combined, especially when opponents see homosexual Muslims as "possessed" by evil spirits or Satan. However, seeing them as possessed displaces the issues they raise outside the arena of debate and discussion of the Qur'an's meaning, for the Muslim community should not debate with possessed persons but rather either "cure" them or suppress them.
62. Abou El Fadl, *Speaking in God's Name*, p. 10 note 8.

Chapter Three

1. Abu Dawud, *Sunan*, vol. 2, p. 857, "Kitab al-Adab," book 42, chapter 122, report 5127. Unless otherwise noted, all citations of hadith are from the six standard Sunni collections published in Liechtenstein by Thesaurus Islamicus Foundation, 2000. Volume, page, and report number refer to these publications. In addition, the book (*kitab*) and chapter (*bab*) and report (hadith) numbers are also given to facilitate cross-referencing with other published versions of hadith collections. The six canonical collections in Sunni Islam are: *al-Jami' al-sahih* of Muhammad ibn Isma'il al-Bukhari (died 870), *al-Jami' al-sahih* of Muslim ibn al-Hajjaj (died 875), *Kitab al-sunan* of Abu Da'ud Sulayman al-Sijistani (died 889), *al-Jami' al-sahih* of Abu 'Isa Muhammad al-Tirmidhi (died 892/93), *Kitab al-sunan* of Ahmad ibn Shu'ayb al-Nasa'i (died 915), and *Kitab al-sunan* of Ibn Majah Muhammad al-Raba'i al-Qazwini (died 887). To these six collections are occasionally added other works that have not quite achieved the same degree of authority, most notably the *Musnad* of Ahmad ibn Hanbal (died 855).
2. Scholarly training in hadith studies has been largely snuffed out by the vagaries of twentieth-century history. Colonial occupation closed down many higher madrasas and poverty keeps them closed, and others are reduced to ideological boot-camps rather than acting as centers of Islamic humanism as they used to.
3. For example, a hadith that Abu Sa'id Al-Khudri (died 683) reported relates that the Prophet said, "Do not write down anything from me except the Qur'an. He who has noted down anything from me apart from the Qur'an must erase it!" This hadith is translated in Siddiqi, *Hadith Literature*, 49; it is preserved in Muslim, *Sahih*; it is discussed in Virjee, *Introduction to Hadith*, p. 69. In another incident, the Prophet once came to Abu Hurayra (died 678) and others while they were writing down his sayings and asked what they were writing. They replied that they were writing down sayings that they heard from him but he said, "A book other than God's book?" So Abu Hurayra and his group gathered what they had written and burnt it all; see Juynboll, *The Authenticity of the Tradition Literature*, p. 50.
4. When Ubayy ibn Ka'b narrated reports about Jerusalem on the authority of the Prophet, 'Umar admonished him. Ubayy called upon other companions to bear witness that he had heard what he was narrating from the Prophet, and they supported him. He objected to 'Umar, "Are you accusing me with regard to the

hadith of the Prophet of God!" and 'Umar replied, "O Abu Mundhir [Ubayy's nickname], by God, I was not accusing you [of lying], but I hated to think that the hadith of the Prophet was being manifest." Virjee, *Introduction to Hadith*, pp. 71–72. Upon his deathbed, 'Umar advised the Muslims to follow many sources of guidance in making decisions (the Qur'an foremost, followed by the opinions of the Prophet's companions and also the example of Christians and Jews) but he does not mention hadith as a reliable guide; as recorded in Ibn Sa'd, *Tabaqat*, vol. 3, p. 243, and discussed in Juynboll, *Muslim Tradition*, p. 26.

5. Ibn Hazm, *Asma' al-Sahabat*, p. 37. Another of the Prophet's family, 'Ali ibn Abi Talib, was suspicious about reports: see Siddiqi, *Hadith Literature*, pp. 189–190.
6. Virgee, *Introduction to Hadith*, p. 72. On Ibn Mas'ud, see al-Jazari, *Ghayat al-Nihaya*, pp. 548–549; he was one of the leading Qur'an reciters who learned the scripture directly from the Prophet and helped spread memorization and beautiful recitation of it among the companions.
7. Writing down hadith was not an independent development prior to law, contrary to what theorists of Islamic law often portray. Rather, legal necessity drove the compilation of hadith. This is clear from how the Umayyad Caliph 'Umar the Second (died 720) ordered the first collection of hadith in an official manner. As an imperial ruler, he wanted to impart uniformity to jurists' decisions across various regions. Abu Bakr ibn Muhammad ibn Hazm (died 737) and Muhammad ibn Muslim ibn Shihab al-Zuhri (died 742) are among those scholars who compiled hadith at 'Umar the Second's behest, though their compilations are not now known. Several learned Muslims seem to have independently written down small compilations of hadith, called *Sahifa* or *Musannaf*.
8. Legal works such as *al-Muwatta'* compiled by Malik ibn Anas (died 795) assumed that the behavior of Medina's residents perpetuated what the Prophet's followers did, which reproduced what the Prophet's companions did before them, which was in harmony with the Prophet's own actions or decisions. Early jurists wrote texts similar to that of Malik, such as Ibn Jurayj in Mecca, al-Awza'i in Syria, Sufyan al-Thawri in Kufa, Hammad ibn Abi Sulayman in Basra, Hushaym ibn Wasit and Ma'mar in Yemen, and Ibn Mubarak and Jarir ibn 'Abd al-Hamid in Iran.
9. Muslims today are familiar with Ibn Hanbal as the founder of a "Sunni legal school" – the Hanbali school – named after him. However, Ibn Hanbal was primarily a hadith collector rather than a jurist. He answered the need, first articulated by al-Shafi'i, for hadith with an explicit and documented chain of narrators linking the information reported to the Prophet. Others also composed *musnad* texts, but for modern debates on hadith it is standard to refer back to the compilation of Prophetic hadith by Ibn Hanbal before all others. Other *musnad* texts are by Ubaydallah ibn Musa al-'Abasi in Kufa, Musaddad ibn Musarhad in Basra, Asad ibn Musa al-Umawi and Nu'aym ibn Hammad al-Khaza'i in Egypt, in addition to Ishaq ibn Rahawayh and Uthman ibn Shaybah.

10. Insisting on an *isnad* filtered out many reports that claimed to give information about the Prophet's behavior but did not have a full chain of transmission back to the Prophet's own time. Such reports may or may not convey genuine information about the Prophet's words or actions, but there is not way to confirm that in the absence of an *isnad*. However, the mere presence of a full *isnad* is no foolproof guarantee that the report is genuine, for once it became necessary to state the *isnad* of a report explicitly, *isnads* could be manufactured to support reports. Hadith scholars admit that this happened but do not agree to what degree forged *isnad* may compromise the whole body of hadith. On this crucial point, that an intact *isnad* is not proof of the genuiness of the report to which it is attached as evidence, see Siddiqi, *Hadith Literature*, p. 200.
11. Al-Bukhari's motivation to write this masterpiece of hadith scholarship was recorded by later admirers: "When al-Bukhari saw these works [the *musnad* works] transmitted as a single collection comprising both the authentic and the good, and many that even had weak reports in them, he endeavored to collect all the authentic reports into one. The words of his teacher, Ishaq ibn Rahawayh, when he was talking to a group among whom al-Bukhari was present, strengthened his ambition: 'If only you had compiled a concise book comprising the authentic reports of the Prophet ... ' Al-Bukhari said, 'This touched my heart, and I began collecting the Comprehensive Book of Authentic Reports [*Sahih*].'" See Virgee, *Introduction to Hadith*, p. 74.
12. Al-Bukhari surveyed over 600,000 reports attributed to the Prophet which he collected during 40 years of travel for this sole purpose. Of these, he selected only 7,275 reports as authentic, after applying the most stringent tests of reliability to the narrators and the links between them. His contemporary, Muslim ibn al-Hajjaj, made a comparable effort by surveying 300,000 reports attributed to the Prophet and selecting only 4,000 as authentic and reliable.
13. The later hadith scholar al-Daraqutuni (died 995) demonstrated the weakness of 200 reports that al-Bukhari had included as authentic; see Siddiqi, *Hadith Literature*, pp. 93–101. Muslim's collection is generally not considered as comprehensive as al-Bukhari's, mainly because the former's section of reports on the meaning of various Qur'anic verses and the circumstance of their revelation is not as complete as the latter's. However, Muslim was more explicit in explaining his criteria for authentification and more precise than al-Bukhari in recording the *isnad* and its variations.
14. These later collections became known as *sunan* texts (collections of reports of each Prophetic example) or *jami'* texts (comprehensive collections of hadith). Four of them achieved renowned status: the texts of Abu Dawud, al-Tirmidhi, Ibn Maja, and al-Nasa'i.
15. Shi'i theologians and jurists developed their own corpus of hadith with different criteria; they included as authentic guidance reports about not only the Prophet but also his descendants who were imams, but they excluded as corrupt any reports narrated by companions or followers who opposed Imam 'Ali and his

family members. Yet Shiʿi and Sunni scholars faced the same difficulty ascertaining which reports were authentic.

16. Brown, "Criticism of the Proto-hadith Canon," offers an excellent example of a tenth-century scholar who both admired and critiqued the hadith collections of Muslim and al-Bukhari which became cannonical in Sunni circles.
17. Virgee, *Introduction to Hadith*, pp. 20–21.
18. Ibn Hazm, *Muʿjam Fiqh Ibn Hazm al-Zahiri*, vol. 1, p. 56.
19. Ibid., pp. 56–57. The famous medieval scholar al-Suyuti wrote a book on the subject – *al-Azhar al-Mutanathira fi al-Ahadith al-Mutawatira* – in which he found only 121 hadith that qualified as absolutely confirmed (*mutawatir*); even these were the subject of disagreement by later scholars, who claim some of these reports are weak and others are forged. Ibn Hiban and al-Harith say that *mutawatir* hadith are non-existent; al-Nawawi asserts, "They are very few to the point of almost not existing."
20. Ibid., p. 58.
21. Medieval estimations rate somewhere between 80 and 120 reports as *mutawatir* but, of the two most restrictive and authoritative collections, the *Sahih* of al-Bukhari contains 2,775 reports and the *Sahih* of Muslim contains 7,748 reports. So most of the reports in *sahih* collections that are often regarded as reliable are in fact not *mutawatir* at all.
22. Hadith scholars developed a category for hadith of lesser reliability, calling them *mustafid* or "extensively narrated," meaning a report narrated by more than two or three reporters on every level (it is often called *mashhur* or "well known"). These have multiple chains but do not live up to the criteria of *mutawatir*, which should have so many chains of narration that they are mutually confirming and assure that no error in the exact transmission of information has occurred.
23. Khalifa, "Hadith Matn Criticism".
24. There are hadith in which the Prophet is depicted condemning Khariji rebels, a sectarian purist movement initiated during the civil war at the battle of Siffin in 657 (twenty-eight years after the death of the Prophet Muhammad), when they deserted the army commanded by the vice-regent ʿAli and eventually assassinated him. Related sectarian groups battled Islamic governments in regional guerrilla wars for many generations, and later Sunni theologians branded them heretics; it is no wonder that reports were in wide circulation picturing the Prophet condemning and opposing Khariji heretics and that Sunni scholars would allow them into the corpus of hadith. But linguistically it is not possible that the Prophet actually said what these reports claim, because the term "Khariji," referring to sectarians or heretics, did not exist during his lifetime.
25. Some reports picture the Prophet condemning the Qadariyya who supported free will and human initiative in debates in the Umayyad era, or predicting the rise of the ʿAbbasid dynasty. These groups did not exist in the time of the Prophet and so from the content of their *matn* the reports can be judged to be later fabrications attributed falsely to the Prophet. Similarly, *matn* analysis is used to dimiss reports

that link the coming of the Mahdi with the eventual conquest of Constantinople, failed assaults on which were launched in 674, a full fifty-four years after the Prophet's death, and were not abandoned until fifty years later.

26. The most famous book about poetry and song, which records many stories of the Prophet, his companions, and their society, is *Kitab al-Aghani* by Abu al-Faraj al-Isfahani (died 967). The first biography of the Prophet, *Sirat Rasul Allah*, was written by Muhammad ibn Ishaq (died around 783) and edited and circulated by Ibn Hisham (died around 840). Both genres were preceeded by several books on the Prophet's military campaigns, called *maghazi*. Hadith scholars disparaged these genres, but in fact they relate sayings of the Prophet's companions, followers, and family in much the same way that hadith do, the only difference being that the other genres valued the information these reports provide over their chain of narration, and incorporate the information rather seamlessly into a full narrative whereas hadith emphasize the explicit chain of narration in an attempt to certify the information, thereby isolating the information conveyed from its context in history. Both kinds of literature drew from the same body of information: sayings about the Prophet that circulated orally among the Prophet's community after his death.
27. Mernissi, *The Veil and the Male Elite*, pp. 42–81; Barlas, *Believing Women*, pp. 42–62.
28. Al-Jawziyya, *Rawdat al-Muhibbin*, p. 400. As a Hanbali scholar, Ibn Qayyim al-Jawziyya strongly supports the validity of hadith over and above legal reasoning, but admits that some reports are of weak authenticity.
29. Patani, *Tadhkirat al-Mawdu'at*, p. 171.
30. Ibid. On Ibn 'Abbas as a narrator of hadith, see Ibn Hazm, *Asma' al-Sahabat*, p. 40. Ibn Qayyim al-Jawziyya, al-Suyuti, and other medieval scholars composed similar books on fabricated hadith to try to cull fabricated and weak reports and reinforce their contention that reports in general were reliable.
31. Kugle, "Sultan Mahmud's Makeover," pp. 38–40.
32. Zafeeruddin, *Islam on Homo-sexuality*, p. 78.
33. Reporting on Islamic attitudes to homosexuality, gay and lesbian rights organizations pick up references and unwittingly give them authority they do not deserve, as in the International Lesbian and Gay Association's report on the *shari'a*, which quotes this report: <www.ilga.info/Information/Legal_survey/middle%20east/supporting%20files/sharia_law.htm>. Contemporary debates on homosexuality obscure the ambiguity inherent in the Islamic tradition. Contemporary upholders of "orthodoxy" tend to deny the existence of ambiguities of which medieval scholars were not afraid. Once reports were written down and gathered into collections that achieved canonical status, they became difficult if not impossible to remove, even if they are revealed to be outright forgeries. In that sense, hadith represent "tradition" by exerting a force of inertia against reform or progress, even if by criteria both traditional and rational there is overwhelming evidence that change is necessary.

34. Patani, *Tadhkirat al-Mawdu'at*, p. 171, discredits this report, on the authority of al-Suyuti's analysis of fabricated reports, entitled *Al-La'ali' al-Masnu'a fi al-Ahadith al-Mawdu'a* (*The Book of Artificial Pearls about Fabricated Reports*). Al-Nuwayri, *Nihayat al-Arab*, vol. 2, p. 210, cites the report as authentic with the following *isnad*: from Talha ibn Zayd, from Burd ibn Sinan, from Abu al-Munib, from 'Abdallah ibn 'Umar. On 'Abdallah ibn 'Umar as a narrator and the number of reports linked to him, see Ibn Hazm, *Asma' al-Sahabat*, p. 38.
35. Zafeeruddin, *Islam on Homo-sexuality*, p. 77.
36. Ali, *Sexual Ethics and Islam*, pp. 75–78. The Qur'an enjoins Muslims to avoid the "enormous sins" but assures them that lesser sins can be forgiven (Q. 4:31); the Qur'an pointedly does not specify what are "enormous sins," hence a whole genre of moralistic literature by Muslim scholars.
37. Rowson and Wright, *Homoeroticism in Classical Arabic Literature*, p. 25.
38. See Rowson, "Gender Irregularity as Entertainment."
39. Patani, *Tadhkirat al-Mawdu'at*, p. 171.
40. Ibid.
41. Ibid., p. 7.
42. Ibid., p. 8.
43. Juynboll, *The Authenticity of the Tradition Literature*, pp. 63–99, summarizes the acrimonious modern arguments over Abu Hurayra's authenticity as a hadith narrator.
44. Estimates of the time Abu Hurayra spent around the Prophet's household range from twenty-one months to three years – this a matter of grave debate, since his authenticity as a narrator depends upon his witnessing the activities of the Prophet.
45. Ahmed, *Women and Gender in Islam*, pp. 64–78.
46. Al-Bukhari, *Sahih*, vol. 3, pp. 1212–1213 – "Kitab al-Libas," book 77, chapters 61–62.
47. Ibid., chapter 62, report 5948; as translated by Rowson, "Effeminates of Early Medina," p. 64.
48. Muslim, *Sahih*, vol. 2, p. 946 – "Kitab al-Salam," book 40, chapter13, report 5820. The report is also recorded in Ibn Hanbal, *Musnad*.
49. Rowson, "Effeminates of Early Medina," p. 67.
50. Al-Bukhari, *Sahih*, vol. 3, p. 1213 – "Kitab al-Libas," book 77, chapter 62, report 5947.
51. Ibid., report 5946.
52. Abu Dawud, *Sunan*, vol. 2, p. 686 – "Kitab al-Libas," book 33, chapter 35, reports 4108–4112.
53. Ibid., vol. 2, p. 826 – "Kitab al-Adab," book 42, chapter 61, report 4930.
54. Rowson, "Effeminates of Early Medina," p. 66.
55. Al-Qurtubi, *Tafsir al-Jami' fi Ahkam al-Qur'an*, vol. 7, p. 244, narrates this report – including the name of the man punished but not an *isnad* – as part of his juridical interpretation of Lot's story in Q. 7:80. The report and the man's name are related by al-Munajjad, *al-Hayat al-Jinsiyya*, p. 34.

56. Rashid Rida mentions Fuja'a as an apostate in his interpretation of Q. 5:54. See Rida, *Tafsir al-Manar*, vol. 6, p. 437.
57. Schmitt, "*Liwat* im *Fiqh*," p. 68.
58. Ibn Hanbal was inspired by the jurist al-Shafi'i, who argued that the only *sunna* Muslims needed to follow was that of the Prophet, rather than the organically developing practice of the people of Medina or the locally emerging consensus of regional legal schools. However, al-Shafi'i allowed that the practice of the Prophet's companions did provide guidance for jurists if there was no verse from Qur'an or report from the Prophet that contradicted the companion's practice.
59. Ibn Hanbal's *Musnad* recorded any report with a chain of narration leading back to the Prophet, regardless of whether it was confirmed by other reports, whether its narrators were judged reliable, or whether its content contradicted other reports. In this way, the floodgates were opened to reports claiming to be from the Prophet, about two and half centuries after the Prophet had died.
60. Ibn Hanbal, *Musnad*, vol. 1, p. 300.
61. Ibid.
62. Berg, *The Development of Exegesis in Early Islam*, gives an excellent overview of the "common link" method of hadith analysis.
63. Motski, *Origins of Islamic Jurisprudence*, pp. 287–289, discusses how Ibn 'Abbas was known in his time primarily as a jurist and not as a narrator of hadith.
64. See for example the comment of Abu Dawud, *Sunan*, vol. 2, p. 747 – "Kitab al-Hudud," book 39, chapter 29, report 4464, of which some of the *isnad*s end with 'Ikrima but are assumed to lead back to the Prophet via Ibn 'Abbas.
65. Ibn Sa'd, *Tabaqat*, vol. 5, pp. 212–216. For a summary of 'Ikrima's reception by Muslim scholars, see Schacht, "Ikrima, Mawla Ibn Abbas," and also Juynboll, *Muslim Tradition*, pp. 55–57.
66. Ibn Sa'd, *Tabaqat*, vol. 2, p. 133.
67. Al-Jazari, *Ghayat al-Nihaya*, vol. 1, p. 515.
68. Al-Maqrizi, *Mukhtasar al-Kamil*, p. 577.
69. Ibid., p. 578.
70. Al-Harawi, *Al-Masnu' fi Ma'rifat al-Hadith al-Mawdu'*, p. 103. Sa'id ibn al-Musayyab's student, the premier jurist Malik ibn Anas, was not satisfied with narrating hadith on the authority of 'Ikrima, and Muslim did not use his hadith in his *Sahih*, as discussed by the hadith scholar 'Ali al-Qari al-Harawi (died 1605).
71. Ibid.
72. Ibid.
73. Vaglieri, "Ibn 'Abbas, Abdallah."
74. Al-Jazari, *Ghayat al-Nihaya*, vol. 1, p. 515.
75. Al-Maqrizi, *Mukhtasar al-Kamil*, p. 578.
76. Ibid.
77. Wellhausen, *The Religio-political Factions in Early Islam*, p. 87.
78. 'Ikrima was exposed to the comparatively moderate Khariji ideology of the group known as Sufriyya. He was in Basra during the years when his owner, Ibn 'Abbas,

was the governor of that city. In Basra, the Khariji movement went underground after the central government suppressed it. The most extreme Kharijis argued that all must fight against non-Khariji Muslims and extremists even attacked fellow Kharijis who refused this suicidal militancy. Wellhausen, *The Religio-political Factions in Early Islam*, p. 23, describes their zeal: "They wish to save their souls by fighting the impious community with total lack of consideration for themselves and others. They are renowned enemies of the unified community ... Whoever deviates from the path of rightesousness by his actions is an unbeliever ... whoever takes one false step has fallen off from Islam."

79. Madelung, "Sufriyya." The Sufriyya was a breakaway group that believed fighting was necessary only when one could win, otherwise one should harbor subversion quietly while maintaining strict ascetic morality. The more militant Kharijis derided them as *sufr al-wujuh* – "yellow-faced" – owing to their parsiminous asceticism and refusal to join an open revolt doomed to failure; thus their sect got the name "Sufriyya." As other Khariji groups left Basra to form guerrilla bands, the Sufriyya remained in Basra, spreading their ideology in quiet subversive ways by trying to shape emerging notions of Islamic piety.
80. Lewinstein, "Sufriyya in North Africa." Occassionally, the Sufriyya fomented armed uprisings, but usually only when the central government persecuted them or tried to suppress their separatist communities. When they gained strength among various Berber tribes, the Sufriyya groups tried to conquer leading cities (like Qayrawan in Tunisia, Tlemcen in Algeria, and Tangier in Morocco). Conquest of urban centers largely failed, and Sufriyya groups were pushed into mountain and desert regions, where they built sustainable communities (like the caravan center of Sijilmasa in southern Morocco). Thus, unlike the more militant Kharijis, the moderate separatists were able to survive in tense discomfort with more mainstream Muslims, such that in Berber regions of North Africa, such as Algeria, moderate Khariji communities exist today.
81. Lewinstein, "Making and Unmaking of a Sect," especially note 44.
82. Malik, *Muwatta'*, p. 323 – "Kitab al-Hudud," book 41, chapter 1, report 1512.
83. The version of the Qur'an that is today widely accepted was officially collected after 'Umar's death, by the third caliph, 'Uthman.
84. Ibn Maja, *Sunan*, p. 372 – "Kitab al-Hudud," book 21, chapter 12, report 2659.
85. Mernissi, *The Veil and the Male Elite*, pp. 70–76.
86. Al-Maqrizi, *Mukhtasar al-Kamil*, p. 453.
87. Ibid., p. 569.
88. Abu Dawud, *Sunan*, vol. 2, p. 747 – "Kitab al-Hudud," book 39, chapter 29, report 4465.
89. Siddiqi, *Hadith Literature*, p. 201.
90. Ibn Hanbal, *Musnad*, vol. 1, p. 309.
91. Like the term "sodomy" (*liwat* or *lutiya*), the juridical term of "lesser sodomy" (*lutiya sughra*) was projected backward from jurists' discussions into a hadith

report, presented as the words of the Prophet; see Ibn Hanbal, *Musnad*, vol. 2, pp. 182, 210.

92. Siddiqi, *Hadith Literature*, p. 201.
93. In the context of a curse upon some Jews, see Q. 4:47–52, and a curse upon some Jews and Christians, see Q. 2:87–89.
94. 'A'isha was left behind during a journey and was rescued by a young man; back in Medina, hypocrites took advantage of 'A'isha's negligence and misled even some staunch Muslims in the Prophet's own family.
95. Ibn Hanbal, *Musnad*, vol. 1 p. 317.
96. Schmitt, "*Liwat* im *Fiqh*," p. 68.
97. Al-Tirmidhi, *Sunan*, vol. 1, pp. 394–395 – "Kitab al-Hudud," book 13, chapter 23, report 1526. A variation with different wording exists in Abu Dawud, *Sunan*, vol. 2, p. 747 – "Kitab al-Hudud," book 39, chapter 29, report 4466.
98. Abu Dawud, *Sunan*, vol. 2, p. 747 – "Kitab al-Hudud," book 39, chapter 29, report 4467. A variation with different wording exists in al-Tirmidhi, *Sunan*, vol. 1, p. 395 – "Kitab al-Hudud," book 13, chapter 24, report 1527.
99. Ibn Hanbal, *Musnad*, vol. 3, p. 382. See also al-Tirmidhi, *Sunan*, vol. 1, p. 395 – "Kitab al-Hudud," book 13, chapter 24, report 1529; and Ibn Maja, *Sunan*, p. 372 – "Kitab al-Hudud," book 21, chapter 12, report 2660.
100. Al-Maqrizi, *Mukhtasar al-Kamil*, p. 446.
101. For example, see the reports in Muslim, *Sahih*, vol. 1, pp. 149–150 – "Kitab al-Hayd," book 4, chapter 17, reports 794–795.
102. Yip, "Negotiating Space with Family and Kin," p. 366, writes, "Significant social–cultural and religious factors constitute the framework within which they [non-heterosexual Muslims in the U.K.] negotiate relations. These factors are the strict religious censure of non-heterosexuality (specifically homosexuality) based on various Islamic written sources, the pervasive cultural censure of homosexuality as a 'Western disease', the expectation of marriage as a cultural and religious obligation, the respect for parents, and the maintenance of family honour (*'izzat*) particularly in the close-knit kinship network."
103. The Qur'an is the best display of the Prophet's own character. His wife 'A'isha is reported to have said (in a hadith!) that "The Prophet is the Qur'an walking." She meant that the best of his character and integrity are inherent in the Qur'an, more intensely and more authentically than in any other source of knowledge. One suspects that, although 'A'isha is the source of over 2000 purported hadith, she would agree that the Qur'an communicates the Prophet's character more clearly and forcefully than any report handed down to posterity by fallible women and men.

Chapter Four

1. Kugle, *The Book of Illumination*, p. 65.
2. Adang, "Ibn Hazm on Homosexuality," p. 11. Ibn Hazm had abandoned the Maliki school of law for the more radical reformist stance of the Zahiri legal school – see Adang, "From Malikism to Shafi'ism to Zahirism."

3. All quotations by Omar Nahas are from an interview with S. Kugle in Amsterdam (June 25, 2005), unless otherwise noted.
4. In Arabic, see Nahas, *Al-Junusiyya* [*Homosexuality: Toward a Method for Interpreting Homosexuality from the Perspective of a Muslim Homosexual Man*]; and, in Dutch, *Islam en Homoseksualiteit* [*Islam and Homosexuality*] and *Homo en Moslem – hoe gaat dat samen?* [*Homosexual and Muslim – How Does that Go Together?*].
5. All quotations from Rasheed are from an interview with S. Kugle in Amsterdam (February 5, 2006). His name has been changed to protect his security.
6. Ramadan, *To Be a European Muslim*, states that being a faithful Muslim and being a responsible citizen of a Western nation is not only possible but an Islamic obligation.
7. Abou El Fadl, *Speaking in God's Name*, p. 12.
8. See Kugle, "Framed, Blamed and Renamed," for a discussion of how colonialism, nationalism, and fundamentalism have affected Islamic law and conceptions of the *shari'a*.
9. Ali, "Progressive Muslims and Islamic Jurisprudence," p. 167; Abou El Fadl, *Speaking in God's Name*, pp. 32–33.
10. Tayob, "The Function of Islam in the South African Political Process," p. 144.
11. Abou El Fadl, *Speaking in God's Name*, p. 141.
12. I thank my teacher and friend, Vincent Cornell, for helping me to understand this meaning of the *shari'a* as he taught me about Islamic law.
13. Abou El Fadl, *Speaking in God's Name*, pp. 55–56.
14. Al-Qurtubi, *Tafsir al-Jami' fi Ahkam al-Qur'an*, vol. 7, p. 244, gives this report including the name of the man punished but does not give an *isnad*, as part of his juridical interpretation of Lot's story in Q. 7:80. Al-Nuwayri, *Nihayat al-Arab*, vol. 2, p. 206, gives the report on the authority of Muhammad ibn al-Munkadar with *isnad*. The man's name is related also by al-Munajjad, *al-Hayat al-Jinsiyya*, p. 34.
15. Shaban, *Islamic History*, pp. 21–22.
16. Some Arab tribes pledged allegiance to "rival prophets" like Musaylama of the Hanifa tribe in the region of Yamama, or Tulayha of the Asad tribe, or al-Aswad al-'Ansi in Yemen.
17. Khalid ibn al-Walid was known for his heroism and ferocity as Sayf Allah, "The Sword of God."
18. Al-Bukhari, *Sahih*, vol. 3, p. 1452 – "Kitab al-Ahkam," book 94, chapter 35, report 7276.
19. In Arabic, al-Tabari, *Tarikh*, vol. 3, p. 264–5; in English, see al-Tabari, *History of Tabari*, vol. 10, pp. 79–81.
20. Lane, *Arabic–English Lexicon*, vol. 2, p. 2340.
21. Al-Tabari, *Tarikh*, vol. 3, p. 264.
22. Ibid.
23. It is not clear what was the ultimate aim of al-Fuja'a – to live the piratical life of a highway robber or to set himself up as a territorial strongman.

24. Ibn Hanbal, *Musnad*, vol. 1, p. 217.
25. Mernissi, *The Veil and the Male Elite*, pp. 180–188.
26. There is controversy over whether *mut'a* (temporary marriage) was forbidden by the Prophet Muhammad or by 'Umar, the second *khalifa*. The controversy impacts juridical decisions on this institution's legality, but this legal point is complicated by Sunni–Shi'i disputes over the legitimacy of 'Umar's serving as *khalifa*. This book will discuss *mut'a* in more detail in Chapter 5.
27. Many early Islamic sources, from Qur'an and hadith, blame Jewish communities for being in error or falling into misguidance. To quote these sources is not to defame Jews as people, so readers are warned to understand this discussion of Islamic appropriation of Judaic custom as a historical argument rather than an intercommunal blame game. Among Muslims, a long debate began in the classical period about whether Muslims scholars should rely upon Judaic sources – texts and interpretations – in explicating their own religious tradition. This study takes a position in this intra-Muslim debate, rather than taking a position on the question of whether Judaic customs are good or bad in themselves.
28. Mernissi, *The Veil and the Male Elite*, p. 75.
29. Musallam, *Sex and Society*, p. 23.
30. Barlas, *Believing Women*, p. 40; and Wadud, *Qur'an and Woman*, p. 20.
31. Mernissi, *The Veil and the Male Elite*, pp. 73–75.
32. Ibid., p. 76.
33. Musallam, *Sex and Society*, pp. 15–16.
34. Adang, "Muslim Writers on Judaism," p. 164.
35. Saul Olyan, "'And with a Male You Shall Not Lie the Lying down of a Woman,'" p. 410.
36. Al-Nuwayri, *Nihayat al-Arab*, vol. 2, p. 206.
37. See Dutton, "Amal versus Hadith in Islamic Law," on the practice of the people of Medina and how it rivaled the later concept of reports specifically about the Prophet. Later legal theorists invented technical terms to differentiate these sources of authority: "hadith" would be reserved for reports about the Prophet and *khabar* would be applied to reports about his companions and followers. However, Malik did not distinguish between these types of reports, because he wanted to record the practice of the people of Medina.
38. Lecker, "Biographical Notes on Ibn Shihab al-Zuhri." Muhammad ibn Muslim ibn Shihab al-Zuhri (died 742), known simply as Ibn Shihab or al-Zuhri, is among the first compilers of hadith at the behest of the Umayyad ruler 'Umar the Second (died 720).
39. Malik, *al-Muwatta'*, p. 323 – "Kitab al-Hudud," book 41, chapter 1, report 1512. The narrator of this report is Yahya ibn Yahya al-Laythi. In Arabic, the exact wording of the decision is "Malik sa'ala Ibn Shihab 'an al-ladhi ya'malu 'amal qawm lut, fa qala Ibn Shihab – 'alayhi al-rajm ahsana aw lam yuhsin."
40. Motski, *The Origins of Islamic Jurisprudence*, p. 255, notes that in Mecca as well as Medina jurists used reports in a rather carefree way, assuming that they reflected

the Prophet's directives even if they did not quote the Prophet directly or were not supported by a full *isnad.*

41. Malik, *al-Muwatta'*, p. 323 – "Kitab al-Hudud," book 41, chapter 1, report 1512. For a different version of 'Umar's claim, see ibid., p. 322 – report 1510.
42. 'Umar ibn al-Khattab insisted that there was a verse in the Qur'an stipulating that mature men and women should be stoned for adultery or fornication. He insisted upon this to his dying day, whereas most other Muslims recognized the command to stone for adultery as a decision of the Prophet which is not dictated by the Qur'an. 'Umar insisted that he himself had recited during worship a verse of the Qu'ran that explicitly called for stoning of adulterors. In 'Umar's time there was heated argument over exactly what constituted the Qur'an and how to properly recite it, raising controversies over pronunciation, grammar, and syntax. Most Muslim agree that it was after 'Umar was murdered, during the reign of the third *khalifa* 'Uthman, that an official version of the Qur'an was compiled in written form.
43. See the discussions on heterosexual adultery in Malik, *al-Muwatta'*, p. 324 – "Kitab al-Hudud," book 41, chapter 1, reports 1515–1518.
44. One Maliki jurist who tried to show how decisions of his school were rooted in the Qur'an (despite their actual evolution from the custom of the elders of Medina) was Muhammad al-Qurtubi. For critical discussion of his method of Qur'an interpretation, see Kugle, "Sexuality and Sexual Ethics."
45. Al-Qurtubi, *al-Jami' li Ahkam al-Qur'an*, vol. 7, p. 243. See also al-Tirmidhi, *Sunan*, vol. 1, p. 395 – "Kitab al-Hudud," book 13, chapter 24, report 1528. This was the judgment of early jurists like al-Nakha'i, 'Ata' ibn Abi Rabah, and Ibn Musayyab, who contradicted Malik and his followers.
46. Al-Shafi'i argued that the Prophet Muhammad's every decision was divinely inspired and protected from error, by interpreting the verse that describes Muhammad: *Your companion [Muhammad] does not err or go astray, nor does he speak from personal desire* (Q. 53:2–3).
47. The historian of Islamic law Joseph Schacht stated it best: "Two generations before al-Shafi'i, reference to the tradition from companions and followers was the rule, to traditions from the Prophet himself the exception, and it was left to al-Shafi'i to make the exception his principle." Schacht, *The Origins of Muhammadan Jurisprudence*, p. v – as cited and confirmed in Motski, *Origins of Islamic Jurisprudence*, p. 295.
48. Abou El Fadl, *Speaking in God's Name*, pp. 190–191.
49. Shafi'i prohibits masturbation in his *Kitab al-Umm*; for discussion see Ali, "Money, Sex, and Power."
50. Musallam, *Sex and Society in Islam*, pp. 33–34.
51. Ibid., p. 108.
52. Approximately fifteen percent of Sunni Muslims follow the Shafi'i school; it became well established in Egypt and Yemen, from where it spread through maritime trade to coastal communities around the Indian Ocean. Most Muslims

along the coast of East Africa (from Somalia to Cape Town), South India, and Sri Lanka are Shafi'i in orientation, as are Muslims in South-East Asia (Indonesia, Philippines, and Malaysia).

53. The European Council for Fatwa and Research is funded primarily by the Maktoum Charity Foundation and is supported by the royal family of Dubai. On Shaykh Qaradawi's influence in Europe, see Caeiro, "Transnational 'Ulama'."
54. Al-Jazeera, *Shari'a and Life* (June 8, 2006), episode entitled "Fitrat allah fi khalqi-hi." Translation from Arabic transcript provided by al-Jazeera is by S. Kugle.
55. Ibn Hanbal's opinions hardened in opposition to Mu'tazili theologians who adopted concepts and rhetorical strategies from Greek philosophy in order to assert the supremacy of one God who is unique, transcendent, and just.
56. Since the Islamic Revolution in 1978, Iran has had a state policy of executing gay men, which its jurist-rulers justify through the Ja'fari legal school. Though Shi'i Iranians are usually quick to distinguish themselves from their Sunni neighbors, in the case of execution of gay men the Iranian legal arguments parallel the Hanbali legal school's.
57. Rashid Rida was a Syrian intellectual of the Islamic modernist tradition pioneered by Jamal al-Din al-Afghani and Muhammad Abduh. Like his predecessors, he focused on the relative weakness of Muslim societies vis-à-vis Western colonialism, blaming Sufi excesses, the blind imitation of the past (*taqlid*), the stagnation of the ulama, and the resulting failure to achieve progress in science and technology; see Kerr, *Islamic Reform*.
58. Rida admits that for the majority of interpreters "the immorality" in this verse means heterosexual fornication, but claims it is taken by some to refer to sodomy between two men (*liwat*). Al-Shafi'i argued that this verse addresses those among men who commit adultery with women, but Jalal al-Din al-Mahalli and Jalal al-Din al-Suyuti, *Tafsir al-Jalalayn*, vol. 1, p. 73, argued that the dual pronoun made it more likely to refer to two men who committed fornication together in an act of sodomy (*liwat*). Rida cites this *Tafsir* as his source for his unorthodox opinion.
59. Rida, *Tafsir al-Manar*, vol. 4, p. 438.
60. Qutb began life as a secularist, novelist, and bureaucrat in Egypt. He earned a master's degree from the University of Northern Colorado in education (1948–50), and his experience there led him to denounce Western civilization as decadent; upon returning to Egypt he joined the Muslim Brotherhood (al-Ikhwan al-Muslimin) and worked to radicalize its ideology.
61. Calvert, "'The World Is an Undutiful Boy!'"
62. Inspired by Qutb, a group of the Muslim Brotherhood broke away to form a militant sect, al-Takfir wa'l-Hijra, which accused the Egyptian government and the majority of the population of not being Muslims, and assassinated Anwar Sadat in 1981.
63. Sayyid Qutb's ideas were promoted in Saudi Arabia by his brother, Muhammad Qutb, who was released from jail in Egypt and became a professor of Islam in Saudi Arabia. He published his brother's work and taught Ayman al-Zawahiri, the

spiritual advisor of Osama bin Laden of the al-Qa'ida movement. On Sayyid Qutb's life and theories, see Haddad, "Sayyid Qutb;" see also Moussalli, *Radical Islamic Fundamentalism.*

64. Qutb, *Fi Zilal al-Qur'an*, vol. 4, pp. 274–275.
65. Qutb cites a report from Abu Dawud, *Sunan*, vol. 2, p. 737 – "Kitab al-Hudud," book 39, chapter 23, reports 4415–4416; the original source specified that the report's context is heterosexual fornication and adultery.
66. Qutb, *Fi Zilal al-Qur'an*, vol. 4, p. 275–276.
67. Qutb's interpretation is ideologically authoritarian rather than traditionally authoritative in the terms presented by Abou El Fadl, *Speaking in God's Name*, pp. 91–94.
68. Qutb, *Fi Zilal al-Qur'an*, vol. 4, pp. 277–278.
69. Al-Qurtubi, *Tafsir al-Jami' fi Ahkam al-Qur'an*, vol. 7, p. 244.
70. Ibid.
71. Al-Jassas, *Ahkam al-Qur'an*, vol. 2, p. 363.
72. Ibid.
73. Hanafi law is followed by most Sunnis in Eastern Europe (Bosnia through Turkey), Central Asia (Iraq through eastern China) and South Asia (Afghanistan through Bangladesh) and it informed the official policy of the Ottoman, Uzbek, and Mughal empires in medieval and early modern times. However, some Muslims from South Asia have been influenced by the Deobandi movement, which abjures traditional Hanafi jurisprudence in its politicized confrontation with modernity and verges toward a more ideological approach informed by Hanbali-influenced Wahhabi or modern Salafi teachings. In this sense, the Deobandi scholar cited in Chapter 3, Mufti Zafeeruddin, does not accurately reflect the classical Hanafi legal school's approach but is more in line with Sayyid Qutb and other Salafi or Wahhabi neo-traditionalists.
74. Zahiri scholars refered to Q. 16:103 to defend their methodology that Muslims should follow the clear and apparent meaning of the Qur'an.
75. Ibn Hazm, *al-Muhalla*, vol. 9, p. 519.
76. Adang, "Ibn Hazm on Homosexuality," p. 20.
77. Ibid., pp. 21–22. Adang's article unfortunately uses the term "homosexuality" when she means sodomy. It is clear that Ibn Hazm does not address homosexuality as sexual orientation, but rather addresses specifically the act of anal penetration between men. Otherwise, Adang's analysis of Ibn Hazm's legal decisions in *al-Muhalla* is a very accurate presentation of the Zahiri jurist's complex critique.
78. Ibn Hazm demonstrates that there was no *ijma'* on this issue, and in addition he asserts that *ijma'* is not a legal principle at all; if jurists agree on a legal decision because it is based upon the explicit wording of the Qur'an or authentic hadith, then that decision is binding because of its textual source, and if the jurists' consensus is on a decision that has no textual source then it is invalid for that reason. In Ibn Hazm's view, *ijma'* is not a valid legal principle.
79. Ibid., p. 26.

80. Ibid., pp. 26–27.
81. The Arabic of this report is "al-sihaq zina al-nisa' bayna-hunna." The *isnad* of this report is Ahmad ibn Hanbal, from Abu Qasim ibn Muhammad ibn Qasim, from his grandfather Qasim ibn Asbagh, from Muhammad ibn Wadah, from Hisham ibn Khalid, from Baqiya ibn al-Walid, from 'Uthman ibn 'Abd al-Rahman, from 'Anbasa ibn Sa'id, from Makhul, from Walitha ibn al-Asqa', from the Prophet Muhammad. According to Ibn 'Adi, at least three of these narrators (Baqiya, 'Uthman, and 'Anbasa) are of doubtful trustworthiness, or are accused of outright lying; see Ibn 'Adi, *Makhtasar al-Kamil*, pp. 201–202, 551, 577.
82. Ibn Hazm, *al-Muhalla*, vol. 11, pp. 390–391.
83. Ibid., p. 392.
84. Ibid.
85. Ibid., p. 393
86. Ibid., p. 394.
87. Ibid.
88. Ibn Hazm, *Maratib al-Ijma'*, pp. 8–10. Ibn Hazm lists other jurists' concepts of consensus, which he finds compromised and corrupt: "Some jurists have claimed that consensus covers some issues that are not in fact covered by it. A group of jurists consider the opinion of a majority to be consensus. Another group holds that consensus is determined by evident lack of dispute about an issue, even if they have not definitively agreed that there is no difference or dispute. Others count as consensus the opinion of a companion [of the Prophet] transmitted in a report that is well-known and wide spread as long as no other companions are known to have disagreed with it, even if disagreement is found among followers and later generations of Muslims. Others count as consensus the opinion of a companion if no other companions disagreed even if transmitted in a report that is not well-known or widespread. Other groups of jurists consider the opinion of the elders of Medina to constitute consensus, or alternatively the opinion of the scholars of Kufa. Other jurists count as consensus whatever opinion out of two or more possibilities their own teachers or the generation preceding them upheld."
89. Ibid., p. 178. He notes at the end of his text, "The reader of our words should know that there is a great difference between my saying 'they come to consensus' and 'they agree.'"
90. "Cleaving together" most likely means sexual caress without penetration. There is some ambiguity in the Arabic word *lizq*. Its application to sexual acts is not supported by other texts known to the author. However, caressing is linked closely to masturbation, as both acts are sexual in nature and can lead to orgasm without genital penetration. However, it is penetration that determines – in Ibn Hazm's view (and that of most jurists) – whether a sexual act is licit or illicit. In this sentence – in contrast to the two previous sentences – Ibn Hazm leaves unclear whether those engaged in these sexual acts are a same-sex couple, a heterosexual couple, or an individual engaged in self-stimulation.
91. Ibn Hazm, *Maratib al-Ijma'*, p. 131.

92. Ibid., p. 65.
93. Ibn Hazm, *Mu'jam Fiqh Ibn Hazm al-Zahiri*, vol. 1, p. 47–48.
94. Adang, "Ibn Hazm on Homosexuality," p. 30. See also Adang, "Women's Access to Public Space."
95. Al-Qurtubi, *Tafsir al-Jami' fi Ahkam al-Qur'an*, vol. 7, p. 243. Other Maliki jurists outspokenly rejected the Zahiri positions of Ibn Hazm, such as Qadi Abu Bakr ibn al-'Arabi, who said that the Zahiri school is made up of imbeciles who are imagined to be of a level that they are not, and who speak with a discourse that no jurist understands but which their brethren in the heretical Khariji movement latch on to by saying, "There is no ruling but God's ruling." See Ibn Hazm, *Maratib al-Ijma'*, p. 4.
96. Al-Qurtubi, *Tafsir al-Jami' fi Ahkam al-Qur'an*, vol. 7, p. 248.
97. Ibid., p. 243.
98. Masud, "Muslim Jurists' Quest for the Normative Basis of Shari'a," p. 8.
99. Ibid., p. 9.
100. Masud, *Shatibi's Philosophy of Islamic Law*, p. 73.
101. The Shi'i jurist al-Hilli (died 1277) put forward similar arguments in order to regulate and reform the decisions enforced by Shi'i communities.
102. Rahman, *Islam and Modernity*, p. 39. For a discussion of this reformist lineage as the "values approach" to Islam, see Muzaffar, *Muslims, Dialogue, Terror.*
103. For his critical assessment, Rahman was driven from his position as director of the Islamic Research Institute in Pakistan under accusation of heresy, and took refuge in the U.S., where he taught Islamic studies at the University of Chicago.
104. Taha, *Second Message of Islam.*
105. Mahmoud Taha was not just a legal theorist but also a democratic reformer who engaged in party politics, and for his efforts was assassinated by the proponents of Islamic fundamentalism in Sudan. His major follower, the legal theorist Abdullahi an-Naim, sought refuge in the U.S. and teaches about Islamic law at Emory University. Both Mahmoud Taha's and Fazlur Rahman's ideas flourished in North America and influenced a younger generation of Muslims internationally.
106. The full text of his call for a moratorium can be found at <www.tariqramadan. com>.
107. Kamali, *Equity and Fairness in Islam*, pp. 8, 29.
108. A moratorium on the death penalty in the name of Islam would benefit homosexuals in those few Muslim-majority countries where executions actually happen, like Iran and Saudi Arabia. But it is hardly relevant to lesbian, gay, and transgender Muslims in secular democracies who are not in danger of the death penalty by Islamic law. Spokespersons in Muslim minority communities refer to the death penalty to emphasize moral condemnation, with the effect of suppressing such people, stifling open discussion of the issues, and encouraging families to ostracize or abuse members who might be homosexual or transgender. Rhetoric involving the death sentence has no legal force but imposes a kind of social death through marginalization and ostracization.
109. Kamali, *Equity and Fairness in Islam*, p. 24.
110. Ibid., pp. 120–121.

111. Masud, "Muslim Jurists' Quest for the Normative Basis of Shariʿa," p. 8.
112. Wadud, *Inside the Gender Jihad*, p. 236, addresses this issue in the context of sexually transmitted diseases like H.I.V./A.I.D.S., pointing out the injustice of a woman's having to submit to intercourse with her legal husband without being able to assert conditions such as insisting on contraception that could prevent the spread of disease. The feminist activist Asra Nomani also raises the issue, as a human right, regardless of circumstances such as contagious disease; on Nomani's "Islamic Bill of Rights for Women in the Bedroom" see Ali, *Sexual Ethics and Islam*, pp. 70–71.
113. Abou El Fadl, *Speaking in God's Name*, pp. 57–58.
114. Senturk, *Islam and Human Rights Fellowship Program*, at Emory University: <www.law.emory.edu/IHR/recep.html>. Senturk notes that the other Sunni legal schools lacked the universal concept of human rights and allowed that sanctity is due to the citizenry only by virtue of faith or treaty rather than inhering in their essential humanity.

Chapter Five

1. Abu Tarab, *Carousing with Gazelles*, p. 2, offers this translation of Abu Nuwas's poem.
2. Ali, *Sexual Ethics and Islam*, pp. 5–6; see also Ali, "Progressive Muslims and Islamic Jurisprudence."
3. Outside of the five countries included in this study, the pattern of legalization is bewilderingly complex. The first same-sex civil union was granted in Denmark in 1989, and Norway and Sweden legalized same-sex civil unions soon after. Civil unions were legalized in France in 1999 and in Germany and Portugal in 2001 and in Belgium in 2002. In 2005, Spain legalized same-sex marriages without the intermediate step of allowing civil partnerships. In Latin America, Argentina was the first country to allow civil unions, in 2002. Among British Commonwealth countries, New Zealand recognized civil unions for same-sex couples in 2004 (without allowing them the right to marry) whereas neighboring Australia has moved to legally ban same-sex marriage. Among former Soviet dependencies, Hungary recognized same-sex civil unions on equal par with unmarried heterosexual cohabitants in 1995, followed by Croatia, which recognized same-sex civil unions in 2003. Legalizing same-sex unions and marriages in countries where Muslims are a minority affects Muslim-majority countries, emboldening gay and lesbian activists to speak up or inciting neo-traditionalists to denounce the West as debauched and immoral.
4. Ibn Hazm, *The Ring of the Dove*, pp. 21–22.
5. Crompton, "Male Love and Islamic Law in Arab Spain," p. 147.
6. Nussbaum, *Sex and Social Justice*, p. 300.
7. Ibid., p. 314.
8. One exception to the hetero-exclusive system set up by Muslim jurists is in the issue of legalizing sex with one's slaves. There was some ambiguity about whether

same-sex acts with a slave were legal; see Schmitt, "*Liwat* im *Fiqh*," for a discussion of the ambiguity between a man's right to own another man (with ownership understood to justify demanding sexual intercourse) and a man's being forbidden to have sexual intercourse with another man.

9. Ibn Hazm, *The Ring of the Dove*, p. 23.
10. Ibid., pp. 23–27.
11. All quotations from Daayiee Abdullah, here and subsequently, are from an interview with S. Kugle in Washington (November 16, 2005).
12. The idea that love for another human being forms a bridge to love for God is found in many Sufi writings: *Sawanih* by Ahmad Ghazali (died 1126), *Ruba'iyat* by Awhaduddin Kirmani (died 1237), and *Mathnawi-yi Ma'anwi* and *Diwan-i Shams-i Tabrezi* by Jalaluddin Rumi (died 1273) accept that homoerotic love can play the same role as heterosexual love.
13. Bouhdiba, *Sexuality in Islam.*
14. The Qur'an does not impose dress codes for men or women, but enjoins modesty for both. However, it does discuss women's dress in some detail, mentioning items of clothing common in seventh-century Arabia such as a head-cloth and directing women to wear it in a way that covers their chest. Among Muslims, therefore, we find that men's clothing changes according to culture and custom with greater ease than women's clothing. See El Guindi, *Veil*, pp. 66–76, on the Qur'anic terms for dress and cultural expressions of modesty.
15. The Qur'an forbids a man to "inherit" a wife against her will – in many ancient cultures a brother inherits his dead brother's wife as if she belonged to the husband's family rather than having a contract with the husband alone. The Qur'an forbids a man from marrying a woman who has had intercourse with his father or other close male relative (Q. 4:19). It forbids a man from marrying his close female relatives (Q. 4:23) and from marrying women who are currently married to someone else (Q. 4:24). It forbids a man from repudiating his wife by "turning his back" on her, declaring that she is like his mother, yet refusing to divorce her.
16. Ahmed, *Women and Gender in Islam*, pp. 117–118. The Qur'an requires the husband to give the wife something of value (*sadaq*) before intercourse (Q. 4:4) which will become her property that he cannot claim, even if the marriage runs into trouble (Q. 4:20–21). The Qur'an allows divorce but urges men to provide for their divorced spouse and avoid causing her harm (Q. 65:1–3). Remarriage is encouraged after divorce or death of a spouse, but with careful attention to the parentage of any pregnancy that might be residual from the former partner (Q. 2:228–234).
17. Al-Jazeera, *Shari'a and Life* (June 8, 2006), episode entitled "Fitrat allah fi khalqi-hi." All quotations from Shaykh Qaradawi in this chapter come from this interview.
18. Haeri, *Law of Desire*, p. 23.

19. Wadud, *Inside the Gender Jihad*, p. 133, discusses how issues of children's legitimacy have reinforced gender-differentiated roles in heterosexual Islamic marriages.
20. Musallam, *Sex and Society in Islam.*
21. Haeri, *Law of Desire*, p. 35; see also Ali, *Sexual Ethics and Islam*, pp. 6–9; and Shaikh, "Family Planning, Contraception and Abortion in Islam."
22. Ali, *Sexual Ethics and Islam*, pp. 56–58.
23. I know of some heterosexual Sunni couples in North America who have engaged in temporary marriage, citing that fact that it is legal in the Shi'i school of law; such couples keep this practice secret, for fear that their Sunni family or community will accuse them of prostitution or fornication.
24. Haeri, *Law of Desire*, p. 34.
25. Ibid., pp. 36–37.
26. Ibid., p. 37.
27. Ibid., p. 39. Much evidence indicates that the Prophet originally held that women can give themselves in marriage by their own independent legal agency, to the extent that the marriage is invalid if a father arranges it without the explicit consent of his daughter. However, this agency was gradually eroded in Islamic practice that allowed a father to extend his authority over a daughter up till and including her marriage. Some Muslim communities discourage a bride from being present at the contract-signing and delegate authority over her to her father or elder male relative.
28. Ibid., p. 47. In the classical *shari'a*, the husband must sleep with his wife at least one in every four nights and they must have intercourse at least once every four months. The jurists who forged the classical *shari'a* felt that male sexuality was totally different in quality and intensity from female sexuality. Men's need for satisfaction was assumed to be constant and immediate, whereas women's need was assumed to be infrequent or of lower intensity so that it was possible for her to endure long periods without intercourse. Men's access to multiple wives or concubines allowed men more frequent sexual intercourse than any single wife, who was allowed intercourse only with her husband.The juridical assumptions run counter to popular imagination in medieval Islamic communities where, in moral discourse and literature, women are pictured as sexually voracious and incapable of restraint.
29. Divorce (*talaq*) is the legal prerogative of the husband in the classical *shari'a*, and he can take his divorced wife back into marriage (with or without her consent) within a certain window of time. Women can initiate dissolving the marriage (*khul'*) only with the consent of the husband or in extraordinary cases such as a husband's insanity or contagious illness; in such a case, she must return the value of the bride-price to the husband to "ransom herself" and be released from contractual obligations (Q. 2:229). Mutual separation (*mubarat*) occurs when both partners dislike each other; in this case the wife must return some portion of her bride-price to symbolize the end of the contract, as in dissolution of marriage.

Annulment is possible if any prerequisites of the marriage contract are fraudulent or faulty; either party can initiate annulment.

30. Ali, *Sexual Ethics and Islam*, p. 94.
31. The conventional wording in Arabic is for the female marriage partner to offer, "zawajtu-ka nafsi ..." which the male partner accepts with "qabiltu al-zawaj min-ki ..." If a female marriage partner were to offer herself to a woman, the pronouns in the wording would alter very slightly, so that one female partner would offer, "zawajtu-ki nafsi ..." and the other would accept with "qabiltu al-zawaj min-ki ..." If a male marriage partner were to offer himself to a man, the pronouns would also alter very slightly so that one male partner would offer, "zawajtu-ka nafsi ..." and the other would accept with "qabiltu al-zawaj min-ka ..." The example of the standard *nikah* contract is taken from Hartford and Muneeb, *Your Islamic Marriage Contract.*
32. In conventional *nikah*, the offer, acceptance, and exchange of value must be witnessed by two adult male Muslims who are sane (or by one man and two women who fulfill the same condition). Same-sex *nikah* would probably not differentiate between female and male witnesses, but simply require that two adult, sane Muslims act as witnesses.
33. Muhammad al-Shaybani, an influential follower of Abu Hanifa, dissented from his master's opinion on the matter of a male guardian in marriage. But most Hanafi jurists follow Abu Hanifa and hold that a male guardian is not necessary.
34. Ali, "Progressive Muslims and Islamic Jurisprudence," p. 169.
35. All quotations from Tamsila, here and subsequently, are from two interviews with S. Kugle in London (June 14–15, 2005).
36. If the wife in a heterosexual *mut'a* became pregnant, she would have to have an abortion (which was generally allowed in *shari'a* before the 120th day of pregnancy), convince her partner to enter with her into a permanent formal marriage, or rely on the sincerity of her male partner to publicly acknowledge their temporary marriage and accept paternity of the child along with maintenance of her and the child. The child would be assumed to be legally fathered by the *mut'a* partner unless he disavows being the father.
37. Motski, *Origins of Islamic Jurisprudence*, pp. 142–144, cites 'Ata's decision as recorded in 'Abd al-Razzaq's *Musannaf.*
38. Temporary marriage is practiced by the largest group of Shi'a Muslims, the Ithna-'Ashariyya or "Twelver Shi'te" community, who constitute a majority in Iran and Iraq, a powerful minority in Lebanon, and an influential minority in Pakistan and India and Afghanistan.
39. Nahas, *Islam en homoseksualiteit*, p. 53, discusses contentious interpretations of this phrase "cutting the path."
40. Esack and Chiddy, *Islam and AIDS.*
41. As a compromise measure, some gay Muslims seek a marriage of convenience with a lesbian woman, just as lesbian Muslims may seek the same with a gay man. See Akram, "Muslim Gays Seek Lesbians for Wives."

42. "Human Rights for Minorities Not up for Bargain: Muslim Canadian Congress Endorses Same-Sex Marriage Legislation," <www.muslimcanadiancongress.org> (February 1, 2005).
43. The Washington State legislature House passed H.B. 2661, called the "Anderson–Murray Antidiscrimination Bill," and Governor Gregoire signed the bill into law on January 31, 2006.
44. Iwasaki, "Tolerance Sets the Tone at Services."
45. Tariq, "My Road to Wisconsin Was Paved with Good Intentions."
46. Fatima Mernissi's research is the strongest statement of this idea from a feminist perspective, linking the emerging rule of elite men to the suppression of democratic values and women's authority in the generation after the Prophet Muhammad's death.
47. Dabashi, *Authority in Islam*, documents varieties of resistance to Arab kingship from positions that came to be called Shi'i or Khariji.

Chapter Six

1. Murata, *The Tao of Islam*, pp. 235–236. I have modified Murata's translation to remove gender references from God and pronouns that stand in for God. This is because her interpretation of this text – and others in Ibn Arabi's tradition – does not go far enough toward comprehending how radical their challenge is to patriarchal constructions of gender. For a cogent critique of Murata's conservative assumptions about gender, see Shaikh, *Spiritual Cartographies of Gender*.
2. Ibn Hazm, *Mu'jam Fiqh Ibn Hazm al-Zahiri*, p. 37 – in the introduction by Muhammad al-Muntasir al-Kattani,
3. Translation of these verses is taken from Sells, *Approaching the Qur'an*, p. 86.
4. Barlas, *Believing Women in Islam*, pp. 93–99, expands upon the groundbreaking feminist critique by Riffat Hassan of the idea of a masculine God in Islam.
5. See for example, Tapinc, "Masculinity, Femininity and Turkish Male Homosexuality."
6. For definition and clinical discussion if the term "gender dysphoria" see the website of G.I.R.E.S. (Gender Identity Research and Education Society) at <www.gires.org.uk>.
7. The term "hermaphrodite" is derived from the name for two Greek deities: Hermes who is male and Aphrodite who is female. As a compound of their two names, it denotes a person who has both male and female genitalia in one body.
8. For more detail on the role of eunuchs in Islamic culture, see Marmon, *Eunuchs and Sacred Boundaries*, and Ayalon, *Eunuchs, Caliphs and Sultans*.
9. In Arabic, the term *mukhannath* is derived from a word for skin that is folded back upon itself, like the folds of fat on the waist of a reclining odalisque. Linguistically, the term suggests an inversion of the norm (like turning something inside out) and also a languidness in posture; see Lane, *Arabic–English Lexicon*, vol. 1, p. 814, and also Rowson, "Effeminates of Early Medina."
10. Bouhdiba, *Sexuality in Islam*, documented and discussed these *mutarajjulat* or

masculine women. I have been forced to coin a new term "emmasculine woman" to parallel the more conventional "effeminate man." The new term sounds very close to "emasculate," which means to remove from a man his masculinity. This is providential, because in patriarchal societies emmasculine women, who behave like men, are perceived to threaten men and emasculate them, a threat more perceived than real.

11. See Nanda, *Neither Man nor Woman*, and also Reddy, *With Respect to Sex*; for a more journalistic account, see Jaffrey, *The Invisibles.*
12. Abd al-Rahman Jami, *Nafahat al-Uns wa Hadrat al-Quds*, p. 613, preserves this couplet of al-Sulami in his biography of the famous female Sufi, Rabi'a of Basra, who was often admired by her male colleagues as "a man in the body of a woman."
13. For a discussion of the grammatical gender of the noun "spirit," see Sells, *Approaching the Qur'an*, pp. 183–197.
14. Al-Jazeera, *Shari'a and Life* (June 8, 2006), episode entitled "Fitrat Allah fi Khalqi-hi."
15. Bagemihl, *Biological Exuberance*, documents a bewildering variety of same-sex behaviors and gender-changing patterns in animal species, from simple invertebrates to mammals that are human beings' closest cousins in genetic pattern and intelligence, such as apes, whales, and dolphins. His book changes the baseline of debate over what kind of sexual and gender displays are "natural."
16. See, for example, the medical sociological study by Money, *Love and Love Sickness.*
17. Stowasser, *Women in the Qur'an*, pp. 87, 167 note 16. On eunuchs in Byzantine society (including Egypt before the Arab–Islamic conquest) see Herdt, *Third Sex, Third Gender*, chapter 1; and also Ringrose, *The Perfect Servant.* Christian societies of Egypt and Ethiopia may have been especially receptive to eunuchs, for the Apostle Phillip supposedly converted to Christianity an Ethiopian eunuch who was the powerful treasurer to the Ethiopian Queen (see the Bible, Acts 8:27). The Gospel according to Matthew pictures Jesus preaching that "Some are born eunuchs and some are made eunuchs by men. Yet others make themselves eunuchs for the sake of the kingdom of God."
18. Stowasser, *Women in the Qur'an*, p. 96.
19. Ibid., p. 112, translates this gossip taken from hadith recorded by Ibn Sa'd, *Kitab al-Tabaqat*, vol. 8, p. 154–155.
20. Ibid., p. 112.
21. Ibid., p. 113, drawing hadith again from Ibn Sa'd, *Kitab al-Tabaqat*, pp. 154–155. In later generations, this pattern was confirmed in Islamic law, which rules that a female slave who bears a male Muslim owner a son is legally recognized as the mother of his child (*umm walad*), and so her status changes: she is protected from being sold off or married off to another man, and upon the owner's death she is freed.
22. Rowson, "Effeminates of Early Medina," p. 66.
23. Ibid., p. 81
24. Ibid., pp. 83–85.
25. Ibid., p. 66.

26. Ibid., pp. 87–88.
27. Sanders, "Gendering the Ungendered Body," p. 79
28. Ibid., p. 78.
29. Ibid., p. 81
30. Ibid.
31. Musić, "Queer Visions of Islam," and Ali, *Sexual Ethics in Islam*, chapter 5. Many thanks to Rusmir Music for generously sharing his master's degree research, upon which this discussion of Egyptian and Saudi cases is based.
32. Afsaneh Najmabadi (author of *Women with Mustaches and Men without Beards: Gender and Sexual Anxiety of Iranian Modernity*) discusses how the Iranian government's acceptance of sex-change operations is liberating for transgendered people but dangerous for homosexual men and women, as sex-change surgery is often promoted (or enforced) as a "cure" for homosexuals. See Najmabadi, "Transing and Transpassing across Sex–Gender Walls in Iran."
33. Taha and Magbool, "The Pattern of Intersex Disorders and Gender Assignment in the Eastern Province of Saudi Arabia," p. 18.
34. Ibid., p. 21.
35. Skovgaard-Petersen, *Defining Islam for the Egyptian State*, p. 325; see also Ali, *Sexual Ethics and Islam*, pp. 93–94.
36. Skovgaard-Petersen, *Defining Islam for the Egyptian State*, p. 331.
37. Ibid., p. 334.
38. Ibid., p. 330
39. Ibid., p. 332.
40. Ibid., p. 326.
41. The Khomeini regime commissioned a Shi'i jurist, Hussayn Ali Muntazeri Najafabadi, to write a standardized legal text justifying its Islamization of national law around issues of sexuality and sex acts: in Arabic, *Kitab al-Hudud* [*The Book of Divine Punishments: On the Subject of Adultery, Sodomy, Tribadism and Collusion*].
42. Harrison, "Iran's Sex-Change Operations."
43. Ibid.
44. McDowall and Khan, "The Ayatollah and the Transsexual."
45. Al-Jazeera, *Shari'a and Life* (June 8, 2006), episode entitled "Fitrat Allah fi Khalqihi."
46. Alan Stern is a scientist at the New Horizons space mission to Pluto based at the Southwest Research Institute in Boulder, Colorado; quoted in Overbye, "So What Is a Planet?"
47. Chang, "Unraveling the Moon's Mysteries."

Conclusion

1. An-Na'im, *Toward an Islamic Reformation*, p. 9.
2. The central ethical and religious teaching of Islam is *tawhid*. In belief, *tawhid* asserts the radical monotheism that God is singular and unique with no partners or associates. In theology, *tawhid* means perceiving radical monotheism as the

single teaching of many Prophets. In social life, *tawhid* means urging a plurality of people to come into a harmonious unity. In personal life, *tawhid* means struggling with alienation and fragmentation in each person, urging others and oneself through honesty and sincerity into a more unified whole. *Tawhid* in general means assessing honestly the alienation, violence, egotism, and hypocrisy that keep people fragmented and societies unjust.

Bibliography

Abdul-Ghafur, Saleemah, ed. *Living Islam Out Loud: American Muslim Women Speak.* Boston: Beacon Press, 2005.

Abou El Fadl, Khaled. *The Place of Tolerance in Islam.* Boston: Beacon Press, 2002.

——. *Speaking in God's Name: Islamic Law, Authority and Women.* Oxford: Oneworld, 2001.

Abu Laylah, Muhammad. *In Pursuit of Virtue: The Moral Theology and Psychology of Ibn Hazm al-Andalusi with a Translation of His Book* Al-Akhlaq wa'l-Siyar. London: Ta-Ha, 1998.

Abu Tarab, Jaafar, trans. *Carousing with Gazelles: Homoerotic Songs of Old Baghdad by Abu Nuwas.* London: iUniverse, 2005.

Adang, Camilla. "From Malikism to Shafi'ism to Zahirism: The 'Conversions' of Ibn Hazm," in Mercedes Garcìa-Arenal, ed. *Conversions islamiques: Identités religieuses en Islam méditerranéen.* Paris: Maisonneuve & Larose, 2001.

——. "Ibn Hazm on Homosexuality," *Al Qantara* 24 (2003), pp. 5–31.

——. "Muslim Writers on Judaism and the Hebrew Bible from Ibn Rabban to Ibn Hazm," Ph.D. dissertation, Katholieke Universiteit Nijmegen, 1993.

——. "Women's Access to Public Space According to al-Muhalla bi-l-Athar," in Manuela Marin and Randi Deguilhem, eds. *Writing the Feminine: Women in Arab Sources.* London: I. B. Tauris, 2002.

Ahmed, Leila. *Women and Gender in Islam.* New Haven: Yale University Press, 1992.

Akram, Ayesha. "Muslim Gays Seek Lesbians for Wives: Social Pressures Push Some into Sexless Marriage," *Religion News Service* (June 24, 2006).

Ali, Kecia. "Money, Sex, and Power: The Contractual Nature of Marriage in Islamic Jurisprudence of the Formative Period," Ph.D. dissertation, Duke University, 2002.

——. "Progressive Muslims and Islamic Jurisprudence: The Necessity for Critical Engagement with Marriage and Divorce Laws," in Omid Safi, ed. *Progressive Muslims: On Gender, Justice and Pluralism.* Oxford: Oneworld, 2003.

——. *Sexual Ethics and Islam: Feminist Reflections on Qur'an, Hadith and Jurisprudence.* Oxford: Oneworld, 2006.

Ayalon, David. *Eunuchs, Caliphs, and Sultans: A Study in Power Relationships.* Jerusalem: Magnes Press, 1999.

Bagemihl, Bruce. *Biological Exuberance: Animal Homosexuality and Natural Diversity.* New York: St. Martin's Press, 1999.

Barlas, Asma. *Believing Women in Islam: Un-reading Patriarchal Interpretations of the Qur'an.* Austin: University of Texas Press, 2002.

Berg, Herbert. *The Development of Exegesis in Early Islam.* Richmond, England: Curzon Press, 2000.

Boswell, John. "Concepts, Experience and Sexuality," in E. Stein, ed. *Forms of Desire.* New York: Routledge, 1992.

Bouhdiba, Abdelwahab. *Sexuality in Islam.* London: Saqi Books, 1998.

Brooten, Bernadette. *Love Between Women: Early Christian Responses to Female Homoeroticism.* Chicago: University of Chicago Press, 1996.

Brown, Jonathan. "Criticism of the Proto-hadith Canon: Al-Daraqutni's Adjustment of the *Sahihayn*," *Journal of Islamic Studies* 15(1) (2004), pp. 1–37.

Caeiro, Alexandre. "Transnational 'Ulama', European Fatwas, and Islamic Authority: A Case Study of the European Council for Fatwa and Research," in Stefano Allievi and Martin van Bruinessen, *Production and Dissemination of Islamic Knowledge in Western Europe.* London: Routledge, forthcoming.

Calvert, John. "'The World Is an Undutiful Boy!': Sayyid Qutb's American Experience," *Islam and Christian–Muslim Relations* 2(1) (2000), pp. 87–103.

Chang, Kenneth. "Unraveling the Moon's Mysteries," *International Herald Tribune* (August 10, 2006).

Crompton, Louis. "Male Love and Islamic Law in Arab Spain," in Stephen Murray and Will Roscoe, eds. *Islamic Homosexualities: Culture History and Literature.* New York: New York University Press, 1997.

Dabashi, Hamid. *Authority in Islam: From the Rise of Muhammad to the Establishment of the Umayyads.* New Brunswick, New Jersey: Transaction, 1989.

Doi, Abd al-Rahman. *Shariah: The Islamic Law.* London: Ta-Ha, 1984.

Dutton, Yasin. "Amal versus Hadith in Islamic Law," *Islamic Law and Society* 3 (1996), pp. 1–40.

El Guindi, Fadwa. *Veil: Modesty, Privacy and Resistance.* Oxford: Berg, 1999.

Engineer, Asghar Ali. *Islam and Liberation Theology: Essays on Liberative Elements in Islam.* New Delhi: Sterling Press, 1990.

Esack, Farid. *The Qur'an: A Short Introduction.* Oxford: Oneworld, 2002.

——. *Qur'an, Liberation and Pluralism: An Islamic Perspective of Interreligious Solidarity against Oppression.* Oxford: Oneworld, 1997.

—— and Sarah Chiddy. *Islam and AIDS: Between Scorn, Pity and Justice.* Oxford: Oneworld, 2009.

Fierro, Maribel. "Women as Prophets in Islam," in Manuela Marin and Randi Deguilhem, eds. *Writing the Feminine: Women in Arab Sources.* London: I. B. Tauris, 2002.

Haddad, Yvonne. "Sayyid Qutb: Ideologue of Islamic Revival," in John Esposito, ed. *Voices of the Islamic Revolution.* Oxford: Oxford University Press, 1983.

Haeri, Shahla. *Law of Desire: Temporary Marriage in Shi'i Iran.* Syracuse, New York: Syracuse University Press, 1989.

Hamer, Dean et al. "A Linkage between DNA Markers on the X Chromosome and Male Sexual Orientation," *Science* 261 (1993), pp. 321–327.

Al-Harawi, 'Ali al-Qari. *Al-Masnu' fi Ma'rifat al-Hadith al-Mawdu'*, ed. 'Abd al-Fattah Abu Ghudda, 2nd edn. Beirut: Mu'assasat al-Risala, 1978.

Harrison, Frances. "Iran's Sex-Change Operations," BBC News (January 5, 2005), <http://news.bbc.co.uk/go/pr/fr/-/1/hi/programmes/newsnight/4115535.stm>.

Hartford, Hedaya and Ashraf Muneeb. *Your Islamic Marriage Contract.* Damascus: Dar al Fikr, 2001.

Herdt, Gilbert. *Third Sex, Third Gender: Beyond Sexual Dimorphism in Culture and History.* New York: Zone Books, 1996.

Ibn Hanbal, Ahmad. *Musnad.* Beirut: al-Maktab al-Islami Dar al-Sadir, 1969.

Ibn Hazm al-Andalusi. *Asma' al-Sahabat al-Ruwat wa ma li-kulli Wahid min al-'Adad*, ed. Sayyid Kurdi Hasan. Beirut: Dar al-Kutub al-'Ilmiyya, 1992.

——. *Al-Ihkam fi Usul al-Ahkam*, ed. Ahmad Shakir. Cairo: Matba' al-'Asima, n.d.

——. *Kitab fi Ma'rifat al-Nasikh wa'l-Mansukh*, printed in the margins of Jalal al-Din al-Mahalli and Jalal al-Din al-Suyuti. *Tafsir al-Qur'an.* Cairo: Matba' al-Taqaddum al-'Ilmiyya, 1910.

——. *Maratib al-Ijma' fi al-'Ibadat wa'l-Mu'amalat wa'l-Mu'taqidat.* Beirut: Dar al-Kutub al- 'Ilmiyya, n.d.

——. *Al-Muhalla*, ed. Ahmad Muhammad Shakir. Beirut: al-Maktab al-Tijari, 1960.

——. *Mu'jam Fiqh Ibn Hazm al-Zahiri*, ed. Muhammad al-Muntasir al-Kattani. Damascus: Kulliyat al-Shari'a, 1966.

——. *The Ring of the Dove: A Treatise on the Art and Practice of Arab Love*, trans. Anthony Arberry. London: Luzac Oriental, 1994.

——. *Al-Usul wa'l-Furu'*. Cairo: Dar al-Nahda al-'Arabiyya, 1978.

Ibn Sa'd, Muhammad. *Kitab al-Tabaqat al-Kabir*, ed. Carl Brockelmann. Leiden, the Netherlands: Brill, 1904.

Iwasaki, John. "Tolerance Sets the Tone at Services: Faithful Gather for Gay Rights," *Seattle Post Intelligencer* (May 12, 2006).

Jaffrey, Zia. *The Invisibles: A Tale of the Eunuchs of India.* London: Phoenix, 1996.

Jakobsen, Janet and Ann Pellegrini. *Love the Sin: Sexual Regulation and the Limits of Tolerance.* New York: New York University Press, 2003.

Jamel, Amreen. "The Story of Lut and the Qur'an's Perception of the Morality of Same-Sex Sexuality," *Journal of Homosexuality* 41(1) (2001), pp. 1–88.

Jami, 'Abd al-Rahman. *Nafahat al-Uns wa Hadrat al-Quds.* Tehran: Intisharat Itla'at, 1373 AH.

Al-Jassas, Ahmad al-Razi. *Ahkam al-Qur'an.* Beirut: Dar al-Kitab al-'Arabi, 1978.

Al-Jawziyya, Ibn Qayyim. *Rawdat al-Muhibbin wa Nuzhat al-Mushtaqin*, ed. Ahmad Ubayd. Damascus: n.p., 1930.

Al-Jazari, Muhammad. *Ghayat al-Nihaya fi Tabaqat al-Qura'*. Cairo: G. Bergstaesser, 1932.

Juynboll, G. H. A. *The Authenticity of the Tradition Literature: Discussions in Modern Egypt.* Leiden, the Netherlands: Brill, 1969.

——. *Muslim Tradition: Studies in Chronology, Provenance and Authorship of Early Hadith.* Cambridge, England: Cambridge University Press, 1983.

——. "Sihak," *Encyclopedia of Islam*, 2nd edn., vol. 9, pp. 565–566.

Kamali, Muhammad Hashim. *Equity and Fairness in Islam.* Cambridge, England: Islamic Texts Society, 2005.

Kerr, Malcolm. *Islamic Reform: The Political and Legal Theories of Muhammad 'Abduh and Rashid Rida.* Berkeley and Los Angeles: University of California Press, 1966.

Khalifa, Mohsen. "Hadith Matn Criticism: A Reconsideration of Orientalists' and Some Muslim Scholars' Views," M.A. thesis, Universiteit Leiden, 2001.

Kugle, Scott Siraj al-Haqq, trans. *The Book of Illumination: Kitab al-Tanwir fi Isqat al-Tadbir by Shaykh Ibn Ata Allah al-Iskandari.* Louisville: Fons Vitae, 2005.

——. "Framed, Blamed and Renamed: The Reshaping of Islamic law in Colonial South Asia," *Modern Asian Studies* 35(2) (2001), pp. 257–313.

——. "Sexual Diversity in Islam," in Vincent Cornell, Gray Henry, and Omid Safi, eds. *Voices of Islam*, vol. 5. Westport, Connecticut: Praeger, 2006.

——. "Sexuality, Diversity and Ethics in the Agenda of Progressive Muslims," in Omid Safi, ed. *Progressive Muslims: On Gender, Justice and Pluralism.* Oxford: Oneworld, 2003.

——. "Sultan Mahmud's Makover: Colonial Homophobia and the Persian–Urdu Literary Tradition," in Ruth Vanita, ed. *Queering India: Same-Sex Love and Eroticism in Indian Culture and Society.* New York: Routledge, 2002.

Lane, Edward. *Arabic–English Lexicon: Derived from the Best and Most Copious Eastern Sources.* Cambridge, England: Islamic Texts Society, 1984.

Lecker, Michael. "Biographical Notes on Ibn Shihab al-Zuhri," *Journal of Semitic Studies* 41 (1996), pp. 21–63.

Le Vay, Simon. "Difference in Hypothalamic Structure between Heterosexual and Homosexual Men," *Brain Research* 253 (1991), pp. 1034–1037.

Lewinstein, K. "Making and Unmaking of a Sect." *Studia Islamica* 76 (1982), pp. 75–96.

——. "Sufriyya in North Africa," *Encyclopedia of Islam*, 2nd edn., vol. 9, pp. 766–768.

Madelung, W. "Sufriyya," *Encyclopedia of Islam*, 2nd edn., vol. 9, pp. 766–768.

Al-Mahalli, Jalal al-Din and Jalal al-Din al-Suyuti. *Tafsir al-Jalalayn* [or *Tafsir al-Qur'an al-'Azim*]. Cairo: Muhammad Ali Sabih, n.d.

Al-Maqrizi, Taqi al-Din. *Mukhtasar al-Kamil fi al-Du'afa' wa 'Ilal al-Hadith by Ibn 'Adi.* Beirut: Dar al-Jil, 2001.

Marmon, Shaun Elizabeth. *Eunuchs and Sacred Boundaries in Islamic Society.* Oxford: Oxford University Press, 1995.

Masud, Muhammad Khalid. "Muslim Jurists' Quest for the Normative Basis of

Shari'a," Inaugural Lecture as Director of Institute for the Study of Islam in the Modern World in the Netherlands, 2001.

——. *Shatibi's Philosophy of Islamic Law.* Islamabad: Islamic Research Institute, 1995.

Al-Maturidi. *Kitab al-Tawhid.* Beirut: Dar el-Machreq Editeours Sarl, 1982.

McDowall, Angus and Stephen Khan. "The Ayatollah and the Transsexual," *The Independent* (November 25, 2004).

Mernissi, Fatima. *The Veil and the Male Elite: A Feminist Interpretation of Women's Rights in Islam*, trans. Mary Jo Lakeland. Cambridge, Massachusetts: Perseus Books, 1991.

Money, John. *Love and Love Sickness: The Science of Sex, Gender Difference and Pair-Bonding.* Baltimore: Johns Hopkins University Press, 1980.

Motski, Harald. *The Origins of Islamic Jurisprudence: Meccan Fiqh before the Classical Schools*, trans. Marion Katz. Leiden, the Netherlands: Brill, 2002.

Moussalli, Ahmad. *Radical Islamic Fundamentalism: the Ideological and Political Discourse of Sayyid Qutb.* Beirut: American University of Beirut, 1992.

Al-Munajjad, Salah al-Din. *Al-Hayat al-Jinsiyya 'ind al-'Arab: min al-Jahiliyya ila Awakhir al-Qarn al-Rabi' al-Hijri* [*Sexual Life of the Arabs: From Pre-Islamic Times until the End of the Fourth Century after Hijra*]. Beirut: Dar al-Kutub al-Jadid, 1975.

Murata, Sachiko. *The Tao of Islam: A Sourcebook on Gender Relationships in Islamic Thought.* Albany: State University of New York Press, 1992.

Murray, Stephen and Will Roscoe, eds. *Islamic Homosexualities: Culture History and Literature.* New York University Press, 1997.

Musallam, Basim. *Sex and Society in Islam: Birth Control before the Nineteenth Century.* Cambridge, England: Cambridge University Press, 1983.

Musić, Rusmir. "Queer Visions of Islam," master's thesis, New York University, 2003.

Muzaffar, Chandra. *Muslims, Dialogue, Terror.* Selangor, Malaysia: International Movement for a Just World, 2003.

Nahas, Muhammad Omar. *Homo en Moslem – hoe gaat dat samen?* Utrecht: F.O.R.U.M. Institute voor Mutliculturele Ontwikkeling, 2005.

——. 2001. *Islam en Homoseksualiteit.* Amsterdam: Bulaaq, 2001.

——. *Al-Junusiyya: nahwa namudhaj li-tafsir al-junusiyya* [*Homosexuality: Toward a Method for Interpreting Homosexuality from the Perspective of a Muslim Homosexual Man*]. Roermond, the Netherlands: Arabica, 1997.

An-Na'im, Abdullahi. *Toward an Islamic Reformation: Civil Liberties, Human Rights and International Law.* Syracuse, New York: Syracuse University Press, 1990.

Najmabadi, Afsaneh. "Transing and Transpassing across Sex–Gender Walls in Iran," *Women's Studies Quarterly* 36(3–4) (2008), pp. 23–42.

Nanda, Serena. *Neither Man nor Woman: The Hijras of India.* Belmont, California: Wadsworth Press, 1999.

Nussbaum, Martha. *Sex and Social Justice.* Oxford: Oxford University Press, 1999.

Al-Nuwayri, Ahmad bin 'Abd al-Wahhab. *Nihayat al-Arab fi Funun al-Adab.* Cairo: Dar al-Kutub al-Masriyya, 1964.

Olyan, Saul. "'And with a Male You Shall Not Lie the Lying Down of a Woman': On the Meaning and Significance of Leviticus 18:22 and 20:13," in Gary David Comstock and Susan E. Henking, eds. *Que(e)rying Religion: A Critical Anthology.* New York: Continuum, 1997.

Overbye, Dennis. "So What Is a Planet?" *International Herald Tribune* (August 17, 2006).

Patani, Muhammad ibn Tahir. *Tadhkirat al-Mawdu'at.* Bombay: al-Maktaba al-Qayyima, 1924.

Al-Qurtubi, Muhammad ibn Ahmad. *Al-Jami' li Ahkam al-Qur'an* [or *Tafsir al-Jami'* or *Tafsir al-Qurtubi*]. Cairo: Dar al-Katib al-'Arabi, 1967.

Qutb, Sayyid. *Fi Zilal al-Qur'an* [*In the Shade of the Qur'an*]. Beirut: Dar Ihya' al-Turath al-'Arabi, 1962.

Rahman, Fazlur. *Islam and Modernity: Transformation of an Intellectual Tradition.* Chicago: University of Chicago Press, 1982.

Ramadan, Tariq. *To Be a European Muslim.* Leicester: Islamic Foundation, 1999.

Razi, Fakhr al-Din. *Mafatih al-Ghayb.* Cairo: n.p., 1927–1935.

Reddy, Gayatri. *With Respect to Sex: Negotiating Hijra Identity in South India.* Chicago: University of Chicago Press, 2005.

Rida, Muhammad Rashid. *Tafsir al-Manar* [or *Tafsir al-Qur'an al-Hakim*]. Cairo: Dar al-Manar, 1952.

Ringrose, Kathryn. *The Perfect Servant: Eunuchs and the Social Construction of Gender in Byzantium.* Chicago: University of Chicago Press, 2003.

El-Rouayheb, Khaled. *Before Homosexuality in the Arab–Islamic World, 1500–1800.* Chicago: University of Chicago Press, 2005.

Roughgarden, Joan. *Evolution's Rainbow: Diversity, Gender, and Sexuality in Nature and People.* Berkeley: University of California Press, 2004.

Rowson, Everrett. "The Effeminates of Early Medina," in Gary David Comstock and Susan E. Henking, eds. *Que(e)rying Religion: A Critical Anthology.* New York: Continuum, 1997.

——. "Gender Irregularity as Entertainment: Institutionalized Tranvestism at the Caliphal Court in Medieval Baghdad," in Sharon Farmer and Carol Braun Pasternack, eds. *Gender and Difference in the Middle Ages.* Minneapolis: University of Minnesota Press, 2003.

—— and J. W. Wright, eds. *Homoeroticism in Classical Arabic Literature.* New York: Columbia University Press, 1997.

Sakr, Ahmad. *Matrimonial Education in Islam.* Lombard, Illinois: Foundation for Islamic Knowledge, 1991.

Sanders, Paula. "Gendering the Ungendered Body: Hermaphrodites in Medieval Islamic Law," in N. Keddie and B. Baron, eds. *Women in Middle Eastern History.* New Haven: Yale University Press, 1991.

Schacht, Joseph. "Ikrima, Mawla Ibn Abbas," *Encyclopedia of Islam*, new edn., vol. 3, p. 1081.

——. *The Origins of Muhammadan Jurisprudence*, 5th edn. Oxford: Oxford University Press, 1979.

Schmitt, Arno. "*Liwat* im *Fiqh:* Männliche Homosexualität?" *Journal of Arabic and Islamic Studies* 4 (2001–2), pp. 49–110.

—— and J. Sofer, eds. *Sexuality and Eroticism among Males in Moslem Societies.* New York: Harrington Park Press, 1992.

Sells, Michael, trans. *Approaching the Qur'an: the Early Revelations.* Ashland, Oregon: White Cloud Press, 1999.

Senturk, Recep. "'I Am Therefore I Have Rights': Human Rights in Islam between Universalistic and Communalistic Perspectives," *Muslim World Journal of Human Rights* 2(1) (2005), article 11.

Shaban, M. A. *Islamic History: A New Interpretation, A.D. 600–750.* Cambridge, England: Cambridge University Press, 1974.

Shaikh, Sa'diyya. "Family Planning, Contraception and Abortion In Islam," in D. Maguire, ed., *Sacred Choices: The Case for Contraception and Abortion in World Religions.* Oxford: Oxford University Press, 2003.

——. "Gender Justice: Muslim Women's Approaches to Feminist Activism," in Omid Safi, ed., *Progressive Muslims: On Gender, Justice and Pluralism.* London: Oneworld, 2003.

——. *Spiritual Cartographies of Gender: Ibn Arabi and Sufi Discourses of Gender, Sexuality and Marriage.* Forthcoming.

Siddiqi, Muhammad Zubayr. *Hadith Literature: Its Origin, Special Features and Criticism.* Calcutta: Calcutta University, 1961.

Skovgaard-Petersen, Jakob. *Defining Islam for the Egyptian State.* Leiden, the Netherlands: Brill, 1997.

Stowasser, Barbara Freyer. *Women in the Qur'an, Traditions and Interpretation.* Oxford: Oxford University Press, 1994.

Al-Tabari, Muhammad. *History of Tabari,* trans. Khalid Blankenship. Albany: State University of New York Press, 1993.

——. *Tafsir al-Tabari,* ed. Bashar 'Awwad. Beirut: Mu'assasat al-Risala, 1994.

——. *Tarikh al-Tabari: tarikh al-rusul wa'l-muluk.* Cairo: Dar al-Ma'arif, 1962.

Taha, Mahmoud. *Second Message of Islam.* Syracuse, New York: Syracuse University Press, 1987.

Taha, Saud and Gady Magbool. "The Pattern of Intersex Disorders and Gender Assignment in the Eastern Province of Saudi Arabia," *Saudi Medical Journal* 16(1) (1995), pp. 17–22.

Tapinc, Huseyin. "Masculinity, Femininity and Turkish Male Homosexuality," in Kenneth Plummer, ed. *Modern Homosexualities: Fragments of Lesbian and Gay Experience.* New York: Routledge, 2002.

Tariq, Ambreen. "My Road to Wisconsin Was Paved with Good Intentions: A Muslim-American Reflection on the Civil-Union Ban," *MuslimWakeUp* (December 9, 2006) <www.muslimwakeup.com>.

Tayob, Abdulkader. "The Function of Islam in the South African Political Process: Defining a Community in a Nation," in Abdulkader Tayob and Wolfram

Weisse, eds. *Religion and Politics in South Africa: From Apartheid to Democracy.* Münster: Waxmann Verlag, 1999.

Vaglieri, L. Veccia. "Ibn 'Abbas, Abdallah," *Encyclopedia of Islam*, 2nd edn., vol. 1, p. 40.

Virjee, Nazmina, trans. *Introduction to Hadith by 'Abd al-Hadi al-Fadli.* London: I.C.A.S. Press, 2002.

Wadud, Amina. *Inside the Gender Jihad: Woman's Reform in Islam.* Oxford: Oneworld, 2006.

——. *Qur'an and Woman: Rereading the Sacred Text from a Woman's Perspective.* New York: Oxford University Press, 1999.

Wellhausen, Julius. *The Religio-political Factions in Early Islam.* Amsterdam: North-Holland, 1975.

Yip, Andrew. "Negotiating Space with Family and Kin in Identity Construction: The Narratives of British Non-heterosexual Muslims," *Sociological Review* 52(3) (2004), pp. 336–349.

Zafeeruddin, Muhammad Miftahi. *Islam on Homo-sexuality: The First Authentic Book on the Evils of Homosexuality (the Practice of the People of Lut) Containing Discussion in the Light of Qur'an, Hadith, History and Medicine*, trans. Azhar Ali Zaidi. Karachi: Darul Ishaat, 1999.

——. *Nasl-Kushi: ghayr-fitri jinsi maylan ya'ni 'amal qawm lut aur us ke dawa'i ki qabahat o mafasid par pehli muhaqqiqana kitab* [Killing the Lineage: The First Scholarly Book on Unnatural Sexual Attraction, Meaning the Act of the People of Lot, and Its Advocates' Repugnance and Sinfulness]. Deoband, India: Salim, 1982.

Glossary of terms from Arabic (and other Islamic languages)

adamiyya: humanity – the state of being fully human, bearing rights and deserving protection.

ahad (also called *wahid*): a *hadith* report that is solitary, having only one chain of narration with no other independent chain to confirm its authentic transmission.

ahl al-kitab: people of scripture – members of other monotheistic religions besides Islam.

'aqd: a legal contract, for example a marriage contract (see *nikah*).

'azl: premature withdrawal from sexual intercourse so as not to ejaculate in the partner's body (known in Western medical texts by the Latin *coitus interruptus*) as contraception.

bagha: desire for egoistic satisfaction or covetousness.

bigha': prostitution.

bahima: a four-legged domestic animal, like a cow or sheep, specified in condemnations of bestiality (*wati' al-bahima*).

din: moral challenge – to live uprightly and fulfill one's duty, the Islamic term for "religion."

fahisha: immorality or transgression.

fatwa: a legal decision offered by a Muslim jurist.

fiqh: Islamic jurisprudence based on the legal norms developed by Muslim jurists in medieval times.

fitna: social disruption or temptation to sin.

fitra: one's original nature.

fuqaha' (plural of *faqih*): Muslim jurists.

furuj (plural of *farj*): bodily orifice – meaning genitalia, especially in reference to female vulva.

ghulam: male slave – later taken to mean a youth or "boy" (as opposed to *jariya* – female slave or "maid").

hadd: boundary – a crime whose punishment is specified exactly in the Qur'an.

hadith: oral reports of the Prophet Muhammad's teachings and behavior later written down as normative texts.

hijra: in South Asia, a person born with male sex organs and raised as a boy who identifies as female, taking on female behavior, name and dress, and voluntarily undergoes a ritual castration to remove both testicles and penis (compare to *khasi*).

hukm: command – the explicit meaning of a clear scriptural text that obliges a Muslim to act.

husur: chaste – a person who does not have sexual intercourse due to ascetic purity, for example John the Baptist (Yahya in the Qur'an).

ihsan: to do what is good and beautiful through moral actions.

ijma': consensus of jurists on a particular ruling or issue.

ijtihad: struggle to ascertain what is right – intellectual effort and ethical discretion in the interpretation of religion.

'illa: rationale – the common factor that allows a legal analogy between one thing and another (in Latin *ratio legis*).

irba: hidden sexual desire – used in the Qur'an to describe men who "have no wiles with women" and feel no sexual attraction toward women.

irtidad: apostasy – rebelling against authority by renouncing one's allegiance to Islam.

'isma: sanctity and inviolability.

isnad: chain of narration – a list of people who have reported a *hadith* until it was written down, by which the report can be judged to be authentic or not.

istihsan: preferring what is beneficial – a legal technique to abandon an established ruling in favor of an alterative ruling that gives a more beneficial result.

istimna': masturbation – sexual pleasure by manipulation rather than penetration.

istislah: favoring the public good – a legal technique to decide an issue in favor of human welfare rather than in accord with past precedent. Sometimes called *maslaha mursala* if the ruling to promote the common good is to the intent of the divine lawgiver even in the absence of scriptural text.

jihad: struggle to fulfill one's commitments, personal or communal, often applied to conflict or military engagement.

kaba'ir (plural of *kabira*): "enormities" or grave sins that God will not forgive.

kafir: infidel (see *kufr*).

khabar: report relating the acts and opinions of Muhammad's companions or followers.

khalifa: successor to the Prophet and ruler of the Muslim community.

Khariji: Muslim puritan rebels against early Islamic rulers.

khasi: eunuch – a person born with male sex organs and raised as a boy until castrated (usually by removing the testicles).

khul': divorce – an act by either husband or wife to dissolve a marriage contract.

kufr: infidelity – rejecting the Prophets and calling their message a lie.

liwat: anal intercourse – legal term for "the act of the people of Lot," corresponding to English "sodomy." *Lutiya* has the same meaning.

lizq: cleaving together – intimate embracing to give sexual pleasure without genital penetration.

luti: legal term for a man who engages in anal intercourse, corresponding to English "sodomite."

Lut: Lot, in Arabic pronunciation – a relative of Abraham whom Muslims consider to be a Prophet sent to the "Cities of the Plain" (Sodom and Gomorrah in the Torah and Bible).

madrasa: institute of Islamic education.

mahr: bride-price – money paid by a man to a woman to contract a legal marriage.

marfu': a *hadith* report whose chain of narration ends with a companion or follower of the Prophet but not directly to Muhammad himself (in contrast to *musnad*).

maqasid: essential principles of Islamic law that define the goals of legislation.

mukhannath: effeminate man who is anatomically male but dresses and acts as female.

mushrik: idolater – one who associates a thing or person with God and replaces the worship of God with worship of that thing or person (an act called *shirk*).

musnad: a *hadith* report whose chain of narration leads back to the Prophet Muhammad.

matn: the content of a *hadith* report or the information it conveys (in contrast to *isnad*).

mut'a: informal marriage based on a finite time and oral contract (called "temporary marriage").

mutarrajula: woman who behaves like a man in speech, gesture, gait or dress.

mutawatir: a *hadith* report that has multiple and continuous chains of narration which mutually confirm its reliable and authentic transmission from the Prophet Muhammad.

mu'tazili: a school of Islamic theology that upheld the value of human reason in understanding the nature of God and divine will.

mawdu': a fabricated *hadith* report with a chain of transmission that is false.

nafs: person or soul – or in Islamic law it means "a life."

naskh: abrogation – a command later overruled or rescinded. When applied to the Qur'an, abrogated words are recognized as an integral part of scripture but their legal meaning is not applied because of a later command.

nass: clear and unambiguous words, applied to scriptural sources (like the Qur'an or *hadith*).

nikah: marriage – acceptable sexual intercourse legalized by a contractual relationship.

qatl: killing – illegal homicide and also legal execution for a crime.

qiyas: analogical reasoning – used in Islamic jurisprudence to relate an authoritative ruling in a clear situation to an ambiguous situation, thereby making a new ruling.

Qur'an: the eternal recitation – the unique and inimitable speech of God as transmitted by the angel Gabriel to the Prophet in the Arabic language; later written down as a book, it is the Islamic scripture.

rajm: stoning to death – in the *shari'a*, punishment for fornication if the perpetrator is adult and married; also a punishment for sodomy in some schools of Islamic law.

sa'ada: felicity – happiness in this world and salvation in the afterlife.

sadd al-dhari'a: prevention of harm – a legal technique to forbid something that is legal if it might lead to something that is illegal.

sahabi: companion of the Prophet Muhammad – one who met, saw or heard the Prophet.

shakila: disposition – traits or characteristics that are more or less innate.

shari'a: way of behavior obligated by a religion – religious law based upon scripture and Prophetic example. Most often applied to the Islamic system of ritual and legal norms, but each religion has a *shari'a* based upon its prior revealed scripture.

shahwa: desire for sensual gratification or pleasurable consumption.

sihaq: rubbing – a legal term for same-sex acts between two women (corresponding to the English term "tribadism") consisting of *sahq* (genital rubbing between two women) or *raf'a* (a woman's "mounting" another).

sunna: exemplary custom – especially the example of the Prophet Muhammad.

sura: form – the outer appearance of a person or thing.

tabi'a: constitution – physical or genetic material that determines one's temperament.

tafsir: commentary on the Qur'an or explanation of its meaning.

talaq: divorce – enacted by a husband to terminate a marriage contract unilaterally.

taqlid: imitation of one's parents, community elders, or exemplary jurists in Islamic behavior (contrast with *ijtihad*).

tawhid: making God one and one only – belief in monotheism and action to assert divine unity.

ta'zir: punishment for a crime at the discretion of the ruler, not stipulated by the Qur'an or other scriptural text.

'urf: local custom or cultural tradition.

usul al-fiqh: sources for deriving legal rulings based on religion (including scripture, oral reports of the Prophet, analogical reasoning, and consensus of the jurists).

zawj: mate – one of a pair of corresponding things, including a marital spouse.

zina: fornication – illicit sexual intercourse between a man and woman.

zani: fornicator – one who has illicit sexual intercourse.

zann: speculative opinion in Islamic law and theology, contrasted to decisive proof (*qat'*) based on the most explicit and authoritative scriptural sources.

Index

Terms from Arabic (and other Islamic languages) are given in *italics*.

B

C

N